A Rascal by Nature,
A Christian by Yearning

A Rascal by Nature,
A Christian by Yearning

A Mormon Autobiography

...

LEVI S. PETERSON

THE UNIVERSITY OF UTAH PRESS
Salt Lake City

The Defiance House Man colophon is a registered trademark
of the University of Utah Press. It is based upon a four-foot-tall,
Ancient Puebloan pictograph (late PIII) near Glen Canyon, Utah.

10 09 08 07 06   5 4 3 2 1

LIBRARY OF CONGRESS CATALOGING-IN-PUBLICATION DATA
Peterson, Levi S., 1933-
   A rascal by nature, a Christian by yearning : a Mormon autobiography
/ Levi S. Peterson.
      p. cm.
   Includes bibliographical references and index.
   ISBN-13: 978-0-87480-851-3 (cloth : alk. paper)
   ISBN-10: 0-87480-851-0 (cloth : alk. paper)
   1. Peterson, Levi S., 1933- . 2. Mormons—United States—Biography.
3. Mormon authors—20th century—Biography.   I. Title.
BX8695.P49A3 2006
289.3092—dc22
[B]
                                              2005036650

Cover photo of Levi Peterson courtesy of Jeffrey Thompson, Bellevue,
Washington.

◆ ◆ ◆

To my grandsons, Lars and Hans,

and to that host of other loved ones

and friends, named and unnamed

in these pages, who have contributed

to my happiness and well-being.

• • •

Contents

Photographs follow page 214

...

Acknowledgments

THIS WORK HAS BEEN NEARLY TWO DECADES in preparation. I owe a great debt to many loved ones, friends, and colleagues who have contributed to its appearance. I thank Althea, my wife, who has lived it with me and encouraged me to write it. I thank John Sillito, James F. Cartwright, and Patti Umscheid, who have stored and cataloged my letters, diaries, and manuscripts in the Weber State University Archives. I thank the members of three writing groups for their encouragement and for their helpful critique of the many versions through which this work has evolved. In Utah, these friends were Linda Sillitoe and John Sillito, Bruce and Donna Jorgensen, Dennis and Valerie Clark, John and Karla Bennion, and Gene and Charlotte England; in Washington, they were Brent and Susan Todd, Rob and Cheri Van Wagoner, Tracie Lamb and Bruce Smith, Kathleen and Chuck Petty, and Annette and Scott Bowen. I thank two reviewers of my manuscript, William Mulder and Mary Lythgoe Bradford, whose recommendations have been crucial to its publication. I thank Lavina Fielding Anderson, who urged me to submit my manuscript to the University of Utah Press and who has encouraged my writing career from its earliest moments. Finally, I thank Peter H. DeLafosse, acquisitions editor at the University of Utah Press, for his cheerful efficiency.

A Rascal by Nature,
A Christian by Yearning

My Ancestors

I WILL INTRODUCE MYSELF WITH A FEW FACTS. I was born and raised in Snowflake, a Mormon town in northern Arizona. I have lived most of my adult life in the cities of the American West. Although I consider myself a religious person, I know very little about God. At first I intended this book to be about wilderness, but as I wrote it, it became an autobiography with many themes. Among these themes are wilderness, my vexed and vexing relationship with Mormonism, my moral and emotional qualities, and my family. I hesitate to call the last of these more important than any other. Nonetheless, I feel obliged to begin by explaining my family—vast, multilayered, and tenacious in looking after its own.

Most of my ancestors that I know anything about were pioneers. I grew up venerating all pioneers. Everyone in Snowflake venerated the pioneers. We believed the settlement of the American frontier was a grand and noble enterprise, a major contribution to the history of civilization. I presently hold a more chastened view of the pioneers. It is easy to project the ills of modern America upon the pioneers who founded it, and in fact many historians and anthropologists find it mandatory to do so. It is an indisputable fact that settlers of European origin or descent displaced the Indians, exterminated the buffalo, plowed the prairie, cut down the forests, fought and assassinated one another on a regular basis, and discriminated grossly against blacks, Asians, and Hispanics. However, if blame has to be apportioned, it would seem the living representatives of a flawed civilization deserve a far greater share than their dead ancestors. The pioneers were heroic in this sense, if in no other: the settling of the frontier was neither easy nor safe, yet they persisted. They took risks, suffered hardships, and endured in uncertain enterprises far beyond the capacity of most of their secure, well-fed descendants even to imagine.

Some of my pioneer ancestors kept journals, and my family is awash with written accounts of their lives. Much of what I learned about them, however, came from the spoken lore of the family. No one impressed the past on me more forcefully than my mother. With a sure instinct for the dramatic and crucial, she repeated the tragedies, triumphs, adventures, narrow escapes, sacrifices, and amazing devotions of her ancestors—and of my father's ancestors, too, because, like many Mormon wives, she adopted the duty of researching her husband's line as well as her own.

My mother's first known paternal ancestor was John Savage, who came to America as a private soldier in the British army that captured Quebec in 1759. After the Battle of Quebec, he deserted from the army and fled to southwestern Massachusetts, which at that time was the edge of settlement. He married a quarrelsome red-haired Irish woman, fathered four children, and escaped by the skin of his teeth when his wife betrayed him to British officers at the beginning of the American Revolution. One of his sons, Daniel Savage, married Sally Parrish and migrated to central New York, and by 1835 one of Daniel and Sally's sons, Levi Savage Sr., had married Polly Haynes and migrated to western Michigan. In 1843 Levi, Polly, and their children were baptized Mormons, and with their conversion a new motivation must be factored into their westering impulse.

The Mormons gave a religious turn to the general enthusiasm of the American nation for Manifest Destiny. With unblinking self-confidence, they asserted that the New Jerusalem they intended to build in Missouri would dominate the entire world throughout the Millennium. In the meantime, they gathered converts successively to Kirtland, Nauvoo, and Salt Lake City, and from Salt Lake City they extended a Mormon corridor of towns and villages into southern Idaho and northern Arizona. As a result, some of my ancestors would inhabit impoverished frontiers where the blindest of optimism would never have led them simply because they were called by ecclesiastical authority to extend the borders of the Kingdom of God.

When the Mormon exodus from Nauvoo began in 1846, Levi and Polly left Michigan with wagons and ox teams and joined the saints on the Iowa plains. The following winter found the Mormons in shanties, dugouts, and wagon boxes, suffering from malnutrition and despair. During January of that infamous winter, Polly died at a camp on Mosquito Creek, near Council Bluffs, while giving birth to male twins, who also died. Nobody knows the precise spot of their graves, and in truth very little is known about Polly other than what I relate here. Her name is inscribed, along with many others, on a monument in a Mormon cemetery near Council Bluffs. My wife and I viewed that inscription in the company of my mother and some of my siblings in the summer of 1961. My mother spoke of our little-known ancestor with the deepest of grief. I recognized then, and will confirm now, that a fierce, proud grief lies at the core of the Mormon identity, cemented there by the hardships, smothered aspirations, and truncated lives of our pioneer ancestors. Anyone wishing to understand Mormonism must remember it was a religion created by pioneering.

About five months after Polly's death, Levi departed for the Rocky Mountains, accompanied by his ten-year-old son, Matthew, who probably drove one of the ox teams, and by a young woman, Jane Mathers, who served as cook and camp helper. The company with which these three traveled, one of a very few allowed to migrate during the summer of 1847, arrived in the Salt Lake Valley two months after the vanguard company on July 24.

The eldest son of Levi Savage Sr., Levi Savage Jr., arrived in the Salt Lake Valley by a circuitous route only three weeks after his father. This Levi, twenty-two, had joined the Mormon Battalion on the Iowa plains during the summer of 1846 and had participated in the Mexican War by marching with the battalion to Santa Fe, Tucson, and San Diego. In 1848, Levi Savage Jr. married Jane Mathers. In January 1851, Jane bore a son named Levi Mathers Savage, who would become my grandfather. In December 1851, Jane died of erysipelas and was buried in the nearly vacant Salt Lake cemetery. Today a simple granite stone marks her grave among a veritable forest of markers and monuments.

Jane had left her family in Michigan at seventeen and joined the saints in Nauvoo. When she departed, carrying all her goods in a bundle made of a kerchief, a six-year-old sister followed, calling her name. She hugged the little girl and sent her back to her waiting parents. None of the family ever saw her again. In Nauvoo,

Jane was immediately married as the second wife to Milo Webb, whose first wife mistreated her severely. Jane left this man about the time the Mormon exodus from Nauvoo began and, as it would appear, found refuge with the Savage family on the Iowa plains. During the following summer of 1847, Jane was among the very few women whom Brigham Young allowed to migrate to the Salt Lake Valley. It would please me to believe that Jane was strong spirited and simply insisted on going along. However, Brigham Young wasn't impressed by spunk in women. Most likely, he allowed Jane to migrate to remove her from the vicinity of Milo Webb and his first wife, whose relationship with Jane was glaring evidence that the plural marriage Brigham Young was promoting didn't always work.

As for Levi Savage Jr., he may be appropriately called a Mormon Odysseus. In 1852, less than a year after Jane's death, Brigham Young called this young widower on a mission to Siam. He left his little son with a sister and departed on a journey that led him in a complete circumnavigation of the earth. He made his way horseback to Los Angeles, took a ship to San Francisco, and sailed to Calcutta. From there he found passage to Rangoon but never reached Siam. He spent depressed months living as a total dependent upon kind English colonials. He converted no one. In fact, he rarely preached the Gospel and at last considered himself fortunate merely to receive passage on a vessel bound for New York.

From New York, he made his way by rail to Florence, Nebraska, the current marshaling point of the saints for the crossing of the plains. This was August 1856, and he had been gone from the saints for four years. He found them moved by a new enthusiasm. It was, they asserted, the Lord's will that the handcart be used to transport immigrants to Zion—requiring the immigrants not only to walk the fifteen hundred miles to the Salt Lake Valley but at the same time to pull such food, clothing, durable goods, and little children as a two-wheeled cart would hold. Levi warned the members of the Willie company that the season was too far advanced, but when he was shouted down, he joined their fated trek, earning himself a place in Hubert Howe Bancroft's *History of Utah*. Bancroft quotes him as saying, "Brethren and sisters, what I have said I know to be true; but seeing you are to go forward, I will go with you. May God in his mercy preserve us." There is nothing of such eloquence in his journal, but his entries nonetheless record the worsening circumstances of the company stranded by early storms on the high Wyoming plains: "October 24, 1856. This morning found us with thirteen corpses for burial. These were all put into one grave. Some had actually frozen to death. We were obliged to remain in camp, move the tents and people behind the willows to shelter them from the severe wind which blew enough to pierce us through. Several of our cattle died here."[1]

Among the rescued survivors of this debacle were an English widow and her two daughters. Levi soon married this widow, and when her daughters reached maturity, he also married them. He migrated southward from Salt Lake City, pausing for a year or so in one village or another. At one moment he pioneered in Kanab near the Arizona border. During an Indian uprising, he retreated to Toquerville, a hamlet in the desert near St. George, where he spent the rest of his days eking out a scant living from a few irrigated acres among the lava outcroppings of LaVerkin Creek. When the federal government intensified its prosecution of Mormon polygamists, he patiently accepted his fate, serving six months in the Utah penitentiary during the winter of 1887–1888 for illegal cohabitation with his plural wives. Following his release, he was required to situate his three wives in separate residences. He was not a prominent man, nor, if I believe his sparse and ungrammatical journal, was he educated. But he was a representative saint. He went through it all: the march of the battalion, a circumnavigation of the globe for the purpose of preaching the Gospel, the handcart passage, pioneering in southern Utah, and imprisonment for practicing polygamy, that peculiar institution of Mormonism.

His son Levi Mathers Savage grew up to be an intelligent and serious-minded man. He yearned for a mission, and when a call came to go to the frontier in northern Arizona, he was ready. In 1871 he and his wife, Marintha Wright, journeyed by wagon to Sunset, a United Order village under the direction of Lot Smith. One day Wilford Woodruff, an apostle hiding from federal marshals, sat with Levi on the banks of the Little Colorado and persuaded him, over the strenuous objections of Marintha, to obey the principle of plural marriage. Levi took Lydia Lenora Hatch, my grandmother, to St. George by wagon and was united to her in the temple there by an ecclesiastic wedding, which had no legal standing. In the meantime, Marintha, pregnant with their third child, rampaged, attempting to set fire to the colony's wheat stacks. Lot Smith had her bound to a chair, and when a wagon going to Utah came by, he put her and her children into it. That was the end of my grandfather's first family. Marintha raised her children among relatives in northern Utah and after twenty years of bitter estrangement secured a divorce from Levi.

Levi Mathers Savage also married Hannah Adeline Hatch, a younger sister of my grandmother. He and his two wives lived in northern Mexico for a while to escape federal prosecution for illegal cohabitation. Forced from Mexico by political turmoil, they returned to northern Arizona in 1890, and Levi was soon installed as bishop of the new colony of Woodruff at the confluence of the Little Colorado and Silver Creek, about twenty miles north of Snowflake. For twenty-six years he remained bishop of Woodruff—a bleak, windblown, impoverished hamlet. He was released only after his son informed the General Authorities of the Mormon Church that his father was kept a prisoner to duty by a stake president who could not dispense with his leadership in Woodruff. Levi supervised the building of a dozen dams on the Little Colorado. All of them washed out. When he left Woodruff, he said he wanted never to see it again. He spent his last days doing temple work in Salt Lake City, often walking the seven miles to the temple. He died of pneumonia at eighty-three and was buried in the Salt Lake cemetery. My grandmother is beside him, and only a couple of yards away lies the grave of his mother, Jane Mathers. The return of my grandfather to the city in his old age is deceptive. Most of his life he was a groundbreaker, either in wilderness or at its edge.

My grandmother, called Nora, was the only one of my pioneer ancestors whom I knew personally. For a half-dozen years she lived in my childhood home in a condition of obese senility. Throughout a bright, bitterly cold January day in 1946, I watched her die, unconscious and gasping convulsively. I judge her chief influence on me to have been indirect. Through my mother, she bequeathed me a free-floating grief, which has always accompanied my worst pathological moods. She lost four of her seven children. The first of the four was an infant daughter whom she bore near the same time Adeline bore a daughter. Adeline couldn't nurse hers, so my grandmother nursed both. Adeline's baby fed vigorously, while Nora's dwindled and died. A six-year-old daughter and a ten-month-old son died of diphtheria in Mexico. When my grandparents fled Mexico, my grandfather obliterated all sign of the graves. He assured my grandmother he could find them again, but they never went back. Finally, an eleven-year-old son died from a kick in the head by a supposedly gentle horse. As I say, Nora passed her grief on to my mother, and my mother, having added to it her own grief over the death of my brother Alma, passed it on to me. No tragedy touches me as deeply as the death of a child.

My grandmother's sister wife, Adeline, lies in the red, wind-stirred soil of Woodruff cemetery. None of her five children died. Otherwise she was not as fortunate as my grandmother. She was bedridden during most of her married life, suffering from a bad back, dizzy spells, and vague internal pains. Her compensation lay in spiritual experiences, which are detailed in her remarkable journal. She knelt in prayer circles with other women. She anointed, administered, and prophesied. She spoke in tongues and interpreted them. She received miraculous healings and portentous promises for herself and her children. Though infrequent, these moments of rejuvenation gave her mind something to dwell upon during tedious bedridden hours.

My pioneer ancestors on my father's side provide a less momentous history. My father's parents, Andrew Peterson and Anna Marie Pherson (called Mary Ann in America), converted to Mormonism in Sweden and, engaged to be married, set out for the United States by sailing vessel in 1862. While their ship took on German immigrants in the mouth of the Elbe River, the ship's captain persuaded them to be married at once. Reaching America, they traveled by rail to Omaha and joined a wagon train headed for Utah. On the plains my grandfather was stricken with mountain fever and took my grandmother's place in a wagon while she walked and sometimes drove the oxen. One night she found him far from camp in a delirium and with great difficulty persuaded him to return. She also had to cook and do camp chores for the man whose wagon they used. Sometimes this man would sit on a rocking chair fondling his new plural wife while Mary Ann cooked their supper over a campfire.

My grandparents settled in Lehi on the northern shore of Utah Lake, where they lived quiet, respectable lives. They became the parents of ten children, of whom seven survived to adulthood. They assisted his parents and her widowed mother to migrate to Utah, where they too lived out their days. As for the epic experience of crossing the plains, my grandmother claimed that it had ruined her health and for the rest of her life required a cup of medicinal coffee before getting out of bed every morning.

My ancestors help explain me. Knowing them, I know myself more completely. Because they came from northern Europe, I am fair skinned and possessed of what was once a thick thatch of blond, curly hair, which gradually darkened, thinned, and finally turned white. I am six feet in height, capable of remaining lean without too much difficulty, and generally of sound physical health though possessed of sun-sensitive Scandinavian eyes that developed cataracts by the time I was forty. I am energetic and purposeful yet, like my father, prone to anxiety and depression. Perhaps I inherited my instinct for disbelief from my Swedish forebears. If so, the gene must have been recessive until the accidental recombination of my conception brought it forward, for the evidence is that, with the possible exception of my father, all of my known ancestors had a prominent instinct for believing.

I have wondered whether I inherited my taste for wilderness from my ancestors. In fact, more than twenty years ago I wrote an essay propounding that idea.[2] By definition, pioneers were people who lived where the domesticated was rudimentary and wilderness abundant. I thought it possible that my ancestors preferred wild places and passed that instinct on to me. That would be one way of explaining the perpetual discomfort I feel in an urban environment. However, I have come to believe this hypothesis is more useful as a metaphor than as a historical interpretation. A more demonstrable hypothesis is that my ancestors sought the wilderness for economic reasons. Clearly, most pioneers went west in search of unpreempted wealth—furs, hides, precious metals, timber, and land for farms, ranches, and speculation. It was farms my ancestors sought. Some of them moved so restlessly from farm to farm on successive frontiers that I might easily argue that they had a genetic propensity, not for an intimacy with the wild, but for economic failure. Unable to succeed in existing settlements, they struck off for the latest frontier where, as rumor had it, better opportunities awaited.

I can't dissociate their image in my mind from the image of the continental wilderness that America once was. Collectively, they saw it in its near-pristine condition. I feel its unutterable beauty more intensely because I see myself among them. They helped ruin the continental wilderness too, making tracks across it, clearing trees for farms, grazing their livestock on grasslands. I feel the tragedy of its destruction all the more intensely for belonging to them. I hear my ancestors in the surf breaking on the Plymouth shore. I walk with John Savage along the trail from Canada to Massachusetts. With his sons I pass over the mountains and enter the forests of western New York and Ohio. I winter at Council Bluffs. I choke on the dust of the Platte trail. I see the valley of the Great Salt Lake from Little Mountain. I herd sheep on the red cliffs beyond Kanab. I weather the winds of spring on the Little Colorado. The American wilderness is my emotional domain, granted by birthright, and when I awaken from imagination, I recognize that with its destruction I have suffered a personal loss. Unquestionably, my ancestors have made me a westerner. Their migrations ended in Utah and Arizona, making the interior West the region of my heart. I have always been restless living anywhere else.

My ancestors also bequeathed me a love for family. From my earliest memory, I have understood that a family extends widely, composed of dozens of overlapping nuclear units, including grandparents, uncles, aunts, and cousins as well as parents and siblings. From almost as early, I have understood that a family has mystical dimensions, receding into the past and projecting into the future, being composed of persons dead and unborn as well as persons currently alive. My ancestors, having, as I say, an instinct for believing, suffered and sacrificed for a quaint, controversial religion. For that reason I am, emotionally speaking, an indelible Mormon. For whatever it is worth, I take comfort in the solidity of the foregoing facts. I feel owned, recognized, and accepted by my parentage. I am no orphan, haunted by the question of who begat me. Thanks to knowing my ancestors, I feel well planted, fully rooted, and in many ways at home with myself.

··· 2

That Failed Anthropologist,
My Father

MY FATHER WAS NAMED JOSEPH after the founder of Mormonism.[1]
Born in 1874, he grew up on a farm in Lehi, Utah, steeped in a culture that made its calculations in acreage and animals and fervently
propounded that prosperity, if not wealth, lay in a farm or a ranch.
In his teens he herded sheep for his older brother and learned to
drink coffee, smoke cigarettes, and read dime novels, vices from
which his mother saved him, in the fall of 1892, by persuading
him to enter Brigham Young Academy. There he met a culture that
valued books and ideas and opened a livelihood through teaching.
He would prove a competent but restless teacher, forever pulled
toward farming.

He graduated from the academy in 1897 with a bachelor of
pedagogy degree. He had been especially interested in science, and,
with the encouragement of his mentors, he considered going east
to continue his education, perhaps with a view toward someday
teaching in a college or university. Instead of going east, however,
he accepted a teaching position in his hometown of Lehi, and at
Christmas of 1897 he married Amanda Andelin, who was also the
child of Swedish immigrants. My father and Amanda made a handsome couple, as their wedding portrait shows. They sit stiffly in
formal attire, he with a mass of dark, wavy hair and a solemn, boy-
ish face, she with her hair tied into a bun on top of her head and an
innocent repose upon her countenance.

In September 1898 my father was called by the Mormon
Church to be principal of a struggling stake academy in Snowflake,
Arizona. He traveled by train via Colorado and New Mexico, dis-

embarking in Holbrook, thirty miles north of Snowflake. Amanda followed in December with their six-week-old son, Arley, in her arms. Upon his arrival, Joseph learned that, although the bricks for an academy building were on hand, the trustees were locked in a dispute as to its location. He supervised and taught in the grade school that year. The next year he opened the academy by scheduling classes for the first year of high school in the social hall and church house. The new academy building was completed in 1901. Although he had been forewarned of rowdy teenage boys, he had no trouble establishing discipline. He was articulate and dignified yet pleasant and open to all comers, whatever their station, fulfilling this frontier community's ideal as to what a man of learning should be. Although he was only twenty-four years old and possessed of a diploma defined today as a high school degree, people instantly called him Professor Peterson, a title he retained for the rest of his life. Amanda also adapted well to Snowflake. She was, if anything, even more pleasant and sociable than her husband and could sew beautifully. For whatever it is worth, she and my father introduced round dancing to Snowflake, the town having hitherto, as Joseph reported in his letters, practiced only square dancing.

It pleases me to imagine my father's early years in that country. I won't call him a pioneer because he was a generation behind those who had first founded settlements. Yet when he arrived in northeastern Arizona, white culture had made only minor changes in the wilderness. Small towns were scattered along the railroad and along the Little Colorado and its tributary Silver Creek. Rolling plains, well grassed in those days, stretched away on either side of the temperamental and intermittent Little Colorado. To the north, the plains gave way to the erosions of the Painted Desert. To the south they gave way to juniper-covered hills, and those hills gave way to the White Mountains and the Mogollon Rim. Cattle grazed everywhere, and from time to time my father saw cowboys, duly appareled with felt hats, bandannas, boots, and revolvers. The cowboys for the most part worked for the large Hashknife outfit, a subsidiary of the railroad.

Snowflake, one of the larger towns, lay in a widening of the Silver Creek valley. Fields stretched between town and the creek. Irrigation ditches and maturing cottonwoods lined the streets. There were eighty or ninety homes ranging from simple unpainted log cabins and lumber shacks to two- and three-story edifices of locally fired redbrick. Behind the houses were gardens, barns, coops, and corrals. In the center of town stood a meetinghouse with a steeple. These signs of domestication failed to banish the wild. Junipers, sagebrush, and prickly pear crowded the boundaries of the town. Overhead stretched a vast sky. A cold, disagreeable wind blew all spring long. Wilderness percolated through open doors and seeped under windowsills.

I also like to imagine my father's first encounter with the Native Americans of northeastern Arizona, who I suspect helped direct his ambition to a career in the new science of anthropology. The White Mountain Apache reservation lay forty miles south of Snowflake. The Navajo reservation lay an equal distance to the north. Some miles farther to the north were the Hopi pueblos. Upon arriving in Holbrook on his first day, he might have seen a Navajo clad in buckskin moccasins, wool pants, velvet shirt, and high, round-domed Stetson, his hair tied into a bun at the nape of his neck and his chest adorned by a necklace of silver and turquoise. This man's skin would have been coppery, his hair jet black, his eyes marked by a hint of an ancestral Asian slant. His bearing would have been colored by a primordial grace whose existence, so I imagine, my father had never before even guessed at.

My father attended his first Hopi snake dance in August 1899, at either Walpi on First Mesa or Mishongnovi on Second Mesa, where it is known that snake dances were held that year. From the cliffs at the edge of the mesa, he watched the progress of Hopi racers across the distant valley floor soon after dawn and looked on while costumed celebrants dusted the arriving racers with sacred cornmeal. With a variety of other white onlookers, he loitered through a hot day until, in the late afternoon, dancers from the Snake and Antelope societies emerged from their kivas. They wore kilts, headbands, moccasins, and turtle-shell rattles, and they had geometric designs painted in white and black upon their torsos, arms, and faces. They formed pairs and, chanting and stamping the earth in rhythm with a drummer, shuffled past a small brush shelter, where each pair received a writhing snake—a rattlesnake or a bull snake or occasionally a snake of a rarer species. While one held a snake in his hands and teeth, his companion positioned himself a little behind, stroking the other's back with eagle feathers, as if it were important to soothe not the twisting snake, but the man who held it. After they had dropped the snakes in a writhing heap within a circle of cornmeal, runners grasped them by the handful and dashed away in the four cardinal directions to deposit them at shrines on the valley floor, where, so the Hopi believed, they would crawl into dens and crevices and inform the forces of the Underworld of the Hopi need for rain.

I have modeled these hypothetical details upon H. R. Voth's observations of snake dances held at Oraibi on Third Mesa in 1896, 1898, and 1900, published in 1903 with dozens of astonishing black-and-white photographs.[2] The ceremony my father witnessed in 1899 would not have differed much from those Voth describes at Oraibi. A Mennonite missionary with an anthropological bent, Voth was of course dedicated to the extinction of the traditional culture that he so carefully described in this and a half dozen other anthropological works.

I surmise that by the time of watching the Hopi snake dance, my father had settled on the pursuit of a university degree in anthropology with an emphasis upon the Native Americans of the Southwest. There is no question of his having made that determination by 1903 when, with his teaching mission completed, he and Amanda began a circuitous return to Utah by way of Berkeley, where he intended to take courses for an indefinite period at the University of California. By now they had three children, Leora having been born in 1900 and Andelin in 1903, a few months before their departure for Berkeley.

There's a small photo of my father taken by a studio in Berkeley. He's very handsome. He wears a double-breasted suit and white collar and tie. His hair is rich, brown, and curly and parted just slightly left of the middle. He wears a trim, pointed beard and full mustache in the style of Louis Pasteur. This was perhaps by more than coincidence. He may indeed have wished to appear as a man of science.

At that time, the university was growing rapidly in every department. It boasted a cluster of august stone and brick buildings, pleasant walks, wooded retreats, and a Greek theater where lyceums and pageants held forth. My father enrolled in classes during the summer and fall sessions of 1903 and the spring and summer sessions of 1904. His major was anthropology, in which his principal instructor and adviser was Alfred L. Kroeber, fresh from Columbia with a Ph.D. taken under Franz Boas, a father of American anthropology. According to Kroeber's wife and biographer, Boas transmitted to Kroeber his extraordinary esteem for threatened Native American cultures, which Kroeber in turn, as I surmise, transmitted to that hopeful but ultimately failed anthropologist, my father. "To the field then!" wrote Mrs. Kroeber by way of explaining her husband's bent of mind. "With notebook and pencil, record, record, record. Rescue from historylessness all languages still living, all cultures. Each is precious, unique, irreplaceable, a people's ultimate expression and identity, which, being lost, the world is made poorer as surely as it was when a Praxitelean marble was broken and turned to dust."[3]

Although Kroeber preferred fieldwork among living Native American cultures, he established an ambitious program for collecting the archaeology of vanished cultures in California and contiguous areas in the United States and Mexico. Initially he did this on funds provided by Phoebe Apperson Hearst, widow of mining magnate George Hearst and mother of William Randolph Hearst. A regent of the university, Phoebe Hearst was the founding patron of the new museum of anthropology, where she deposited her own considerable collection of classical antiquities, purchased in Europe. Among the earliest excavators retained by Kroeber was my father, who engaged in extensive digging in northern Arizona following his unplanned return to that arid region.

My father withdrew abruptly from a full schedule of courses early during the fall session of 1904, citing ill health in his petition to the university for honorable dismissal. His affliction, which would recur throughout the rest of his life, seems to have centered in his digestive system, and so many of his sons and grandsons have suffered ulcers and colitis that it is reasonable to suppose he was responding to stress by experiencing gastrointestinal pain.

Besides the usual stress of deadlines and grades, he probably suffered from a conflict between his religious faith and the brash secular science of his professors. Following is a story my mother often told. In class one day my father asked the professor whether the existence of God wasn't at least a possibility. "But, my dear man, we don't need God!" the professor replied. He meant that God as a physical force is not necessary among the postulates that account for the functioning of the universe. My mother always went on to quote my father as saying that, if he had stayed at Berkeley, he probably wouldn't have remained a Mormon. So he had to leave, being unwilling to exchange his Christian mythology, with its prospect of redemption beyond this world, for the mythology of secular science, which, for all its heroic self-assertion, left the human creature poised at death upon the brink of nothingness.

As my father and Amanda prepared to depart for Utah, a telegram arrived from the stake president in Snowflake asking my father to return as principal of the academy. His disillusioned successor had chosen to quit midterm. This wasn't a missionary call, but an offer for regular employment. My father and Amanda decided to accept. He was thirty and she was thirty-two, and they were casting their lot irrevocably with northern Arizona. As for my father's feelings about the return, I extrapolate his ambivalence from a letter he wrote my mother in 1924 from Berkeley, where he had returned to attend summer school.

> I don't know, dear, whether I want to go back to the wilds of Arizona or not. I liked it when I was here before and I like it now. The conviction forces itself on me frequently that I would have been happier and more contented if I had established myself in some city when I was young.... Don't misunderstand me to mean that I don't like the people out there [in Arizona], because I do. I love them. But there are so few of us and things have been so uphill.[4]

On their return to Snowflake in 1904, my father and Amanda bought a small house and resumed their place in the town's social life. In 1906, they added Earland to their family. In my opinion, they would have done well to spend the rest of their lives in these circumstances, with a modest but secure cash income from teaching and an irrigated lot with fruit trees, an ample garden, and a pig, chickens, and cow. My father was restless at the academy, however, and continued to think of himself as ill. He supposed, as he wrote a friend, that ranching or some other line of outdoor life would be better for him than his duties as principal and teacher. Though he performed those duties well, there was undoubtedly a tension in articulating subject matter before students for hour after hour, to say nothing of disciplining the unruly among them. Accordingly, in 1906, he agreed with five other men to found a town next to a small lake in the pine forest thirty miles south of Snowflake. According to our family lore, he proposed the name of Lakeside, which the others accepted. In the summer of 1908 my father quit the academy for a second time, apparently intending never to return. That fall, the family moved to Lakeside, where my father and Amanda took out a homestead of eighty acres a mile northeast of town. Within a couple of months of their moving, another son, Elwood, was born. Thus began a new era in the history of their family.

In the meantime, my father spent the summers of 1906, 1907, and 1908 excavating prehistoric ruins along the creeks and dry washes of central Navajo County and shipping artifacts and skeletons to Kroeber in California. He drew a map locating some forty ruins of varying size and importance, of which he excavated ten. Most were near watercourses that are now dry and perhaps were intermittent even in the period of occupancy. Fallen walls, stoneware, and pottery shards made the ruins easy to find, and a plenteous array of petroglyphs decorated nearby sandstone cliffs. In fact, the vertical walls of Silver Creek canyon north of Snowflake hold thousands of these simple yet often startling representations. My father's correspondence with Kroeber indicates that he succeeded best in his search for materials within deeply buried residential rooms where local pothunters had not yet dug.[5] He mentions teams of men he had hired to do the digging. Sometimes he himself engaged in the excavation. In August 1906, he shipped fifteen cases and three crates of specimens to Berkeley, in July 1907 thirteen boxes and nine bales, in July and August 1908 twenty-four boxes. The more than three hundred specimens that he shipped consisted of stone axes and mallets, arrowheads and spear points, grinding stones and mills, pottery ware of many sizes and shapes, awls and other bone objects, human skeletal remains, and, oddly, the complete skeleton of a turkey, apparently buried with rites.

I myself examined some of these specimens in the museum of anthropology as I concluded a year of graduate study at the University of California at Berkeley in 1961. They were contained in twenty or thirty drawers in a large storage area filled to the ceiling with long rows of drawers. In the summer of 1992, the museum mounted an exhibit of materials acquired through the generosity of Phoebe Apperson Hearst. Among the displays was a modest glass case containing artifacts collected by my father. As it turns out, the collection he assembled is larger than any other made by excavators funded by Mrs. Hearst.

Thereafter, my father maintained a hobbyist's interest in the anthropology of Native Americans in northern Arizona. He built a small but select personal collection of artifacts. He often attended the public ceremonies of Navajos and Apaches as well as Hopis. In his later travels as county school superintendent, he conversed with both whites and Native Americans about the traditions of the latter and accepted invitations to visit the government schools at Keams Canyon and Whiteriver. He also made Native Americans the subject matter of some of the poetry and high school pageants he wrote in his later years. *Geronimo,* the pageant he wrote and directed for the class of 1939, compresses the Spanish conquest, the era of the mountain man, and the subjugation of the Apaches by the U.S. cavalry into the single lifetime of the famous Apache war chief Geronimo and his fictitious lover, Yucca Blossom. "They take our ponies, feed on our pastures, pen us on reservations," says Geronimo of the whites, "and if we dare to be men they imprison or murder us." General Crooke, an officer who pursues him, though not without sympathy, replies: "You must yield to civilization."[6]

In this way my father voiced the dilemma regarding traditional Indian culture experienced by even the best intentioned of whites. I am sure he took satisfaction in knowing the bones and artifacts he was uncovering in 1906, 1907, and 1908 would join the Greek and Roman antiquities with which Phoebe Apperson Hearst was aggrandizing the reputation of a new Oxford in the West, and I do not doubt that he regretted the demise of traditional culture among living tribes. Whites have been feeling guilty over the displacement of Native Americans for a long time. James Fenimore Cooper first alluded to that tragedy in *The Pioneers* of 1823, then made it the center of *The Last of the Mohicans* in 1826. The tragedy extends to those tribes who have managed to survive that displacement and even in some cases to increase their numbers greatly. All of them have lost touch with their ancestral culture. For example, the Hopis whose ancestors my father watched perform an authentic snake dance in 1898 have forgotten how such a dance must proceed, and, even if they hadn't, they no longer believe that the snakes will ask the deities of the Underworld to cause rain to fall on Hopiland.

My father's contribution to the demise of traditional Native American culture in northeastern Arizona was made chiefly in the classroom, and it probably would have had the same impact even if he had thought it desirable to help them retain their traditional culture. They couldn't retain it because they were constantly exposed to the technology and premises of white culture. The Euro-American culture confronting the Native Americans wasn't static. It was becoming ever more complex, ever more potent against simpler cultures, and formal education hastened the process. A dutiful and competent teacher, my father assisted in this process by introducing his young white charges to the rudiments of science, mathematics, logic, and grammar, making them more conversant with capital and finance, more tolerant of the specialization of labor, more dependent on machines and manufactured goods. As one school term succeeded another, each new generation of students left his classroom slightly more advanced in culture, slightly more removed from the primordial, than its predecessor, making it ever more certain that the Native Americans who associated with them would interpret their own culture as irrelevant and outdated.

Moreover, my father's sympathy for Native Americans did not transfer readily to me when I was young. I recall how repelled I was during the summer of 1947 when, as a boy of thirteen, I first observed a snake dance at one of the Hopi pueblos. The small fields of corn and squash at the base of the mesa did nothing to relieve the sere, barren monotony of the surrounding desert. I was astonished at the very existence of these fields, there being no creek at hand, no irrigation ditch full of rich brown water. The pueblo itself, with its walls of rock and mud, seemed a raw, unalleviated extension of the desert. Nor was I impressed by the ceremony. The dancers, who struck me as ludicrously decorated with daubs of paint and tufts of feathers, milled about in evident confusion before finally forming a revolving circle. The snakes they carried in their hands or mouths were mostly nonvenomous with perhaps one or two rattlesnakes among them. Long afterward, upon reading Voth's descriptions of the ceremonies at the turn of the century, I would realize that in 1947 I was witnessing a communal ceremony in the midstages of dying.

I had no idea as a child how culturally distant I was from these people. What little I knew about them I gathered not from my father, who died when I was nine, but from chance reading. The Book of Mormon said their brown skin was a curse. Many of them lived a camp life and wore soiled clothing. Many of them spoke English haltingly. Some of them didn't speak it at all, a sharp contrast with today, when almost all of them are fluent in English and few of them know their ancestral tongue. I hope I have outgrown my prejudice, having come to regard brown, black, and white skin as equally desirable. As for the traditional culture of Native Americans, I have learned to respect it, chiefly through reading about the Hopis. I respect it above all because it existed in harmony with wilderness.

The Hopis maintained an astonishingly complex ceremonial calendar throughout the entire year. The snake dance my father viewed followed eight days of rites conducted largely within the kivas of the Snake and Antelope societies, where the celebrants prayed and made prayer sticks, engaged in the ritual smoking of a pipe, and practiced new songs and dance patterns for the ninth day. The major point of their elaborate ceremonies was the control of nature. Given their circumstances, the greatest threat facing them was drought. Having done all that their limited technology allowed by way of actual control of nature, they resorted to sacred gestures, motivated by the conviction that a human rite, if it were correctly performed, could affect the annual progress of the sun, the formation of rain clouds, the banishment of disease, the relief of pain, and the fertility of their own bodies as well as of the seeds they planted.

What attracts me to all this is its intimacy with the wild. Their rock houses and small cultivated fields did not sever the Hopis from nature. Nor did their mythology alienate them from wilderness. They endowed natural objects with spirit. They made shrines at springs and in crevices where worshipers could pray or sprinkle sacred cornmeal. A culture that projects such intense meaning onto natural objects is itself an element of the wild. It doesn't merely coexist with wilderness. It is wilderness.

The death of traditional Indian culture is a major subplot in the tragedy of the lost American wilderness. If the anthropologists among whom my father at one moment aspired to take a place could do nothing to prevent the loss, at least they helped preserve knowledge about that culture. Unfortunately, that knowledge serves to remind me of the alienation from the wild of modern Euro-American culture. It is probable that a highly developed culture and wilderness are essentially inimical. If so, the culture in which I live is fated to a future I don't care to live to see. In the meantime, I can't fault my father for his part in the demise of traditional Native American culture any more than I fault myself for not engaging in the impossible task of restoring it. Though he died too soon to instruct me in Native American lore, I was led to it through my interest in his life, and for that, as well as for many, many other things, I thank him.

··· 3

The Ranch

MY FAMILY HAS ALWAYS CALLED THE HOMESTEAD that my father and Amanda took out in 1908 "the ranch," a term that borrows something of the glamour of cattle raising. Their intention, however, was to develop it into a farm. My father bought a share in a small sawmill and helped saw the lumber with which he built a house with walls twelve feet high and a pyramidal roof. At first there were no battings over the exterior siding and wind whistled through the cracks. The family used an outdoor privy and hauled water from the lake or took it from a nearby creek. After a year or two they dug a cistern in which they stored drinking water from an irrigation ditch. The exterior of the house, never painted, eventually took on a dark, weathered look. As far as I can remember, I never spent a night in the place, which burned down in 1962.

Today Lakeside is a resort for affluent refugees from the summer heat of Phoenix and Mesa. It forms a single town with Pinetop along a three- or four-mile stretch of highway with gutter and curb, motels, supermarkets, fast food restaurants, and a blaze of neon signs. Hundreds of vacation homes are scattered through the surrounding forest, which, after a century of fire suppression, is dense with thickets of small pines. In 1908, the forest consisted of mature ponderosa pines with clean lower trunks and high, asymmetrical limbs. There was little understory, and people could see in all directions. Native grass sprouted among black igneous rocks. People sometimes saw a bear or a cougar in the forest, to say nothing of the more abundant wild turkeys and elk. On a corner of the ranch, a tiny creek formed a meadow thick with wild irises. The family called the place Flag Hollow and often went there for picnics. The wind that blew all spring in Snowflake blew here too. Moist air from the Gulf of Mexico produced a rainy season during the late summer. Before a storm, silvery white clouds boiled thousands of feet into the air. Sunsets were radiant, and the vast night sky twinkled with limitless stars.

During the busy fall of 1908 someone talked my father into campaigning for a seat in the Arizona territorial legislature. It says something for his prominence that he won. Christmas of 1908 was the leanest their daughter Leora could ever remember; they were essentially living without cash. In January 1909, as my father departed for a two-month session of the legislature in balmy Phoenix, Amanda and their five children moved into the incomplete ranch house to begin a mandatory residence on the homestead in order to prove up on the claim. Snow blew through the cracks, and Amanda changed the baby's diaper between the stove and a screen made of blankets draped on chairs. At chore time, she put on my father's pants and rubber boots and went out with ten-year-old Arley to chop wood and to milk a runty range cow a friend had lent them. Their nearest neighbor was a mile away. If Amanda was frightened, the children didn't know it. They remembered her as calm and competent.

My father returned from the legislature in March 1909 and got on with the spring plowing and the construction of fences, coops, and pens. Financial necessity bore down on the family, and in September 1909 my father resumed the principalship of the academy at Snowflake, his replacement having lasted only a year. For the next four years, my father was with his family only summers and weekends. While school was in session, he rented lodging in Snowflake and on Friday nights rode the thirty miles to Lakeside on a trotting horse named Maud. He boasted of having made the trip in as little as three hours and fifteen minutes. He may have enjoyed moments of reflection on these solitary rides through a juniper forest that gave way to piñon and then to ponderosa. Overall, his rides were probably tedious. On dark nights he may have been afraid, totally dependent on Maud to keep her footing. However, when he saw a full moon rising on the faraway eastern rim of the world, as I myself used to see it, I do not doubt he felt the ecstasy of being alive.

During this period he added a fourth year of high school to the academy's curriculum. He also became involved in the construction of a new academy building. The brick building finished in 1901 was gutted by fire on Thanksgiving night of 1910. Classes went on without interruption in the town social hall, the church house, and even private homes. The brick walls were torn down, and a new structure of hewn stone from a local quarry was built. This building, dedicated in 1913, still stands on the campus of the high school at Snowflake. When I was in high school in the 1940s, it was called the Peterson Building. A large portrait photograph of my father hung on an auditorium wall. Whenever I have met his former students, they have been effusive in their praise of his teaching. But what struck others as masterful teaching may have struck him as perfunctory. He sometimes said that he could have been happy as a full-time farmer. Furthermore, he seems to have undervalued education as an end in itself. In keeping with the pedagogy of his time, he believed its purposes were to form character and prepare one for earning a living. He had an intellectual bent, yet he did not urge his children to delve into the scientific or humanistic traditions of higher education, as may be seen in a letter he wrote Arley from Snowflake on his twelfth birthday urging him to study hard in grade school so that he could succeed in the academy. "If you do this," he writes, "I will try to give you an education in Agriculture or Stockraising in some good school or college."[1] If he had ever had faith in learning as an end in itself, he had left it behind.

According to Arley, our father was a good farmer. He read books and pamphlets on scientific farming and consulted with professors of agriculture at the University of Arizona at Tucson on techniques of dry farming. He applied one such technique, for example, by having Arley harrow the fields in the early spring to seal in the winter's moisture. He wasn't afraid of hard work, often having his fields plowed and planted before the neighboring farmers. He took pride in being able to plow an acre of land in a single day with his team of small horses. He marshaled the entire family to clear the igneous rocks that freezing and thawing repeatedly forced to the surface; scattered piles of the black stone slowly grew among the fields. As for Amanda, she continued to work outside in his absence. She and Arley built an aboveground root house of double lumber walls insulated by sawdust where they kept potatoes, carrots, turnips, and squash without freezing. She read articles in *Farm and Fireside* and other magazines on how to keep her hens laying eggs in the winter. Among other things, she hung up cabbages where the chickens could peck them.[2]

In September 1913, having proved up on the homestead, the family moved to Snowflake for the school year. There, in March 1914, their sixth and final child, Wanda, was born. When school adjourned, my father resigned from teaching for a third time, and the family returned to Lakeside, optimistic enough to take out a $1,700 farm loan with which to make improvements on the ranch and buy fourteen head of range cattle. This farm loan would hang over the family well into my mother's era, the interest ultimately amounting to much more than the original. It was, in fact, a major irritant in my mother's life. In 1912 my father had twelve acres under cultivation, raising, as he reported when proving up on the homestead, "one hundred thirty bushels of oats and one ton of alfalfa, and also five hundred pounds of potatoes and some corn." He valued his total improvements, including house, barn, granary, and fences, at $1,010.[3] In light of that, the loan of $1,700 seems improvident. My father and Amanda's homestead, like hundreds of others taken out during the first two decades of the twentieth century, had little potential beyond mere subsistence, a fact to which they remained oblivious for a long time.

The ranch was a symbol as well as an economic reality. They were as happy with their expectation of prosperity as they might have been with prosperity itself. The ranch had an idyllic beauty in the summer. It gave them a sense of high purpose. It gave them standing in Lakeside, where they had a close, friendly relationship with the other families, being intimately involved in all their church meetings and socials. They were no poorer than anyone else. Their children were healthy. In short, the ranch defined who they were and what they aspired to and stood as a concrete embodiment of that transcendent happiness that human beings instinctively expect of life until age and experience have disabused them.

Economic reality seems to have asserted itself enough that my father was willing to campaign for the office of county school superintendent during the fall of 1914. He won and in January 1915 began to spend his weekdays in Holbrook, the county seat nearly sixty miles north of Lakeside. Navajo County was about 230 miles long and 50 miles wide. Its northern half lay within the Navajo and Hopi reservations, whose schools were supervised by the Bureau of Indian Affairs. Even so, my father's jurisdiction covered an immense territory. There were substantial schools in a number of towns and a host of one-room schools scattered widely throughout the southern half of the county. My father visited all these schools periodically, probably once a year. He facilitated these visits, as well as weekend trips to Lakeside, by purchasing a Model T Ford shortly before taking office. The farm loan must have financed this car, at least indirectly. There were no paved roads in Navajo County and very few graveled ones. Our family lore is full of mechanical failures, flat tires repaired on the spot, steep hills requiring all passengers to disembark and push, and roads made impassible by mud and flash floods.

In the spring of 1915, Arley and Leora graduated from the eighth grade in Lakeside. Arley was sixteen, Leora fourteen. Years earlier, Amanda's niece, Pearl Potter, teaching in Lakeside's one-room grade school, had put Arley back two grades and Leora one. I suspect this was for the purpose of helping Cousin Pearl, as she insisted on being called, manage her other pupils rather than for the academic improvement of Arley and Leora. In the fall of 1915, my father and Amanda decided they could not afford to send Arley and Leora to Snowflake to attend high school at the academy—a fact that astonishes me when I consider that my father was the foremost representative of education in the county. So that year Amanda and the children lived on the ranch again, and my father commuted by automobile from Holbrook whenever he could. I suppose he recognized they could not realize their ambitions for the ranch without Arley's labor, and Amanda was happy enough to keep her family intact as long as possible.

A year later, in the fall of 1916, they had a change of heart and sent Arley and Leora to Snowflake for their freshman year at the academy. Amanda remained on the ranch with the four younger children. They sold the fourteen head of range cattle to a judge in Holbrook, evidence, I think, that they were beginning to admit the poor prospects of the ranch. They may have turned the proceeds of the sale toward the everyday expenses of a family divided among three towns. Indirectly at least, the sale must have helped them pay for the house they bought in Holbrook in the fall of 1917. For the next two school years the family lived in Holbrook with at least some of them returning to the ranch each summer.

Holbrook figures so little in family lore that I was an adult before I realized my father's first family had dwelled there for two years. Then as later, Holbrook was one of the most barren, unwatered, downright ugly towns within the boundaries of the United States. Small frame houses sat on bare, desolated lots. South of town ran the Little Colorado, sandy and dry most of the year but dangerously full of muddy, roiling water when torrential rains fell upstream. Trains rumbled by on the Santa Fe tracks night and day. Farmers, traveling salesmen, Hispanic track workers, Indians, and cowboys from the surrounding ranges sauntered the commercial district. Mormons, dominant in most of the upcountry towns, were a distinct minority here.

The domestic life of the family must have gone on pleasantly enough in Holbrook. They were together with a regularity they had rarely experienced before. Sometimes Amanda accompanied my father on his school visits around the county. The only existing photograph of the entire family shows them in the Model T. In this photograph and several others from the Holbrook era, Amanda appears thin, even wiry, and very tan and windblown. Her hair, somewhat wispy, is tied in a bun on top of her head, her favorite way of keeping it. She looks kind, competent, and durable. Across the ninety years that have passed since these photographs were taken, I intuit the strength and loveliness of her personality. Nonetheless, she could carp at her children, if we believe Leora, who says Amanda scolded her for reading too much and neglecting her household chores.

Amanda deemed the rangeland ballad "Streets of Laredo," which refers obliquely to a dying cowboy's visits to a brothel and gambling den, to be indecent and wouldn't let her children sing it. My father shared her standard of decency, believing implicitly in the high-minded ideals he urged upon students in classroom and assembly hall. A long single-spaced letter he typed to Arley in August 1916 summarizes the virtues Arley was to adopt and the vices he was to eschew. Our father warns that smoking will damage Arley's intellect, for he has seen bright boys who "have lost their reason and been sent to insane asylums" because of tobacco. He spends an entire page on masturbation. This habit, which he calls "self abuse or secret vice," leads to addiction, a weakening of the male sexual organs, inferior offspring, and an inability to sire children.[4]

My father was, I believe, a good parent but perhaps not as calm and equable as Amanda. He could not abide a stubborn child, and sons from both his first and second families, Elwood and Roald, report whippings that went to the point of brutality. With Elwood the issue was five cents missing from his savings, which he had spent on forbidden candy. When Amanda asked where the money was, Elwood said he didn't know. Amanda turned him over to our father who began switching his buttocks with a willow. Elwood refused to speak or cry, and the beating went on and on. When our father stopped, he sent Elwood to bed.[5] I once saw my brother Andelin beat one of his sons with a belt, and I have wondered lately whether Andelin took example from our father. However, our father said he never spanked Wanda. I don't remember him ever spanking me. All his children recall that his first response, positive or negative, to any request they made would be his last. He never changed his mind. It is also true that he nursed his children tenderly when they were ill and entertained them often with stories, songs, and such feats as balancing a chair on his chin.

All the family except my father went to the ranch during the early summer of 1919. He came for the Fourth of July celebration. When it was over, he took Amanda and Wanda back to Holbrook. Amanda wanted to bottle currants, available from peddlers in Holbrook. They promised to join the other children in Lakeside for Pioneer Day on the twenty-fourth of July. On that day, my father phoned saying Amanda was ill and asking Retta Hansen, a practical nurse and Amanda's best friend, to come to Holbrook to care for her. My father later recorded that she had influenza. A couple of doctors apparently disagreed. One diagnosed Amanda's disease as typhoid; the other said it was congestion and inflammation of bowels and the bladder with enlargement of the liver and spleen. Neither doctor helped her. Three weeks passed. Retta, who had a large family, wanted to go home, but Amanda wouldn't let her. Unable to admit Amanda was dying, my father didn't have the children come see her. Very early on August 16, Amanda told him she was chilling. He went outside and pumped water to heat and pour into bottles for packing around her. When he came back, she said, "You are too late, Papa," and died. It was a great agony to my father that he had not had the children come. Retta sorrowed while she washed Amanda's hair and laid out her body. Aunt Janette Smith, an elderly widow of the stake president who had first brought my father to Snowflake, donated temple clothes she had been saving for her own burial. My father bought a beautiful white plush casket on credit.

They took Amanda's body to Lakeside that night, arriving at sunrise on August 17. The funeral was held in the schoolhouse, which served for church meetings as well. After the service the casket was opened, and everyone filed by to view the body. Leora demurred but our father insisted. "Her face looked peaceful and lovely, but her stomach was swollen," Leora writes.[6] Our father held Wanda and let her look down on her mother. "She looked very natural to me, just like she was sleeping," Wanda remembers. "I did notice that she had a small fever blister between her lips."[7] They buried her in a new cemetery immediately west of the lake. Pines and oaks gave the plot an uncultivated beauty. I doubt the bereaved family paid any attention to that. I feel most palpably their unspoken protest over surrendering those precious remains to the gravelly clay.

Amanda's mother came from Utah and stayed a couple of weeks. Leaving the cooking and dish washing to Leora, she mended clothes and refurbished worn quilts. When school started, my father moved the six children into two rented rooms in Snowflake. He stayed in Holbrook during the week, coming to Snowflake on weekends. Arley, Leora, and Andelin went to high school every day, Earland and Elwood to grade school, and Wanda to Cousin Pearl's house. The children didn't engage in rebellious or unlawful behavior, didn't sulk, fret, or grieve aloud. A few days after Amanda's burial, Leora found thirteen-year-old Earland crying on the back step of the ranch house. She never saw him cry again. On that occasion she wanted to put her arms around him and comfort him. She didn't, inhibited by what she calls her "Swedish reserve." According to her autobiography, Leora's sense of loss was enormous; an essential ingredient to happiness was gone and would not be restored until she married and had children of her own twenty years later. "Dreams of my mother continued every night for years, then tapered off to two or three times a week, then gradually less for many more years, but never ceased entirely, even to this day. They were frustrating, heartbreaking dreams, often took strange and unlikely angles. Sometimes I thought she was forced to live away from us against her will; again she had left us because she wanted to."[8]

After Christmas, my father came down with the flu and soon had what the family has always called a nervous breakdown, occupying the boys' bed in the rented rooms in Snowflake for nearly four months. While an associate covered his duties at the courthouse in Holbrook, his children and kind neighbors nursed him. Arley, Leora, and Andelin took turns sitting up with him at night. Leora writes: "He could not endure anything for long. He would ask me to read to him, and after a couple of pages would order me to stop. He could stand no more. He was wracked with pains, he shifted positions, went into cold sweats that soaked him through. He wept, he despaired. Thinking he might die also, he told me where all his papers were and what to do about them."[9]

Arley and Leora graduated from high school in May 1920. My father sent the boys to the ranch to begin spring plowing. By the first of June, feeling better, he followed with Leora and Wanda. "We were a sad little group," writes Leora, "bereft of the pivot around which we had always revolved, she who had been the heart and soul of the homestead, and the center of our existence."[10] While the boys farmed and Leora kept house, our father convalesced. He sat in the sun, puttered in the barnyard, took walks, and rode horseback, always accompanied by six-year-old Wanda. He returned to his duties in Holbrook in the fall, but when his term had expired at the end of the year, he went back to the ranch. Although Leora calls 1921 "a starvation year," the family was actually in for a three-year period of near starvation. A national recession had set in. Arley and Andelin earned a little cash from brief jobs. Otherwise the family had to depend on the produce of the farm, much of which had to go toward the farm loan payment. In his unpublished reminiscence Elwood recalls the diet of these hard times: "We ate 'blue filling' I guess probably Andelin's name for hot water colored a little with a little milk with sugar in it. Corn bread or hot baking powder bread with it. I can remember a good many meals of parched corn crushed in a hand sausage grinder with water and sugar on it or possibly, if we were lucky, some milk."[11]

Times were too hard to allow Andelin to return to school in Snowflake. So the foremost representative of education in Navajo County had one son who never finished high school. When Earland graduated from the Lakeside grade school in May 1922, they had to assemble decent attire from the combined wardrobes of Arley and Andelin. The Model T had worn out and couldn't be replaced. Yet life wasn't altogether bad, and slowly they recovered their spirits. They attended church, dances, and holiday celebrations and enjoyed the solicitude of good friends. Retta Hansen had them to her house for Thanksgiving and Christmas dinners. My father's brother Hyrum had bought the homestead just east of theirs; he, his wife, Anna, and their growing brood of strapping boys made companionable neighbors. During the fall of 1922 my father ran for the office of county supervisor and won the part-time position, which brought in a little cash. For the next two years he made monthly trips to Holbrook.

The family circle began to dissolve. Arley married Coral Shumway in October 1922, and Andelin married Bessie Rhoton in June 1923. In the fall of 1923 Leora went away to a business college in Los Angeles, an expense our father met by selling a crop of potatoes at Whiteriver. As 1924 dawned, he and his other children moved to Snowflake where he took a position teaching English, vacated midyear, at the stake academy, which would become a public high school at the beginning of the next academic year. Approaching his fiftieth birthday, he was revived in spirit and had some cash. He had been writing to a much younger divorced woman in Salt Lake City with near indifference for three years. He had not seen her in person for four. A friend from Snowflake mentioned that he intended to ask this woman to marry him. My father suddenly decided to write something more than a friendly letter, and a new era began in his life.

I understood very early in childhood that the family to which I belonged had been reconstructed from remnants. I have always been curious to know the histories of those remnants, one of which I have summarized in this chapter. I am particularly glad to be more intimately acquainted with Amanda, whom my father loved deeply and whom six of my elder siblings called mother. I pondered Amanda at an early age. My mind had an image of her from photographs. When the wind crooned in the eaves and I was alone in our house, I thought of Amanda and made connections between her and things remote, mysterious, and sad. Even now, it is a sobering thought that my father didn't need any more children than those he had by Amanda. Had she stayed in Lakeside that fateful summer, had she not gone to Holbrook to bottle currants, she and my father might have gone on with their happy marriage, retiring to the ranch and finding comfort in the role of grandparents, and my immediate brothers and I might never have been born.

··· 4

My Mother's First Marriage

MY MOTHER CONFIDED THINGS IN HER CHILDREN while they were still very young, so I can't say exactly how old I was when I began to learn about her first marriage. It was one of the stories she was most likely to tell, elaborate and many faceted and rarely to be completed in a single telling. Long before she became old, it had dawned on me that her brief marriage to N. J. Smith was an extraordinary saga, full of conflict, suspense, and puzzling hints of hidden traits in her personality. Any telling of this lengthy story was above all a confession of a dreadful mistake on her part, and her predominant emotion in telling it was a deep, immitigable shame. That she never recovered from this shame, not even in her old age, only whetted my appetite for knowing how she had been led to make such a mistake.

Born on December 21, 1892, in Woodruff, a hamlet about twenty miles north of Snowflake, my mother was named Lydia Jane Savage. Her father was Levi M. Savage, longtime bishop of Woodruff, and her mother was Lydia Lenora Hatch, called Nora. My mother considered the domicile of her father's other wife, Hannah Adeline Hatch, called Addie, as her own, mingling with her half brothers and sisters with as complete a familiarity as with her full siblings. The routines of the family were rural. Lydia learned to cook and sew indoors and milk cows and tend chickens and pigs outdoors. Once she stumbled and fell while carrying the brimming chamber pot of her maternal grandmother, who lived across the street, and she watched in amazement as waves of urine surged across the plank floor of the kitchen.

The pieties of the family imprinted themselves indelibly upon Lydia's character and, indirectly, upon mine. Profoundly ethnocentric, Levi and his wives were suspicious of "outsiders," as they called those who were not Mormon, and contemptuous of Jack Mormons, as they called less-than-faithful Mormons; without hesitation, they consigned both these categories of malefactors to the lesser glories in the hereafter. Obedience to authority was an unwavering principle with them; it was this trait, in fact, that held them in Woodruff. In an era when many good Mormons smoked or drank tea and coffee, Levi and his wives practiced the Word of Wisdom with an exactitude impressive even by modern standards. They resorted to the rituals of healing through prayer for the slightest ills. They believed in dreams, visions, and spiritual manifestations, and they abhorred profanity and swearing. They expected the return of the Savior within their lifetime and kept their temple robes ready to put on at the moment of his appearance.

My mother attended grade school in Woodruff, graduating from the eighth grade at fifteen. Her mother kept her at home one more year before allowing her to attend high school in Snowflake. My mother liked her classes at the academy and did well enough to be selected to deliver the farewell oration at her class's graduation in 1912. She took classes from Joseph Peterson, principal of the academy. Oblivious to her future connection with him, she shared in Snowflake society's veneration of this man, a veneration she would not lose throughout nineteen years as his wife.

In the fall of 1912 my mother returned to Snowflake to enter a newly instituted fourth year of high school. There she met a man recently come from Mexico, Jessie N. Smith III, usually called N. J. to distinguish him from his father and his illustrious grandfather, first president of Snowflake Stake and one of the most influential Mormons in northern Arizona during pioneer times. My mother was impressed by the Smith name, a fact she would repeat over and over to explain why she had consented to marry N. J. At thirty, he was ten years my mother's senior. He didn't have a job and he smoked, which precluded the temple marriage my mother's parents expected. She went to her father for advice, expecting—and wanting—him to forbid the marriage. He said blandly, "Well, men can stop smoking." Thrown back on her own judgment, she proceeded. She and N. J. were married by a judge in Holbrook on January 20, 1913. Her mother attended the ceremony. Her father did not, and she took his absence as an overt, if belated, expression of disapproval.

Following the ceremony, the newly married couple returned by wagon to Snowflake where N. J. established my mother in one of the rooms his mother had rented in a hotel. Leaving her to sob alone in the room, N. J. spent the evening with the proprietor of the hotel. Later she conjectured that his absence on this evening, and on every other evening of the following week, had to do with his fastidiousness about smoking in the presence of his mother and his wife. She attributed his refusal to let her go rabbit hunting with him during that week to the same motive. He seemed to have no need for conversation with her. She told me they rarely quarreled. In fact, they didn't talk at all except about perfunctory matters.

Within a couple of weeks of their wedding, she persuaded him to take a job as a carpenter in St. Johns, about forty miles east of Snowflake. Here she found a new reason to be dissatisfied with him. He wasn't troubled by unpaid bills. Once, with rent and an account at a grocery store in arrears, he spent his paycheck on a set of red cut-glass dishware. He was astonished that she wasn't pleased. She describes their furniture in her autobiography: "I had next to nothing and no window curtains. I did have a bed, several chairs, a table, kitchen stove, and tubs for washday with a good washboard."[1] That she found N. J. constantly irritating may be inferred from the vindictive pleasure she took in recounting the following story over and over to her children. Someone had told him turpentine served well as a medication for hemorrhoids. While she watched, he dosed himself with turpentine. He shrieked and, on all fours, climbed over the bed and went across the floor barking like a dog.

Lenora was born in St. Johns in December 1913. My mother often told me she had envied men for their greater freedom until she had her first child. Motherhood was an instinctive joy with her. When Lenora was about six weeks old, N. J. rented a wagon and they went to Snowflake to visit his mother. While there, my mother went to a high school assembly to show off her baby. She sat by Joseph Peterson's wife, Amanda, pregnant with Wanda, and afterward went about the campus with her. Presumably neither woman had a premonition that the infant Lenora and unborn Wanda were destined to become stepsisters.

By midsummer of 1914, N. J.'s carpentering job had ended, and his brother found him a part-time job hauling parcel-post mail from Holbrook to St. Johns. N. J. moved to Holbrook, and my mother went home to live with her parents in Woodruff, which lay on the road between Holbrook and St. Johns. About every two weeks, N. J. stopped by Woodruff to spend a night and, as I judge, to exercise his connubial right with his wife. He was present on the night in early April 1915 when the town's dam in the Little Colorado washed out. From that memorable occasion my mother dated the conception of her daughter Mary, as she often told me. While staying in Woodruff, my mother entered a church-sponsored essay contest that she hoped would pay her way to Salt Lake City where, if N. J. could stop smoking and earn enough money to buy himself a ticket on the train, they could be married in the temple. She won the contest, but no ticket to Salt Lake City materialized, which was probably just as well, considering that N. J. could neither stop smoking nor buy his own ticket. Obviously she still hoped to rehabilitate her husband. She was enormously ashamed of him, deriving no status from him in any social circle she cared about. Ironically, I owe my existence to N. J.'s addiction to nicotine, which kept him from a temple marriage to my mother. My father would never have married her had she been already sealed in the temple to another man.

Not long after the dam washed out, N. J.'s mail-freighting job ended. He had another job of sorts in Holbrook—meeting trains and directing travelers to certain hotels. Apparently it was on the strength of this job that my mother took up domicile with him in Holbrook. However, it proved not much of a job. "Very few passengers ever got off," my mother writes in her autobiography, "and those that did were fairly well informed where to go or were met by their own parties. That left N. J. with many hours on his hands. These he spent in the local pool hall."[2] The little family rented a single room and, as in St. Johns, accrued unpaid bills. During my mother's mandatory ten-day confinement following Mary's birth in January 1916, N. J. committed an unpardonable dereliction of duty. My mother had been delivering eggs to local households for her father. During her confinement, N. J. delivered the eggs and promptly spent the proceeds, amounting to fifty dollars. My mother angrily insisted that the sum be restored without her father knowing it had been spent. A chastened N. J. sought help from a brother, who arranged a loan from a prosperous Mormon in nearby Joseph

City. N. J. and my mother took a room in this man's house, and, while N. J. carpentered to pay off the loan, my mother did housework to pay for their board and room.

This brief period was, if not happy, at least promising because N. J. was engaged in honest labor and separated from his disreputable cronies in the taverns of Holbrook. However, when he had paid off the loan, N. J. asked his brother to drive him to Holbrook, where he continued to meet trains and lounge in taverns. My mother accompanied him on the trip to Holbrook but didn't stay, having secured a dilapidated room in Joseph City. During the return drive to Joseph City, she sobbed uncontrollably. Her brother-in-law asked if she meant to divorce N. J. She said no. Later, when she had, he would accuse her of lying. The truth is that to this point she had rejected the possibility. This was 1916, and a woman couldn't divorce a man for the mere fact that he lounged in pool halls and sired children he couldn't support. The depth of her inhibition against divorce may be judged by the unconcealed shame with which, as I have said, she endlessly repeated the story of her first marriage to her children.

In the immediate aftermath of N. J.'s return to Holbrook, my mother decided she would have to earn her own living. With her three-year high school diploma, she could qualify for a teaching certificate by passing a state examination, for which she now began to prepare. In the meantime, divorce had indeed entered her mind, possibly put there by the brother-in-law's question. One Sunday she fasted and prayed all day. "I told the Lord that I would do anything that he told me to do," she writes. "So many times I had prayed to the Lord to direct my life but up to this day I had never felt like I could face a divorce. So always that had been a block in my path. But today I had said and meant it that anything the Lord would tell me I would do."[3] This was not a decision to seek a divorce but merely a promise to obey God should he instruct her to seek one. She would agonize over this matter for months, constantly seeking direction from God or his servants, her church leaders. There was little in her social conditioning to make her believe she had the power to make such a decision on her own, having been trained from infancy to seek God's direction even in inconsequential things.

The next day my mother's sister Ruth, who had just returned from a mission, came to Joseph City to speak at a special conference. The sisters had a long conversation during which Ruth found my mother thinking not of divorcing N. J., but of teaching school while remaining married. Ruth pointed out that my mother couldn't teach if she continued having babies. My mother replied that she knew of women who had large families while teaching school. Later on the same day, while Ruth visited friends, my mother again engaged in fervent prayer with the following result. "Then it came to me and I formulated a plan. I must never again have wifely relations with N.J. That was the word that I got and the thing I must live by. I do not know if I thought of this in terms of a divorce but from that minute on it must hold. Never again could I be his wife."[4] My mother regarded this as a clear and unmistakable revelation, of which she spoke to me so repeatedly and with such conviction that I believed for forty years that she had had no further connubial relations with N. J. from that moment forward.

About two weeks after Ruth left, N. J. made his way to Joseph City. He probably wanted to see Lenora and Mary. Undoubtedly he also counted on having sex with his wife, who probably refused. In any event, an open discussion of separation ensued. "When he was finally convinced that I meant it, he said that I could not take Lenora with me. He would keep her. Here was a new angle."[5] Obviously, leaving N. J. was a complicated matter. With negotiations barely begun, he had already checked her. Nonetheless, my mother wrote her mother asking to come home. Nora, who happened to be in Idaho visiting her other daughter, had received a small legacy and proposed that she and Lydia spend a month doing genealogical research in Salt Lake City. They would take turns tending my mother's daughters and going to the genealogical library. N. J. was agreeable to this proposal on condition that, when her stay in Salt Lake was over, my mother would go to Parowan in southern Utah where his mother presently lived and where he now intended to go. Nora sent my mother money for her fare, and N. J. raised his fare by selling the few household effects he and my mother had acquired.

My mother spent the month of June and more than a week of July in Salt Lake City, confused beyond description. It seemed clear she was never again to have sex with N. J. yet not clear whether she was to take the drastic step of divorcing him. She wrote the president of Snowflake Stake, Samuel F. Smith, a son of the pioneer stake president Jesse N. Smith and therefore an uncle to N. J. and, by virtue of having married Nora's half-sister Lulu Hatch, an uncle to Lydia herself. Samuel's reply is extant. On the one hand, he reminds her that in the Sermon on the Mount Jesus forbids divorce for any reason except adultery. On the other hand, he cites Brigham Young's opinion that a woman can leave a man who has become unbearable and unworthy. He warns that divorce will distance her even further from the indispensable blessings of a temple marriage—necessary in the Mormon worldview for the higher levels of glory in the hereafter. "If you are sure that you do not want to be sealed in the Temple to your husband—taking every chance that you must take without him, then you may be justified in a separation."[6] In short, the letter did nothing to resolve her confusion.

A few days after the letter came, my mother took the train for southern Utah as promised while Nora returned to Idaho for a brief extension of her visit with her other daughter. N. J. met the train at Lund and conveyed my mother to Parowan where his mother had prepared a pleasant supper. As the evening wore on, my mother suddenly realized that a point she had thought settled in Joseph City—that she and N. J. were to have no further sexual relations—was not settled at all. She writes: "Dark came late at that time of year, but as soon as preparations were made for bed I was filled with a great fear. I knew with great emphasis that I would or should never be N.J.'s wife again. Nonetheless we occupied the same room and the same bed for about 2½ months."[7]

I had this account orally long before I read it in her autobiography. Invariably she prefaced the fact that she had to share a bed with him with her certainty that the Lord had ordained there be no further sexual intercourse between them. I could conclude only that she had obeyed God's counsel. I marveled at her determination—and at the tension that must have existed between them—as night after night they undressed and got into the same bed to sleep as chastely as a brother and sister. It was only as she approached ninety and had fallen into a mild senility that she shocked me one day by casually mentioning that on the last night of their sleeping together they had made love. This so violated my prior understanding that I asked then and later whether what she had told me was true, and she said it was. Thereafter, I asked my siblings whether they knew about it. Only Lenora said she did. She sent me a copy of a letter my mother had written Nora about a week after arriving in Parowan. My mother mentions her great fear upon going to bed with N. J. on the first night. She says things have happened twice that shouldn't have. She says she longs for living on a higher level and calls herself weak and erring. She asks Nora to pray for her and to write her long Gospel letters full of religious instruction.[8]

My mother was in an anomalous position. This man who couldn't afford a house to keep her in or groceries for her table had brought her home for keeping to his mother. The transfer of the scene of contention between my mother and N. J. to Parowan had greatly strengthened his hand, for his mother would be a competent and willing caretaker for Lenora should my mother decide to go through with the threatened separation. My mother writes: "Day after day I wrestled in the spirit and prayed mightily night and day to be guided. Where should I go? What should I do? My days were a constant prayer. To leave one of my precious children seemed impossible. Still I knew that my life with N.J. must end. I continually told the Lord I would do whatever he told me to do. But if the answer was to leave my daughter, either one of them, I hardly saw how I could live."[9]

After a couple of weeks, Nora sent more money, and my mother traveled by train to Idaho for a brief visit, leaving Lenora with N. J.'s mother. The purpose of this visit was a second patriarchal blessing that a maternal uncle gave her in hopes that it would clarify her course of action. This visit may also have been a kind of time-out for additional coaching by her mother in the war of wills being waged between her and N. J. When my mother returned to Parowan, Nora accompanied her and stayed for about a week before traveling on to rejoin her husband in Arizona. During this week, Nora advanced abundant arguments to N. J.'s mother as to why my mother should be allowed to leave and take Lenora with her. N. J.'s mother remained unpersuaded.

A resolution to Mother's turmoil was closer than she had imagined. One night in late August she and N. J. lay in their bed the entire night talking about the grievances they held against one another.

My mother was surprised how many N. J. held. She was particularly astonished to learn that he resented her inability to sing well. Discussing their future, she conceded that if she left him, she would leave Lenora behind and when Mary was older return and exchange Mary for Lenora so that they could each know both their daughters. It was at the end of this wakeful night that the instance of lovemaking occurred of which my mother informed me in her old age. Immediately after that event had transpired, the couple arose and N. J. prepared to depart for a week in the mountains working at a brother's sawmill. He shook my mother's hand and asked whether she would be gone when he got back. She said, "I guess not." It was, however, the last time they would ever see each other.

A day or two later, rereading her recent patriarchal blessing, my mother was struck by a previously overlooked sentence: "In due time the Lord will make known unto you through his servants his mind and will concerning you and your affairs in life."[10] It occurred to her she must write again to Samuel Smith, her stake president. She wrote a letter and walked to the post office intending to mail it but was deterred by an emotion that, then and later, she interpreted as a directive from God. A little later on the same day a man traveling by wagon to St. George stopped for dinner at the Smith home. Learning that he would pass through Toquerville, where her father's brother lived, she asked for a ride. N. J.'s mother agreed that it would make a nice diversion for my mother and the girls to spend a few days with this uncle. My mother packed a few belongings and, as she left town, mailed her letter to Samuel Smith with the added information that his reply must be sent to Toquerville. Neither her letter nor her uncle's reply is extant, but a crucial sentence from his reply is quoted in a letter she wrote her parents on September 6, 1916: "If I understand the situation and conditions existing between you and your husband & I hope I do, you would better take your two children, both of them and go to your parents."[11] This positive advice from a church leader was all the catalyst she needed. Her letter of September 6 informed her parents that she would arrive in Holbrook by train on the following Monday, the same day when, as she candidly told them, N. J. expected her in Parowan. She also told them she would have to travel a roundabout route to the railroad because she expected that N. J. would be in Cedar City, through which the direct route ran.

She was fleeing in a literal sense, taking Lenora as well as Mary despite a promise to do otherwise. She had reason for anxiety because if N. J. had thwarted her escape, she had little recourse. Whether or not a court would have sided with N. J. in a custody dispute, my mother feared that it would. Furthermore, there would have been little safety even in flight had it not been for the approval and assistance of two men, her stake president and her father. She lived in an era when women had few powers.

She took a stage from Toquerville to St. George and stayed overnight with her father's sister. Well before dawn she left St. George on a buckboard that carried mail to Enterprise. Following approximately today's state highway 18, their route led west of the Pine Valley Mountains, over which, as my mother told me many times, a sickle moon stood as they left St. George. While the buckboard jolted and twisted in rutted tracks, my mother held Mary in her arms and supported Lenora at her side. In the afternoon, they passed the site of the Mountain Meadows massacre, which the driver pointed out. My mother knew the dark lore of that bloody event because her ancestors had immigrated into southern Utah shortly after its occurrence and one of her sisters had married a grandson of John D. Lee, a major participant in the massacre.

At sundown the buckboard reached the village of Enterprise on the Utah-Nevada border. The next morning she rode in an automobile carrying mail to Modena on the Union Pacific line. She got a meal from a kind woman who let her stay in her house till sundown, when she went to the depot. It was chilly and the station agent offered to let her sit inside. She declined, preferring to sit on a bench outside for reasons I don't understand. She opened her suitcase and laid Mary in it and held Lenora on her lap. At two in the morning she boarded a train, and for the first time in days she began to feel secure.

Her autobiography says she reached Holbrook at ten o'clock that same morning. It was probably at ten o'clock of the day after because she had to change trains in Barstow and the entire trip was close to five hundred miles. In any event, she made Holbrook safely and took the mail buckboard to Woodruff, arriving at last in the refuge of her parents' home. N. J. sent a telegram that day, which is extant. Dated September 15, 1916, it reads: "Mrs. Lydia S. Smith. Wire me your purpose and intentions at once. So I will not have to call you back by law. N.J. Smith."[12] She asked her father what she should do. He told her to ignore the telegram. She heard no more from N. J., who, besides lacking the means to hire a lawyer, likely feared the moral authority of her father.

My mother was divorced from N. J. in 1918 by the same judge who had married them. She writes: "I stood in the same room and in the same spot when he gave the divorce as I had stood when I was married to N.J. Oh! The sorrow of it all. But I believe it was a great schooling to me."[13] N. J. did not contest the divorce, and Lenora and Mary remained in her custody. She was twenty-three when she fled N. J., and twenty-five when she was divorced. She did not remarry till she was thirty-one.

My mother's first marriage influenced me in innumerable ways. I'm not ashamed of it, as she was. I feel her despair over having ruined her life and her incredulous joy upon marrying my father. Above all, I feel the unspoken humiliation of her utter dependence on other men to effect her escape from N. J. If I have a single overriding emotional response to the saga of my mother's first marriage, it is anger against my own gender for the dominance it has maintained, and continues to maintain, over women. Knowing my mother so intimately, I couldn't fail to respect women as the full equals of men.

··· 5

The Family I Was Born Into

CONSIDERING EVERYTHING, I AM ASTONISHED that my mother and father ever married. It seems incredible that my mother persisted in her letter writing during four arid years and that my father, when he at last felt moved to remarry, believed his options narrowed to her and one other slightly less eligible woman. As far as my mother was concerned, this had nothing to do with chance. For her, it was unmistakably God's will and doing.

After escaping from N. J., my mother lived with her parents in Woodruff for a couple of years. She passed a teacher's examination and took a position teaching in a one-room school in a tiny ranching community. At the beginning of her second year at this school, she was visited by county school superintendent Joseph Peterson. This was 1919, and he had lost his wife only a few weeks earlier. In January 1920 she conversed with him again at a teacher's convention in Winslow. Although he was nineteen years her senior, these brief encounters awakened her to the hope of marrying him, as she told me later.

My mother soon had reason to doubt whether even God could bring about such a miracle. Before the school year ended, her father wrote from Salt Lake City, where he and Nora had moved a year earlier, informing her that Nora was ill and asking my mother to come help take care of her. When the summer of 1920 came, my mother reluctantly obeyed. Though Nora soon recovered, there was no talk of my mother returning to Arizona. Securing a temporary certificate by attending summer classes at the University of Utah, she taught as a substitute teacher in nearby school districts for three years. Although her prospects for marriage seemed bleak, she initiated a correspondence by writing my father about her credentials.

When he replied, she followed with another letter, having no other pretext than friendship. He answered under the same cautious pretext, showing an interest that, in the desultory correspondence that followed, proved considerably more tentative than hers. He often allowed weeks to lapse before answering her letters. In December 1923 another widower from Arizona wrote my mother a proposal of marriage. Playing her new trump card skillfully, my mother wrote asking my father whether she should accept this proposal. My father knew of it already because the man had confided it to him. Jolted from his complacence, my father responded with a proposal of his own, which he made conditional upon her answers to what he called "frank, perhaps blunt" questions:

> You have been married, another man is the father of your children. Do you still have a lingering love for that man, or do you *feel* & *know* that you can love me more? There could be such a thing as that man having a feeling of returning to his first love and children. In that event I wouldn't want you ever to be sorry. Have you ever been *sealed* to your former husband or any other man? If so, how do you propose to solve that problem?[1]

My mother replied that she harbored no latent affection for N.J. and had not been sealed to him by a temple marriage. In later years she candidly judged that it was this that induced my father to choose her over another young widow with whom he had maintained a long correspondence.

Their wedding took place on August 21, 1924, in the Salt Lake temple. Before the ceremony, my mother was interviewed by the entire quorum of twelve apostles on the question of having Lenora and Mary sealed to my father rather than to N. J. When she insisted, they consented, and in Mormon eyes, the girls became my father's daughters for eternity. No other formalities of adoption were ever considered necessary. With the help of neighbors, Nora put on a wedding dinner, following which, according to Mary, my father held my mother upon his lap. Leaving the girls with their grandparents, my father and mother spent three or four days in Lehi visiting his brothers and sisters, his parents being by now deceased. In later years my mother gave no sign of regarding this as anything less than a satisfactory honeymoon. Then they retrieved the girls, said good-bye to Levi and Nora, and departed for Arizona by train. They put the girls in an overhead Pullman berth, and Mary, who deems herself to have been an awkward child, prone to dropping bottles of milk and stumbling when there was nothing in her path, fell out in the middle of the night.

In Snowflake they rented rooms in a two-story house and settled in for the 1924–1925 school year with a composite family consisting of Earland, eighteen; Elwood, sixteen; Lenora, ten; Wanda, ten; and Mary, eight. Lenora and Mary called my father Papa, and Wanda called my mother Mother. Earland and Elwood called her Aunt Lydia. If there were serious frictions between them, none of the participants ever admitted it in my presence. I think my parents were determined to show no favorites. Lenora and Wanda remember my father holding them, sobbing, on either knee, while he adjudicated a squabble between them. Mary recalls Lenora and Wanda forcing her to occupy the middle spot in the bed they shared. My mother made the girls take turns at washing dishes and sweeping floors. Wanda often dallied till she was late for school, and her teacher came by to see whether the new stepmother was being abusive. I don't think Wanda resented the discipline. As an adult she spoke of our mother with unfeigned affection.

My father's reputation as a teacher grew, and he continued to be known as Professor Peterson. In October 1924, he was called to be first counselor to stake president Samuel F. Smith, a position he held till 1939. The call was unanticipated by its giver as well as its recipient. While waiting for a stake conference to begin, President Smith sat on the stand pondering who should be his new first counselor. When my father walked into the meeting hall, President Smith said to himself, "That's my man." Needless to say, my father's prominence ensured my mother of considerable status. She was almost immediately called to the stake Relief Society board and a little later served as a counselor in its presidency. She liked to tell of a woman at church who saw her holding my father's hat on her lap while he sat on the stand as befitted his new position. The woman commented, "Well, look at the heights you have come to!"

My parents' first child, Alma, was born in May 1925. In Alma, my father's children by Amanda and my mother's children by N. J. sensed a blood relationship with each other that had hitherto been lacking, and the instinctive fervor of their love for him spilled over into their affection for each other. When school adjourned a week or two later, the family moved to the ranch at Lakeside for the summer, taking their piano and sewing machine. My father immediately departed for a summer session at the University of California. Suppressing whatever trepidation she may have felt for entering upon Amanda's territory, my mother attacked the dilapidated, soiled ranch house with vigor. Marshaling the children, she scrubbed floors, calcimined walls, and routed bedbugs with repeated applications of kerosene. One day when Arley, married and living in his own house in Lakeside, tried to recruit Earland and Elwood for tilling crops in the ranch fields, they said they had to haul water from the creek for wash day. "Aunt Lydia uses too much water," Arley grumbled. Obviously my father returned from summer school to find neglected fields but an improved ranch house. The family returned to Lakeside for four more summers. Those were rich summers for the girls, who swam in the creek, roamed the woods, and fraternized with local boys, who included the sturdy, handsome sons of my father's brother Hyrum and his wife, Anna.

Arley and Andelin and their families often gathered with my parents' family for dinners and celebrations in both Lakeside and Snowflake, gatherings from which Leora was at first absent, being at college in Salt Lake City. By the time my brother Charles was born in January 1927, the extended family was developing a two-tiered nature in which the offspring of my parents mingled as peers with the offspring of their older siblings.

Though the family was happily ascendant and expanding, it was fated to its share of grief. In early 1927, soon after the birth of their third child, Andelin's wife, Bessie, died and was buried in the Lakeside cemetery. In March 1927, Arley and Coral buried a stillborn daughter there. In August 1928 my father and mother's first born, Alma, died of dysentery and was buried beside Amanda.

No other death has had the impact on me of Alma's. My mother recounted its details over and over with such great sorrow that I for one internalized a deep and ineradicable grief. Alma contracted dysentery, possibly caused by unhygienic ways of processing milk and other foods or by the family's drinking water, collected in a cistern from an irrigation ditch. Suffering from intense cramps, Alma vomited, had diarrhea, and slowly dehydrated. The nearest hospi-

tal was Albuquerque where, had they set out immediately with
him, he might have been saved. My mother said it never occurred
to her to take him there. On one cold, rainy day my father held
Alma by the cookstove and sang him all the songs he had learned
in sheep camp. My mother showed him a pair of new shoes and a
pocket knife she had bought for him. At one point she said, "Oh,
Alma, you are awfully sick, aren't you?" He replied, "I don't want
dead." Startled, she took this as evidence that the angel of death
was present in the house. The next day, frantic because he was suffering so much, she asked my father and Arley to give him a blessing and tell God to take him if necessary but to spare him from
pain. My father refused to ask God to take him. Nonetheless, they
gave the suffering boy a blessing, and Arley asked that God's will
be done. All that I have narrated so far can be found in my mother's autobiography. What she left out of that account was the following, which she told to me many times with great emphasis.
After the men's blessing, she retreated to the orchard north of the
ranch house and, praying aloud, relinquished Alma to God, promising to restrain her sorrow if God would keep him from suffering
long. When she returned to the house, he was no longer in pain.
Shortly there was a strange rattling in his breath, and he died. She
believed herself sustained by angels for a week following Alma's
death. Then all support crashed, and a devastating and perpetual
grief fell upon her. Long afterward, she wondered whether she had
bargained away his life too soon and too easily.

Many times that winter in Snowflake, my father came home
from school and took the family for a ride in their Model A—his
way of distracting them from gloom. More important, he relented
on his determination to have no more children. He was, my mother
told me many times, a man of great self-control. Deciding that two
children were enough for an aging man, he had steadfastly re-
frained from sexual relations with her following Charles's birth.
However, within two months of Alma's death, Roald was conceived. Two years later it was Leon. Nearly two and a half years
later, it was I, the last of a combined total of thirteen children for
my parents.

During the spring of 1929, my father and mother bought a dilapidated frame house in Snowflake for six hundred dollars. It was

on a barren, unfenced lot above the ditch. Outside were a privy, a sagging barn, and a pigpen. They had to reglaze most of the windows, patch broken plaster, and pipe in culinary water from a main in the street. The next year they fenced the lot and began to plant trees, currant bushes, and grapevines, which they had to irrigate with culinary water. In a couple of years they added a large front room and an indoor bathroom to the house. Earland and Elwood graduated from high school and left home before this house came into the family, but for the rest of my father and mother's children, it became home. Roald was born in this house on July 14, 1929; Leon on July 21, 1931; and I on December 13, 1933. Lenora, Wanda, and Mary finished high school and got married while living in this house.

My father had to be persuaded to buy the house in Snowflake. He had counted on teaching for only a few years and then returning to the ranch. My mother opposed Lakeside for various reasons, among them perhaps the poverty awaiting them on the ranch and the many associations with Amanda she encountered there. The telling reason, however—the one that proved persuasive with my father—was the better prospects for raising a family in Snowflake. They judged Lakeside's grade school to be inferior to Snowflake's, and it had no high school. There was also the nebulous matter of Lakeside's disrepute. Snowflake, the center of Mormonism in Navajo County, did not lack for pride and self-esteem. Its citizens looked down on their confreres in the smaller Mormon towns for their poverty, uncouth manners, and supposed proclivity among their young men toward rowdy and ungodly behavior. My mother, a native of the humble outlying village of Woodruff, would have been more sensitive to the social disadvantages to their children of living in Lakeside than my father, who had both the skill and the disposition to mingle with the socially disfavored without harming his status among the socially elevated. In any event, my mother's will on this matter ruled, and with the purchase of the house in 1929, my father entered upon the last full decade of his life with a reorientation to Snowflake. By 1935 he had deeded the ranch at Lakeside to his children and bought a small, undeveloped farm on Silver Creek about two and a half miles south of Snowflake. He deeded each of Amanda's six children about thirty acres of the Lakeside land. He deeded each of my mother's six children five acres and agreed with my mother that the farm on Silver Creek would be divided among her children, as it eventually was. Andelin, married to Bessie's sister Goldie and well on the way toward siring nine more children, moved his family into the ranch house. Eventually, Andelin acquired most of the ranch from his siblings.

The farm on Silver Creek, which the family always referred to as "the Field," was to have enormous influence on me and my immediate brothers. Its seventy acres were split by the creek, along which grew a willow patch thick as a jungle. Near the bottom of our property, a wall of mortared rock diverted water into a ditch through a wheel-and-screw headgate. We called this "Rock Wall," another term with the force of a proper noun in the family lexicon. About a hundred yards below our property, a dam of concrete and rock diverted the water into another ditch. The top of the dam was a roadway by which we crossed to the east side of the farm. During the growing season, our milk cows pastured on the east side of the creek, which meant we had to cross the dam at least twice a day, whether we milked the cows in the pasture or whether we drove them home at evening and back in the morning. Half a dozen times a year, usually during the rainy season of July and August, cloudbursts upstream sent floods down the creek, making the dam crossing spectacular if not downright dangerous. The inadvertent effect of this dam was to make our farm susceptible to floods of extraordinary volume, which historically have occurred every three or four years. The 1930s were, however, an exceptionally dry decade, and my father owned the farm for five years before becoming fully aware of its susceptibility to floods.

Despite the Great Depression, I believe the 1930s were one of the happiest decades in the lives of both my parents. I was not present to witness the beginning of the decade, but I turned seven as it ended and the conditions into which the family grew during that decade were those that I took as stable, fixed, and given. Of all the influences on my future psyche, conscience, and worldview, none was greater than my family during this period.

In photographs from this era, my father appears as solemn, silvery haired, affixed with prominent ears, and always clad in suit, vest, white shirt, and tie. These photographs have superseded whatever unaided memory I might retain of his face.

I suppose he liked the prominence in which he stood at church and in school. As a member of the stake presidency, he sat in a position of honor on the stand at church, where as I clearly recall, he often slept. At school his reputation was such that he had merely to enter a classroom to quiet a crowd of chattering students. He assigned and graded themes and taught English and American literature, which he had studied during three summer sessions at Berkeley during the 1920s. He tried his hand at writing poetry, telling my mother that he believed he might have done something significant had he started earlier. His poems are in the tradition of Tennyson and Longfellow, further evidence that he belonged, temperamentally and culturally, to the nineteenth century. His poetry was highly esteemed in our family. It was with some disillusionment that I admitted, late in my graduate studies of literature, that his production of poems was so diminutive and little known that he scarcely merited the title of poet. None, so far as I know, were ever published.

His creative bent also showed itself in the pageants that he wrote and directed for performance by the senior class as graduation neared. The most notable feature of the pageants was their setting, the Pioneer Sink, the largest of a score of natural sinkholes among the junipers about ten miles northwest of Snowflake. This depression, an inverted parabola whose bottom was about a hundred yards across, had excellent acoustics. On a hot and sometimes windy Friday evening in May, the citizenry of southern Navajo County congregated on rock seats descending the sides of this sink to witness a drama of such dimension that troops of horses were often involved. The pageant of 1938, titled *The Adventures of the Red Cross Knight,* featured a dragon constructed of painted cloth stretched over a frame of metal rings, propelled from inside by a number of senior boys. I recall this creature coming down a trail into the sink, spitting fire from its mouth. I remember driving alone with my father in our Model A to rehearsals at the sink. On one trip he allowed me to play with a toy cap pistol that was to be used in the pageant; on another, he gave me a grape lollipop.

Contributing to my father's happiness during the 1930s were his many friends. All his life he showed himself to be gregarious, enjoying people and having a natural curiosity about them. I recall a number of instances when he took me along on some errand or another in the Model A and lingered so long conversing with an acquaintance he happened to meet that I whined and wheedled to go home—uselessly, I might add, because my father was not a man to be hurried by a child. Undoubtedly these chance excursions with my father were instructive. One day, as he and I arrived home in the car, he asked me to open the gate to the driveway, which I did with some difficulty, being at most five years old. As the car rolled past me, he said, "Thank you." I also said, "Thank you." "No," he said gently, "you say, 'You are welcome.'" Thus I learned how to be gracious to those who have thanked me. How many hundreds of other things did I learn from him without remembering my debt?

My father was particularly devoted to a handful of friends with whom he shared intellectual interests. These included the county agricultural agent, a partially retired lawyer, and an osteopathic physician, with whom he formed a club that met one evening each month. The physician, Neil Heywood, served as our family doctor. Indirectly, he was our relative because his first wife, long dead by my time, had been my mother's half sister. He was a Mormon but perhaps not a believer, rarely if ever attending church. Though said to be color blind, he raised elegant flowers on the church grounds as well as on his own lot. He was a skillful practitioner of general medicine, and Snowflake was lucky to have him. Every two or three years he vaccinated all the students in the grade school, an event to which I looked forward with nothing less than sheer terror. His services to our family were considerable. He delivered all the babies born in my parents' house, bandaged wounds, sewed up lacerations, and examined us when we had high fevers. I suppose my parents paid for his services before my father's death. Afterward, I am sure he gave his services free of charge to my mother. Quite early, I took Dr. Heywood as a model for what I wanted to become. I had a toy doctor's kit, and I often told people I was going to be a doctor when I grew up. It says much about my father that he had this somber, intelligent, and serviceable man as one of his closest and most intimate of friends.

As for my mother, she seems plain, almost severe, in the photographs of her years with my father. She had a prominent nose and a long chin affixed to a jutting lower jaw. She had very wide hips and long arms. Her hair was fine, thick, and auburn, and remained so even in her old age. In my early boyhood, she wore a corset when dressing up and adorned her face with powder, rouge, and lipstick. She wore round, brass-rimmed eyeglasses. Her palms and fingers were rough and cracked from housework (though, strangely, all the more comforting for that fact when she rubbed a sick child with alcohol or ointment), and she habitually lathered her hands with glycerin upon going to bed.

She spent a long period on her knees in secret prayer beside her bed both night and morning. From her I conceived of God as attentive to my welfare, and I recall having very amicable feelings toward this solemn, grand personage who dwelled out of sight but not out of earshot. However, I also gathered from her that God would brook no trifling with the Commandments. One Saturday while she waxed the hardwood floor in the front room, I cut a slice of bread and broke it into bits on a plate, then carried it into the front room and offered her a morsel in imitation of the priests and deacons who prepare and pass the sacrament on Sunday. My mother reacted with an emotion close to horror. "Never, never pretend that you are doing sacred things," she pleaded with deep consternation, as if I had reached out a hand to steady the ark and was in imminent danger of being struck dead for sacrilege.

I hasten to say that much of the civilizing I have undergone along the line of affection, loyalty, and interest in my fellow human beings I owe to my mother. Over and over she communicated an unconditional love for me during my formative years, infusing me with a propensity to affirm and take pleasure in human beings rather than to injure or begrudge them, a contribution to my adult personality very worth having.

There were reasons my mother might have considered herself unhappy. I have the impression that I saw my mother cry many times during my early childhood, though specific memories are hard to evoke. I do recall once coming silently into the kitchen and observing her at the counter sobbing while she tenderized a steak by pounding it with a large butcher knife with a vehemence that I took to express anger. If the 1930s were nonetheless a happy decade for her, it was because the welfare of her family, pursued with indefatigable intent, was her joy. With both guilt and gratitude I recognize that her chief happiness consisted of seeing her family sheltered, fed, groomed, and sent about their daily doings with equal doses of affection and discipline. Though my father earned a paycheck, it was my mother who made the family economy function. Unquestionably, the routines and rhythms of our home revolved around her. She was a prodigious worker, going to bed around midnight and rising well before dawn seven days a week, twelve months a year. Predictably, she slept in church, falling off within five minutes of taking her seat. It was the duty of anyone sitting next to her to awaken her for partaking of the sacrament. She also talked to herself a good deal while working alone in the kitchen. During warm weather when the interior doors of the house were kept open, I often roused from my sleep and heard her engaged in dialogues with herself. Her voice was animated and inflected with a friendly civility, as if she spoke to a person upon whom she wished to make a positive impression. There is something pathetic in this memory, suggesting as it does that she lacked, as my father most decidedly did not, the conversation of peers.

Being the first out of bed, she built whatever fires were necessary: one in the kitchen cookstove year-round, another in the dining room stove if the weather was cold, another in the bathroom stove if it was Sunday morning and we were to take our weekly bath. On rising in cold weather, the rest of us pulled on our pants and clustered in the warm dining room to finish dressing. My father, in pants and union suit, sat with his toes curled up to keep them off the cold linoleum. Before breakfast we went out to do chores, milking the cows, feeding milk from a bucket to the weaned calves, feeding slop to the pig, feeding mash and the mixed grains we called scratch to the chickens, and chopping wood. My earliest outdoor job was getting in a pan of chips to use for kindling for the next day's fires. Chores done, we gathered in the dining room for family prayer. We knelt before our chairs or the couch that occupied a corner of the room, and our father designated one of the family to pray aloud. When it was his turn or our mother's, the prayer might go on at great length, and there was some danger while Leon and I were very young that we would forget that we were involved in a sacred activity and begin provoking one another. We sat then at the table, and our father designated some other person to "say the blessing on the food," as we called it, a combination of thanking God for our food and asking that he bless it to our health and welfare. (I was an adult before I heard the term *grace* applied to the blessing on the food.) Breakfast consisted of cooked cereal, usually cracked wheat with sugar and cream, eggs fried in butter, buttered toast with jam, and a glass of milk. After my father's death and my mother went back to college in the summer to renew her teaching certificate, she took courses on nutrition and added a serving of vitamin C to our breakfast, usually a small glass of canned tomato or grapefruit juice, which she bought by the case at Safeway in Holbrook.

The family ordinarily reassembled for the noon meal, both the high school and the elementary school being within a block and a half of our house. In winter, when the cows no longer pastured at the farm, someone had to drive them from the corral to a ditch for water before our noon meal, a duty that devolved upon me at an early age. We called the noon meal dinner, lunch being something we carried along when forced to eat away from home. The menu included a meat or meat substitute (beans, cottage cheese, or macaroni and cheese, the latter always baked with bottled tomatoes), a couple of vegetable dishes, bread and butter, milk, and a dessert consisting of fresh baked cobbler, pie, or cake if my mother had disposed of time to prepare it, or bottled fruit if she hadn't. My father again called on someone to say a blessing on the food, but at least we were spared the ordeal of family prayer. Not so at supper, as we called our evening meal, when again, after performing the evening chores in the backyard or at the farm, we assembled in the dining room for family prayer, another blessing on the food, and finally a simple meal of leftovers or bread and milk.

Over the years the seating pattern at the dining table varied. I recall a period when I sat between my father and mother, duly isolated from Leon, two years older than I, with whom I conducted a running quarrel. On the whole mealtimes were happy. I remember the sheer pleasure in early summer of having little green onions from the garden to eat with our bread and milk at supper. One such summer evening the setting sun slanted in through the open doors from the adjoining bedroom. It bathed the room in a strange yellow light, touching me with a transcendent joy. I remember a similar light while playing out-of-doors after supper one evening.

Just a little before full darkness, I rounded a corner of our house and unexpectedly met my father. I don't recall any words. I do recall being swept up by the deepest love and reassurance simply from meeting him in the gloaming. I had such moments with my mother too. I recall approaching her one day while she sat at the sewing machine patching overalls. I don't remember what I asked her. I do remember the tenderness and affection that transfused her face while I made my request. I did not doubt I was loved. From all appearances, it was a happy moment for her too.

In the winter we stayed indoors after supper, doing homework or playing. I don't recall helping our mother with the supper dishes, though I was recruited at an early age to wash the breakfast dishes. My father, for his part, moved directly from the supper table to the couch in the corner, where he dozed till bedtime with his hands folded on his mounding belly. He usually had a toothpick in his mouth. On Friday evenings for one or two winters after I entered school, we listened to *Gang Busters* on our radio. Our radio could receive very few stations and those only at night, KSL from Salt Lake City being one of them. The duty of getting us to bed fell upon my mother. I was not always cheerful about giving up the pleasures of the day. I recall kneeling behind the warm dining room stove—so it must have been winter—appearing to offer my secret prayer as instructed by my mother, but in this case offering instead a silent and angry repetition of the word *shit, shit, shit,* till I had taken up the expected time of a secret prayer.

I was afraid of the dark and hated to go to bed alone. Ordinarily Leon went to bed with me and all was well. On bitterly cold nights our mother heaped quilts upon the bed and tucked us in with a warm flatiron wrapped in flannel at our feet. For several years, Leon and I entertained ourselves by taking turns at inventing stories long after our mother had given us a good-night kiss and closed the door behind her. One cycle of stories was about the local justice of the peace and the proprietor of a small grocery store, who always figured as a pair in our comic narratives. We looked down on the justice of the peace because of his corpulent paunch and a white stubble of whiskers that, despite being a barber by profession, he seemed always to wear. We looked down on the grocer because of his snorting intonations and demeanor of high seriousness.

I have been describing what, at age five or six, I took to be the fixed rhythms of our family's life. In retrospect, I see that our routines were in transition throughout the 1930s as our house emptied itself of one generation of my parents' children and filled with another. All my half siblings were married by the end of the decade, Elwood to Lucilia Smith, Lenora to Marion Hansen, Earland to Arlene Oliver, Mary to Glenn Brown, Wanda to Lewis Tenney, and Leora to George Schuck. Be it said that from my earliest memory I associated with a plentiful supply of nephews and nieces only a little less intimately than with my immediate brothers.

My married sisters returned to our house to have their babies. Toward the end of the decade Mary came home to live for almost a year before returning for a time to her estranged husband. She lived in the one-room washhouse behind the main house with her son and daughter, whom my mother cared for during the day while Mary cleaned houses for a pittance. About the same time Lenora left her two-year-old son, Marion, in my mother's care for two winter months while he convalesced from pneumonia. Some of the orphaned children of my mother's sister Adeline and her husband, Byrum Pace, lived in our house for extended periods during the 1930s. Toward the end of the decade my widowed grandmother, Nora, came to live with us. My parents turned their bedroom over to my grandmother and installed their bed in our front room, which thereafter had to double as our formal living room and their bedroom. My father sometimes bickered with my grandmother on politics and religion at the dinner table, a practice of which he repented when she suffered a debilitating stroke. My grandmother, as I remember her, was senile, obese, and capable of only a ponderous, shuffling ambulation. A dozen times a day, when my brothers or I passed the heavy red cedar rocking chair she occupied in our dining room, she caught us by an arm and asked our name. My mother grieved that her younger children never knew their grandmother in her competence.

The congestion in our home affected my mother more than my father because, as I have said, it was she who organized our household. While illnesses and accidents worried my father as much as my mother, the duties of nursing fell more strongly on her. He himself was often ill with colds and an upset stomach, while my mother

was rarely ill. We boys cycled through the usual childhood diseases, chicken pox, whooping cough, measles, and mumps, which,
though common, weren't inconsequential. Every year or so a child
would die of them in town. Roald and I were susceptible to sore
throats, and our mother had Dr. Heywood remove our tonsils
within weeks of our father's death—our father having forbidden
the operation because of its risks. A gauze cone was placed over
our nostrils, and ether was dripped onto it. My last sensation before passing into oblivion was of suffocation.

We had our share of accidents. At three I drank from a cup of
fly spray that had been left on the kitchen counter and became unconscious. Obviously I revived. Leon and I were swept out of the
back of the pickup by a hayrack that slid off when our father drove
around a corner in the lane approaching our field. I fell from the
running board of the pickup in a pasture one day, and a rear wheel
ran over my ankle. I ran after the pickup, trying my best not to
limp because my father had ordered me not to ride on the running
board. Another time, when Charles was bringing the pickup to a
stop, I misjudged its speed and jumped from the running board. I
got up from the gravel with the skin peeled back from one of my
knees. One Sunday morning Charles spilled scalding water on my
ankle while I sat on the kitchen floor polishing shoes for church. I
lost a patch of skin about the size of a half-dollar.

Roald nearly drowned once at Rock Wall while our father
stood guard, unaware that the suction of the ditch headgate had
trapped him underwater. A big girl who happened to be swimming
there at the same time grabbed him by the hair and pulled him to
safety. On another occasion, Roald slashed his thigh while crawling through a barbed-wire fence. Fearing that our father would
punish him, he swore Leon and me to secrecy, and we rode home
from the farm without telling. At home Roald told our mother, and
shortly he found himself in Dr. Heywood's office. The wound,
clamped and sutured, left a vivid scar six inches long and nearly an
inch wide.

Roald was once run over by a cow that he and Charles were
trying to corner. All of us were thrown from horses at one time or
another. Our father's judgment, sound in most matters, suffered a
blank when it came to horses. He kept a riding horse named Bolly,

known to bolt and run when startled, and he forced us all to ride it. Roald later told me I turned blue in the face from screaming when my father placed me on Bolly for the first time.

Our parents both relied on whipping as a form of discipline. Roald came in for more than his share. Roald, who from my earliest memory was rhapsodic, inventive, and evasive of work, engaged in a war of wills especially with our father. One winter day while trying to knock a large icicle from the eaves of our house with a broom, he broke a window. Our father asked him why he had broken the window. Rather than giving the true reason, Roald said, "Because I wanted to." He persisted in this answer, and our father whipped him severely and sent him to bed without supper. Roald's intransigence perhaps earned him the privilege of traveling to Utah with our parents when they brought my grandmother back to stay at our house not long after Roald had slit his leg on the barbed-wire fence. Roald later conjectured that our father, astonished by his refusal to inform him of the wound, took him on the trip by way of reconciliation.

I do not recall that my father ever whipped me. My mother, however, made up amply for the lack. One day when I was perhaps no more than three, I escaped through a hole in the fence around our lot and headed toward Bushman's store with its array of candy, passing by a deep and, for a little child, dangerous ditch along the way. I recall seeing my mother bearing down upon me about the time I reached the bridge across the ditch. She drove me home like an animal, switching my legs and buttocks every time I lagged enough for her to catch up with me. I assume my mother's whippings elicited the desired behavior from me, but they also left me with a fund of resentment that even today, more than sixty years later, I cannot entirely efface. My resentment perhaps benefited two-year-old Marion whom my mother spanked one day for defecating in his overalls. Her whipping increased in severity as anger grew on her. At last I said, "That's enough now." She said, "Well, I guess it is," and stopped. My mother was compassionate but overworked and therefore all too willing to give in to the prevalent convention of improving children's behavior through whipping.

My parents did not disagree with each other in the presence of their children. However, they were both strong willed. My father had the upper hand, being older and more experienced and privi-

leged by the fact that he was male and her former teacher. By custom if not by law, he controlled the family finances, consulting her,
I am sure, but frequently ignoring her wishes. I surmise that she listened respectfully to many of his opinions and even adopted some
of them. He seems to have been able to allude to his religious
doubts without alarming her. What counted with her was that he
was scrupulous in his practice of Mormonism and a vocal proponent of its moral values. I am sure it was from him that she picked
up the belief—anomalous among Mormons—that there was no dis-
harmony between the theory of organic evolution and the book of
Genesis. Similarly, he may have influenced her in matters of politics. Like him, she became a New Deal Democrat, though she had
been raised a Republican and had brothers who were still rabidly
denouncing Franklin D. Roosevelt when I knew them in the 1960s
and 1970s. In her later years, she inclined toward Republicanism,
influenced like most other Mormons by the increasing conserva-
tism of the Mormon hierarchy. Nonetheless, she never adopted the
blind opposition to government-sponsored welfare that character-
izes Mormonism today and always spoke respectfully of the stimulus and hope that the federal relief programs had brought to a
discouraged America during the Great Depression.

My mother's respect for my father's opinions had its limits.
They bickered on certain issues, he insisting on his rightness with
increasing vehemence and she at last retreating from the room, calling over her shoulder, "Just because you say it's so doesn't neces-
sarily make it true." I don't know how often this happened, nor do
I know the kind of issues involved. In one case she told me about,
their disagreement had a comic yet pathetic outcome. When an
uncle, her mother's brother-in-law, ran for office in a county election, my father badgered her incessantly over his incompetence. At
last, stifling her sense of family loyalty, she heeded her husband's
admonition and voted for his opponent—only to have my father
admit later that, being certain the uncle would lose by a humiliat-
ing margin, he had voted for him.

I judge that my mother had more reason to be unhappy than
my father. The intensity and duration of my own unhappiness as
an adult have led me to suspect that I imbibed a good deal of it
from this hardworking, selfless woman, she and I being equally unconscious of the transfer. Still, as I say, overall she considered her-

self happy. Her participation with my father in the generation and nurture of a large, vigorous family was profoundly fulfilling. Her identity melded with her family's identity. The happiness and success of her loved ones were her happiness and success.

I am grateful to have been born into a happy family. It was a blessing to have parents who were basically respectful of each other, able to hide their animosities from their children, and capable of mingling affection with discipline. It was a blessing to have elder siblings who were surrogate parents and to have immediate siblings and a multitude of nephews and nieces who were peers and companions as well as rivals. It was a blessing to grow up with the sense that a large, inclusive family is a fixed feature of the cosmos, its ranks filled with persons to whom you can rightfully turn for any necessity.

··· 6

How Green Was Her Valley

MY FATHER RETIRED FROM TEACHING in the spring of 1939, having just turned sixty-five. He had been released from the stake presidency early in 1939 after the stake president suffered a debilitating stroke. He supplemented a paltry teacher's pension of fifty dollars a month with a twenty-dollar monthly stipend for supervising the stake welfare store. He hoped to extract whatever else his family required from the farm.

The welfare store was across the street from the elementary school where, three months short of six, I started the first grade in the fall of 1939. Sometimes after school I went across the street to beg a penny from my father. If he gave it to me, I bought candy at Bushman's store. When my mother protested that the candy was ruining my appetite for supper, my father replied that he hadn't the heart to refuse me.

Before retiring, my father had rented out the farm. Now he began to develop it in earnest, relying for help on Charles, who turned twelve in 1939. They built fences, laid out new fields, and dug ditches to water them. My father had acquired a couple of work-horses and an array of horse-drawn implements—a plow with a single share, a harrow, a furrow marker, a cultivator, a hay mower, and a hay rake.

He also traded in his Model A on a worn-out orange and black Chevrolet pickup. Riding with him in this vehicle gave me my in-veterate need to own a pickup. It also induced me to believe that a malfunctioning automobile was inherently beyond repair. The win-dow on the driver's side wouldn't roll up, the brakes went out with repeated crossings of the overflowing dam, and the generator failed to charge, leaving the pickup without lights or starter. For extended periods, it had to be stopped by gearing it down, and it had to be parked on a hill so that it could be started by rolling. If necessity required that it be driven at night, my father pulled over to the shoulder and waited till approaching cars had passed.

My mother often repeated the rural adage that a family farm raised children if nothing else. Charles was probably the chief beneficiary of this dubious process. My father recruited him as a chief assistant at an early age, turning the milking over to him at seven or eight. Adult responsibility made Charles reliable and competent but perhaps augmented his stress. I recall being cuffed and kicked by him from time to time, probably with due provocation on my part. He shouted eloquent obscenities in the corral or behind the team of horses when our father was not present. This expressive vocabulary was not lost on his younger brothers, who absorbed it all and in time found use for it. Even then, Charles knew he wanted to be a farmer. He says he liked farmwork at an early age.

It was otherwise with me. I suffered sheer despair when, hoe in hand, I gazed down a row of corn as long as a football field or contemplated an interminable day of tramping hay. Still, farmwork could be fascinating as well as tedious. The mower's reciprocating blade, lined with sharp triangular teeth, was a lethal-looking thing. I liked to follow the mower afoot, watching it fell a continuous swath of dark green alfalfa about six feet wide. Once a cottontail rabbit lurched from that falling wall of alfalfa, its legs cut off and its screams terrible to hear. The rake was an ingenious device, perhaps twelve feet wide with high spoked wheels and long curved tines that picked up the dried alfalfa and dumped it into cocks. My father, Charles, and Roald loaded the cocks by pitchfork onto a rack on the pickup and trailer while Leon and I tramped the hay into place. More hay meant more cows, and for a period we sold milk and butter to neighbors, and my mother got into the production of a bitter, almost inedible cheese. We also operated a separator in our washhouse and sold cream to creameries in Phoenix. Corn and alfalfa were the most reliable crops, though my father also tried oats, wheat, and potatoes. We always had a large vegetable garden, sometimes at the farm, sometimes on a rented plot below the ditch in town. My mother took chief responsibility for the gardens. It was from her that I learned gardening.

For children on furlough from work, the farm was a magical place. Mysterious things stirred beneath the surface of the brown, placid creek. Herons waded its sandbars, hunting frogs and small carp. Red-winged blackbirds warbled in the reeds. Scouring rush grew along the ditches, its joints amenable to being made into whistles. Enticing trails entered the willow patch, only to lose themselves among a sea of leafy boughs and stinging nettles. One summer Roald, Leon, and I—under Roald's inventive direction—built a jungle hut in the willow patch and slept there overnight. At the periphery of our arable land, cottontail rabbits bounded for shelter among rocky ledges. Beyond our fence on the east was a hill that gave a view of vast plains stretching away on all hands to a distant horizon flecked by knolls, buttes, and mesas. In the rangeland beyond the hill was a large outcropping of rock where, having seen the movie *Gunga Din,* we pretended that we were Hindus fighting the British, again under Roald's inspiration. Roald was a consummate play master whose suggestions constantly fueled the imagination of his younger brothers.

Near the end of the summer of 1940, a fierce hailstorm struck late one afternoon. Clouds of an eerie copperish hue gathered, a furious wind arose, and soon sheets of rain and hail slanted in at an oblique angle. The storm was worse at the farm, where my father, Charles, and Roald were milking cows on the east side of the creek. Pelted by hailstones an inch in diameter, they abandoned their milk buckets and, crawling under a barbed-wire fence whose strands flashed with blue electricity, retreated to the pickup. When the rain and hail had abated, they struck out for home afoot, the pickup having refused to start. Holding hands, my father in the middle with a son on either side, they waded through a frothing torrent pouring over the lip of the dam. Though the flood was far from cresting, they were lucky to make it to the other side. Wet, cold, and tired, they arrived home well after dark, relieving the anxiety of those of us who waited there.

Hail severely damaged gardens and field crops for miles around, and on our farm, floodwater added to the loss. Elevated by the dam, water overflowed the creek bed, turning our cultivated fields into a great, muddy, slow-moving lake. This was the first flooding of the farm my father had experienced. Thereafter, as I have said, inundations of our arable land occurred on the average of every three or four years, usually during the rainy season of July or August. From what Charles related to his siblings nearly fifty years later, I judge the worst effect of this flood to have been upon our father's emotions. Soon after it had happened, he confided to Charles that of all the events of his life to that point, only the deaths of Amanda and Alma had filled him with greater grief. He said not even the deaths of his own parents had touched him so deeply. In Charles's opinion, this was because the flood had put a definitive end to his dream of a prosperous, family-supporting farm. He could see that no matter how intelligently he laid out his fields and leveled the land, no matter how scientifically he selected and cultivated his crops, a single cloudburst upstream could drastically reduce the harvest.

I am not sure whether, in this episode, our father lost his faith in the agrarian ideal altogether or merely in his individual realization of it. In either event, it shows the amazing durability of his belief that a person could attain prosperity and happiness on a family farm. I can understand his holding to this faith as a young man because it was in the air upon the late frontier where he grew up and he had not yet had time to disprove it. But it astonishes me that, long before the hailstorm and flood, he had not seen clearly that any farm he had the means to acquire, whether by purchase or homesteading, would provide little more than a scant subsistence. Like other faiths, the agrarian ideal was beyond the testimony of facts and common sense.

During the following year, 1941, my father became aware of a growth on one of his testicles. My mother told me, long afterward, that it felt exactly like a knot of baling wire. I can't imagine how a knot of baling wire might feel, but she always repeated the word *exactly* with great emphasis. At that moment, I knew only that my parents would go to Phoenix for an operation shortly after Christmas. On the last Sunday of November, the new Snowflake church house burned, my brothers and I watching the conflagration from the roof of a chicken coop. The church, a handsome structure of chiseled yellow native sandstone, was gutted, and the town had to settle grimly down to the business of rebuilding it. On another Sunday, two weeks later, the Japanese attacked Pearl Harbor. While we were in sacrament meeting in the elementary school auditorium, someone came in to announce the attack. The next Saturday, December 13, 1941, my father baptized me in the icy water of Silver Creek just above the dam. I recall vividly the sensation of my feet sinking into the silted bottom. I also recall my mother wrapping me in a warm blanket as I emerged from the creek.

The Christmas of 1941 was the leanest I can remember. A tree, duly decorated, stood in the front room. As usual, our mother filled a large stocking for each of us with nuts, candy, homemade doughnuts, and an orange. My only gift of any interest was a kit for constructing a small model airplane from solid wood. It required some carving, and I never completed it. The gloom of our parents' departure hung over the house. They left the day after Christmas, leaving us in Mary's care. Mary had been living in Overgaard, a sawmill town, on a second trial of her marriage to Glenn Brown. She now had three children, the last being only a couple of months old. In my father's absence, I was confirmed a member of the Mormon Church and blessed with the gift of the Holy Ghost by my eldest brother, Arley, on the first Sunday of January 1942.

My parents were gone for six weeks. Though some winters in Snowflake are sunny, I can remember only cold, gloomy days during that one. One day, probably a Saturday, Leon and I walked across the grade school grounds under a cold, lowering sky. I recall being depressed. That's all there is to the memory. Attendance at school was a merciful distraction. I was in the third grade and enamored of my teacher, Melba Flake, who read us long, entrancing passages from *Kazan, Dog of the North*.

The surgeon removed at least one and perhaps both of my father's testicles, opened his abdomen, and promptly sewed him up. He told him the cancer had not spread, and upon recovery, he could go home in peace. Privately the surgeon told my mother the cancer had spread widely, and she could expect my father to die within one to two years from cancer of the lungs. My parents had stayed in a motel in Phoenix before the operation. Afterward, fully aware that the family economy wouldn't bear such an extravagance, my mother went wild with worry over the expense of staying on in the motel. Another of the many instances of divine intervention my mother would note throughout her life occurred when friends of Wanda invited my mother to stay in their home while my father convalesced in the hospital.

When spring came, my father went on with his farming at a much reduced pace. He followed the progress of World War II closely, lamenting that he was not able to deliver patriotic speeches on behalf of the war effort as he had done upon the entrance of the United States into World War I. Inevitably, the war affected us all. We saw it in the newsreels at the Wednesday and Saturday movies and in the photos and articles of *Life* magazine to which my parents subscribed. Food rationing affected our supply of sugar. As for meat, dairy products, and canned goods, we produced most of our own, so were unaffected by rationing. As a farm family, we qualified for a generous tire and gasoline quota. Numerous young men from Navajo County departed for the war, including Arley's son Max and Andelin's sons Larry and Lorenzo, who were destined to return safely. From across Navajo County several dozen young men were killed. A family in Snowflake lost a son in the Japanese conquest of Wake Island, whereupon his angry brother volunteered for the Marines. Later he too was killed. Another family lost two sons whose airplanes were shot down over Europe.

My father turned sixty-nine in April 1943. He complained that spring of a pain in his lungs, and he felt very fatigued. On a Saturday in June, he and my mother drove to McNary to consult a doctor, passing through Lakeside on the way. The day was calm and clear, and the countryside was magnificent. Viewing its beauty, my father grumbled at my mother for having influenced him to abandon Lakeside as his domicile. After examining him, the doctor told him bluntly that he had cancer of the lungs and there was nothing to be done about it. On the return drive, his hands were icy, his face ashen, and his lips blue. At home he went immediately to bed. The next afternoon my mother sent me with a note asking a member of the high priests' quorum to assist in administering the rite of healing to my father. I recall how hopefully I went on this errand. The blessing had no effect.

In the meantime, family members who lived in far-away places were alerted that they must gather. Arley, Elwood, and Mary lived in Snowflake. Andelin was in Lakeside; his wife, Goldie, a practical nurse, came to Snowflake and helped at my father's bedside. Leora and George had to drive from Abilene, Texas, where George was stationed at an army base. Borrowing gasoline stamps from friends, they arrived in time for our father to recognize Leora, only hours before he died. Earland and Arlene came from El Paso, where Earland worked in the assay office of the Phelps Dodge Copper Company. He drove across the border into Mexico and filled cans with enough gasoline to get to Snowflake and back. Wanda lived in Glendale, a suburb of Phoenix. She brought Lewis Jr., her six-month-old son. Lewis Sr., who didn't come, may have been at a construction site in Mexico. Lenora and Marion came from Poston on the lower Colorado River where Marion was helping to construct an internment camp for Japanese Americans from California.

My father died about nine o'clock on the evening of Thursday, June 17, 1943, five days after the trip to McNary. It had been a hot day, and heat still lingered in our house. A day or two earlier my father had said, "It seems there ought to be something that can be done for me." He could have lived several weeks longer if his good friend Dr. Heywood had tapped the water from his lungs. Warned that it would only prolong his suffering, my mother decided against the procedure. I don't know whether she consulted my father on the matter. Now, on this hot evening, he lay in a semiconscious condition. From time to time, he roused and, assisted by his daughters-in-law Goldie and Arlene, heaved himself to his elbows and took great gasping breaths of air. His lungs were nearly full, and he was drowning. I had this from Roald, who watched him die. I don't think my mother wanted me in the room, and I had little incentive to be there. Wanda, holding her six-month-old son in her arms, found the scene very hard to bear. Trying to console our dying father, she said, during one of his moments of rousing, "Father, you should be proud of the big family you have." He replied by quoting a line of poetry: "Oh, why should spirit of mortal be proud?" Wanda retreated to Arley's house, unable to watch any longer.

As dusk fell, I loitered outside, crying while I gazed at the lights of an itinerant carnival that had set up on the block north of ours. Leon approached and asked why I was crying. I said it was because I wanted to go to the carnival and couldn't. He berated me for crying about such a trivial thing when our father lay dying inside the house. Actually I was crying for our father, but I couldn't inform

Leon, my arch antagonist as well as my most intimate companion, of that fact. It was from a curious sense of vulnerability that I hid my grief. At the exact moment of our father's death I was seated at the dining table eating a bowl of stew. The door between the dining room and the bedroom where he lay was open, and I heard something of a stir and a murmur among the many adults gathered there. I knew it was the end, and I went into the bedroom where Leora clasped me in a close, unrelenting hug. Immediately the house bustled with the preparation of the body. Goldie placed coins over my father's eyelids. Somebody shaved him—Earland, I think. My cousin Marna, Uncle Hy's adolescent daughter, squeezed lemons in the kitchen for a mixture of lemon juice and saltpeter, which was applied to my father's face to keep it from turning black. They laid the body out on sawhorses and planks in the front room. Someone got ice, and they packed bottles of ice around the body to keep it from putrefying. The activity cheered us up.

The funeral was held two days later in the high school gymnasium, which, as I recall, was crowded. People came by our house shortly before the funeral to view my father in his coffin. I cried at the beginning of the funeral till my mother whispered that crying would give me a headache. I don't know why that should have stopped my weeping, but it did. One of the hymns at the funeral was "Oh, My Father," a traditional Mormon hymn composed by Eliza R. Snow. To this day I invariably remember my father, often with tears, when I hear that haunting hymn. Another hymn, sung by a male quartet, was "Come, Lay His Books and Papers By," composed for the funeral of Karl G. Maeser, the church educational official who had called my father to Snowflake to become principal of its academy in 1898.

> Come, lay his books and papers by, He shall not need them more;
>
> The ink shall dry upon his pen, So softly close the door.
>
> His tired head, with locks of white, and like the winter's sun
>
> Hath lain to peaceful rest tonight—The teacher's work is done.

After the funeral, his body was conveyed to Lakeside and buried next to Amanda. I leaned against a pine tree just a few feet from the open grave, watching while the coffin was lowered into a board box and the box nailed shut. My older brothers filled the grave. It was a strange sensation to hear the thudding of earth upon the pine box. I had expected they would bury him; I hadn't expected the incredulity and horror I felt upon observing them do it. I would have nightmares about being buried alive for a long time afterward, early in the night, just as I was drifting off to sleep. I imagined myself waking the next morning to discover that I lay beneath a pine lid and six feet of earth. I pounded on the lid and shouted, but no one could hear me. I will add that I was claustrophobic from my earliest memory. Wild terror seized me when Roald and Leon gleefully shut me in our bedroom closet. To this day, I ride elevators uneasily.

Returned to Snowflake, I played in the backyard with Gale, Lenora's daughter of my age, whom I loved passionately. A thunderstorm had passed through while we had been in Lakeside for the burial, and we made roadways in the soft, moist soil with matchboxes that we pretended were bulldozers. Lenora, Gale, and Marion Jr. stayed for a few days after the funeral, an arrangement that pleased me greatly. On the day they left, Lenora played from sheet music at the piano and sang a haunting song about an Indian princess made captive in the land of the sky-blue water. I felt empty and listless when Lenora and her children drove away. My mother's sister Ruth came soon afterward from Oakland, California, to stay for a week, a considerable sacrifice for a mother of eight children of her own. The morning after Aunt Ruth had gone, my mother sat on the edge of her bed in despair over the prospect of raising her boys without her husband's help. It occurred to her to sing a hymn. She sang "Ere You Left Your Room This Morning," a hymn about the strength to be derived from prayer. From that moment she felt capable of the task ahead.

Within a week or two of my father's death, I bravely agreed after the morning milking to drive the cows to the field astride Bolly, our erratic riding horse. After a couple of days of making the trek without incident, I became bored. One morning, once I was well under way with the cows, I pulled from my pocket an advertisement I had torn from *Life* magazine that had a jingle I wished to memorize. When the paper rattled, Bolly bolted, scattering the cows and pounding along in the barrow pit beside the highway at a dead run. Terrified, I leaped off and plowed into the earth, luck-ily suffering no more than a bruised forearm. Bolly stopped and stood peacefully. Gathering the dangling reins, I led him behind the plodding cows. My brothers came along in the pickup, and we hoed weeds till afternoon. When I got home, I told my mother about the runaway. Strange emotions played across her face. That very morning, as she informed me, a classmate of mine, Charles Bushman, had been dragged to death by a horse; he had tied its lead rope to his waist while attempting to saddle it. The terror on my mother's face half persuaded me it was I who had been killed. On the day of Charles Bushman's funeral, I asked her if I could take flowers to the viewing. She said yes. I vacillated in our iris patch, terribly ambivalent. When at last I made up my mind and went, bearing a fistful of irises, I arrived too late. Knocking at the house where the viewing had been held, I could hear a funeral hymn being sung in the high school gymnasium across the street, where, days earlier, my father's funeral had been held. Utterly dis-appointed, I went home. Years later I would recognize what I had hoped to settle by viewing the corpse in Charles's coffin. Was it he or was it I?

I was most keenly aware of my father's absence at the supper table. I'm not sure just why I sensed an empty place at that meal more than at breakfast or dinner. However, I was not aware of mourning extensively. If I was depressed, it was intermittently. In retrospect I judge that if I had to lose a parent at nine, it was better to lose my father. Though my mother was vulnerable to anxiety, she met practical hardship with resilience and determination. She suffered no such breakdown as afflicted my father in the aftermath of Amanda's death. Fortunately, Lenora and Marion and their chil-dren moved permanently to Snowflake in September. They had been studying the Book of Mormon and had decided construction camps were not a good environment. They parked their camp trailer on our lot, using our bathroom and disposing of the wash-house for an overflow room. I was ecstatic with this turn of events. In the meantime, our domestic routines went on almost precisely as before under the direction of my mother. She now called on some-one to say the family prayer while we all knelt at our chairs or to say the blessing on the food at the table. She directed our chores and kept an eye on the progress of the farm, which fared as well as before under Charles's capable management.

My mother's anxiety over money was eased when she became the teacher of the fourth grade at the elementary school in September 1943. In her estimation, this was another divine intervention in her life. However that may be, the school district was able to renew her long-lapsed teaching certificate on an emergency basis, thanks to the exigencies of the war. My mother would remain in the classroom for the next seventeen years, renewing her certificate by attendance at summer school. Slowly and with considerable hardship to herself, she would acquire a bachelor's degree and build herself a modest retirement. The immediate dislocations created by her teaching didn't strike me as much of a handicap. At the outset, Leon and I were still attending school in the same building in which she taught. The greatest disturbance fell upon Nora, who stayed sometimes with her sister May Hatch Decker and sometimes with us. For a couple of winters my mother hired housekeepers on a part-time basis. One was a woman from Clay Springs, who rode the school bus into Snowflake each morning. She had a cracked front tooth, spoke with a Texas twang, and could cough up phlegm and spit it out our back door with magnificent energy. I attribute to her my own mastery of this useful skill.

I don't know whether my mother worked harder now, but she certainly had to manage her time more carefully. She shifted the washing of clothes to Saturday and recruited her sons more vigorously into housework. Outside I learned to milk, a matter of conditioning the hand muscles. Inside, I washed the breakfast dishes and swept and mopped floors. I also learned to build fires, fry eggs, and cook cereal. My mother was a conscientious schoolteacher, staying late almost every afternoon to tutor the slower students. She especially helped the children of the Spanish-speaking section hands who lived along the railroad tracks. They were grateful for her help. She also checked spelling and math papers almost every school evening. She usually dozed off while doing so, took a half-hour nap, then went back to checking papers. As always she retired late and was up very early.

When working alone in the kitchen at night, she went on talking to herself. Sometimes after a period of meditative silence she would utter a new and unfamiliar phrase: "How green was my valley!" The word *valley* puzzled me. The only context in which I knew the word was our lot, which sloped to the south into a wide, shallow ravine. From the perspective of my childhood, the well-worn path that ran from the house to the woodpile at the bottom seemed long and steep. We called this bottom "the valley." That is what came to my mind when I overheard my mother mutter, "How green was my valley!" However, our valley was anything but green. It grew native bunchgrass, tumbleweeds, and a hardy breed of wild gourd, which often figured in my play. At length I asked my mother what she meant by this utterance. She explained she had seen a movie of that title while staying with Wanda's friends in Phoenix shortly after my father's operation. Although I quickly forgot whatever details about the movie she imparted, I understood clearly, and never forgot, that the movie had summarized and expressed the beauty of her years with my father. Ever after, whenever she repeated those words to herself—and it must have been often, for I have a vivid memory of them—I understood that she was meditating on her life with my father and, by her utterance, pronouncing it fulfilling, sacred, and irreplaceable.

The movie, based on a novel by Richard Llewellyn, has been available in videocassette for a long time. Fearing it would depress me, I put off renting it until shortly before I began to write the present chapter. A Twentieth Century Fox production directed by John Ford, the movie follows the gradual disintegration of a large, happy family in a coal-mining district of Wales. Quaint by present standards, its plot is episodic and melodramatic—for example, the miners march en masse every day between the pit and home singing grand choral music. Near the end, the family's amiable tyrant of a father, injured in a mining accident, dies in the arms of his youngest son. As the movie closes, the adult voice of that son says in retrospect: "Men like my father cannot die. They are with me still, real in memory as they were in flesh, loving and beloved forever. How green was my valley!"

I see my mother in a dark theater. My father, convalescing in a hospital, has been told he will recover. My mother knows he will die soon. Her long grief has already begun. The movie addresses her condition closely, emphasizing both the joy and the brevity of family relationships. It suggests that nostalgia is a sufficient compensation for tragic loss. My mother knows better than that. Remembering her happy years with my father is no compensation for their imminent end. But the imminence of their end has thrust upon her the full intensity of their beauty. This movie has evoked that beauty and given her words to express it. How green was her valley.

··· 7

A Piratical Fraternity

IN FEBRUARY 1944 MY MOTHER AND I TRAVELED with Lenora and Marion and their children to Glendale, a cotton-farming town at the outskirts of Phoenix where Wanda and Lewis lived. It was my first visit to the Salt River Valley and the first time I ever saw the Sonoran Desert with its thick, sere vegetation composed of mesquite, creosote, and cactus. I was astonished at the balmy weather and the lettuce and radishes already growing in Wanda's garden. Squadrons of military aircraft from a nearby training field flew over, reminding us that the nation was at war.

We also stayed overnight in Mesa, where Gale and I were baptized for the dead in the Mormon temple. That night my mother and I stayed with my mother's sister Louie Ison, a widow. The three of us slept in a double bed, I in the middle. Before turning out the lights, Aunt Louie, always a voluble talker, pointed out what she called the cameos on her knotty pine ceiling. On our way home, we had a hamburger in Globe at dusk—an event rare enough in my life for me to remember it—and passed over the snowy Mogollon Rim long after dark. I awoke in the back seat and gazed out at the car lights reflecting off deep walls of snow. In one of those transcendent moments that occur even to children, I sensed the deep mystery of being alive.

Soon afterward, Marion traded his car for a used bobtailed truck, which he used to gather, saw, and sell juniper firewood. Marion also helped us with the farmwork. One day he put me and Marion Jr. on our workhorses, Jack and Ned. I was delighted to discover that my mount was amenable to my directions, and from that moment considered myself able to ride horses. A bald, sturdy man with thick wrists and large hands, Marion had a cheerful, optimistic personality. He loved children and knew how to interest and entertain them. At family gatherings for many decades I have seen him surrounded by hordes of shouting, excited children. I am grateful for the model of good-natured competence that he provided me in the absence of my father.

In the spring of 1945 the family acquired a new riding horse, a bay filly of classic quarter-horse configuration. When Charles and Roald went after the filly, she stood apart from the other horses in the pasture. For this reason Roald named her Gypsy, it being his fancy that gypsies are solitary. Charles and Roald set about immediately to break her, an easy task because she was anything but excitable. Gypsy and I were destined to spend many an hour together, and I came to know, if not appreciate, her indolent personality well.

Within a couple of weeks of our acquiring Gypsy, Charles was drafted into the army. He had turned eighteen in January, a half year after graduating from high school. On the day he left, Charles sought me out in the backyard to say good-bye. We both wept. I was astonished that my old animosities toward him had given way to grief over his departure. Roald, fifteen and nearing his adult height of six foot four, now took charge of the farm. With our acquisition of Gypsy, his romantic bent turned toward things western. He ordered a saddle and custom-made cowboy boots from Texas and began training Gypsy to rope, sometimes practicing illicitly on calves he encountered while riding for pleasure on nearby ranges.

On August 11, 1945, the day of Japan's surrender, I began to deliver newspapers on Gypsy, carrying the two-sided news bag over the cantle of our ancient frontier-era saddle. On the first few days that followed, I delivered newspapers with an inexplicable anxiety that when I got home my mother would have disappeared. Soon I divided the route, which included the entire town, with Gale, who delivered papers on a bicycle. We delivered two newspapers, the *Arizona Republic* and, in considerably fewer numbers, the *Phoenix Gazette*. My earnings were not munificent, about ten dollars a month from my half route. Still, that was ten dollars a month I had not had before, and I never again felt poor. Though I spent most of it on necessities, I began to indulge myself in a daily candy bar.

Charles came home for a furlough near the time of the Japanese surrender. Andelin drove us to Winslow to pick him up and to send him away again. At the station, crowded troop trains clattered by in both directions, causing me to wonder, young as I was, why troops from the West were being sent east and troops from the East were being sent west. Charles was on his way to Yokohama, Japan, where he would serve in the army of occupation for a year.

I entered the seventh grade in September 1945. My grade card shows that I received a D in wood shop that year. My task in wood shop was to square a board by means of a trisquare and plane. Invariably I planed too much off one corner and left the other high. I suspect the real reason for the D was that I talked and trifled with my fellow students during wood shop. I was always very sociable in school.

Someone decided that the seventh graders had to learn to dance. A teacher from one of the other grades who was adept in music spent an evening at the piano in the school auditorium, instructing us in what she called a waltz: two steps forward, one to the side, two steps forward, one to the side. These mechanical steps, suited only to music of slow tempo, were all I ever acquired by way of dancing. They served me well enough through high school and college. I have rarely danced since. As for the seventh grade, all I can remember is that at a dance held on a Friday evening I roistered in the hall with other boys instead of dancing, ending by getting one of them to chase me and crash through the plate glass of the front door of the school, which I slammed shut on him while he was in hot pursuit.

I turned twelve in December 1945 and, like other Mormon boys of that age, entered the Boy Scouts of America and was ordained to the office of deacon in the Aaronic Priesthood. I proved to be a lackluster Scout. I passed from Tenderfoot to Second Class but never managed to meet all of the qualifications for First Class. I recall that I failed to build a fire with only two matches at a jamboree at a neighboring town. I whittled shavings for tinder as instructed, but apparently not enough. Unlike me, Roald was a very successful Scout. Becoming a patrol leader, he secured permission to use a defunct pool hall on our block as a patrol den. At the beginning of World War II, he and his patrol sorted scrap metal from an abandoned logging railroad and earned enough money to buy uniforms, sleeping bags, and rucksacks. When it came our turn, both Leon and I used Roald's sleeping bag and rucksack. I never owned or wore any article of Scout clothing. As infrequent and unsuccessful as my scouting ventures were, they gave me my later interest in backpacking.

My maternal grandmother, Nora, died on a bright but exceedingly cold January day in 1946. Obese, senile, and nearly immobilized by a stroke, she had become increasingly paranoid during the fall of 1945. One evening in January she was so distraught that my mother called in Dr. Heywood, who gave her a sedative shot that put her to sleep. The next morning she remained in a coma. I stayed home from school that day and watched her gasp convulsively for hours. At last her breathing stopped. Even at twelve I recognized that watching a person die is an exceptional experience. Following her funeral, my mother's brother Parley accompanied the coffin by train to Salt Lake City, where my grandmother was buried beside her pioneer spouse, Levi Mathers Savage. I remember how depressed I was after the funeral as I saddled Gypsy and set out under a lowering sky to deliver newspapers. I recall too that my grandmother's coffin was a metallic gray. Years later, anxious over an imminent trip away from home by jet plane, I had a nightmare of being suffocated in an airplane whose color was of the same metallic gray.

I bought a used bicycle in the spring of 1946 and began intermittently to deliver newspapers with it. The lay of the town was such that I had to pump uphill against the perpetual spring wind, greatly hindered by the double bag of newspapers hung over my chest and back. The used bicycle soon broke, and Leon and I both ordered new bicycles from Sears. Overall, my bicycle was a liberating machine, and I rode it to many destinations. One day Leon, Gale, Marion Jr., and I rode our bicycles to the Taylor airstrip where we paid a returned war veteran one dollar apiece to give us a ten-minute flight in a two-seated Aerocoupe. The pilot strapped us in two at a time. He circled Taylor, flew north along the creek, and banked low over the church house in Snowflake. I ended my flight with a sense of disbelief, being somehow unable to conceive of myself as one ordained to travel by air.

I attended a weeklong Scout camp in the White Mountains during the summer of 1946. Marion was scoutmaster, and the Scouts rode atop their high-piled gear and bedrolls in the back of his truck. Pine trees shaded our camp along the bank of a clear, rushing river. We were divided into patrols, and each patrol cooked its meals in common. I shared a pup tent with my cousin Dale Hatch, who had been one of my best friends for years. Anxious over being away from my mother, I stayed close to camp and didn't participate in many of the available activities, which included swimming, hiking, merit-badge acquisition, volleyball, fishing, and so on. Busying myself with making my tent tidy, I constructed a railing from a small tree trunk and neatly outlined a curving path from the campfire to the tent with rocks. On the last night of camp I was surprised to be given an award as the most industrious Scout. Our toilet was an open pit without walls. The best way to use it was to pull your pants off one leg and straddle the pit. Reluctant to defecate in such public circumstances, I wandered off into the forest where I dropped my pants and squatted on the needle-covered ground, paying no attention to the innocuous presence of foot-high stems bearing shiny dark green leaves in clusters of three. Within a day or two of arriving home, I had a seriously blistered outbreak of dermatitis on my hands and within the crack of my buttocks. I went to bed, and Dr. Heywood gave me a shot of some kind and prescribed a drying lotion that did little to ease the fiery itching. I emerged from a weeklong ordeal thoroughly conditioned to recognize and avoid poison ivy.

Roald, Leon, and I were often at the farm during the summer of 1946, with Roald once again in charge. I helped with the night and morning milkings, proving neither more nor less hygienic than my brothers. I recall plucking many a mote of dry cow manure from a foaming pail with a none-too-clean finger, a practice that did not deter us from selling milk to some of our neighbors. Though milking was tedious, the cows were often entertaining. Each had a name—Pet, Pippin, Sally, Jerse, Blackie, Flossie, and so on—and each had a personality. Sally was irritable and kicked at the least provocation. However, she gave a high yield, and her teats were easy to milk. Jerse, on the other hand, was placid and long-suffering but had stubby, gristly teats requiring an exhausting squeeze. It was a pleasure to hear our cows belch and watch a lump rise up their long throats and see their jaws begin to chew a cud. Sometimes I toyed with them by falling to the ground and writhing in mock agony, causing them, good souls that they were, to gather around me, mooing anxiously and wanting to help.

I often had the duty of escorting a cow in heat to a bull kept by John T. Flake on his farm not far from ours. One eager cow didn't wait till I had opened a gate but tried to go through a barbed-wire fence, where she stopped, half in and half out. While the amorous bull lowed gently at her head, I shoved mightily at her rear till I had pushed her through the fence. I ordinarily allowed the cow and bull at least an hour of lovemaking before I separated them, reasoning that a number of couplings would increase the chance for fertilization. I recall once trying to stimulate the bull's penis with a long stick after he had jumped the cow a time or two and seemed to fall into lassitude. The bull was a Jersey, a breed noted for truculent males. Luckily this bull tolerated my intervention.

During the summer of 1946, we had six or seven dogs around our place because Gale's female dog Snowball had a batch of adolescent pups. One day at the farm this pack of dogs surrounded a skunk in a rabbit bush. Attracted by the commotion, Leon and I methodically caught each dog and tossed it into the bush with the skunk, from which each canine ignominiously scrambled, drenched with skunk scent. Roald wouldn't let them into the pickup for the ride home, and they all had to run the two and a half miles. The pups eventually disappeared, though another batch soon materialized. No one in Snowflake considered spaying or neutering pets. The result was a perpetual congregation of male dogs around a female in heat somewhere in town.

I entered the eighth grade in September 1946, a year during which my mother taught at nearby Taylor. I was going on thirteen. One moonlit fall evening after a Scout meeting, I gathered with a mixed group of my own age in front of a girl's house at the far end of town. By arrangements I no longer recall, one of the girls and I ended up in a shed across the street long enough to exchange a few kisses, and I slunk home full of guilt. The next morning Arley's son Van and I rode our horses eight or nine miles south along the highway toward Showlow till we met the Peterson trail drive, if I may honor the two-day transfer of fifty or sixty head of cattle from summer pasture on the national forest at Lakeside to winter pasture around Snowflake by calling it a trail drive. This must have been one of the last of these semiannual drives. At any rate, they ended before I was considered competent to make the complete two-day drive. Each was preceded by a minor roundup and followed by a session of branding, earmarking, and castrating. During one of the drives, a horse named Blaze was killed by a speeding automobile, and the rider, Andelin's son Scott, went flying over a juniper tree and landed unharmed, still seated in a saddle set free by broken cinches.

Andelin came the closest among my father's sons to becoming a true cattleman. But even he didn't come very close. He earned his living chiefly by working as a self-taught land surveyor and a highway maintenance man. Still, we all understood the glamour of the cowboy. The western movies we saw at the Wednesday- and Saturday-night movies reinforced the romance of cattle raising, but they didn't create it. It was in the air in Navajo County and had been from the beginning of white settlement. The Mormon pioneers who settled on Silver Creek were much more influenced by the cowboy tradition than were their counterparts in the villages of Utah and Idaho. This was the terrain of the infamous Hash Knife outfit, a subsidiary of the Atchison, Topeka, and Santa Fe Railroad, whose range included every other section for a swath extending forty miles on either side of their track across northern Arizona. Snowflake was also on the periphery of the Pleasant Valley War of the late 1880s, a bloody feud over horse theft and grazing rights centered in the pine country southwest of the Mogollon Rim. The summer I was thirteen I read Earle Forrest's *Arizona's Dark and Bloody Ground,* which informed me about the lynching of Stott, Scott, and Wilson by unidentified vigilantes on the Mogollon Rim and the death of four Blevins brothers in a shootout with Sheriff Commodore Perry Owens in Holbrook. This wasn't abstract history like the adventures of Prince Henry the Navigator and Marco Polo whom I had learned about in the fourth grade. This was my history. I remember from before my father's death a church picnic in the junipers north of town where, by the blaze of a entire juniper tree that had been set afire, I first heard a townsman sing "Home on the Range," and I understood this song was about me and my land. For no more than a seven-mile stretch, the narrow valley of Silver Creek was farm country. If you went over the rim of the valley, east or west, you were in rangeland. Cattle, windmills, salt licks, and barbed-wire fences were everywhere.

Though I never acquired the skills of a cowboy, as Roald and some of Andelin's sons did, I have a treasured memory of riding with Andelin and his sons Scott, Jack, and Derl on a November morning out to their winter section southwest of town. The sun glittered on yellow native grass. Andelin's boys shouted and raced their horses. Their long-legged dog Prodg barked and ran this way and that, happy just to be alive. Andelin wore a battered narrow-brim Stetson and work shoes. I don't recall ever seeing him in cowboy boots. I wore no cowboy boots because I owned none. I remember that Andelin had a resonant, impressive voice. My other siblings say he had a lively sense of humor, a large vocabulary, and an enormous capacity for storytelling. Andelin would be the next of my siblings after Alma to die. This was while I was on my mission and before I had time to fraternize with him as an adult. Of all my siblings except Alma, I knew Andelin least well. That may be the reason my ride with him and his boys on a frosty, glittering November morning remains so vividly with me.

Charles returned from Japan and was discharged from the army during the fall of 1946. As a souvenir, he had shipped home a bolt-action Japanese army rifle with a long bayonet. A new affection existed between Charles and his three younger brothers. One fall evening he wrestled with all of us at once in the backyard. I don't remember who vanquished whom. Minutes later he and I were chasing each other around the yard. Hotly pursued, he took shelter in the corner of the front porch located close enough to the entrance to the house that he could pull the screen door in front of himself, barring my access to him. I scooped up an armful of brown elm leaves from the lawn and threw them over the top of the screen door, showering him with debris. He broke into hearty laughter over my clever coup. This is my first memory of ever playing with Charles. It was nice having him home that winter. In March 1947 he departed for a mission to Sweden, and I didn't see him again till I was fifteen.

In late April 1947, I contracted scarlet fever and was quarantined for three weeks in my mother's bedroom where I shared her bed. It was a great comfort to have her beside me when I awoke from perfervid, phantasmagoric dreams. For about a week I had a desperately high fever. Dr. Heywood prescribed a course of sulfa pills. I was required to drink great quantities of water with these pills, which posed the danger of ruining the kidneys. I don't suppose the sulfa had any effect. After I began to feel better, I read my school assignments with the result that I returned to school well ahead of my fellow students in all subjects. I graduated from the eighth grade at the end of May 1947. My mother bought me a new sports jacket and pants for graduation. There was a banquet for graduates and parents in the recreation hall of the church following the awarding of diplomas. One of my classmates rewrote the words of a currently popular song "The Old Lamp Lighter of Long, Long Ago." We sang: "This is the night we've all looked forward to for eight long years you know / When we could graduate and then to high school go." I was assigned to give a joke, which I took from a book of jokes at our house. An Irish bachelor was asked to comment on his sister's newborn infant. The punch line was that he called the child a hard drinker. In the telling, I quoted him as saying the child was a hard sucker. No one laughed.

In June 1947, at the age of forty, Marion departed for a two-and-a-half-year mission to Denmark, a sad event for me as well as for Lenora, Gale, and Marion Jr. At least he left them comfortably settled into the three-bedroom house he had finished across the street westward from my mother's house. Lenora had been hired to teach business in the high school the next year. At the same time, having graduated from high school, Roald went to work for the Forest Service to earn money for college, leaving Leon in charge of the farm. Not quite sixteen at the beginning of the summer, Leon ran the risk of being ticketed for illegally driving the new Ford pickup our mother had bought by cashing in war bonds. I recall that Arley drove the new vehicle from the dealer in Holbrook. I was the only one at home when he arrived, and he forthwith instructed me on how to change a flat tire, particularly emphasizing that I must tighten two lug nuts on opposite sides in order to seat the wheel properly. I never change a flat tire without thinking of his lesson.

Lenora and my mother attended college at Flagstaff that summer. Both were destined to years of attending summer school before acquiring a degree and permanent certification. From Monday morning till Friday evening, Leon and I prepared our own meals and generally looked after ourselves. I felt very lonely without my mother, and I resented Leon's supervision in the farmwork. I was far from a cooperative assistant. During a fistfight in the kitchen one morning, I battled with such ferocity that Leon felt obliged to throw me to the floor and, standing over me, kick me in the ribs if I offered to get up and begin again. On another occasion when we had waded the flooding dam to catch the workhorses and return across the creek for a day of mowing alfalfa, Leon asked me to carry one of the bridles. I refused. Incensed by the symbolic injustice of my refusal, Leon thrust one of the bridles into my hands. I dropped it. He picked it up and hung it over my shoulder. I pushed it off. He tied the reins to my wrists. I collapsed and lay on the ground. He dragged me, howling and cursing, along the dusty lane. I don't remember how the episode ended, but I have no doubt the alfalfa was mowed.

I suppose conflict was to be expected among boys living in our inescapable intimacy. During my earliest childhood, my three brothers and I shared two beds in a single room. Later, when the washhouse was finished, Charles and Roald often slept there. Each of us had a small closet for shirts and pants and a single drawer in a dresser for socks and briefs. Neither the closet nor the drawer could be locked. We ate at the same table, vied for a single bathroom, and did outside chores together. In winter our indoor activities were confined to the dining room and kitchen, the only rooms normally kept warm. The kitchen, I will add, was very small.

By the end of the summer of 1947 I had been delivering newspapers for two years, sometimes as I have said by horse, sometimes by bicycle. I would go on delivering papers for another two years. Delivering papers was an educational experience. For one thing, while loading my bags with papers in front of the store where the daily White Mountain Lines bus from Phoenix dropped them, I often became absorbed in reading the front page, devouring a candy bar while I read. I also came to know the town intimately, delivering papers to a substantial majority of the hundred or so houses in town. In my mind I can still proceed along each street, house by house, and tell you who lived in each.

The worst part of my job was the monthly collection. Record book in hand, I tediously knocked on every door. Often no one was at home, and I had to try again the next day. When I succeeded in finding them in, most people paid. A few, however, told me to come back next week. When I did, they often told me to come back the week after that. I constantly carried three or four unpaid subscriptions for months before I got around to terminating them. In essence I was paying for their newspaper from my meager earnings because the Phoenix newspapers presented me with a monthly bill for the papers put in my hands. The newspapers proudly advertised their delivery boys as "little businessmen." *Victims of adult economics* would have been a better term.

Another problem was discovering, as I neared the end of my route once or twice a week, that I was short a paper or two. This was an uncanny phenomenon because, when I counted the papers at the beginning of the route, I always had enough. I can't explain it even now. All too often, the next-to-last house on my route went without its paper. I am surprised to this day that the family who lived there never canceled their subscription—though the husband scolded me regularly when I collected there. To his credit, he always paid promptly. Our house, the last, never went without. I enjoyed reading the comics too much for that. Those were the days of Dick Tracy, Gordo, Little Orphan Annie, and Buck Rogers. Blondie and Dagwood were around in those days as well.

I was scolded for other misdemeanors too. Gypsy sometimes ate people's flowers or defecated on their sidewalk. One afternoon the proprietor of the store where the bus left the papers thrust a scoop shovel in my hands and made me clean up the accumulating pile of horse dung at the side of his store where I tied Gypsy while stuffing my bags. I also had a penchant for breaking off a switch from the hanging boughs of weeping-willow trees in front of people's houses, for which I was often scolded. I preferred a sturdy, curving branch that would serve both as an effective whip for my indolent mount and as an aid to fantasy. While delivering on Gypsy, I found it natural to place myself in a heroic drama about a cavalry officer, and a sturdy, nicely curving willow branch made a perfect saber. I especially liked to lash the groaning Gypsy into a reluctant gallop across a vacant lot, where, with paper bags flapping on my saddle, I thrust, parried, and slashed with my saber.

Morally speaking, I was an interesting mix of good and evil as I prepared, at the age of thirteen, to enter high school. I considered myself a religious person. Ignoring momentary flashes of doubt, I affirmed the Mormonism in which I had been raised. However, I hated sermons from my earliest consciousness. The lay preachers of Snowflake Ward relished doctrine and high-sounding phrases, and many a good farmer, called on to open or close a meeting, turned his prayer into a lengthy disquisition on the Gospel. My mother was mercifully narcotized during all this by sleep. Unluckily I lacked the ability to sleep in church in those days. For distraction, I made dolls from a handkerchief, drew pictures on bits of paper, and counted dots on the high ceiling. Long before the meeting ended, I languished in unrelieved misery.

Still, Sunday had its redeeming traits. Sunday dinner was the best of the week, with fried chicken or roast beef, mashed potatoes, gravy made with cream, buttered vegetables, and pie with a tender, flaky crust or cake with deep, rich chocolate icing. When sacrament meeting finally adjourned in the late afternoon, I was free to seek friends, and we played raucous games in the street or backyard. The church also accounted for much of the social life of the town. It sponsored Friday- or Saturday-night dances, especially in the summer when school was out, and organized the observance of holidays. Children often attended adult dances, and some of the older men practiced the pioneer custom of dancing with any willing female, including teenage girls. On the Fourth of July the town fathers fired a charge of dynamite at dawn. A patriotic program, street games, and a dance followed through the course of the day. Pioneer Day on the twenty-fourth of July was an even bigger event, featuring a parade, a grand barbecue, and a two-day rodeo with boxing matches and evening dances. On Thanksgiving night there was the Wood Dance, admission to which men and boys earned by hauling, sawing, and splitting a winter's supply of juniper for the town's widows and spinsters.

I loved these celebrations. My parents, siblings, and friends were animated by a festive spirit, and their pleasure kindled a combustion in me. No solitary animal, I was happiest when others were happy. A child needs only the slightest excuse for feeling happy. I wanted things with a feverish intensity, my appetites being as yet wild and unschooled by admonition or experience.

At the rodeos, I escaped from the car and circled the arena afoot, excited by all the commotion. A loud speaker blared "The Yellow Rose of Texas" or "Blue Shadows on the Trail." I peered into pens where broncs stood with heads drooping in deceitful ease. I passed a camp of Apaches from the White Mountain reservation, who had arrived in a half-dozen horse-drawn wagons. I viewed a cavalcade of dudes, sun-burned Jewish youths from the East who summered at a nearby guest ranch operated by Mormon ranchers. I watched the calf roping, the team tying, the bulldogging, the horse racing. The contestants were from Snowflake and nearby towns. Some were skilled, some inept. That made no difference to me. Amid rising dust and bawling critters, I was amazed, excited, and electrified.

It was the church that made this possible. The bishop appointed a Pioneer Day committee and called on others to help out in putting on the parade, program, barbecue, rodeos, boxing matches, and dances. If I were looking for a new church, I'd find one that puts on rodeos. A church that puts on rodeos has a lot going for it.

The church also instructed me in Christian mythology, giving me a metaphysics view and worldview as well as a mode of worship. Despite my aversion to sermons, the church managed to teach me a good deal of doctrine and theology. Some of my early catechists were duly appointed by the church—my primary teacher, my Sunday-school teacher, and later, when I had turned twelve and been ordained a deacon, my priesthood-meeting instructor. My instructors in priesthood meeting were always men. Most of my other teachers were women. They were invariably better prepared and more impressive than the men.

I also received a lot of informal instruction. My brothers were adept at translating adult language into juvenile concepts. For example, Roald informed me that God could see through concrete. Though I doubted Roald at first, I later adopted his view. One night after Scout meeting, a town loafer who was loitering outside the church declared that according to an apostle preaching in the latest

General Conference, the Second Coming would occur within the decade. "You boys better get your house in order in a hurry," the loafer said. Because of this, I suffered anxiety for several years over the fast approach of the Great and Dreadful Day of the Lord. This loafer was an agent of the church, albeit self-appointed. As an institution of religious instruction, the church isn't limited to those who occupy pulpits or who sign certificates of baptism and ordination. It includes anyone who fancies himself or herself an authority.

Following is a confession of my faith during my early teens, the credo of a Christian child from Snowflake. I believed God the Father, God the Son, and God the Holy Ghost were distinct personal and corporeal entities. I believed my Heavenly Father had a spouse, my Heavenly Mother, and they were the parents of my spirit in the preexistence. I believed the preexistence still thronged with unborn spirits waiting to be assigned to the mortal body of a newly conceived child. I believed that human couples who persevered in righteousness were destined to become celestial parents of spirits and creators of worlds in the manner of our Heavenly Father and Mother. I believed the Bible and the Book of Mormon were the Word of God, equally tedious and incomprehensible. I believed that Joseph Smith had been a true prophet of God and that the existing president of the church, Heber J. Grant, was his successor. I believed that faithful prayer could move mountains and heal the sick, though I had never witnessed an actual miracle. I believed it wicked to drink, smoke, swear, masturbate, or peer into the blouse of a nubile girl sitting in the desk next to mine at school. Predictably, in certain moods I believed myself damned. In more congenial moods, I fancied I stood in good odor with God. The key to winning God's grace was self-denial. I believed in self-denial. I simply wasn't very good at achieving it.

For example, I went on a daylong excursion in the summer of 1947 with five or six other deacons during which a good deal of evil talk and mischievous behavior transpired. Our quorum adviser took us to Second Mesa in the back of his pickup to watch a Hopi snake dance. At a store on the way, one of the boys stole an entire carton of Walnetto caramel candies. Mile after mile we released a litter of candy wrappings into the roiling dust behind the speeding pickup.

This half century later, I can recall clearly the ten or twelve boys who were my classmates at church and school for year after year. I can recall clearly their older brothers who were my older brothers' classmates. While the older boys looked down on the younger and made scathing commentary on them, their influence upon us was enormous. The boys of Snowflake created a counter-culture whereby they collectively resisted the domestications of adult society. My brothers and I were members in good standing in this piratical fraternity. We had a conscience, knew right from wrong, and cheerfully sought the wrong. Returning from movies after dark, we wrote our names with urine in the dust of the graveled street. If one of us broke wind, we followed a frantic ritual. If the one who had broken wind shouted "Safety!" before someone else could shout "Jiggers!" all was well with him. But if someone else shouted "Jiggers!" first, all present were commissioned to pinch the wrongdoer while he counted from ten backward, whistled, and shouted "Bulljo!"

When insulting our enemies with a birdie, we did not merely offer an elevated middle finger but pulled down the fingers on ei ther side to resemble testicles below an erect penis. It took muscular conditioning to get one's side fingers to take this position quickly, important because in offering insults, timing is everything. So under the tutelage of my brothers, I practiced for weeks one summer to perfect my ability. I am pleased to report that this skill, once acquired, never departs. From my brothers I also learned how to use obscene words, smoke bark-and-paper cigarettes, and induce an orgasm in a male dog. Often as not my brothers and I aided and abetted one another in truancy from duty at the farm. I recall trips to the shitting tree (as we called it) with Roald and Leon when we should have been hoeing corn. This tree was a cottonwood in the willows along the creek where we could sit comfortably with our bared bottoms over one limb and our feet upon another and gaze down between our legs at the minor torrent of urine and feces falling upon the earth. Once while we were thus engaged, a coyote trotted through the clearing beneath us. It was the first coyote I ever saw in the wild. Speaking of wild things, I had some inkling while I was a boy that my mind was partly wild. It wasn't that I had any notion of instinct or innate impulse or the dark jungle of the id. Adults ordered me not to behave so wildly, so I knew the wild was something to be disapproved of and repressed like sin, vice, and rudeness. I had no idea how impossible it is for any human being to stop behaving wildly.

Predictably, I suffered a great deal of guilt for the barbarities in which I engaged. I bullied a smaller classmate after school one day and threw him to the ground. He broke into piteous wails, and my belligerence collapsed in an accession of remorse. I recall stealing four pennies from the toy box of a neighbor boy. Mother smelled my guilt and asked me what I had been up to. I pulled the pennies from my pocket, and she made me return them. One day I saw a key on our kitchen counter. For no good reason I put it in my pocket. Later that day, which must have been a Saturday, I loitered with friends on the elementary school grounds. The janitor ordered us off the premises. I pulled the key from my pocket and gave it to him, saying I had found it on the school grounds. He was a stern man, and I wanted to placate him. The next day Charles and Mother were in a great stir because the key to the chicken coop was missing. I realized where the key was but said nothing for fear of punishment. The search for the key went on for several days, and eventually the padlock had to be cut off. In the meantime I suffered the torment of the damned.

Guilt has been one of my gifts. I excel in it. I feel guilty for all the ills of our time: for the extinction of species, the exhaustion of natural resources, the abuse of women and children, the suppression of minorities, and the general malice of human nature. Guilty characters come naturally to my fiction. Guilt seems the heart of any good conflict. As for avoiding guilt by achieving saintly behavior, that seems a quality far beyond my capacities. Somehow I gathered from the culture in which I grew up—and especially from that small but crucial part of it represented by my mother—the nature of sainthood. But, as the following chapters will attest, it has been an elusive ideal.

8

High School

I ENTERED SNOWFLAKE UNION HIGH SCHOOL in September 1947. About a third of the school's 250 students came from Snowflake. The rest were transported by bus from a half-dozen outlying towns. I took a class in agriculture from my brother Elwood, which included instruction in woodworking as well as in farming. I joined the Future Farmers of America (FFA) and received instructions on etiquette when it came time for that club's annual banquet. That was the first time anyone had ever told me that you should lay your napkin across your lap and delicately dab the food from your lips with it from time to time. In fact, I don't recall using napkins in my childhood home. I also learned that formal dinners required an excess of cutlery. I had known the difference between a pitchfork and a manure fork in the barnyard. Now I discovered the difference between a salad fork and dessert fork on the dinner table.

In wood shop, I built a rabbit pen with a floor of spaced slats that supposedly would allow the droppings to fall through. The droppings tended to pile up on the floor, however, and the rabbits chewed on the slats till some of them became perilously thin. I got into rabbit raising by a circuitous route. I stole some pigeons from a neighbor's barn and traded them for a buck and a doe, which I housed in a pen I built from scrap boards and pieces of chicken wire lying around our place. Soon the doe had babies and began to fight the buck. I built another pen for him, then bought several more does for which I built more ramshackle pens. I began to read government pamphlets on rabbit raising, which I got through my class in agriculture. I liked to watch the rabbits eat and drink or simply lie at rest in a corner of their cage. They empowered me, making me feel more like an adult. If Leon hadn't vetoed the idea,

I would have erected a sign over our garage bearing the words *Petersons' Rabbitry.*

Late in my freshman year, my mother persuaded me to slaughter one of my rabbits for the dinner table. One Saturday morning I wandered our lot carrying a club in one hand and dangling a fryer rabbit by its hind legs from my other hand, trying to get up the courage to knock the animal on the head. As a little child I had reacted with horror to the slaughter of our pigs, and something of that horror still lurked in my feelings. At last, with palpitating heart, I struck the dangling rabbit on the head. That was a moral fall of sorts. From then on the deed came easy, and I regularly butchered rabbits for our table.

During that same spring of 1948, I accompanied the high school Glee Club to Flagstaff for a music festival. My musical abilities were such that I barely qualified for the last slot in the roster of those privileged to attend. I worried about being away from my mother for two nights but generally went through the experience in good spirits. Staying in a motel and ordering my own meals in a restaurant made me feel grown up. I also encountered my first pornography. One of my classmates had bought a tiny telescope that, if you held it to a light, showed the image of a beautiful nude blonde. It took my breath away to realize I was looking at a photograph and not simply a drawing. I coveted the tiny telescope but didn't dare offer to buy it. That would have seemed an utter capitulation to the forces of darkness.

As school ended in 1948, a senior girl and junior boy had to get married, a fact that stunned me. It had not occurred to me that persons near my own age could beget babies. Having a new and compulsive fodder for my fantasy life, I began to construct long, repetitive daydreams about getting the girl pregnant with whom I was currently in love. I could easily spend three or four days in creating one of these repetitive dramas, taking it up or laying it down in my imagination according to the practical demands of the moment. These episodes always ended with my marrying the pregnant girl. I imagined in great detail the scenes in which she and I advanced toward our illicit consummation. I took similar pleasure, once the episode had progressed to the point of my knowing of her pregnancy, in imagining scenes in which I eluded her irate male relatives. At last, apprehended and forced to agree to a wedding, I approached the girl with contrition and a confession of true and lasting love. She forgave me for my earlier reservation, and we were wed with our mutual relatives in attendance. With that, I ended this fantasy and shortly began a new one differing only in its particulars.

As these fantasies indicate, I possess a narrative imagination by instinct. From my earliest memory, I have entertained myself by creating imaginary episodes. Those I describe here also indicate that I relish the scandal of shotgun weddings, which predictably figure prominently in some of my fiction.

The first girl who figured in these fantasies was Barbara Jean Ellsworth from Showlow. Toward the end of our first year in high school, she had asked me for a date to the annual coed dance—an eventuality that plunged me into an ardor of an intensity hitherto unknown to me, the result, I suppose, of puberty. Barbara Jean's demeanor, I will emphasize, was always entirely proper. I dated her about once a month during the following year, depending on Leon to take me along on a double date in the family pickup. On these occasions, Leon's date rode in the middle of the bench seat while Barbara Jean sat on my lap, an arrangement in which I rejoiced. Barbara Jean was willing to dance body to body, and she always allowed me a good-night kiss at her doorstep. I can't overemphasize the significance of that single once-a-month kiss, a privilege that I interpreted as evidence that Barbara Jean was as much in love with me as I was with her.

In retrospect, I see that, while she regarded me as useful for friendly conversation, she didn't share my ardor. Well before the end of my sophomore year, I was experiencing such little success in arranging a monthly date that my fantasies about her became listless and unrewarding, and I soon abandoned the attempt to date her altogether. I don't recall being resentful or bitter. I must have gone through a period of mourning, though I was quite adept at that time in repressing painful emotions. I do know that Barbara Jean, with her lithe, shapely body, her fine brunette hair, her vibrant personality, stands enshrined in a thinly populated archive of my memory dedicated to romantic love. Through mutual friends, I have followed her subsequent life as a Mormon wife and mother with admiration and respect.

I emerged from my freshman year well into the adolescent process of shifting from my family to my peers as the focus of my social concerns, though, for good or evil, my peers happened to include members of my extended family. My best friends were my nephew Dwain, second son of my brother Elwood, and my third cousin Dale Hatch, to whom I was related on the side of my maternal grandmother. Dwain and Dale lived next door to each other. A vacant block, covered by native grass and yucca, lay between their houses and mine. They came by for me on their way to movies, dances, and church meetings, and we often helped one another milk cows and irrigate our gardens.

I entered my sophomore year of high school in the fall of 1948. I again sang in the Glee Club, and I served as sophomore class reporter on the staff of the school paper, the *Lobo's Howl*. I won first prize in a contest for writing Christmas stories both my sophomore and my junior years, for which I received a book at the annual awards day. I have no memory of paying much attention to my grades. However, I must have done reasonably well because for my sophomore and junior years I appear in the yearbook photo of the local chapter of the National Honor Society, and somewhere among my mementos I still have that organization's small gold pin.

Charles returned from his mission to Sweden during the late spring of 1949, released early because of Roald's imminent departure for a mission in Canada. Charles took over the farm during the summer of 1949, and I helped him while Leon, freshly graduated from high school and intent on financing a year at Brigham Young University (BYU), stacked lumber on contract at a sawmill at Overgaard. Charles too planned to enter BYU. Though his prospects were considerably eased by the G.I. Bill, he expected to make enough money from an acre of cucumbers to buy a used car. The three of us were at home at night, cooking for ourselves during the week because our mother, as usual, was enrolled in summer school at Flagstaff.

In early August Charles and I harvested a first light picking of cucumbers. Before our next picking, however, a cloudburst sent a flood down Silver Creek, inundating our farm. Our alfalfa had been recently cut and therefore was not much affected. In the cornfield, stalks listed in the direction of the current but afterward went on growing. Only the cucumbers were ruined. Charles immediately took a job stacking lumber with Leon, earning enough to buy a 1941 Oldsmobile before he and Leon departed for BYU. In the meantime I took over most of the work in the barnyard and at the farm and divested myself of my newspaper route—its income to be replaced by the proceeds of selling milk to our neighbors, which my mother had customarily turned over to the eldest son at home.

Charles and Leon left for BYU in mid-September, and my mother and I were left alone at home. At first I was successful in ignoring our loneliness. That early fall of 1949 was beautiful: frosty nights, sunny days, yellowing cottonwoods along the creek, fields of silver stubble. I was exhilarated by my new responsibilities and privileges. I had taught myself to drive our Ford pickup one day at the farm when Leon had left the key in the ignition. Now, three months short of sixteen, the legal age for getting a driver's license, I had to drive in order for the family economy to function. My mother, who had not learned to drive till she was forty, had an instinct for doing bad things with a car and avoided driving whenever possible.

I arranged to have our field corn chopped into silage and assisted in transferring it from the field to our silo in town. I had our last cutting of alfalfa baled and hauled it home to our barn. Then I transferred the livestock—four milk cows, a steer destined for beef, and two horses—from the pastures on the east side of the creek to the cultivated west side, where they grazed for a month or so on the alfalfa and corn stubble. In the meantime, I carried on with the daily chores, milking the cows at the farm and feeding the pig and chopping wood on our lot in town.

A junior at the high school, I decided to go out for football, a show of valor that I soon regretted. I liked scrimmage, but there was very little of that and much by way of drills and practices. One drill that I especially abhorred required that I scoop up a kicked football and run downfield against an oncoming wave of defenders, composed, as it seemed to me, not of puny, inexperienced neophytes like me but of brawny veterans of last year's A-squad. As the fall wore on, I fancied I would try out for the basketball team with better chances for success. However, duck season opened at noon on the Friday when tryouts were scheduled, and I had by then become passionate about hunting. I skipped tryouts and stalked and shot seven ducks sitting on ponds and the creek. In retrospect, I judge I took the better action. I simply wasn't a good athlete.

I became fast friends with Howard Ramsey that fall, a non-Mormon boy from the other end of town with whom Dwain had begun to fraternize. Howard was impulsive, witty, and perhaps too candid and public in his remarks on persons he didn't like. His father and two uncles, Depression-era migrants from Missouri, owned a sawmill and logging operation in Chevelon Canyon about seventy miles west of Snowflake. By the time I knew Howard, both of us still fifteen, he had operated bulldozers and logging trucks, giving him a precocious competence that made me trust him to a degree I now consider imprudent. On a Sunday afternoon, after he and I and Dwain had driven with some girls out into the rangeland to devour stolen watermelons, I held a sizable chunk of melon rind at arm's length above my head and allowed Howard to shoot it with a .22 rifle from a distance of about fifteen yards.

By an arrangement between my mother and the principal, I left school a little early each afternoon for completing the harvest at our farm. One pleasant consequence of the extra time was that I did a good deal of hunting. After rabbit season opened in September, I made various sorties over unimproved roads through the rangeland around Snowflake, stopping to reconnoiter along likely outcroppings of sandstone where cottontails made their burrows. One evening I got home so late that I had to skin and gut a couple of cottontails by the light from our dining room window. A little later, when I came in from milking, my mother was frying the rabbits for supper.

On another rabbit hunt, I saw a herd of antelope in a wide grassy valley rimmed by junipers. Maybe twenty of the tawny-and-white pronghorns wheeled and began an easy lope down the valley toward a barbed-wire fence. I watched with excitement, anticipating that, one after another, they would gracefully leap the fence with scarcely a break in their stride. I was shocked when they skidded to a halt and, three or four at a time, fell to their knees and crawled under the fence. On the other side, they resumed their flight, and after a minute or two they passed from sight over the far rim of the valley.

I was aware even then that I had acquired an appetite for nature—an appetite that in retrospect I attribute to Snowflake. As a community, Snowflake prepared me for life in an advanced urban civilization. As a place, it gave me a taste for the wild. I have lived only in cities since leaving Snowflake, choosing to do so in order to pursue a profession. However, I have been ill at ease in every one of them, largely, I think, because accumulations of people and their domestications obliterate all signs of the wild. Snowflake, a town of fewer than a thousand, conditioned me to expect an equal mingling of the wild and the domesticated. Growing up, I had no idea that civilization is antithetical to wilderness. I assumed you could enjoy both.

Perhaps unfortunately, I felt no dissonance between my appreciation for the wild and my growing passion for guns and hunting, which I must also attribute to a boyhood in Snowflake. Throughout my junior year in high school, I applied the same intensity to the literature of guns and hunting that I had applied to the literature on raising rabbits a couple of years earlier. I bought and read *Sports Afield* and *Outdoor Life,* and I studied Stoeger's *Shooter's Bible,* a sales catalog with an enormous inventory of handguns, shotguns, and rifles described in technical detail. For ten dollars I bought a .20-gauge bolt-action shotgun that had a malfunctioning magazine and had to be used as a single shot. Upon acquiring it, I stalked a roost of vultures in a cottonwood tree in our willow patch and downed one of them from its perch. I remember my disgust at seeing its writhing intestines, laid open by the blast. However, I recall no remorse over the wanton destruction of the bird. Another afternoon, I saw in a neighbor's corn patch a feral house cat that had been haunting the vicinity for a long time. Moving stealthily through the corn, I succeeded in killing the cat with another blast from the shotgun. At home a day or two later I saw a feral cat that frequented our lot. I got my .22 from the house, cornered the cat in our garage, and shot it. Without actually intending to make myself into a cat killer, I nonetheless shot or was present while my friends shot something close to thirty cats during the following year. On at least two occasions, the mothers of girls with whom my friends and I fraternized asked us to dispose of litters of baby cats.

I have often pondered this period of bloodletting in my life without arriving at a satisfactory explanation for it. Killing cats may have been a way of forcing myself to grapple with the moral implications of hunting for sport, which I was getting into. I was perhaps something like a mountaineer who takes to rock climbing as a way of overcoming a fear of heights. It was as if, by killing cats, I could quell a streak of mercy deep within me that seemed inconsonant with the requirements of hunting.

I hunted turkey and deer that fall with Marion and Marion Jr., using a borrowed .30-30. My anticipation of these hunts was close to uncontainable, a fact that helps explain the intensity of the following experience. It was after dark on the evening before the turkey hunt, and I was at the farm, sitting at the flank of a cow and stripping the last drops of milk from her teats. A bright moon stood high in the sky. I heard a distant sound, which quickly magnified into the quacking of ducks. Suddenly I saw two ducks pass between me and the moon, rocketing on with plaintive voices toward an invisible haven on the nearby creek. My emotions were vivid and complex. I was suspended in delight, rich anticipation, and the ineffable mystery of being alive. I was at one with the staccato flight of the ducks, the glowing moon, and the frosty October shadows around me.

While hunting deer on the Mogollon Rim a couple of weeks later, I became separated from Marion and his son and had to find my own way back to the pickup. Riding behind a mounted rancher who had given me a lift on the back of his saddle, I saw five or six does disappearing over a ridge. I had never before seen either deer or elk in the wild and had worried over my ability to distinguish them. The sight of these animals allayed that anxiety. I was struck by their graceful beauty and knew intuitively that they were deer and not elk.

By the time the big-game season ended, I had decided to buy a high-powered rifle of my own. I began to save about ten dollars a month toward this end and began to study my *Shooter's Bible* and the hunting and shooting magazines with renewed concentration. In May 1950, I bought a new but entirely unadorned Remington bolt-action .30-06 for a little more than ninety dollars. Though it had a recoil that made me flinch every time I shot it, I never regretted my purchase. I considered this rifle the essence of beauty, often taking it from my closet to stroke, fondle, and contemplate while it lay upon my bed with a row of gleaming brass cartridges beside it.

As was customary for Mormon youths, I attended seminary during my first three years of high school—seminary being a daily class in the Mormon religion that met in a small stone building on the corner of the high school campus. During my junior year, the instructor recruited my class into a fund-raising campaign for an end-of-the-year trip to Salt Lake City. Among our projects was a concession for selling soda pop at the home basketball games in the high school gymnasium. I remember an evening game during the Christmas holidays to which I conveyed eight or ten cases of bottled soda in the back of my pickup. When the game was over, Dale, Dwain, and I went ice skating at a nearby reservoir, taking the remnants of the soda with us. It was very cold that night, probably below zero, and we built a large fire by which we warmed ourselves between bouts of skating. We drank some of the pop, in which ice crystals were forming, and it seemed exceptionally delicious. We skated far out onto the reservoir while the fire receded into a seeming flicker. The great arch of the sky burned with a frozen brilliance, and the wind rushed in our ears. Our skates made a zinging sound, and the ice groaned and popped with the cold.

Cold winters were to be expected in Snowflake, which stood at fifty-six hundred feet. I can remember more than one occasion when temperatures plunged to thirty degrees below zero with an accession of Arctic air over the open plains of northern Arizona. We heated our house with juniper; no wood has a more fragrant smoke than juniper, and I miss it sorely. Our ill-framed, uninsulated house leaked heat steadily, and we stayed close to a stove—backsides warm and noses cold. We slept between flannel sheets and under a heavy stack of quilts. On the coldest nights, when frost accumulated inside the windowpanes, we wrapped heated flatirons in towels and placed them at our feet.

As for the brilliant sky my friends and I skated under on a cold night in late 1949, that too was to be expected. In any season I was aware of the sky in Snowflake. The sun was bright year-round, even in winter. The rise of a full moon over the low eastern horizon was always spectacular. The harvest moon was unbelievably large and golden—maybe ten miles away. There were no streetlights in Snowflake when I was very young. Even later there were no more than a dozen. During the dark of the moon, I saw a stunning sky. Stars glimmered and the Milky Way painted the zenith a chalky white. Everywhere the cosmos burned with a fine, luminescent dust.

My happy mood during the fall of 1949 did not carry over into the early months of 1950. With the holidays behind me and my brothers returned to BYU, I often felt dejected. As the contraction of our family circle bore in on me, I sought out my friends less often and spent more evenings at home with my mother. After supper we often occupied ourselves at the table in the dining room, which, with the adjoining kitchen, was the only space we ordinarily kept warm during the winter.

While she graded school papers, I did homework or read a novel or, with increasing frequency, tried my hand at watercolors. She often paused in her work to recount family lore, most of which I had heard before but invariably came forth with new details. She led herself repeatedly into accounts of Alma's death to which I listened with clenched jaws, struggling to hold my tears. Even her other stories tended to have an elegiac color. My poignant role as the last child at home sharpened during this dark winter. Subliminally, as I now believe, my mother and I were engaged in a requiem ritual, preparing for the time, still a year and a half in the future, when I too would depart.

I retain vivid memories of milking cows in a mucky corral that winter. At night the cows were likely to lie down in their own dung, and I was sometimes obliged in the morning to peel it off their flanks and udders with a table knife before washing them with warm water carried from the house. I recall at least one occasion when a green sediment floated at the bottom of the bucket as I strained the fresh milk through a cloth into gallon bottles destined for our paying customers. Sometimes the cows' teats became so chapped that they bled onto my fingers. Though I treated their teats with an ointment of lard and kerosene, I still had to hobble their hind legs to keep them from kicking while I milked. I enjoyed feeding them hay and silage. They especially relished the latter, gathering eagerly at the corral fence while I carried tubs of silage, steaming from fermentation, up the ladder leaning inside the pit silo.

I regarded it as a major accomplishment that winter to break in a heifer to milk after the birth of her first calf. Following Elwood's advice, I shut her head in the stanchion while she was eating hay, bound her hind legs with both metal hobbles and a rope, and milked her. One morning she refused to enter the shed where the stanchion stood. I chased her up and down the corral, shouting hoarse obscenities and, each time I cornered her, beating her on the head and back with the milk stool. At last, she dashed into the shed. As I followed, I saw, peering over the top of the fence between us, the eyes of our neighbor, the town postmaster. He said, "My, my," and turned away. Nonetheless, I rejoiced in my triumph. The heifer allowed me to lock her in the stanchion, hobble her, and proceed to milk.

At the high school, a rowdy junior from Showlow went out of his way to pick on me during that winter. Between classes he said insulting things and sometimes, while walking behind me, tried to trip me. I ignored him as best I could because the only way to put a stop to his harassment would have been to fight him, and I was afraid of doing that. It appears that my personality invited persecution from aggressive upcountry boys. For one thing, I called attention to myself by being loud voiced and unflagging in an attempt to be witty. For another thing, my aggressive instincts sank among a host of paralyzing considerations when I was confronted by someone other than my brother Leon, with whom, be it said, I often fought with a near total indifference to personal injury.

A year earlier I had threatened to fight a Showlow boy for tousling my hair. Though he was a year younger than I, he called my bluff and I had to meet him behind the gymnasium for a fight. I made a feeble attempt to throw him down. He easily threw me down, and I retreated in abject humiliation. A medieval code of courage existed among the boys of the high school. It was ignominious to refuse a fight, even more ignominious to lose one. I could tolerate my own pusillanimity only by not thinking about it. Decades later, the depth of my residual anger over this matter would astonish me.

It didn't occur to me to resort to weapons in these confrontations. However, I was witness to an incident where a shooting came very close to occurring. During the winter of my junior year, Howard and I took a couple of girls to a dance in Showlow. As we left town after the dance, four young men, all older than we, pulled ahead of us in a car and forced us to slow down two or three times.

Finally Howard rammed their car from the rear. They sped ahead, turned their car across the highway to serve as a roadblock, and, as we approached, opened the doors and climbed out. Howard revved his engine and bore down on them, swerving at the last instant onto the shoulder of the road. Scattering gravel, his car lurched safely past. They followed at high speed. In Snowflake, Howard swung from the highway, leaped from the car in front of his uncle's house, and pulled a loaded .22 rifle from a pickup. Luckily, this show of force proved sufficient, and our assailants chose to drive on. Otherwise, I fear Howard would have pulled the trigger.

There were signs of spring in late February 1950, and then came some beautiful days in early March before the perennial spring wind set in. I went to the farm nearly every afternoon, cleaning ditches, driving the wintering livestock to the pastures on the east side of the creek, and making plans for my first season in full charge of the farm. There were two fields of established alfalfa, where green sprouts were already showing themselves. I intended to hire the plowing of two smaller fields for corn. I myself would do the harrowing, furrowing, planting, and irrigating. I knew how from years of watching and was eager to get on with the process. This Peterson soil, these seventy acres divided by the serene, willow-lined creek, seemed personable and capable of conversation. It was something merely to be abroad upon it, under a wide benign sky, responding to and applying to myself, for the first time in my sixteen years of life, the age-old agrarian parable of the free and self-sufficient yeoman. I sensed an elemental and mystical quality in what I was about, a mingling of my identity with earth, seed, water, and sun. At last I could understand Charles, who forth-rightly aspired to a lifetime of farming.

Quite suddenly, my plans changed drastically. The manager of a planing mill west of town asked the principal of the high school to recommend several boys for immediate part-time employment after school and on Saturday with the promise of full-time work in the summer. The task was stacking strips of green lumber so that they would dry, for which the pay was minimum wage, seventy-five cents an hour. I was one of the boys the principal recommended. The job meant more than a quadrupling of my income, and I wanted to take it. It occurs to me now that my mother agreed to shift my efforts from the farm to a wage-earning job because she was making plans, unknown to me at the moment, for moving to a college town during the coming school year in order to finish her bachelor's degree—an imminent necessity if she wished to remain certified to teach. She would, of course, take me with her. It made sense to rent the farm for the summer and divest ourselves of the milk cows, since no one would be at home during the winter to milk them. Although I continued to milk our cows during the spring and summer of 1950, the job I took stacking strips at the planing mill essentially ended my connection with farming.

At the time I paid no attention to the symbolic significance of this change. Later I saw its meaning. As far as my own activities were concerned, I had migrated from subsistence farming to the industrial age. Snowflake had thrived on a mingling of the two economies from its beginning. Even the simple agriculture practiced by the town's earliest families required plows, shovels, and axes manufactured in Chicago and Cincinnati. In my time, farmers—my father among them—went on applying age-old practices: flood irrigation and sowing wheat by hand, for example. Yet the train that rumbled through town three times a week, the trucks that transported freight and lumber, the cars parked in front of most of the houses, to say nothing of the planing mill where I would be working, bespoke the town's utter entanglement with complicated activities going on in far-away places—banking, investment in stocks and bonds, research and education, ingenious inventions, steel mills, machining shops, and assembly lines. Though textbooks like to give a definitive date for the shift from subsistence agriculture to an industrial, market-based economy, obviously the shift has been jagged, varied, and overlapping.

When school ended in mid-May, I graduated from seminary, which was a three-year program in those days. The following Monday, my fellow graduates and I set out on a weeklong tour of Utah by chartered bus, accompanied by our seminary teacher. This was in effect my first visit to Utah. I had traveled there twice in early childhood but had no memory of those trips. Though the route of Highway 89 through southern Utah may strike tourists from the East as dry and bleak, it struck my eyes, conditioned to the barren plains of northern Arizona, as lush with greenery. I was instantly attracted to the tidy little towns, well-tilled fields, and verdant pastures filled with grazing cattle, horses, and sheep. It was the beginning of my love affair with Utah.

Upon my return, I settled in at the mill, stacking slats from eight to five, with an hour off for lunch, Monday through Friday. Suffering intolerably from boredom, I realized for the first time that innumerable human beings perform such mind-numbing routines, day in and day out for much of a lifetime. Charles and Leon returned from BYU and got jobs stacking lumber again at Overgaard, where they commuted every morning. Mother went to summer school at Flagstaff as usual, being home only on weekends.

One of the most sobering events of my life occurred soon after I began full-time work at the mill. One afternoon, I persuaded fellow stackers Orville Decker and Kelly Willis to go jackrabbit hunting after work. Kelly's best friend and cousin, Scott Flake, decided to come with us. Orville came by for me in an old pickup, which ironically happened to be the same Chevrolet my father had owned before he died. We parked in front of Scott's house, across the street from Kelly's. Our two friends emerged from their houses and climbed into the back. Kelly, who by another touch of irony had recently purchased my bolt-action shotgun, thrust this weapon through the back window, which had no glass, placing the shotgun muzzle up with its forestock resting against the seat beside Orville's .22 and mine. As Kelly stood up, the shotgun went off. There was first a terrible roar in my left ear—the muzzle being only a couple of inches away—and then a hoarse shout from Kelly, "Scott's been shot!"

Scott lay on the ground, kicking spasmodically like a dying rabbit. A piece of his skull, four or five inches in diameter, was missing, and his brain was visible. He was unconscious, and his breathing was labored. Kelly went into his house and phoned Dr. Heywood. A sixty-year-old neighbor came running. She knelt over Scott, repeating with great urgency, "Keep breathing, Scott, keep breathing!" A small crowd gathered, and we told each newcomer what had happened. Someone sent after Scott's parents, who were not at home. Dr. Heywood arrived. He bent over Scott and sprinkled sulfa powder on the wound, whereupon Scott kicked again. I had expected the doctor to do more. Scott's parents arrived and looked at him with impassive faces. They had already been told what to expect. We laid him in the back seat of their car, and they left for the hospital in Holbrook.

This was a Thursday. Mother was still in Flagstaff, and Charles and Leon hadn't returned from Overgaard. I went into my bedroom and knelt beside my bed and asked God, most fervently, to heal Scott. From the instant of seeing his open brain, I had recoiled with guilt. I felt responsible for having sold the shotgun to Kelly, also for having suggested the hunt in the first place. Over and over I had felt the need to put time in reverse and give a new start to the afternoon's events. I had no relief from my prayer. I knew instinctively there was no remedy for a pulverized skull. No amount of prayer, no amount of pulpit talk, could help here. Scott was a goner.

My mother's face was a study in terror when she got home the next afternoon and I told her about the accident. She went to see Scott's mother, who said, "Lydia, it could have been your boy as easily as mine." Scott died on the following Sunday. By then I had recovered my juvenile bravado. Howard, Dwain, and I went driving after church in Howard's car. Chancing on a jackrabbit, we shot it with the rifle Howard had brought along. We made jokes about Scott. We didn't rejoice in his death, but we pretended to be indifferent to it.

• • •

I didn't pay much attention to the Korean War when it first broke out in June 1950. When American and South Korean troops recovered from the earliest reverses and pushed northward toward the Chinese border, it looked like a war of brief duration. However, the intervention of the Chinese forces soon made it obvious that this would be a long, mean war and that I, coming of draft age within a year and a half, would likely have to participate in it. My gusto for playing at war while a child had entirely evaporated. I knew, most decidedly, that I wanted to have nothing whatsoever to do with fighting. I didn't think of resisting or evading the draft, but I resented it deeply.

Toward the end of the summer my mother and I were making plans for moving to Flagstaff so that Mother could complete her bachelor's degree at the college there. Quite suddenly, only a week before we left, our plans changed. My mother's niece Magdalene Pace and her husband, Gove Allen, had offered us, free of rent, a small apartment in their house in Mesa. Mother would attend Arizona State University in nearby Tempe, commuting each day, again free of charge, with Gove, who was a manual-arts teacher at a high school in Phoenix. Another incentive was that we had many other relatives in the Phoenix-Mesa area, including Arley and Coral, and almost none in Flagstaff.

Our apartment at the back of Magdalene's house consisted of a living room, a tiny kitchen, and a bathroom with a shower. Living for the first time in my life in a house with a working hot water tank, I showered so often that I developed eczema, a minor affliction that has remained with me ever since. Our living room doubled as a bedroom, having a single bed, on which I slept, and a sofa, on which Mother slept. Magdalene complained about this arrangement, believing I should concede the bed to Mother's seniority. I felt guilty but couldn't bring myself to refuse the bed when Mother offered it to me. As far as I could tell, she slept soundly on the sofa, which would have been a torture rack for me because it was short and had arms that prevented my feet from hanging over. I usually went to bed before my mother, who retreated to the kitchen for more study. I played a radio while going to sleep—my first constant access to a radio. I listened to Patti Page singing "The Tennessee Waltz" and Louis Armstrong singing "Blueberry Hill." I thought the first incredibly beautiful, and I loved any song by old Satchmo, whose cheerful personality resounded in both his deep, husky voice and his exuberant trumpet.

Although I found my classes at Mesa High School interesting, I never lost, throughout the entire year, my sense of being an alien there. I grant that I liked the Friday-morning assemblies, where incredibly pretty cheerleaders in tiny skirts roused enthusiasm for games. The assemblies were also remarkable for the fact that from time to time, Harvey L. Taylor, the superintendent of Mesa School District, presented a special program on the theme of containing world communism. On such days a large banner reading "Act Now for Democracy!" hung over the stage. Mr. Taylor, who would later become a vice president under Ernest L. Wilkinson at BYU, orated on the virtues of free enterprise and the imminent dangers of militant communism. He emphasized that it was not only the Soviets, Chinese, and North Koreans that we had to fear but also fellow Americans of subversive ways. I knew nothing about Joseph McCarthy and his hunt for domestic communists, but I came to understand something of his doctrines through the ardent preaching of Mr. Taylor. I had no reason to doubt Mr. Taylor's veracity. He had a firm, square jaw and an air of being utterly resolute. I had a good deal of ambition to save democracy. However, I didn't know any communists to resist, and, except for presumably Mr. Taylor, I didn't know anybody else who knew any.

My mother and I attended church at the Mesa Second Ward, whose bishop ordained me to the rank of priest soon after I turned seventeen in December 1950. Thereafter, at the opening of Sunday school or sacrament meeting, I often joined another young man in breaking the bread and water and saying the prayers of the sacrament service. We read the prayers from a printed card. When we made a mistake, the bishop halted us and made us start over. Apparently, God will not sanctify the tokens of redemption unless you get the words just right.

My year at Mesa would have been much more lonely without Arley and his family. Now a contractor building single-family houses, Arley hired his three sons, Max, Leo, and Van, and me for part-time work after school and on Saturdays. Arley was taciturn and undemonstrative, yet I intuited kindness and a quiet cheerfulness in his demeanor. His strongest expletive, uttered when he bent a nail, was "Dadgost it!" He smiled at the constant banter between Max and Leo, though he never joined in. They, for their part, were energetic workers, and their banter didn't interrupt their sawing and pounding.

Van was my most constant and intimate friend throughout my stay in Mesa. He was gregarious and forward and often witty in his conversation yet characterized by certain small miscues in his speech and demeanor that marked him as eccentric. Born prematurely, he had been so tiny and frail that the attending doctor recommended he not be fed and be allowed to die quickly. Coral refused. She fed him with a medicine dropper and, lacking an incubator, placed him in a shoe box on the open door of the oven of their kitchen range. Although he was several years my senior, he and I progressed through grade school and high school together. Of small stature, he was energetic and fairly athletic and always neatly dressed and groomed.

Arley often put Van on tasks with me. Van and I dug the footings for a couple of houses by pick and shovel, and when Arley did brickwork, Van and I mixed mortar and carried hod. Max and Leo carped at Van a good deal. He ignored them or made an appropriate retort. Almost every evening after work, Van and I drove in my pickup to the Dairy Queen on Country Club Drive and bought a ten- or fifteen-cent soft ice cream cone or, rarely, a milk shake or malt, delicacies I had never tasted before coming to Mesa. Van and I often attended a movie on a Friday evening or a church-sponsored dance at the Mezona on Saturday night, where both of us stood among the single boys, looking with longing at pretty girls across the hall.

One Monday morning, as Van stopped by for me on his way to school, he was ebullient because a girl identifying herself as one of the high school cheerleaders had phoned him on the previous evening, telling him how much she liked him and inviting him to look her up at school. I told him instantly it was a hoax. He was reluctant to believe me, and as we parted to go to class, I wondered whether he might not yet seek out the cheerleader. Fortunately, he didn't. Later I confronted the circle of friends who I believed had perpetrated the hoax. One of them, a girl, apologized for the group's behavior, admitting it had been a cruel and thoughtless joke. Needless to say, my loyalty to Van was intense. I knew my companionship made a big difference in the quality of his life, and I felt guilty for leaving him behind when I returned to Snowflake at the end of the school year.

A moderate winter was one of the few benefits of living in Mesa that I was willing to admit. It was a pleasure to walk to school without a coat along an avenue lined with decorative orange trees and date palms. On many Sunday afternoons I roamed the surrounding Sonoran Desert in my pickup, enjoying the sense of being out of the city but having little taste for the kind of wilderness the desert offered. Throughout most of the year, its abundant vegetation—saguaro, ocotillo, barrel cactus, prickly pear, mesquite, and a host of other small, thorny shrubs for which I had no name—was sere and grayish in hue, much of it lacking the chlorophyll that makes other plants green. Though I was surprised and to some degree rejuvenated by the flowering that came after the rains of early spring, it was too brief a showing to attach my affections to the desert.

I probably would have liked Mesa better had I returned for a second year. As it was, my heart remained fixedly in Snowflake, where I returned on visits perhaps a half-dozen times. One of the most notable was at deer season in mid-October. It surprises me yet that Mother allowed me to go. I stayed with Howard, whose parents and siblings were all in Chevelon. On opening day, a Friday, we hunted futilely in the morning and in the afternoon drove to Flagstaff for a football game. After returning to Snowflake late that night, we drove the seventy miles to Chevelon, arriving cold because the heater wasn't working in the car. When we crawled into bed, Howard snuggled up to me as he was accustomed to do with his brother. With a reflex gesture, I leaped out of bed. I don't recall what was said between us as I got back in. I am sure we did no more snuggling. In retrospect, I think Howard was more secure in his heterosexuality than I was.

We hunted on Saturday with Howard's father and on Sunday with Dale and Dwain, who joined us for a long drive over the Mogollon Rim into Pleasant Valley. Only toward evening did we get out of the car near Heber and hunt afoot. As dusk gathered, we jumped a bunch of deer, excitedly construing a couple of does as bucks, which we shot. Leaving our illegal kill behind, we drove on. Thus ended my first deer hunt with the new .30-06 rifle. On Monday morning, after breakfast with Howard, I set out for Mesa, pausing a moment at our house before leaving town. Clouds had come in during the night, and the morning was gloomy. I circled our house, whose doors were locked and whose windows stared with a bleak vacancy. I wept, seized by nostalgia for all the good things that had happened here and would never happen again.

The hearty welcome Howard, Dwain, and Dale gave me on all of my visits that year increased my eagerness for the end of school and our permanent return to Snowflake. I didn't project ahead to the end of the coming summer when I might be leaving again to go to college. I hadn't quite made up my mind that I would go to college—though I had no ideas about what else I might do. The insuperable problem was that, if I went, Mother would be alone, and that didn't seem right. In the meantime, I endured my exile in Mesa as best I could. On a hot evening in May 1951, I attended commencement exercises under the glaring lights of the football field. The next morning, a Saturday, Mother and I loaded the pickup and set out for Snowflake. The brakes seized on the long pull out of Salt River Canyon, luckily at a spot where the road had a shoulder. I was frightened because I had no idea what to do about the problem. I felt very reduced and vulnerable. That's how I have always felt when a car breaks down far from a town. Someone stopped and told us just to wait. When the brakes cooled off, the fluid unlocked and we drove on.

Lenora had opened our house and readied things for our arrival. I unloaded the pickup and in the early evening went happily off to find my friends. School in Snowflake had ended a week earlier, and my friends weren't to be found. Howard had gone to Chevelon for the summer. Dwain had gone on an FFA trip and wouldn't be home for a week. Dale's parents didn't know where he was at the moment. I would probably see him the next day at church. I went home depressed. Only now did it begin to grow on me that my boyhood was beyond recovery.

9

My Early College Years

WITHIN DAYS OF RETURNING FROM MESA in May 1951, I began to log for the Webb brothers on the Apache reservation south of Showlow.[1] Spending nights in Snowflake, I rode to the sawmill and on into the woods every weekday with my sister Mary's husband, Waldo Ray, whom she had married in 1947. I trudged behind Waldo's bulldozer, attaching cables to logs and releasing them after he had dragged them to a landing. The contract was a year-old burn, and the logs were charred and black, which meant that my sweaty body acquired, even under my clothes, a daily varnish of charcoal and dust.

One Sunday morning soon after I went to work in the woods, I awoke from a dream about Marilyn Cardon, a girl with whom I had often conversed during study hall at Mesa High School. Marilyn had short honey-brown hair with a fringe of tiny curls, alert brown eyes, and a pleasant face. It had never occurred to me to date her, and she was not on my mind when I left Mesa. On this Sunday morning in Snowflake, however, I awoke believing myself to be in love with her—just like that, with no warning or premonition. Suddenly I felt incredibly lucky, for love was an elusive treasure. I didn't doubt its reality, its roots being deep and vital within me. The trick was to find its true object, that adorable person who would evoke and return it. I can't say why I was so sure Marilyn Cardon, having evoked love in me, would return it. I was, it must be remembered, only seventeen.

I exchanged perhaps a dozen letters with Marilyn over the summer, and I drove to Mesa and dated her on three or four weekends. I am startled even now at how little time I spent in her actual presence. It was in my daydreams that I knew her. My labor in the woods had become unbearably tedious, and I sought escape through the sexual fantasies that I have previously described. Predictably, my fantasies about Marilyn occurred in serial form, each requiring, while I trudged behind the dusty bulldozer, two or three days to complete. When an episode ended, I began another, precisely like it in its general features. Needless to say, the actual relationship between Marilyn and me was utterly circumspect.

On the last night that I dated Marilyn in Mesa, I parked beside her home and she slid close to me. I kissed her and told her about how I had dreamed of her and had awakened knowing I was in love with her. She said with deep emotion, "No one has ever said that to me before." Nor had I ever said it to anyone before. After that I could not generate my usual erotic fantasies about her. My feelings seemed too sacred, too intense, for the merely erotic. With no other woman have I ever experienced romantic love with the intensity I felt for Marilyn.

In September I went to BYU because Marilyn was going there. Luckily, my brothers Charles and Roald were also there. We stayed in one of the Wymount dorms converted from army barracks, Roald and I sharing a double room and Charles occupying a single. I found a part-time job peeling potatoes in the Wymount cafeteria, which began at five thirty in the morning, seven days a week. I enrolled in a typical freshman schedule, including composition, college algebra, the Book of Mormon, and ROTC, the last in order to avoid being drafted immediately as an infantryman into the Korean War by qualifying for an eventual commission in the U.S. Air Force.

With a population of thirty thousand, Provo was too vast a city for me. Its lawns, sidewalks, and paved streets were oppressive. I got readily lost among its streets, not realizing for an entire year that a person could navigate the city by its quadrant system of signage. I was repelled by city fashions for men. On campus I despised the young men from California and the Wasatch Front who wore pleated flannel slacks, wide-soled shoes, and duck-tailed, flattopped haircuts. As for me, I wore Levi's and flannel shirts to school and a suit, white shirt, and tie to church.

On a couple of evenings during the first week, I borrowed Charles's car and took Marilyn driving. I was very happy and the entire world seemed right. On Sunday we agreed to meet at church. On my way to meeting that afternoon, I realized suddenly I didn't love Marilyn. Just like that. Again, no warning, no premonition. I was devastated and frightened. I walked her to her dorm after church and went back to my room to assess the damage. I had no idea why I was so frightened and dejected. I did know I had been suddenly tumbled from happiness, and I wanted it restored. I prayed with unusual fervor that I would be in love with Marilyn again when I woke up in the morning. But I wasn't.

The next Friday evening we went to a dance. The orchestra played "September Song," that haunting elegy for the dwindling of love's allotted time. We left the dance early and walked to a spot on the edge of campus overlooking the twinkling lights of Provo. Marilyn hugged me and said she was sure now she was in love with me. That her love had confirmed itself even as mine lapsed seemed a bitter discrepancy. It's strange how irony makes a loss harder to bear.

I told Marilyn about my uncertainty with such equivocation that she granted me time to regain my former feelings for her. But by the end of the quarter she broke off the relationship. I went on throughout a dismal, stormy winter, very depressed and brooding incessantly about falling in love with Marilyn all over again. When spring came, I fancied I had, and I looked her up and told her so. She told me she was about to be married to a veteran and returned missionary who lived in my dorm. She wished me well and thanked me for having, as she put it, made a part of her growing up memorable.

Somehow all this had cosmic implications for me. A world where such a thing could happen—where I could be happily in love at one instant and tumbled at the next into an indifference fraught with enigmatic anxiety and despair—was morally amiss. I couldn't quite admit at that moment how wrenching a realignment of ideas I had undergone. I didn't give up on trying to fall in love for a long time after that. But I could no longer rely on what I will call, for lack of a better term, romantic love. I puzzled about it a good deal. I still puzzle about it. Romantic love breaks up as many marriages as it engenders. The only thing certain about it is its uncertainty. It is here today and gone tomorrow.

My mother came to Utah for General Conference in early October, about three weeks after I had arrived at BYU. During an afternoon session she and I sat outside the Tabernacle on Temple Square listening to the sermons over a loudspeaker. I began to tell her about Marilyn. I began to cry, and we retreated to a secluded outside corner of the Assembly Hall. Sobbing bitterly, I said, "It's as if she is dead." Oddly I did feel as if someone dear and close had died.

In retrospect, I can see that the person for whom I wept stood beside me. I couldn't admit this at that moment. I could only recognize that I was homesick. Roald was homesick too, and we fed on one another's longing. Sometimes we walked in the sagebrush foothills between campus and Wye Mountain. Roald would point to the pass leading south from Utah Valley and remind me that home lay in that direction. Home meant our house and lot in Snowflake and the farm on the creek but chiefly our mother. I for one felt dispossessed. Having become, as I esteemed, an adult, I had no right to return to my mother. Years later I would recognize that in my deep and subliminal emotions that fact was equivalent to her death. So I say it was for my mother that I wept on Temple Square on that October afternoon in 1951. Having moved out of her home and having no home of my own, I felt as if she had died.

Although I studied with diligence, I made only average grades during that first college year. I was especially astonished to pass all my tests in college algebra at scores above 90 yet receive a final grade of C. When I protested to my math instructor, he introduced me to the concept of the bell curve. He pulled out his roll, and there I was, in the big middle bulge of the class, entirely deserving, so he said, of a C.

I made two Cs and a B in the three-quarter series of freshman English taught by Olive Kimball Burmingham. I learned to distinguish between *there, their,* and *they're* and to use the subjunctive *I wish I were* in stating a wish or supposition contrary to fact. Though the assigned essays struck me as insufferably abstract, I was influenced by at least one of them, "A Free Man's Worship," by Bertrand Russell. Russell's cheerless description of a nihilistic universe where "all the labours of the ages, all the devotion, all the inspiration, all the noon-day brightness of human genius, are destined to extinction" would soon reappear in my thinking.[2] As for poetry, it came alive for me only when, in her rich, resonant voice, Mrs. Burmingham read it aloud. Sometimes the dismissal bell would awaken me from one of her readings, and I would realize that, for a precious quarter hour, I had been transported from the general gloom of my existence into a fine, high ecstasy.

On the first day of my Book of Mormon class, the instructor bore his testimony as to the truthfulness of Mormonism. A distinct sensation of doubt went through me. This was frightening and added to the fervor of my private prayers. To this point I had believed on the strength of my parents' faith. Now I judged it was time to know for myself.

Assuming the Holy Ghost would not bear witness to a youth of my relaxed and indifferent standards, I repented with a rigor that made my life inconvenient in many ways. I attended all my church meetings and began to read the scriptures. On fast day I fasted from Saturday evening till Sunday evening. I gave up swearing and obscene language. I paid a precise tithe on the meager earnings of my part-time job. I strove to forego levity and mirth and to keep my mind fixed on sober thoughts. I was only partly successful in this endeavor, being easily seduced into banter and jest by my brothers and friends. I averted my eyes from the shapely hips or gaping blouse of a nearby girl. I even stopped masturbating, a monumental act of self-control.

I must qualify this last achievement. I stopped masturbating while thoroughly awake but began to awaken at night in the midst of the act, which I always completed. I esteemed that sleep had rendered my Christian will so inoperable that I need not count this as a sin. It therefore did not figure in my frequent reviews of the inadequacy of my repentance.

In mid-October Charles and I went deer hunting with our Peterson relatives from Lehi. We got up at two in the morning on opening day, drove to a canyon at the south end of the Oquirrh Mountains, and by four were toiling our way up a steep side canyon with flashlights. This was a new and happy experience for me, my first intimacy with a Utah canyon. Our feet shuffled in crisp fallen leaves. Our breath steamed out in measured puffs. Soon an incredible parade of car lights appeared in the bottom of the main canyon below us.

At dawn a vast cannonading of rifles broke out. This was Utah's first either-sex deer hunt, game managers having at last persuaded the public that the deer herds far exceeded the carrying capacity of the winter range. Deer ran everywhere, and I opened fire with thoughtless haste. Soon I had spent all my cartridges but one. I went in search of Charles, hoping to borrow his rifle. Suddenly a doe stepped from a thicket, and I fired my last cartridge. The doe dropped dead and my heart exulted. I know what bloodlust is. It comes from the wild. I neither condemn nor defend it here. What I felt deeply guilty over was not the death of the doe but my fraudulent purchase of a resident hunting license. I felt too poor to pay nonresident fees. But since I didn't have to go hunting, it seemed certain that God, being who he was, would make no extenuation for poverty when he measured my sins.

This was a winter of extraordinary snowfall. Storm after storm dropped a thigh-deep accumulation on campus and town, and temperatures often plunged below zero. Starving deer were everywhere—in the sagebrush of the foothills, in the orchards opposite the dorms, among the hedges and flower beds of city lots. With no galoshes and only a thin coat, I made my way to class along paths corrugated with ice. During the spring thaw an immense avalanche swept off the east flank of Mount Timpanogos, burying the highway in Provo Canyon under a rubble of snow, brush, and snapped tree trunks. I viewed this spectacle and for the first time had some inkling of the energy stored on snowy slopes.

As the thaw continued, water flooded over the banks of rivers and creeks everywhere. Returning from a weekend trip home to Snowflake for Mother's Day, Charles, Roald, and I drove at dawn through a half-mile sheet of floodwater over the highway between Levan and Nephi. Something in the glint of early sun on that slowly flowing water touched my spirit, adding to the accretion of image and emotion that would eventually bond me to Utah.

I logged for the Webb brothers again during the summer of 1952. They put me on an ancient International tractor and raised me a nickel to $1.10 an hour. I set and released chokers for myself, climbing off and on the tractor dozens of times each day. Again I rode to and from the woods with Waldo, listening to country music on the car radio and taking in the bright Arizona landscape. For a while the woods were haunted by memories of Marilyn, for it was here, in my fantasies, that I had known her most intimately.

I fell into a sparse and ascetic discipline that was not entirely unpleasant. In place of the daydreams that had formerly helped make the grueling labor bearable, I substituted serious thoughts about God and religion. I carried a small copy of the Book of Mormon in my lunch box, which I read while Waldo napped at noon. This was my first and only complete reading of the Book of Mormon, whose abstract, repetitious narrative and formulaic sayings did not fatigue me then as they do now. From time to time I came upon profound or instructive utterances that seemed aimed at me. For a while I esteemed I had achieved a simplicity of act and thought pleasing to God, and if ever in my life I believed God would soon vouchsafe me a vivid, indisputable revelation of himself, it was now.

One Sunday I spoke in fast meeting in Snowflake Ward, expressing my hope for a testimony of my own. A childhood friend, Gussie Schneider, sat on a back bench. I noted the rapt attention she paid to my words, and I began to date her. Blonde, trim, and pretty, she was a congenial and flattering conversationalist. From the start I regarded our dating as more than casual, and I quickly found myself in an emotional paralysis, being uncertain whether I wanted to marry her, yet being so attracted to her that I couldn't break away. I brooded over the absence of that quixotic emotion, romantic love, which, had it descended upon me, would have resolved my internal debate in an instant. The conflict seemed to resolve itself when, at the end of the summer, we went different directions, she back to Arizona State, I back to BYU. At the end of the summer, I also abandoned an ambition to become a forest ranger. This had to do with the tedium of logging. I watched rangers marking trees for cutting and estimating the board feet of lumber in the downed trunks and concluded that their job was as enslaving and witless as mine.

During the second week of fall quarter of 1952 at BYU, I became puzzled by seeming omissions in the chemistry professor's lectures. Another student informed me that this class met five days a week rather than the three days I had been attending. The next morning, while peeling potatoes in the cafeteria, I made a sudden, unpremeditated decision. I would become an English teacher like my father. Visiting an adviser, I discovered that my highest aptitude scores were in language and literature. I dropped the chemistry course and enrolled in two courses for English majors. One of the professors, Clinton Larson, expatiated on his own literary enthusiasms and often read us his own baffling free-verse poems. The other, J. Golden Taylor, solemnly read aloud long passages from the journals, sermons, and letters of the American Puritans. I was a fervent acolyte, worshiping both these professors with little reservation, and I must acknowledge that their encouragement had much to do with my development as an English major.

To my astonishment all my grades for this quarter were A. I found the taste of achievement addictive, and from then on I tried hard to make As and usually did. Nonetheless, my initial enthusiasm for literature soon became intermittent, waxing and waning with shifts in my general mood. I had become sensitive to disbelief. Unconsciously attracted to it, as I now see, I sensed its presence in many works of literature and responded with gloom and anxiety. For example, in a later course from Golden Taylor, which featured the Age of Reason in American literature, I noted that Benjamin Franklin and Thomas Jefferson considered Jesus to be no more than a man, though a great one, whose basically deistic doctrines had been corrupted by his followers.

Near the end of fall quarter I had begun to keep a sporadic journal. As winter quarter of 1953 opened I asked in my journal, "Is there or is there not a God?" In early February I visited several professors in their offices, Taylor among them, for guidance in setting up my future course of study. "I wonder if some of these men," I wrote in my journal, "while gaining their knowledge of English…have not lost that which should be the most precious belief in their soul." Going on, I declare my determination not to become like them. "If I can study English literature and remain true to myself and God, fine; if not, I will not trade my soul for an education. I'll dig ditches all my life before I do that!"[3]

During the summer of 1952 Roald had married Luana Field. When I returned to Provo in the fall, I roomed in the dorm with my nephew Dwain, with whom in high school I had been equally forward in rebellious talk and obscene humor. Now my sobriety made us incompatible. For a while he dated a California girl with whom he engaged in heavy petting, an activity over which he exulted in my presence. One Sunday evening he pulled up with the girl in Charles's car. Leaning into the car window, I exhorted them to chastity. After that, the girl denied him the expected liberties, and he seethed with anger at my interference. My zeal for reforming Dwain helped me ignore the fact that during the preceding spring quarter I myself had fallen to the same temptation with a girl whom I had casually dated.

At the beginning of winter quarter, Gussie transferred to BYU, and I began to date her. Instantly I was back in my former conflict, deeply attached to Gussie yet lacking the resolve to marry her. Consequently, I put a good deal of energy into the attempt to persuade God to make up my mind for me. Once I undertook a three-day fast, stalwartly ignoring the food around me while I peeled potatoes in the cafeteria and praying with as much fervor as I could muster. At last, a few hours short of my allotted three days, with no word from God and afflicted by a thumping headache, I gave in to the weakness of the flesh and ate an orange. I am happy if others find inspiration in fasting. For me, it is a quick route into a surly and ungodly mood.

Soon I decided that securing my endowment in the temple might induce God to say clearly yes or no on the issue of marriage. I arranged to have the president of Snowflake Stake ordain me an elder in his hotel room at the conclusion of General Conference in April. In May Roald accompanied me to the Salt Lake temple where I participated for the first time in the ceremony of the endowment. Rushing to make our session, we ignored a man with a flat tire who thumbed for a ride on the highway between Provo and Salt Lake. Roald likened us to the Pharisees in the parable of the Good Samaritan, concerned with the outward trappings of righteousness rather than with its compassionate core.

On a Sunday evening shortly after attending the temple, my mood was such that I proposed to Gussie and she accepted. She phoned the news to her mother, and her mother informed my mother, who resented my failure to be the first to tell her. The truth is that I returned to my dorm frightened by the prospect of marriage and had no spirit for telling anyone about it. So my search for a definitive sign from God went on even as Gussie and I proceeded with our engagement.

During the summer of 1953 I logged for the unionized Southwest Lumber Industries at $1.95 an hour, a considerable improvement over the wage I had earned from the Webbs. While waiting for the woods to open, I pulled green chain at their Overgaard mill for a couple of weeks. A fellow worker on the green chain lacked one of his thumbs. He said one day his wife had warned him that he might chop off a thumb while splitting wood. "And you know," he told me, "pretty soon I did." He was a brother to Rufus Crandall, whom I knew well as a music teacher, chorister, and general provider of musical entertainment in Snowflake. "Rufus made something of his life," his brother told me sadly. "I haven't done a thing with mine." This wistful self-evaluation affected me. Regardless of how threatening higher education appeared, I knew I couldn't abandon it.

Once the woods had opened, I operated a tractor, which, unlike the antique International I had operated for the Webbs, was designed to skid logs. A Caterpillar D-7, it was equipped with a winch and a protective screen over the operator's seat. I even had the luxury of a choker setter, a rotund middle-aged immigrant from west Texas who spoke with an ineluctable southern drawl. One day at lunch my choker setter entered a debate with other workers on the merits of condoms. He said using condoms was like washing your feet with your socks on. He granted they were useful, as he had learned when traveling by bus in the South one time. He had sat by a pretty redhead who accepted his offer to share a hotel room. "She gave me the clap," he said. "You wouldn't have thought it." In subtle ways I persecuted this man. One day at a landing, while he knelt among some logs unlatching chokers, I revved the engine of the tractor with a slight tap on the throttle. It was a joke, of course. Not knowing that, he launched himself directly into the air in a frenzied attempt to get clear of the logs.

Roald, who spent that summer in Snowflake, also got a job logging for Southwest. Morning and night he and I drove the forty-five miles from Snowflake to Overgaard in our mother's pickup. This was a nostalgic road for Roald because it went by the ranch where his high school sweetheart had lived. My brother Leon returned from his mission to Sweden at the end of the summer, too late to earn a stake for his return to BYU. My earnings paid tuition for both of us, with three hundred dollars left over for buying a car. On a hot Saturday in August Roald, Leon, and I drove to Phoenix, and I bought my first automobile, a pale green 1941 Chrysler sedan with a sluggish early version of an automatic transmission.

I continued to agonize over Gussie throughout the summer. I remained in a state of paralysis, unwilling to marry her yet equally unwilling to lose her. I had long talks with Mother about my indecision, and, on her advice, I sought a second patriarchal blessing. If the patriarch had instructed me with authority to marry Gussie, I would have. His blessing, however, consisted of instructions about like those in Chinese fortune cookies. Gussie and I considered breaking our engagement two or three times. With amazing patience she expressed a willingness to go on with it. We had good times together—dances, parties, drives, earnest conversations. Finally, when the summer was over and we had returned to BYU, she put a definitive end to our engagement. This was after church one Sunday morning. I returned to my dorm room and wept bitterly, utterly baffled by my inability to conclude a union with a young woman for whom I had felt so much affection and respect.

I had been spending summers in Snowflake, resuming old routines and basking in my mother's care. Yet each summer I knew, come fall, I would leave, pursuing a dimly understood, less-than-enticing future. I was obliged to leave my mother's home but was having no luck in founding one of my own. I had tried to get married and had failed. Incomprehensible obstacles stood in my way. Romantic love seemed a sham, an illusion. Furthermore, my inability to make a decision whether to marry bespoke a flaw, a malfunction, in my psyche. My enthusiasm for education wavered. I had already become suspicious of literature, which seemed fraught with challenges to my faith. I lived, in short, in a state of inconclusiveness, a condition that I have never found pleasing.

On the positive side, my enforced intimacy with the woods during these summers expanded my awareness of the wild. No one then talked about the pollution and destruction of wilderness. Our bulldozed roads, the furrowed skid paths, the motor oil that we drained on the ground, the stumps and slash of felled trees seemed only a minor irritation on the face of the wild. I sometimes saw elk, deer, and bear. I encountered rattlesnakes, bees, and wasps far more often than I wished to. I often set the brake on the tractor and leaped to the ground with legs churning in a single instant after inadvertently disturbing a nest of bees or wasps. One day my eye fell on a silent, coiled rattlesnake in the roots of a fallen tree whose fangs would have been six inches from my leg had I taken one more step. I am sorry to say that I killed this snake. There was no need for that.

The chief species of tree in the semiarid mountains of Arizona was ponderosa pine. Among abundant thickets of young pines grew scattered specimens of both Utah and alligator juniper and, more rarely, red cedar. I had feelings close to veneration for the aged, cone-bearing ponderosas that had escaped both fire and the woodcutter's saw. There is, in my estimation, no handsomer tree in the world than a mature ponderosa pine with rough bark of reddish brown and irregular horizontal branches graced by long clustered needles. I also loved the aspens I found in rare moist canyon heads. One day I left the tractor and climbed afoot into a steep ravine where, beneath a few towering aspens, a tiny spring watered ferns and lush tall grass. I was enchanted by a strange sense of longevity and participation in things that do not quickly pass away. I had left reality and entered upon the impossible.

Sometimes a spectacular vista opened before me while I worked. Canyons, valleys, hills, ridges, and peaks fell away to a distant mingling with the sky. I could see ridges rising successively one behind the other, each set into relief by the fact that it took on a less intense tone of blue than the one before it. Blue in many shades, it seems, is the color of distance. I was aware of sky and weather at all moments: the fresh elixir of dawn, the dull heat of midday, the ecstasy of sun-silvered thunderheads. After the rainy season began in July, I sometimes drudged through a cold, wet afternoon protected only by a thin denim coat, quite in contrast to the sweaty heat of the usual day. During hailstorms I crawled under the tractor between the tracks where the radiator fan blew warm air onto me. One day I watched a storm approach from a high, remote ridge. I stood with hat in hand while the wind lifted through the trees in a vast orchestration. Lightning flashed and thunder roared, and a wall of rain advanced upon me. Drenched, I felt triumphant in this display of uncontained force.

So it was with ambivalence that I returned to BYU in September 1953. Rooming in the dorm that year with Leon, I came to know him as an adult. One night while going to sleep we heard Debussy's "Claire de Lune" on the radio. Leon said, "I'd give anything to be able to create something that beautiful." I saw a new aspect of his personality and of my own, as well. Sometimes we went to the music library and listened to Massenet's "Meditation" by earphones. Though I had little musical ability, I had identified certain classical pieces as the clearest examples of sheer beauty that I knew.

Charles had married Betty Hayes during the summer of 1953, and they now lived on Charlie Redd's ranch at La Sal, a tiny hamlet of a few houses, barns, and fields set against the timbered slopes of the La Sal Mountains in southeastern Utah. With a degree in animal husbandry, Charles managed Charlie Redd's dairy. He counted on someday having a farm or maybe even a ranch of his own. Leon and I visited Charles and Betty at Halloween and Thanksgiving. I envied Charles. Between a good-natured, competent wife and an outdoor job in a place of stunning beauty, he had everything a man could possibly want. For breakfast Betty fed us unforgettable venison steaks and fried potatoes. We helped Charles in the dairy, went on happy excursions after hay and grain, and hunted cottontail rabbits on a nearby sagebrush plain and grouse in the firs and aspens of the mountains. Southwestward were the Abajo Mountains and the beginnings of the fanciful erosions of Canyonlands. Evenings we heard coyotes in the crisp, clairvoyant dusk. I realized that this place had firmly anchored itself among my emotions. In few other human habitations have I sensed so strongly the presence of the wild.

I took French that year from James L. Barker, a marvelously ugly man of great amiability and pedagogical skill. From Barker I learned the idiomatic nature of all language. There is no such thing as a precise translation from one language to another. I learned when speaking French I had to detach each syllable from the next. "You cannot speak French and remain handsome," Barker often said as he proceeded to distort his blubbery lips into an authentic French sound. However, not even he could teach me to pronounce the deep-throated Parisian r. When I say it, it sounds as if I am getting ready to spit.

By an equal stroke of good fortune I took a yearlong series in Latter-day Saints moral values from B. F. Cummings, a French professor who taught religion on the side. What little hair Cummings had was chopped rather than cut by the unsteady hand of his wife. He had gold-capped teeth and spluttered when roused to zeal. He sometimes wore shoes and socks that were not mates. Once a bit of egg yolk remained on his jacket lapel for a week. He was often unprepared and was likely to stride into class late with an improvised pie chart apportioning moral value in an abstract and, for his students, meaningless way. Nonetheless, I was very attached to him because of his enthusiasm for Mormonism, which he said was the most enlightened, progressive religion the world had ever seen. The important thing was the eternal progression of the self as taught by Joseph Smith, a concept, as Cummings claimed, that motivated human beings to strive toward forever nobler, ever more lofty and ideal behavior. Later I would realize that here was the essence of liberal Mormonism. I would also realize later that liberal Mormonism is not attractive to most Mormons, including the Brethren who direct the church. It is as alien to them as Methodism or the Episcopalian faith.

Toward the end of fall quarter I suffered another crisis of faith. I visited the instructor of my class in neoclassical British literature, Leonard Rice, whose views, as far as I could make out, proceeded from the premises not of a Christian, but of a secular humanist. I told Rice that I doubted God's existence. He said he had discarded certain Mormon beliefs and retained others. He believed in the reality of cosmic good and evil and in the ability of human beings to participate in either. I wrote in my journal: "Dr. Rice also impressed upon me that if I am to lead the intellectual life, then I must develop patience. Patience, waiting for problems to resolve themselves, is the big quieting factor."[4]

Leon and I drove home for Christmas vacation. The weather at Snowflake was almost balmy, and I enjoyed a respite from my internal conflicts. On a hike with a nephew I watched a cottontail rabbit dupe a pursuing dog by performing an instantaneous U-turn in a bush, doubling back while the befuddled dog ran blindly on.

I talked with my mother about the possibility of going on a mission. She wanted me to go, and with the Korean War moving toward a conclusion, draft boards were beginning to issue deferments to missionaries. I was agreeable to the idea. It did not occur to me at that moment that I was an unlikely candidate for a mission. In most moods, I was still a believer. On Christmas Eve I wrote in my journal: "This evening, gazing in a darkened room, with the warm crackling of the fire in the stove, at our Christmas tree, a feeling prompted me to pray, and so I did, merely asking that God give me a soul that could better appreciate the mission of Christ; as I see it, to hold the same love for Christ that he holds for me is one of the ultimate goods."[5]

After Christmas vacation I began to date a seventeen year old named Jerry Brown. Jerry was tall and pretty, having short, curly auburn hair, dark eyes, and a warm, inviting smile. Though she was a senior in high school, she was a flutist in the BYU orchestra. With characteristic speed—before we had gone out on our first date—I decided I would marry her when I returned from my mission. At no time in our yearlong relationship did I think of myself as being in love with her, yet there was an affinity of spirit between us that seemed a more secure basis for a marriage than romantic love. Sometimes we took in a play or lecture on campus or went to a movie downtown. More often we took a drive or a walk, ending up in her living room engaged in a long, earnest conversation. One evening at a fireside in her home, she played "Claire de Lune" on her flute. I recognized she had selected it because she knew I loved it. Even now, nearly fifty years later, the soulful tones of a flute, no matter where I hear them, remind me of her.

I think Jerry suffered as I did from depression, and we found a therapeutic sympathy in one another. She was sensitive to irony and humor yet was generally of a serious bent of mind. She had a hortatory enthusiasm for ideals and principles. Sometimes she would fervently declare that the future of civilization depended upon adherence to principles, which, as she said, were more important than life itself. We talked endlessly, yet there was something prescient and wordless in our relationship, an intuition of mood and opinion in one another that, when it had become explicit, thrilled us, as if it were evidence of a spiritual force that had us in its care.

Jerry's serious-mindedness strengthened my resolve to master my appetites. I entered now, in this, my last year of college before going on my mission, upon a particularly monkish regimen. I had, of course, attempted to live by a rigorous standard of righteousness from the moment of my repentance, as I called it, at the outset of my first quarter at BYU. Although I was not certain of God's existence, I lived as if he not only existed but also kept a meticulous account of my every thought and deed. Any sort of sexual interest in a woman seemed wrong, and I tried hard to contain the instinctive lust that rose daily when I saw the pretty legs of a girl in the seat next to mine in class or glanced at the bobbing breasts of a girl in the hall.

Yet by the time I began to date Jerry I had accumulated an astonishing sexual history, being no stranger to the procedures of fondling a girl's intimate parts and allowing her to fondle mine. On one memorable night I had even made a full-fledged attempt at sexual intercourse with a girl in the front seat of a car. Luckily we didn't know how the deed was done in those circumstances. Nonetheless, from that moment I regarded myself as a fornicator.

As I say, Jerry's fervor for principles inspired me to an even greater mastery of my appetites. I never held her hand, never hugged her, never kissed her. One evening she informed me she had allowed another boy whom she had dated to hold her hand. I said a girl who dated me had to live by my standards of no physical contact even when dating someone else. She accepted this policy. Where had I come by this Victorian ideal? My mother had long urged on me the ideal of kissing my wife for the first time over the altar in the temple. Understandably, then, I proudly narrated my activities with Jerry in my letters to my mother, making a particular point of the spiritual nature, as I termed it, of our relationship.

I can't say why my happiness with Jerry should have seemed an evidence for God's existence, but it did. In my best moods I believed without wavering. Many passages in my journal speak of our relationship as an extension into "the ideal" or into "true spirituality." At this far remove I cannot define precisely what I meant by the word *spirituality*. In concrete terms it simply meant that I was feeling a certain kind of happiness. Somehow that happiness seemed an evidence of realities beyond the material world.

As spring quarter of 1954 opened I enrolled in my third course from Golden Taylor, a course in the literature of the American romantics. I also enrolled in Shakespeare's tragedies from Parley A. Christensen. P. A., as he was called, was a grand old humanist who bore himself with a regal dignity. His gray crew cut bristled, and his thick glasses magnified his eyes. Though a native of Idaho, he spoke in a husky voice with something akin to a British accent, which he had consciously adopted. I had taken Chaucer from him as well, and my esteem for him approached veneration, a fact that made his evident disbelief all the more potent. I wrote in my journal: "He undoubtedly is a wise man, schooled by years of experience and intellectual pursuit. He frightens me however. I fear a similar fate for myself."[6]

I am sure my classes from Taylor and Christensen had much to do with the crisis that I now fell into. But also important was the ambient discussion of organic evolution that went on everywhere on the BYU campus at this moment. I learned a good deal about evolution from students attempting to refute it. Although I would later learn that both my father and my mother believed that evolution and Christianity could be reconciled, at this moment, during the spring of 1954, the premises of my faith did not allow for a figurative interpretation of Genesis. It was an either-or situation: if organic evolution was a fact, then the Christian God did not exist. During my freshman year my geology instructor took his class on a field trip into nearby Rock Canyon. At one point we observed the fossilized shells of marine creatures in a stratum of dark gray limestone common in the Wasatch Mountains. I tried to dismiss the implication of these fossils. The earth had existed much, much longer than the defenders of Genesis asserted. I could continue to believe in a six thousand–year-old earth only by not thinking about the fossils. But as I say, evolution was in the air during the spring of 1954. The refutations I heard failed to impress me. I couldn't resist thinking about those fossils. They had been there a long, long time.

Near the end of April I recorded in my journal: "Why cannot I see or is there indeed nothing to see? My whole life, as ordered up to now is vitally threatened—all desires, all hopes, all joys shall be shattered if the last wall remaining between me and utter disbelief goes."[7] The next day I conceded that I no longer believed in the Christian deity. With this candor came a temporary relief. It did not seem so bad to be a disbeliever. My natural life would go on, made neither longer nor shorter by the fact that I did not possess an immortal soul.

That night I said my customary evening prayer, reasoning, like Franklin or Jefferson, that the impersonal creative force of the universe was worthy of my reverence. I paused at the end of my prayer, realizing there was no logic in finishing my prayer in the name of Jesus as I had always done before. At that instant I remembered a passage from the Gospel of John: "He that believeth on him is not condemned; but he that believeth not is condemned already." With that, I was swept by waves of terror and a hysterical impulse to run. I had no idea to where or from what I wanted to run. I controlled the impulse to run only by what seemed a great exertion of energy. I got onto my bunk, hoping, as I fell into a merciful sleep, that by morning the terror would have dissipated. Unfortunately I awoke to the same desperate impulse to run. I was afflicted by grief and despair as well as terror. I had no appetite and could think of nothing to look forward to. This went on for ten or twelve days. I ground through each day, peeling potatoes, forcing myself to eat a little food, attending class, trying to study. As early as the second day of this episode I concluded that I was to some degree insane.

At the end of this period I bought Joseph Fielding Smith's new book, *Man: His Origin and Destiny,* which attempted to refute evolution by geological catastrophism, the doctrine that the earth's fossil record was laid down not gradually over vast eons but suddenly in a relatively recent series of floods and other natural catastrophes. Having read Elder Smith's book, I wrote in my journal: "Now I must investigate the veracity of our scientists."[8] Science, it appeared, was not solidly against a literal interpretation of Genesis. Perhaps my Mormon faith was credible after all. With that, my intense anxiety dissipated, and I resumed what I might call more normal emotions. However, my swing back toward faith must be described as tentative. I was much sobered about my future and far more wary about what unexplored distress might lie within my unconscious mind.

Of the two worldviews between which I wavered, one postulated a fundamentally domesticated universe, the other a fundamentally wild one. Christianity assumes that the supernatural predominates over the natural, that divine personality reigns, that heaven and hell are realities. The naturalistic view assumes that nature is predominant, that creative force has no personality, that the human spirit does not subsist beyond death. Just before the crisis described above, I ended an entry in my journal with this: "I feel I must have the truth; and yet I am so completely ill equipped to find truth. I shall work—respond to my effort, God. Give me truth or kill me. Life is bitter as gall without you. I do not want to be an animal." Three days later, with the crisis fully upon me, I wrote: "No, I do not want to be an animal, but I suppose that I am one."[9]

Although Jerry and I continued to date, our intimacy was marred by the unspoken recognition of my lapse from faith. On the last evening before I went home for the summer, I was ill at ease with Jerry yet loath to say good-bye. She gave me instruction on sketching, and we created a song at the piano, I devising the lyrics, she the music. When I finally left, she followed me from the door and asked whether I would accept a mission if I were called. I said I didn't know because I didn't know whether I would be teaching the truth. She said something of a rebuking sort, unusual for her. As I started to drive away, she came from the house and stopped me. She apologized for hurting my feelings and said she was for me and not against me.

Before leaving for ROTC summer camp, I tended to a matter of confession in Snowflake. During the General Conference of the previous April I had attended a Saturday-night priesthood meeting in the BYU field house, where the preachments of the Brethren from Temple Square were broadcast, and had heard Joseph Fielding Smith warn that serious sexual sins could not be absolved simply by abandoning them; they had to be confessed to a proper ecclesiastic authority. My heart fell with this injunction. I saw no alternative to confessing myself a fornicator. On a Sunday morning about two months later, soon after I had returned to Snowflake, I called on my bishop. This was one of the most difficult things I ever did. I had no assurance I would not be excommunicated. Had I been excommunicated, I had reason to believe the fact would be announced over the pulpit of my home ward during a priesthood meeting.

The bishop was a tall, robust, bald rancher named Barr Turley, descended on both sides from the pioneer settlers of Snowflake. He invited me into his living room and sat facing me, still chewing his breakfast. This good man listened with astonishment while I confessed myself guilty of fornication. He did not ask for details, nor did he ask me to identify my partner.

"You haven't been doing it lately?" he said.

"No, sir."

"Good," he said. "I respect you for having the courage to tell me about it. Now consider the matter closed. You don't have to tell anybody else about it, not even another church authority."

I was deeply grateful for this succinct management of my confession, which dispelled at once, if not my private guilt, at least my fear of the ignominy and shame that accompany public exposure.

Early in July, Roald hitchhiked from Provo to Snowflake, and he and I drove to March Air Force Base near Riverside, California. We were assigned to a barracks floor with about thirty Texans, drawling, good-natured fellows who were prone to boast and exaggerate just as I had always understood Texans do. I did not find summer camp unpleasant. New sights and a demanding schedule had a salutary effect on my emotions. We rose at dawn, performed calisthenics, and marched to breakfast in a cafeteria, where we were served abundant food. Through the day we attended lectures or made field visits to hangers, repair stations, and radar units. Evenings we relaxed in the barracks, writing letters and reading. At ten, lights dimmed and we went to bed. For me, the most trying aspect of barracks life was the fact that the toilets stood in a long line without stalls or other concealment. I did not mind using the urinals in the presence of others but tried to restrict my use of the toilets to evenings or other times when the restroom was empty.

By an incredible coincidence Jerry's parents left Provo and invested in a small restaurant in Riverside, only ten miles from the air base. On weekends I rode a bus into Riverside and dated Jerry. I was in a more believing mood, and our times together were harmonious. One evening we went to a movie and then talked for a long time under the palms of a Riverside park, unconcerned that the only other persons in the park were men, single and in pairs.

Back in Arizona after summer camp had ended, I worked for Southwest on the Mogollon Rim for three or four weeks. It was during this period that I saw the only mountain lion I have ever seen in the wild, a half-grown kitten. Between jobs I induced Jerry to come stay at my mother's house after her parents had abandoned the restaurant in Riverside and moved to Mesa. Jerry gamely adapted to the rigors of my mother's domicile. She helped my mother cook and wash dishes and studied her genealogical papers with interest. There is no question Jerry won my mother's heart. A harmony of spirit existed between the two women; both were compassionate, serious minded, work oriented, and fervent in their faith. One of my chief regrets over not marrying Jerry is that she pleased my mother so much.

One evening Jerry and I had a long talk at the farm, where we had gone to milk the cow my mother kept. We both wept, releasing pent-up tension. According to my journal, I wept for Judas Iscariot, who, as I said to Jerry, was "a poor wretch who wasn't responsible for what he had done and rather than deserving imprecation and perdition, he of all men needed to be taken into the arms of Christ and comforted."[10] How had I come by this astonishing pity for the most egregious sinner in the entire lore of Christendom?

Guilt for my recurrent disbelief weighed on me. Inwardly I protested the condemnation of disbelief because it did not seem a matter of choice or volition. I have had an empirical bent all my life. For me, belief derives from evidence. A person can't will to believe in the absence of evidence. That's why I prayed so earnestly for a sign that God existed. I had come to feel that most sin has its roots in the unconscious where choice has no play. In priesthood meeting one day I called sin "a psychological morbidity," a heresy for which I was instantly rebuked by a graduate student in chemistry. It was an experimental sally on my part rather than a deeply fixed conviction. Yet it helps explain my pity for Judas.

On the evening before Jerry left Snowflake, my bishop invited me to visit him in his home. As I expected, he called me on a mission, and I accepted. I returned home and asked Jerry to pray with me. We knelt at the sofa in the living room and, as I recorded, "prayed that the obstacles would be removed from before me."[11] This prayer was the climax of my relationship with Jerry. We felt unified and affectionate and very hopeful that God would touch my spirit and make me a believer.

A few days later my stake president interviewed me and asked whether I was morally clean. I said I was. He then asked expressly whether I masturbated. I said I didn't, interpreting my frequent masturbation upon awakening from sleep at night as involuntary and therefore beyond the imputation of sin. The following week Leon and I drove all night to Salt Lake City for my interview with an apostle, Elder LaGrande Richards. Within a few days of our return to Snowflake, Leon departed for service in the U.S. Army, and I did not see him again till he visited me in Belgium almost a year later.

For the final three or four weeks that I was in Snowflake, I had a job stacking green lumber with Dwain at a planing mill. Dwain had also been called on a mission. He went to Salt Lake for a week for the customary orientation at the mission home, then returned to Snowflake to continue stacking lumber while waiting for a visa to Brazil. Rarely has a missionary viewed his approaching service with a more ribald resentment. He denounced the mission home with obscene eloquence. He scoffed at the temple ceremony and said the missionary lesson plans were little better than arm-twisting. When he returned from Brazil two and a half years later, he was so mild and passive that I wondered whether I had ever known him before. From this I learned, if I hadn't known it before, that spiritual transitions can efface whole blocks of a person's former personality.

I was pleased to be called to the French mission, writing in my journal: "I would feel greatly disappointed if something went awry and I was forced to remain here." Reviewing my doubts, I declared: "Now I go out in ardor to preach to other people that my Church is the truth—which very item I doubted myself—and in honesty I cannot say that I know my church is truth, or that Christ yet lives, or that God exists. Yet I feel at ease about preaching such things."[12] In October I quit my job and drove to La Sal for a final visit with Charles, Betty, and the newborn Colette. I helped Charles milk his cows and move a stack of hay. He and I hunted on the mountain and brought home three or four pine hens for Betty's oven. I saw deer in the fields at evening. At night I heard the transcendent yelp of coyotes. The wild beauty of La Sal bore in on me with the deep poignancy of imminent loss.

I returned to Snowflake for a few days. On the day I left for good, I called by the schoolroom where Mother was teaching and said a final good-bye. There had been a sweet harmony between us during these past few weeks. With deep regret I left her standing in her classroom door, little comforted by the knowledge that I was fulfilling her fondest dream by going on a mission.

I stayed overnight with Roald and Luana in Provo before continuing to Salt Lake for a week of indoctrination at the mission
home. I fraternized with year-old Roald Jr. and his newborn sister,
Heidi, regretting already that they would be much changed before
I saw them again. That evening I went to see Jerry, who had returned to Provo to begin her freshman year at BYU. We stood on
her back porch, which overlooked the winking lights of the campus and city. For the first time in the nearly eleven months since we
had begun to date, we hugged and kissed. I felt the most tenuous of
emotions. All along I had treated her as a disembodied soul and
could not now make any shift. Separation loomed in my mind.
Two and a half years seemed interminable. At last I released her
and struck off for Roald's place through the dark orchard below
her house, by no means certain that I wanted to go on a mission.

A Missionary

I WAS TWO AND A HALF DAYS CROSSING the United States by train. The clack of the rails was a new and unnatural sound. In New York I walked up and down Fifth Avenue, visited Times Square, and watched the Rockettes kick high in Radio City.

I crossed the Atlantic on the SS *America* in eight days, sharing a second-class cabin with three other missionaries. I was overwhelmed by the opulence of the dining room—a printed menu with every meal, attentive waiters, an abundant smorgasbord if you preferred to serve yourself. I studied French or walked on deck watching the gray heaving Atlantic under a lowering sky. The ship's propellers throbbed endlessly. Even on deck I felt claustrophobic and longed for land.

I spent three days at mission headquarters at 3 rue de Lota in Paris. This mansion, built by a wealthy clothier, had a marble balustrade and a ballroom that served as a meeting hall for the Paris branch. There was a bidet in the bathroom I used. I puzzled over its utility, concluding at last it was meant for washing feet.

The mission president was Harold W. Lee, a professor of French on leave from BYU, tall, gaunt, and, to my perception, humorless. He asked whether any of the new arrivals played the piano. When no one else spoke up, I cautiously volunteered without informing him that I played with only one hand. On this basis I was sent to La Chaux-de-Fonds, Switzerland, while the other new missionaries were packed off to Belgium to wait for French visas.

I met my senior companion, Russell French, from rural Alberta, about an hour before we boarded a train for Switzerland. While the train rocked along, he asked how old I believed he was. I thought he had to be thirty but tactfully said twenty-five. He said he was twenty-two. It pleased him to be thought older. I dutifully deferred to him as senior companion yet found him irritating in many ways. Once he teased me by refusing to surrender a package that had come to me. He laughed happily while I wrestled him for the package. Coming close to violence, I was left shaken by what I called in my journal "a look at the beast in myself."[1]

La Chaux-de-Fonds was a small watchmaking city in a high valley of the Jura Mountains. Our quarters at 11 rue du College included an entire top floor with a large meeting hall, a kitchen, and a bedroom. There was no bathroom. We washed and shaved at the kitchen sink with water heated on our two-burner stove and used the toilet on the landing below our floor. I did not have a bath during the entire seven months of my stay in Switzerland.

We walked everywhere because Elder French believed bicycles to be dangerous. After he went home, I bought a three-speed Swiss bicycle, which I rode during the rest of my mission. I had been instructed to buy a hat in Salt Lake City. I transported this narrow-brimmed stockman's style hat from assignment to assignment without wearing it. I began wearing a beret in La Chaux-de-Fonds and continued to do so throughout my mission.

On weekdays my companion and I proselytized mornings, afternoons, and evenings, trudging home for lunch and dinner. We knocked on apartment doors and asked permission to enter and present a lesson. Two or three times a day a housewife or watchmaker who worked at home would invite us in and listen to Elder French's standard first lesson. We were seldom invited back. When a tidy, ruddy-faced housewife invited us in, she was likely to offer us mint tea and cookies, which we accepted gratefully.

The winter of 1954–1955 was said to be a mild one. It seemed otherwise to us. Storm after storm dumped snow on the little city. Hedges of snow higher than my head lined the sidewalks and dump trucks transported accumulations of snow from the streets. During a storm we walked in the streets rather than on the sidewalks because avalanches of snow rumbled off the steep roofs with lethal force. Sometimes when I woke in the night, thudding and rumbling from far and near told me a storm was in progress. Soon I would hear the clocks of the city churches strike with a haunting timbre.

I had come out prayerfully, hopeful that the doubts that had troubled my first three years at BYU would be allayed by a speedy witness of the Holy Spirit. Ironically, proselytizing quickly reawakened my doubts. One evening, after we had knocked futilely on doors for hours, we were invited in by a man with wire-rimmed spectacles and bristling gray hair. With his wife at his side, he carefully scrutinized in a well-worn Bible each scriptural passage my companion cited. After inviting us back twice, this couple concluded that the Bible did not support our claims and asked us not to return.

This seemed fair to me. We had asked to explain our position, and they had allowed us to do so. Yet Mormon doctrine, as I understood it, held that they would inherit a lesser salvation by having rejected our message. Quite suddenly, I realized I could not believe in a deity who meted out eternal rewards and punishment of any kind.

With this recognition, my composure crumbled. Surges of terror swept over me, and the hysterical impulse to run that I had experienced six months earlier returned. Once again, despair and unfocused grief mingled with my terror, and, as days went by, I seemed unable to perform simple and routine tasks without an enormous expenditure of inner energy. I had happy moments, but they were few and easy to overlook. In general, I was profoundly unhappy and would continue to be so for the next fifteen months.

My main relief lay in writing about my problems in my letters and journals. I alluded to them with some restraint in my letters to my mother and with more candor in my letters to Jerry. I am sure my gloomy and unorthodox ponderings were a bad dream come true for Jerry, who had hoped my mission would heal my disbelief. I was even more candid in my journal. One February day I granted the seductive appeal of suicide but concluded that "all the returns are not in. . . . I am too ignorant to safely destroy myself. I have not searched far enough." That was written in the morning. That night I recounted a story my companion had told me with pleasure during the day about a stallion's attack upon a gelding on his father's farm. The rage of the stallion and the terror of the gelding depressed me. More important, they made me realize I could not exclude the rage and terror of animals from my cosmic scheme of morality. I remembered Blake's poem "The Tiger," which asks whether the force that created goodness has not also created evil. It was clear that disbelief had made evil a much more complex quality for me. I was troubled not so much by the ambiguity of worshiping a natural force that kills as well as engenders as by the emotional enormity of knowing that evil occurs, irremediably and at all hours of every day, everywhere around me. Recognizing how drastically my worldview had been altered, I concluded: "Reality takes on a strange, new hue. I am not comfortable in it."[2]

Why didn't I go home? Certainly I wanted to. The saving of souls seemed an absurd and empty business, and the dishonesty of advocating a faith no longer my own was a violation of my integrity. I stayed principally for my mother. Her sorrows and deprivations weighed heavily on me, as did my guilt for having grown up and left her. Throughout my mission I wrote her twice a week, always ending my letters with expressions of esteem and gratitude, which I sincerely felt. Her letters reflected little of the anxiety she must have felt for me. She constantly reassured me that God had me in his protective care and would surely make himself known to me if only I would soften my heart and let him enter. I was where she wanted me to be. That's why I put off the matter of going home and got along as best I could.

Roald mailed me the epilogue of Albert Schweitzer's autobiography, *Out of My Life and Thought,* which he had torn from a paperback edition. I read and reread this brief, eloquent peroration on rationality and Reverence for Life to the point of memorizing it almost line for line. In it Schweitzer maintains that the remedy for the decadence into which modern humanity has fallen lies in a return to elemental thinking. Through elemental thinking, said Schweitzer, human beings will be led to affirm life and to recognize that goodness consists of altruistic service to others. Furthermore, they will see that service must not stop with the human species but must extend to all life forms.

I took Schweitzer at his word regarding elemental thought, trying hard to reflect earnestly on the world around me. Without knowing precisely how it was accomplished, I also tried to practice the resignation he said was essential to happiness. The best I could do was think of myself as resigned. I was not immediately aware of any change for the better but could see no other way to dig out of the confusion and despair that were my daily lot. I was impressed that Schweitzer had abandoned a promising career in theology to become a physician and medical missionary to Africa. Throughout my mission, Schweitzer's ideas and example remained the focal point of my attempt to salvage as much of my Christian heritage as possible from the naturalistic worldview I was constructing. Before the end of my mission I had acquired four of Schweitzer's books in hardback English translations. Never again in my lifetime have I experienced the elation over the prospect of reading a book that I felt when I came upon the first of these volumes in a bookstore in Brussels.

On weekdays, as I have said, my companion and I proselytized. On Saturdays we shopped, washed our clothes, and sometimes went to a movie. On Sunday we tended to pastoral duties, holding conventional Mormon services for our flock of about a dozen participating members. Two of these were a couple in their thirties. The others were middle-aged or elderly women. I must comment that music making in the La Chaux-de-Fonds branch left something to be desired. While I plied the keys of a small pump organ with one hand, Elder French kept time with an indecipherable waving of his arm, and the aging female congregation raised a wavering cacophony of praise unto the Lord.

Elder French finished his mission and departed for Canada near the end of April 1955. I stayed in La Chaux-de-Fonds for five more weeks as junior companion to Larry Atwood, also from rural Alberta. Before leaving the mission, Elder French had the satisfaction of baptizing a couple, Monsieur and Madame Cattin, the sole products of our winter-long labor.

On a cloudy Saturday afternoon, accompanied by a half dozen of our female flock, we went by train and bus to an unpopulated shore of Lake Neuchâtel. Clad in white, Elder French and each of the Cattins in turn walked into the gray waters of the lake. To our left, at the northern tip of the lake, was the small, picturesque city of Neuchâtel. Behind us was the timber-darkened wall of the Juras. Before us, across the lake, rose the snowcapped Alps. The wind was fresh in our faces, and clouds scudded across a broken sky. I was keenly aware of the wild in our setting. It seemed to proclaim with irrefutable eloquence that the universe is governed only by nature, which has decreed the finality of death. Against this grim, unheeding grandeur, the rite of baptism struck me as a trifling and futile gesture. Yet I was aware that my associates regarded the rite as a gateway into an infinitely domesticated domain called the Kingdom of God. By small perceptions of this sort, the gulf widened between me and my believing confreres.

Having arrived at some fluency in French, I was transferred to Charleroi, Belgium, and made senior companion in June 1955. My junior companion was Glade Merrill, a former second lieutenant in the U.S. Army, from whom I expected the same unmurmuring obedience that I had accorded my senior companions. I made appointments and decided when and where we would proselytize without consulting him. Elder Merrill grimaced and sighed but otherwise registered no protest against my policy. In retrospect I judge my minor despotism to have been unnecessary. Had I not been so preoccupied by internal conflicts, I could have managed a more democratic partnership between us.

We shared quarters with another set of missionaries, who made daily life more sociable. By virtue of one of the many contradictions within my personality, I had a compulsion to meet the weekly quota of forty-five proselytizing hours set by the mission president. Elder Merrill and I were always at or near the top of the entire mission in proselytizing hours and in sessions where lessons were presented.

Our second-story apartment at 12 rue de la Science consisted of a meeting hall, two bedrooms, a kitchen, and a bathroom. The walls were grimy, and the windows, crowded by other buildings, gave little light. The mattress on which we slept lost its loft within twenty minutes of our going to bed. The rest of the night we slept on the springs. I still marvel over our stolid acceptance of dismal living conditions that could have been easily improved by a little money and paint.

Our neighborhood in Charleroi offered picturesque sights. With a clear, melodious voice a woman with a donkey and two-wheeled cart called her willingness to buy rags, old paper, and metalware—this in streets where diesel-powered lorries roared. Before dawn on Sundays I was awakened by the clopping of horses' hooves and the crowing of roosters as farmers arrived to set up market in a nearby city square. Just around the corner from our apartment was a domed Catholic church into which I sometimes wandered, half attracted and half repelled by vast dark recesses, musty incense, and flickering candles. Here I felt a timelessness unlike anything I had ever felt in a Mormon church.

The Belgian climate alternated between rain and sunshine two or three times a day. My pants were always baggy because they got wet every day below the hem of my plastic raincoat. Once in a while I pressed my pants with no lasting effect. My coat pockets sagged with my French Bible and a variety of tracts and pamphlets. I had what I esteemed a nice suit for pastoral duties on Sunday and two cheap suits I had bought on sale in Salt Lake City for everyday proselytizing. I wore the first of these suits for fifteen months, then discarded it and wore the other for fifteen more.

My companion and I proselytized among the coal-mining suburbs of Charleroi, where narrow cobblestone streets ran between wall-to-wall houses of soot-blackened brick. Industrial buildings, derricks, and small mountains of detritus and overburden marked the coal mines. Housewives in black dresses poured dishwater into the gutters. Many toilets were outdoor privies in the backyard. Some were no more than holes in the ground with two marks for placing your feet.

The local populace spoke a blustery Walloon patois as well as French. They seemed a joyless yet enduring people—survivors, I now recognize, of two world wars. This being Catholic country, people decorated interior walls with crucifixes and stylized images of the bleeding heart of Jesus. Few of them had a Bible. Sometimes they dismissed us for ludicrous reasons. "You want to tell me about God?" said one elderly Walloon woman. "We don't believe in God around here. We just believe in the Virgin." We also met self-declared atheists, mostly socialists who viewed religion as an instrument of economic oppression. "Ah," said one of these, "you want to talk religion with me? He who has bread to slice gets to eat. There! That is my religion."

To my surprise we soon had a handful of steady investigators who attended our branch meetings or sent their children. I baptized two persons from the Charleroi area and was the initial contact for a husband, wife, and adopted nephew who later became stalwarts of the Charleroi branch. All this happened without my bearing a testimony. In fact, I lived in dread of someone asking me directly whether I believed what I was teaching. I would have had to say no. Luckily no one ever asked.

My first baptism, performed in December 1955, was something less than a spiritual experience. The convert was a portly, square-jawed woman of about fifty, Madame Lejeune, who had to hide her connections with Mormonism from a jealous, domineering husband. I don't recall how she secured a letter of consent from him, required in those days for a married woman. The baptism took place in a swimming pool in Brussels where we went by train early one Sunday morning. Arm to the square, I said the baptismal prayer and attempted to immerse her. Survival instincts seized her, and she flailed and kicked. The witnesses said she had not been entirely immersed and required me to repeat the process. It was not until the fourth try, when desperation overcame decorum, that I fell athwart her with my own body and bore her to the bottom.

I had many fulfilling experiences in Charleroi. I believe my behavior appeared generally dutiful and good-humored to my close associates. Inwardly, however, I was overwhelmed by anxiety and despair. Belgium's perpetual clouds and industrial grime contributed to my distress, as did my new role as senior companion. I had arrived in Charleroi with some of the tranquillity that had come to me during my final month or two in Switzerland. One day, soon after arriving, I saw an elderly woman leading a man of about thirty-five who repeatedly bit his own hand. With this sight, the horror of a strictly natural universe returned to me. I felt a similar horror in passing open-air butcher shops where the bulging eyes and skeletal jaws of skinned rabbits with heads attached upbraided me for my former cruelties to animals.

More and more I considered going home. The reasons for not going were unchanged, but I felt more desperate now. In mid-July the mission president came through Charleroi, and I arranged an interview with him. It didn't go well. I told President Lee I didn't believe in Mormon doctrine. I expected him to agree that I shouldn't be a missionary. Instead, he said I had not done enough to get a testimony. I tactlessly asserted that Mormon beliefs were based upon wishful thinking rather than reason. He counterattacked angrily, challenging me to specify a single doctrine that violated the rules of reason. At the moment I could think of none. He went on to ridicule the humorous poems and essays I had sometimes penned on the back of my weekly reports to him, calling them "foolish trash." Feeling both vanquished and humiliated, I began to sob, and with that the interview ended.

Within a few days he wrote me a long, not unkind letter from Paris. On its way, he wrote, was a book that would help me see the foolishness of unaided reason. This book, which I read, did not restore my inclination to believe in Mormonism, but it did undermine my already tenuous confidence that I might somehow secure rational control over my distraught emotions.

Early in August I traveled by chartered bus with missionaries and youths from Belgium to a missionwide conference in Paris. This was a pleasant distraction. There were concerts, folk dances, buffets, and a sunny picnic in the Bois de Boulogne where, incredible as it seems, I had my first taste of paté de fois gras, liberally spread on crusty French bread. Present at this conference was Elder Spencer W. Kimball, who interviewed each missionary. I told the apostle I did not have a testimony, but I did not repeat the mistake I had made with President Lee of insinuating that a testimony might be the product of wishful thinking. Elder Kimball treated me with warmth and kindness but said that not having a testimony was a reflection on me since any honest-hearted person could have one.

I didn't doubt his sincerity. Sometimes, indeed, a shiver of anxiety passed over me while I attended the mandatory testimony meeting that accompanied every missionary conference. What if, after all, my fellow missionaries were right and I was wrong? Nonetheless, I had so little faith that a sentient being heard my prayers that I did not pray for a testimony after my first few weeks in Switzerland. That fact notwithstanding, I went on with what might be called a rational search for evidence of a providential God. All too often I came upon negative evidence. One day while pedaling my bicycle under a misting Belgian sky, I reminded myself that the absence of evidence is not in itself a proof. Only moments later my companion and I knocked on a door where, while it was briefly open, I caught a glimpse of a man writhing in agony on a bed set up in the living room. My despair deepened, for I had no ability to reconcile the concept of Providence with that man's agony.

Returned from Paris, I went on with my usual work in Charleroi with no improvement of mood. Near the end of August, after much vacillation, I mailed a letter to President Lee asking to be released from proselytizing. He urged me to reconsider. "You say that you do not *know* the Gospel is true," he wrote. "Do you *know* that it is false?" He couldn't understand why I should think it dishonest to preach Mormonism. "I cannot think of a single principle we are called to teach which is not uplifting and ennobling to the human race."[3]

I went to see a Belgian neurologist who practiced psychotherapy on the side. This rotund, goateed man, who kept a skull on a shelf, listened to my troubles sympathetically and supported my plan of returning home. He said my problem was just poor communication. If I informed my mother fully of my unhappiness, he predicted, she would not reject me for coming home early. So I wrote the following to my mother:

> How much I dread to hurt you or lose your love.... You once said you thought it better that one be insane than to lose his testimony. If you continue to meet me with an attitude like that you'll get both in me. Mother, love me and don't worry what I believe. I'm through with proselyting. I don't say I'm through with the Church, but I can't stay on my mission. I shall come home to you if you want me, but I must go where I'll be loved.[4]

I had struck the right chord with my mother, who sent back a deeply concerned and compassionate letter. She did not scold or attempt to dissuade me. Above all, she said, I must come home to her and not think of going anywhere else. She included a third of the fare for my ship passage and promised to mail the rest within a few days. I was very grateful, and not a little guilty, for this demonstration of love and generosity. Nonetheless, I couldn't see any happy outcome to my situation. My decision to go home had intensified, rather than relieved, my anxiety. I could anticipate only painful readjustments in a thousand former relationships. I had no plans as to what I wanted to become or what I wanted to do. Clearly, I lacked the stamina for restructuring my life outside the expectations of Mormonism.

I returned to the neurologist who now agreed I should stay on my mission. "You are doing no one any harm," he said. "People are not forced to listen to you. Those who want to listen will get some good from it." I wrote President Lee saying I would like to talk to him again. Back came a telegram saying he would be happy to discuss my problems. I do not remember this talk. It probably occurred in Berne at the dedication of the new Swiss temple in early September. My decision to stay was reinforced by the dedicatory sermon and prayer of the elderly prophet and president of the church, David O. McKay, whom I had always revered.

Though relieved to some degree by my decision to stay, I was far from happy, being angry now as well as anxious and depressed. Neither my mother nor the mission president could grasp that the hypocrisy in which I lived as a missionary was painful. For them, integrity applied only to the believer. It didn't count for the disbeliever. I was especially angry at President Lee. He stood in my mind as the primary enforcer of the bondage my mission represented. I would nurse a grudge against this man for many decades following my return from my mission. Speaking fairly, I know I have burdened him with more than his share of blame. In the first place, it was no single person who kept me on my mission. It was the innumerable Mormons whom I loved and respected. If one person must be singled out, it is myself. Confined by Mormon protocol, I foolishly sought an official release from the mission, which President Lee was unwilling to give. Had I been truly independent, I would have quietly accumulated funds for my passage home, ordered my ticket, and, on the day I took ship, mailed a letter to him informing him of my departure.

Though expedience was my chief reason for remaining a missionary, I found an increasingly important reason in the service to others opened by my proselytizing and pastoral duties. I had been impressed by Schweitzer's assertion that in the impulse toward selfless devotion to others lies a manifestation of the divine in an otherwise mute and mysterious universe. I will not claim great fortitude in charitable service. But to the degree that missionary rules and quotas permitted, my companion and I often returned to visit people who were lonely or ill even though we judged them to be poor prospects for conversion. One whom we visited was an obese old woman whose husband loathed her and whose only son was emigrating to the United States. She often asked whether suicide was permissible. I said no and read passages from the Sermon on the Mount to her. We also visited a former miner who had been mistakenly given a severe caustic at a company infirmary. The caustic had eaten away part of his esophagus and diaphragm, and his heart lay among his entrails, as he proved by making me grasp the throbbing lump through the wall of his abdomen. He said French doctors had promised him comfortable quarters if he would allow them to observe him. He refused their offer, fearing they would kill him—an ironic worry for a man who repeatedly expressed a wish to die.

While in Charleroi I had a visit from Leon, on furlough from the U.S. Army in Germany. We took a bicycle ride into the countryside and ate fruit and cheese we bought along the way. While we lolled in a meadow, a tiny gnat somehow imprisoned itself inside the viewfinder of the snapshot camera I had just bought. After Leon had left, I awoke during the night worrying about the gnat. Remembering Schweitzer's principle of Reverence for Life, I rose and cracked the plastic rim around the viewfinder, freeing the insect. I had not settled just how far you should go with compassionate service. It seemed possible that I might be led, like Schweitzer, to a near total negation of my preferred self-interest. I often felt that I could justify my own existence only by devotion to others.

Jerry Brown continued to write me until nearly the end of my stay in Charleroi. In April 1955, while still in La Chaux-de-Fonds, I had tried to break off our correspondence. Jerry kept writing me, explaining in a letter to my mother: "Sometimes I feel the Lord is holding me responsible to help Levi all I can. This is when I get discouraged and impatient because I don't know what to do."[5] Mother urged me to resume writing, and I did. Then, in December, Jerry said she wouldn't write anymore. I think she had concluded, after I had been a missionary for more than a year, that I would never gain a testimony. As for me, I was aware that being a satisfactory husband for her would mean, as I wrote my mother, "shutting off a certain part of me—the same which here I am forced to hold silent."[6] Thus ended my relationship with an affable, intelligent, and highly principled young woman.

As Christmas of 1955 approached, I helped prepare a gala branch party. Some of the girls I had recruited were on the organizing committee where, to my dismay, they were being treated with open condescension by a girl whose father and mother had been dominant members of the branch for years. This father was a bank teller of pale hue and delicately tapered fingers. The short, stout mother possessed a soprano voice so powerful that it rattled windowpanes during hymns. They invited the missionaries to dinner every Sunday evening—one of our few predictable pleasures in a generally dreary existence. Near noon one rainy December day I called at the family home and, in the presence of the mother, asked the daughter to be more friendly toward the girls who were on the organizing committee with her.

The daughter defended her behavior, and her mother agreed, pointing out that the rules of polite behavior were different there than in the United States. The daughter added, "Nous sommes des intellectuaux, vous savez." I interpreted this to mean, "We are intellectuals, you know," and was thunderstruck by its apparent arrogance. Later I understood that a more accurate translation would have been, "We are of the white-collar class, you know."

Before I left, the father returned home for lunch and saw his daughter's distress. This usually passive man launched into an eerie ten-minute tirade against me and unnamed earlier missionaries who had apparently reproached his daughter for the same reason. "Why do you have to pick on this poor child?" he ranted. "Can't you leave her alone? Can't you give her a little peace?" I crumbled into tears, thoroughly chastened and newly enlightened as to social stratification in Belgium.

In January 1956, I was transferred to Liège where I remained till the end of my mission. My junior companion was Philip Smith, who spoke French fluently from a stay in Beirut with his parents. We were assigned to work in Outremeuse, an island in the Meuse River, which ran through Liège. The paint on the interior walls of the ancient apartment buildings was grimy and peeling, and stairwells smelled of cooking odors and urine. The residents, living on welfare or scant pensions, were more prone than any other population I proselytized among to engage in that old ploy of letting us enter for a first lesson, agreeing to a second, and then failing to be at home when we returned. Although Elder Smith and I remained at the top of the mission in proselytizing hours and missionary lessons, our six months in Outremeuse yielded no harvest. There were no baptisms and no investigators who attended church more than two or three times.

We were lucky to rent a new, freshly painted room in an apartment building far away from Outremeuse, only a few doors below the Mormon chapel on rue de Campine. This room was two levels below the street entrance, yet because of the steep hillside, it looked out into a pleasant garden at the back. It was furnished with a gas plate for cooking, a cold water faucet and small sink, a table, and a bed that stood against a wall during the day. This pleasant room elevated my spirits enormously.

My companion's fluency with French led him to unthinking intrusions into my authority as senior companion. I swallowed my pride and accepted a full sharing of decision making between us. Fortunately we were compatible in our work habits. A tall, skinny fellow, he was a member of a basketball team of missionaries from the Liège district, whose competition with Belgian teams, mostly on open-air courts, brought favorable publicity. I practiced with this team and attended most of its games. My companion was also fond of classical music. Observing his rapture one evening at the home of a member where we listened to a symphony on the innovative technology of a hi-fi player and 33-rpm records, I recognized that I had little instinct for music. In fairness to myself I will report that we attended the Liège opera from time to time where I found myself enthralled by the live performance of works that included *Aida* and *Pagliacci*.

Every morning my companion and I coasted our bicycles down rue de Campine, past Place St. Lambert, and across a bridge to Outremeuse. At noon we pedaled back across the Meuse and had a substantial lunch, our main meal for the day, in the cafeteria of a department store just off Place St. Lambert. There were public restrooms in the department store. I located no others during my fifteen-month stay in Liège. There were pissoirs for men all over the city. Presumably women didn't need to urinate. It was always late at night before we pumped laboriously back up the steep route to our room. One rainy night I looked up to see Elder Smith catch a front wheel in a tram track. He flew through the air with arms outstretched, suffering scrapes, bruises, and a ruined suit.

Someone told me Liège was the Paris of Belgium. I agreed with the sentiment. I liked the clamor and confusion of Place St. Lambert, from which all the trams and buses of an entire region departed. Across the street was the Palais du Prince-Eveque, the giant Gothic palace from which the prince-bishop of Liège had once ruled his domain. I was constantly intrigued by the solemn Meuse. Tall buildings lined its wharfs and quays, and trees billowed over its promenades. On its surface heavily laden boats, fifty yards long, transported coal, ore, petroleum, and heavy machinery. At the end of each boat was a tidy cabin with curtained windows where the operator and his wife lived. Over the deck, drying laundry flapped like flags in the breeze.

By the time the spring of 1956 arrived I had undergone a major change of mood. I attributed my return to happiness to my practice of resignation, as I had grasped this principle from Albert Schweitzer. I was pleased to believe that at last my attempt to reason myself into happiness had succeeded. In retrospect I attribute my happiness to other causes. A congenial companion, a pleasant room, an interesting city, and—very important—the Liège branch, whose chapel, one of only two in the entire mission, had a recreation hall with a stage and a baptismal font in its basement. Forty or fifty persons attended meetings on Sunday, enough to give the branch something of the feel of the wards I had been accustomed to in Arizona and Utah.

Also contributing to my happiness was a clandestine romance with an outspoken, volatile eighteen-year-old girl of the Liège branch. She was short and had black shoulder-length hair, dark satirical eyes, and a beautiful complexion. Because we lived near the chapel, she recruited me and my companion one Saturday in February to help her decorate the recreation hall for the annual Gold and Green Ball. Elder Smith got tired and went back to our apartment to study while I continued to clamber up and down a tripod ladder, taping streamers of gold and green crepe paper to the ceiling as commanded by the loud-voiced girl. The result was I fell in love with her.

Prohibited by mission rules from expressing my feelings, I existed in a splendid frustration throughout the spring of 1956. I was puzzled by the recurrence of this emotion among my feelings and renewed my attempt to understand it. This produced little more than my former perception, that romantic love is an exalted compulsion to cherish and be near your beloved—sexual in its nature yet almost religious in its adulation of the beloved. From the start I doubted our ability to create a happy marriage. Between the two of us was too much of the impulse to rule and too little of the ability to defer to the other. Yet, being in love, I longed for the freedom to explore whether we might not soften that disparity. A year of my mission remained—an eternity, in my estimation. I fretted over the possibility that she might commit herself to someone else before I could speak to her. My worry increased when she arranged to migrate to Utah at the end of the coming summer. I decided to let her know how I felt. There could be no harm, I reasoned, in writing her a letter.

Around the middle of May I wrote the letter, then wrestled with myself for days in a fit of indecision. Finally one morning I dropped it into a mailbox. That very night I found her enthusiastic reply in our mailbox. Thereafter, we exchanged letters every week, hers coming in conventional envelopes without a return name or address. I read them while using the toilet on the floor above our room—the only privacy of which I was certain. Luckily, my companion usually left it to me to gather our mail.

I was mistaken in thinking there would be no other violation of missionary rules. One evening at a church social, she stopped me on the stairway between the recreational hall and the chapel, and we kissed. Another evening she invited Elder Smith and me to dinner. While he dozed on the sofa, she and I washed the dishes in the kitchen with long intimate pauses. On another occasion when we had invited her to dinner in our room, I escorted her upstairs to the street to catch her tram. We embraced in the deserted foyer for some minutes, listening intently for opening doors or approaching feet. Unexpectedly, she asked whether we would marry. My guilt was such that I could only blurt yes. Descending the stairs after she had caught her tram, I castigated myself bitterly for having committed myself to what I feared would be the lifelong disaster of an incompatible marriage.

I dutifully wrote my mother that she was to have a Belgian daughter-in-law. The girl was worried that my mother would resent her for having corrupted my mission. However, my mother feared a future daughter-in-law's antagonism more than a son's violation of missionary rules. She accepted our engagement without a murmur, and soon she and the girl were exchanging letters. In the meantime, in my own weekly letters to the girl, I urged her to anticipate a long engagement after my mission was over so that we could get to know each other better. She, for her part, wanted to get married immediately after my mission. She foresaw no danger whatsoever; being in love was all that mattered. She wasn't at all perturbed by the confession of disbelief I now felt obliged to include in my letters. In fact, she confidently predicted that her own fervent testimony would reignite my faith. I marked this as one more evidence of our incompatibility.

As the summer of 1956 advanced, I was faced with something of a moral crisis, because in August all the French missionaries were scheduled to attend sessions in the Swiss temple and I would be required to undergo a worthiness interview with the mission president. I could see no alternative to an outright lie. My dilemma was partially resolved by an elderly woman who, after a long disaffection from Mormonism, had returned to church at my urging. Instructed to visit this woman, my companion and I had found her on a cot in an attic of a seedy apartment building. She said her bitterness was beyond remedy. When her only son had died during World War II, the local Mormon elders had refused to conduct his funeral service because he had rarely attended church. Only she and a hearse driver attended her son's burial. On hearing this story I pulled a stool close to her cot and read to her from the Sermon on the Mount. On our next visit she agreed to come to church.

She was a portly, untidy person. Strands of white hair straggled from her head, her black coat was soiled, and she often smelled of cooked onions. Yet I respected her greatly. She had participated in the Resistance during the war, hiding downed Allied aviators in a hayloft. One day while eight English flyers hid in the loft, a German patrol paused before the barnyard gate, where she stood. She stared belligerently into the eyes of the patrol leader, saying silently, "If you want to die, sir, just come inside." The officer's gaze wilted, and the patrol went on.

One Sunday after church, this woman stopped me on the sidewalk in front of the chapel. She said: "Frère Peterson, you think people do not notice your attentions to that girl. You think you are being discreet and tactful. But people have noticed. They are talking. It is only a matter of time, and the mission president will transfer you to another city. That will be too bad. It will be a disgrace to you and your good mother." Ordinarily I resented blunt criticism. In this case, however, I accepted the warning with gratitude, knowing that she spoke as my friend. From that instant I decided to alter my relationship with the girl. By letter she and I agreed that we would continue to correspond but would put an end to the hugging and kissing. With that, I had satisfied the niceties of my conscience, and I awaited the temple excursion with only slight moral tremors.

In Switzerland, I attended temple sessions many hours a day, missionaries being required to fill the ranks in order to offer a wider schedule to French-speaking members attending the temple as a part of their traditional August vacation. I informed the mission president during our interview that I was worthy of attending the temple. I was constrained to respect the arcane ceremony of the temple by the deep reverence in which my confreres held it. I wrote my mother: "Even I feel the peace and security of the hushed halls of the temple—the hours of meditation are worthwhile."[7] One day I sat beside the mission president waiting to participate in the washing and anointing part of the ceremony. We wore no other clothing than a thin covering something like a hospital gown. The absurdity of civilized men sitting side by side in a condition of lightly covered nudity struck me. And then, curiously, I experienced a sense of kinship with this man whom I resented more than any other person alive. In our nudity I recognized our mutual status as creatures of nature and the wild.

I also had time to wander Berne and its environs with other missionaries. I rode on a cable car to a view where the Alps were even more magnificent, and I visited the famous bear pits of Berne, looking down upon the hulking brown beasts that shuffled about on their hindquarters begging for food. I also entered a large Gothic church that, to my surprise, had been stripped of its statues and paintings when expropriated by the Protestants during the Reformation. "I suppose," I wrote my mother, "that the silent story of

which these cold stones and barren walls bespoke is a testimony of
the differences and similarities that exist in the two religions [Cath-
olic and Protestant]."[8] Years later, remembering this building, I
would understand better whence derived the antipathy of my fellow Mormons toward art in their churches.

Returning from Switzerland, our bus followed an indirect route,
passing near evening through the Ardennes mountains, where we
paused at the village of Bastogne to see the giant star-shaped monument erected to the memory of the more than seventy-five thousand American soldiers and Belgian citizens who had been killed or
wounded there during the Battle of the Bulge. Reminders of the
war were everywhere in Belgium. Whole blocks in Liège had been
obliterated by V-1 robot planes. One woman told me that in the
wake of the German invasion her little son had picked up a grenade, which exploded. A Belgian surgeon persuaded her to allow
him to euthanize the wounded child with morphine. Her husband
became psychotic and remained so till after the war. In a courtyard
of the citadel above Liège was a bullet-torn post, varnished and affixed with a sign explaining that the Germans had shot prominent
citizens there in retaliation for acts of the Resistance. Behind the
citadel, rows of white crosses in astonishing numbers marked the
graves of these executed citizens. Some people maintain that war is
not instinctive with human beings. My memories of Belgium persuade me otherwise.

A week after our return from Switzerland, I accompanied our
basketball team to a tournament in Ostend. Our hotel stood on the
seacoast a little outside that city. Not being on the team, I had time
for walks along the beach, which was wide and sandy and went on
and on till it passed from sight. Landward were high dunes anchored by grass that waved in a perpetual wind off the sea. The
surf rolled solemnly in and out, and the vast sky was adrift with
flat-bottomed clouds. On these, my first walks ever on a seacoast, I
was filled with reverence for nature and a sense of liberation from
all unrequited desire.

I also entertained myself with a studious hobby I had developed after reading Schweitzer's *In Quest of the Historical Jesus,* a
summary of scholarly attempts during the eighteenth and nineteenth centuries to sift fact from myth in the accounts of the life of

Jesus in the four Gospels. I had decided I could judge Schweitzer's summary only if I myself mastered the Gospels. I therefore began a methodical outline of Matthew, Mark, Luke, and John during my spare moments, pulling a beloved leather-bound Louis Segond translation of the Bible from my breast pocket while riding on a tram or watching my comrades play basketball. I pursued this project far enough to conclude that, while I believed there had been a historical Jesus, I for one could not discern between history and myth in the record of his life.

The girl I have spoken of migrated to Utah in September. In the meantime, she and I had gone on exchanging letters but had otherwise behaved circumspectly. I had come back from Switzerland aware that I was no longer in love with her. I scarcely regretted the vanishing of romantic love, which seemed more enigmatic and capricious than ever. I was sure now that our differences of temperament would prove insurmountable, and I made up my mind not to marry her. Honesty required that I inform her at once. I chose to wait till the end of my mission for fear she would become angry and jeopardize my position as a missionary. This fear seems ironic given that, just a year earlier, I had been asking to be released early from my mission. After she left for Utah, I often wrote of our attachment as tentative and unexplored and urged her to date other men. Upon returning home, I called on her and in a sad, brief interview ended our relationship. I am not proud of my behavior in this matter. As I search for a word to describe it, *pusillanimous* comes to mind.

Late in the summer of 1956 Elder Smith became a senior companion, and my new companion and I inherited the prime investigators and favorable proselytizing area of a couple of transferred missionaries. It was here, amid clean middle-class neighborhoods on the heights overlooking Liège, that I spent the final months of my mission, a happy culmination if for no other reason than that I saw an end to my bondage. Working in this area posed logistical problems, for it required a long, sweaty pump up rue de Campine and offered no restrooms. Fortunately, investigators we had inherited invited us to dinner three days a week, and on the other two a good sister from the branch prepared us a substantial midday meal for a modest sum. My new companion struck me as moody and easily angered. He did not share my urgency to spend long hours proselytizing, and I did not dare press him. My next companion was likable, easygoing, and amenable to my rule as senior companion. Unfortunately, he was transferred quickly because a fourteen-year-old girl from the branch developed a manifest crush on him. His replacement, my last companion, was angry to the point of being dangerous. Ordering me not to wake him, this elder slept till ten or eleven. Sometimes he disappeared for half a day at a time. One day he tried to spill me from my bicycle. One Sunday morning he and I had a fistfight in our room. The fight was salutary, improving his demeanor for about a week. I was told he punched a later senior companion in the kidneys while standing behind him at doors where the companion had knocked. Eventually, he walked away from his mission and joined the U.S. Army in Germany.

I had both good and bad news from home during my final months. My sister Lenora succeeded in bearing a son, my nephew Joseph Hansen, by lying flat in bed from the moment she had reason to think herself pregnant until the child was delivered. In September 1956, my mother was diagnosed with colon cancer and underwent a radical colostomy. In January 1957, my brother Andelin died of peritonitis following an operation for stomach ulcers. These events seemed remote and to some degree unreal to me. At times I wondered whether I had ever had any other life than that of a missionary.

The most memorable personality from my final months was Denise Graitson, an investigator I had inherited from transferred missionaries. A docile housewife of about forty-five, Madame Graitson had the makings of the archetypal convert to Mormonism, destined to undergo great sacrifices for her new religion. She and her husband, who remained a devout Catholic, came from large Catholic families, and he was pressured by both families to exercise the coercions that Belgian law allowed a husband. Some family members urged him to have her declared insane. Two of her sisters who were nuns pleaded with her at great length, one of them informing her that she prayed for her return to Catholicism daily at the tomb of the founder of her order.

I have never felt more nearly worshiped than by this sincere and generous woman. Each week she fed my companion and me an early dinner when we arrived to teach her a lesson. I recall one of her envious sons shouting as we arrived, "Voilá les grands buffeurs!"—"There come the great gluttons!" She did our laundry without charge, and when she delivered it to us on Saturdays, she included a pound of butter. To my surprise her husband allowed their children to attend our Primary and at last gave his written approval for her baptism, stating simply that he recognized her right to decide for herself. A few days before I baptized her, she wrote to my mother that she hoped for an ultimate witness as to the truthfulness of Mormonism at the moment of her baptism. She did not inform me whether she received this witness.

It seemed briefly that she might accomplish the impossible and convert her husband, who attended some evening socials at the branch and spoke with friendly interest to the members and missionaries. I was not present to observe the failure of this miracle, for within a couple of weeks of her baptism, my mission ended. On the Sunday I left Liège in May 1957, Madame Graitson embraced me in the foyer of the church and with tears brimming in her eyes said, "Je vous aime tant"—"I love you so much." I believed she would never forget me.

More than twenty years later, touring Europe with my wife and daughter, I phoned Madame Graitson from the central Liège train station, identifying myself and inviting her to meet us for lunch at Place St. Lambert. She said, in an aged, weary voice, that she was tending grandchildren and would find it difficult to come to lunch. She remembered me only vaguely. Her husband, she said, had run off the Mormons long ago. I thanked her and prepared to hang up. At the last instant her voice brightened and she said perhaps she could arrange to meet us for lunch after all. By then it had struck me that reviving this woman's memory of Mormonism would be cruel. I said a gentle good-bye and hung up.

As I left the mission, I stopped in Charleroi overnight to say good-bye to my friends there. I took a train to Ostend and boarded a packet boat for a crossing of the Channel. I stayed three nights in London, then took a train to Southampton, where I boarded the SS *United States* for a five-day crossing of the Atlantic. The ocean was calm, blue, and reassuring. I read a used paperback copy of *Jane Eyre* I had bought in London and tried my hand at writing a short story. I felt serene and self-confident. I knew I would return to college and continue with an English major. I wasn't certain where. I thought I might transfer to Arizona State in order to be closer to my mother.

On the day I left Liège, the congregation sang a farewell song that promised that our separation would be temporary. That promise notwithstanding, I knew it very unlikely that I would ever see any of those people again. The song utterly destroyed my composure, and I blubbered, rather than spoke, my own farewell remarks. My weeping was a measure of my mission's significance. The anxiety and despair of the first fifteen months were long forgotten. My anger over the coercion that had kept me on my mission was suspended. My carefully nursed disbelief seemed irrelevant. The interest I had found in observing the Belgian scene; the warm friendships I had formed with missionaries, members, and investigators; and the enlargement of my abilities and understanding combined to make me regret the ending of a remarkable era in my life.

··· 11

Althea

I WAS SURPRISED BY ALL THE CHANGES my mother had made at home. The house was stuccoed a creamy yellow. The former living room had been turned into an apartment, and a handsome rock wall was being built on the street front. An irrigation ditch had at last reached the lot, and lettuce and onions flourished in the garden and a new lawn was being planted.

Mother was not reconciled to the colostomy, which, nine months earlier, had removed her entire colon. For the remaining twenty-eight years of her life, she would be mortified by unpredictable rumblings from the aperture in her abdomen. Lenora took Mother and me to Tucson where we visited Roald and Luana and their three children. Roald was in the U.S. Air Force and flying B47 bombers from Davis-Montham air base. Next I went to Provo where Leon and Charles were finishing spring quarter at BYU. Charles and Betty had left La Sal, and Charles was pursuing a master's degree in history, having abandoned his ambition to become a farmer or rancher.

When I arrived, I asked Leon to introduce me to a girl, Althea Sand, who had written me a letter about three months before the end of my mission. He had been dating other girls in her apartment and had left my address on the kitchen counter with the plea that someone write to his faraway missionary brother. Leon has never told me why he did this. Certainly I hadn't asked him to. In any event, Althea decided to write, and by the end of my mission we had exchanged three letters. In the last she told me she was not a Mormon, a fact that made her presence at BYU a matter of curiosity. Born in Iowa, she had grown up in Long Beach, California. She had accompanied a Mormon friend to BYU. After a single quarter,

the friend had left, but Althea stayed, finding her Mormon room-
mates to be comfortable companions.

Althea struck me as beautiful. She was five feet six and weighed
110 pounds. She had blue eyes, a honey-blonde ponytail, a prominent nose, and tanned legs. She went with us to a steak fry in
Charles's backyard that night, and the next day she and I spent the
afternoon and evening together. The day after that, Leon and I
drove to Snowflake in a car he had bought. On the Kaibab, we de-
toured to see the Grand Canyon from the north rim, my first glimpse
of that immense gorge. I was already thinking of marrying Althea.

Lenora's husband, Marion, hired me to operate a bulldozer in
a tree-eradication project on the Apache reservation. His contract
called for clearing a square mile of juniper and piñon on Limestone
Ridge in wild country fifty miles south of Snowflake. Although
Marion had made good money uprooting junipers at lower eleva-
tions by dragging a giant chain between two tractors, he didn't do
well at Limestone Ridge, where the contract required uprooting
the junipers and piñons one by one with a bulldozer in order to
protect a modest scattering of ponderosa pine, esteemed as timber.
The funding agency decided he had to eradicate even the tiny trees
that bent and slid under the dozer without being uprooted. To accomplish this he hired Apache men to follow the tractors, chopping out the saplings with axes. Midsummer he moved his tractor
to a more profitable job and left me and my tractor and the Apache
ax men to finish the project on Limestone Ridge.

Mother kept house for Leon and me that summer of 1957. I
was grateful for the excellent meals she cooked, and I enjoyed many
conversations with her. I sat by her during church and often took
her for a ride after church. Sometimes we climbed the hill next to
our farm and renewed our sense of being at one with the wide Arizona landscape. Unfortunately, I had a compulsion to be unneces-
sarily candid about my disbelief. I had never seen her at such a loss
for words as when I told her I did not believe in Christ. Whatever
freedom I gained from this was short-lived. In general she proved
an indignant and persistent arguer, convinced that I could choose to
believe as easily as I chose to take a bath or seat myself in a chair.

Each Sunday I taught a Sunday-school class of young adults.
One Saturday night I took one of the girls from this class to a

movie. Afterward I alarmed her by explaining Schweitzer's principle of Reverence for Life. For most people, a sympathy for spiders and worms is simply insane. One Sunday a pretty girl from out of town showed up in my class. After class I took her for a ride in my old Chrysler. We ended at the Lakeside cemetery, thirty miles from Snowflake, where we hugged and kissed and I attempted to insert a hand into her bra. She asked me not to. I despised myself for behaving in this manner within sight of my father's grave. That night I wrote Althea a long letter recounting a history of my sexual experiences and speaking candidly of my sexual attraction to any pretty woman. Feeling unfaithful to Althea because of this episode, I determined I would never again attempt physical intimacy of any sort with anyone with whom I was not seriously considering marriage.

Althea stayed at BYU that summer, graduating in the August commencement. During the fall she lived at home in Lakewood, California, a suburb of Long Beach, and worked as a secretary. In January 1958 she came back to Provo, and we were always together after that. In the meantime, I visited her at Lakewood in September, and she came to Snowflake in August and at Thanksgiving. Maybe we were lucky to be together only briefly during these seven months. The letters we exchanged provide a remarkable record of our intimate selves, sometimes eloquent, always candid and demonstrative of a growing trust and affection.

I didn't write with anything close to delicacy about the crucial issues of love, marriage, and sex. In one letter I offered almost clinical detail about the sex act as I understood it from reading. My former indecisiveness about marriage haunted me, and I lacked the good sense to keep the topic from my letters. We exchanged a good deal of talk about books. Althea was more widely read in popular fiction than I. In both high school and college she had finished a novel almost every night. In one letter she spoke eloquently of college having committed her to a lifetime of learning: "It is like dropping a pebble into a clear pool, the comprehension grows wider and wider and the perception deeper. I want to cry in thankfulness that there is a constant awakening and spreading out that never stops."[1]

Inevitably I detailed my disbelief in my letters. "I cannot believe in a God who can interfere in the normal course of nature;

there can be no supernatural if my idea is correct. Miracles do not occur; mysteries do." Sometimes I asserted that our children, should we marry, should not be taught the dogma of any church. She wondered why an issue had to be made of the matter. She had been baptized into the Lutheran faith of her father but in growing up had attended the Methodist church her mother preferred. She liked the fact that her parents made no inquiry into the condition of her faith. We both worshiped the wild, she more heartily and less ambiguously than I. I wrote: "God must be only the shifting currents of force that are manifested to us in the various aspects of physical phenomena." She replied: "Yes—that is why there is a particular pleasure for me in a storm or a wind—'shifting currents of force' are God—the changes of nature, the light of stars and moon—their existence, their movement—God—and so pray to the functioning whole. And feel wonder and mystery and glory and excitement."[2]

At no other period of my life have I lived as intimately—and as destructively—with the wild as I did that summer. Before my arrival on Limestone Ridge, range cattle had been the sole instruments of its domestication. Although their decades-long foraging had undoubtedly reduced the native grasses and allowed the proliferation of juniper and piñon that I helped to reverse, the plot seemed entirely wild when I first saw it. When I left, it was littered with uprooted trees and its soil tracked and furrowed. I was shackled to my tractor by my civilized sensibility: I had a job; I owed my employer an honest day's labor. I suffered tedium; my mind wandered; desultory meditations on many topics unrelated to the wild occurred to me. Nonetheless, it is a fact that my uprooting of trees and tracking the soil did not obliterate the wild from that place. I wrote Althea of the contentment I felt at night while bathing in a cold mountain stream that ran past our camp trailer. Cottonwoods and aspens lined the stream, and the steep walls of the canyon defined a narrow wedge of sky whose bright stars added "mystery and meditation to my bath and its peace."[3]

Bliss and beatitude visited me often. But so did loneliness and fear. Bees and wasps, stirred up by my bulldozer, proved a dangerous annoyance. Once, frantic to quit the tractor before a rising swarm of bees attacked me, I turned a half somersault and landed on my back on the ground. Another time a bee stung me behind the ear, and a lump formed in my armpit. Storms were more than an inconvenience. One afternoon I took shelter from a thunderstorm beneath a large alligator juniper. Soon Marion appeared and stationed his tractor under another tree. I moved my tractor across the clearing and parked beside Marion's. While we talked, lightning shattered the tree I had been under only moments before. Of this I said to Althea: "It is curious how on these moments when we see how close death has come that we are sobered and reflective, and we wonder if some Providence guides our destiny, as if each day death did not go narrowly by, but being undetected, engenders no feeling of awe."[4]

On that same day, after the storm had passed, we followed the tracks of a bear into a thicket and found a calf it had killed and, next to the calf, an enormous pile of bear dung filled with manzanita berries. The ruthlessness of the bear sobered me. I wrote to Althea: "And recognition of this suffering, this evil which nightly drenches the earth with the blood of life that feeds other life, leads us to pessimistic, dark thoughts."[5]

Marion reported the killing of the calf, and within a few days a trapper had concealed traps beneath a tree at the only water hole on the ridge, suspending the rotten hindquarter of a wild burro from a limb to serve as bait. A week later we found beside the road a dead black bear shorn of its ears, which the trapper had taken as evidence of his kill. Now I felt sorry for the bear, recognizing "animals as having a priority equal to that of man, a priority merited by virtue of having life as we have it, of existing as we exist."[6]

Althea's visit to Snowflake in late August was a happy interlude for both of us. After church on Sunday she and I climbed the hill by our farm, and I introduced her to the mesa-rimmed landscape of my boyhood. The next day she accompanied me to Limestone Ridge. We drove home early to attend a wedding reception for Leon and his bride, Gussie Schneider. Some days earlier I had been absent from their wedding in the Mesa temple. "I should have to lie to qualify for a temple recommend," I had written to Althea a few days before the event, "and I am fatigued of that. I think Leon and Gussie understand that and will not feel slighted." There was, I will add, no embarrassment among us over the fact that Gussie and I had been engaged during the summer of 1953. Nor were my friends and relatives anything short of gracious in welcoming this Gentile girl, Althea, who had come to visit me. Many of them now had their first inkling that I had embarked upon a "new life," as I called it in my letters. Well before the end of my mission I had decided I should not marry a conventional Mormon. I had not thought specifically in terms of an outsider till I met Althea, whose importance I can scarcely overemphasize. That summer I justly credited her with giving me courage. "I did not dare effect what I had dreamed of before I had met and talked with you, and felt there...that which would strengthen me enough for the pain and difficulty involved in changing the moral tone of my life."[7]

My final weeks on Limestone Ridge were a valedictory to the mountains of Arizona, for my sojourns in Arizona thereafter would be brief and in the nature of visits. My respect and love for Marion, on whom I had relied so often while growing up, had been reinforced by my summer's experience. I also learned to respect the Apache men with whom I worked. After Marion moved his tractor from Limestone Ridge, we towed the camp trailer to the outskirts of an Apache village called Carrizo, where I stayed alone two or three nights each week. The Apaches lived in simple frame houses with neither electricity nor running water. Some of the women kept treadle sewing machines under bowers made of leafy cottonwood branches. Their traditional religion appeared to be at least partially intact. A white Assembly of God missionary who lived in the village collected Apaches for Sunday services with an old bus. The men who worked with me laughed at him. One day they informed me of a sing to be held that night for a man struck by a rattlesnake, a ceremony the missionary would have regarded as heathenish. Outside the trailer that night I heard chanting from across the creek. Under bright stars I felt in touch with ancient things.

In late September, I spent a week with Althea in Lakewood. Because my aged Chrysler was unreliable, I drove the Chevy sedan Mother had bought from Leon. I drove this car on loan for a year, then bought it from Mother. I was surprised to see that Althea's parents, Arvid and Stella, were inches shorter than Althea. It was clear that Arvid had given Althea what she called her "ski-jump nose." Arvid was a packer in the shipping department of a caster factory, and Stella was a part-time seamstress in a dry-cleaning establishment. They lived in a pleasant two-bedroom house with a separate garage and an enclosed backyard. Their house struck me as much nicer than Mother's. Only later would I learn that Arvid had constructed much of their furniture from scrap lumber that Stella had concealed beneath creatively sewn covers.

Althea took me to Laguna Beach on Sunday, where I swam in the Pacific and lolled in a swimming suit till the sun had turned me a cherry red. At the house I bathed with Arvid's abrasive Lava soap, setting my skin afire. During the following week I settled into a comfortable routine. After Arvid and Althea had left for work, I sat at Althea's portable typewriter in the den till time for lunch with Stella and again through the afternoon till Althea and Arvid returned. Undoubtedly this was good exercise for an aspiring writer. Otherwise it had no result except that, as I learned later, Stella approved of a young man who could discipline himself to eight hours a day on a typewriter. Off and on all summer I had tried to write stories and random pages of description. My ambition was strong, and I was drawn to the drama of Mormon life. I wasn't certain what being a writer meant. My attempts to create plots had struck me as sterile, and I admitted that I needed to serve a long apprenticeship. What seemed clear was that already writing had become important to the new identity I was constructing. It seemed, in fact, a substitute for religious faith. "Do you see," I wrote Althea, "that as my instinctive need of purpose makes itself felt, writing becomes more and more important to me; it has become directional, a base, a determinant."[8]

At the end of my visit, I drove from Lakewood to Provo and stayed a night or two with Charles and Betty. For permanent quarters, I rented an upstairs room in a private home just off the BYU campus. Though uncertain that I had money for an entire year, I did not look for a job. I bought breakfast and lunch at a campus cafeteria and for supper had bread, jam, and powdered milk in my room. I enrolled in ROTC with the intention of securing a commission in the U.S. Air Force the following June. The five-year stint required for flight training posed an obstacle to the doctorate in English to which I now aspired. However, the alternative of being drafted into the infantry for two years seemed worse.

As a senior student, I was given command over a flight of lower-division cadets, whom I drilled with vigorous commands on Tuesday afternoons. On one occasion I was given demerits for failing to march my flight from the main campus to an assembly on the lower campus in a timely fashion. Marching a flight of cadets through the streets of Provo was not a skill that came to me instinctively. ROTC reinforced my dread of nuclear holocaust. War was an eventuality I tried not to think about. One afternoon another student burst into my room with the news that the Soviet Union had successfully launched the *Sputnik* satellite. "Just think," this young man exulted, "at this very moment a man-made object is orbiting the earth!" I did not share his enthusiasm. I had been conditioned from high school days to believe the Soviet Union intended to enslave the world. *Sputnik* seemed an ominous step in that direction.

My favorite class was creative writing from Thomas Cheney, to whom I submitted three pessimistic stories about bereaved women. One of these was a fictionalization of the incident told me by a Belgian woman who had consented to the euthanization of her son, horribly wounded after finding a live grenade in the aftermath of the German invasion of 1940. Compounding this horror, the boy's father became psychotic and remained so till after the war. This story was published in the spring 1958 issue of *Wye*, BYU's student literary magazine. Given its content, its title, "Le Visage de la Vie," suggests that the characteristic features of life are insanity and death. I have published nothing more grim.

As fall quarter of 1957 wore on, my life became less and less pleasant. With an exacting self-discipline I studied for long hours seven days a week. I had dinner once a week with Charles and Betty and also with Leon and Gussie. Generally I felt lonely and surrounded by strangers or mere acquaintances rather than by intimates. I wrote Althea twice weekly and depended on her replying as regularly as she had done during the summer. This was a regimen she was not up to. She worked forty hours a week as a secretary and went to a night class two evenings each week. She was also witness each evening at dinner to a running quarrel between her parents. Unknown to me, Arvid, of a mild and affable personality when sober, drank himself into an irascible mood by the end of each day. Often Althea's letters came three or four days later than I expected. At first I patiently explained how important they were to me. Then I became angry. Two or three times I phoned, and she mailed a letter the next day. Each of us was comforted by the sound of the other's voice. Why didn't I phone more often? My childhood conditioning ordained that long-distance calls were for emergency only. At one point I wrote that our relationship was endangered by her lack of punctuality. She retorted, with an edge of anger, that "you have been on the controlling side in your relationships," a reference, I think, to my inability to make up my mind to marry my previous girlfriends while refusing to free them to go their own way.[9] Following that, I tried to restrain my impatience, which subsided of its own accord as the turn of the year approached, with its promise of Althea's arrival in Provo.

In mid-November the hysterical anxiety that had overwhelmed me in May and December 1954 erupted again—this on a Saturday afternoon while I was in my room reading from *Paradise Lost*. As before, this was a next-to-irresistible impulse to run. The anxiety accompanying this impulse came in surges, and, while each surge crested, it obliterated every other thought or feeling except a desperate determination not to lose rational control of myself.

I left my room and walked about campus under a gray, lowering sky. Other grim emotions afflicted me. I was thoroughly demoralized and depressed and again filled with an inexpressible grief. I had fancied myself immune to such a devastating mood by virtue of resignation. I still clung to the idea that being resigned might soften or ameliorate the mood, yet I could foresee no circumstance that might hasten an improvement. This mood would, in fact, set the tenor of my life for many months to come. I awoke each morning to a mixture of intense anxiety and depression. I had no taste for class and study yet plodded on with my routines out of simple desperation. Sometimes I became distracted by an interesting lecture or, especially in the evenings, by a passage in a textbook. But soon I would remember how miserable I was.

I had told Althea of my earlier bouts of morbid emotion. Reluctantly I now revealed I was in another. All along I had believed her esteem for me required an image of self-confidence, ambition, and intellectual curiosity. I asked her to come to Snowflake for Thanksgiving. At first she said no from consideration of her parents. At

the last moment she sent a telegram saying, "A woman's prerogative—have changed my mind." I drove from Provo during the night
before Thanksgiving, slept a couple of hours, and met Althea at the
bus station in Holbrook soon after sunrise. We returned to Snowflake by way of Woodruff, my mother's birthplace. We climbed
onto the base of the nearby volcanic cone known as the Woodruff
Butte. The early sun sparkled on the frosty grass of the surrounding plain. Driving on, we visited family graves in the barren red soil
of the tiny Woodruff cemetery, where a wild simplicity reigned. We
were happy to be together on this bright, frosty morning.

Returning to Lakewood, Althea wrote a love letter. She had
come to Snowflake, she said, to test her feelings. "I felt an intense
love for you Friday night, Saturday night, Sunday morning—as we
were riding toward Holbrook....The very nondescript way in
which I took the suitcase from your hand and entered the bus—
what a shock it would have been to have followed my impulse,
dropped everything, thrown my arms around you and wailed—'I
don't want to leave you!'" Regarding my dark emotions, which I
had explained in greater depth than ever before, she wrote: "As you
fight to conquer your depression, I feel a pride in you, a respect for
you, that I have never felt for others who had not fought at all."[10]

Soon after Thanksgiving I went to the student counseling service at BYU where I was interviewed by Burton Robinson, a clinical psychologist. Though it seemed an admission of unmanly
dependence, I felt desperate enough to agree to psychotherapy. Because university policy allowed only a few interviews with the
counseling staff, I arranged to enter therapy with Robinson one
evening a week at a private clinic in downtown Provo at ten dollars
for each hourlong session. Though this sum strained my finances, it
was less than half the fee charged by local psychiatrists. These sessions did not begin till January. I recall a desperate Sunday afternoon in December when I wandered to the building that housed
the counseling service and, against odds, found it open and Robinson in his office. With wracking sobs, I expressed the guilt and grief
I felt over having abandoned my mother by becoming an adult.
This surprised me, for I hadn't recognized before how deep an issue
this was with me.

As fall quarter ended, I submitted a paper on ethics in my introduction to philosophy course, taught by a bright, tolerant young professor, Truman Madsen. As a missionary I had been influenced by Schweitzer's search for an ethic that was, as he called it, "a necessity of thought." Throughout my summer on Limestone Ridge I had often meditated on values, worth, and purpose. In a letter to Althea I conjectured that ethics "depend on thought and ultimate belief regarding the mysteries of existence, and not on conscience; conscience is only a secondary consideration, being the night watchmen who warns the moral man of approaching deviation from the line of conduct dictated by the outlook on life." Despite such self-assurance, I often ended my meditations gloomily. "I see no meaning and make no sense," I wrote on another occasion. "I cannot see the end or the value or the meaning of this miracle of life on a whirling planet."[11] This will explain why, in Madsen's course, I looked forward eagerly to the unit on ethics and chose to write my paper on that topic. In it, I examined two sets of opposites: relative ethics versus absolute ethics and ethics as the search for happiness versus ethics as obedience to a moral imperative. The paper ended inconclusively, and Madsen, while granting it an A, said it needed much revision. I had hoped for a dazzling insight that would assure me of my duty and guiding purpose in life. Failing that, I went forward as confused as ever about the nature of morality, guided not so much by rationally conceived principles as by deep, half-subliminal imperatives and guilts.

Althea returned to Provo at the beginning of winter quarter 1958. She rented a squalid basement apartment with three other young women, enrolled in classes, and found a part-time job on campus. For both of us, there was a steady satisfaction in simply being together. On school days we met in the library in the afternoon and studied till closing. On weekend evenings we went to a movie or dance or played Rook with my brothers and their wives. Sometimes we tended Charles and Betty's children while they went out. On Sunday we attended church in one of the large campus wards.

Overall, however, I continued to consider myself unhappy. I became dependent on my weekly therapy sessions with Robinson, where, for an hour, my anxiety and depression disappeared. Robinson, a faithful Mormon, persuaded me that my anxiety was free-floating, that is, it attached itself to all sorts of perceived dangers, many of them remote and unlikely to happen. I told him about my fear of the extinction of the sun, when all life would disappear from the earth. He asked when I expected this to occur. I said in about four billion years. He said that didn't seem like something I needed to worry about. I agreed. This did not quell my anxiety, which simply gravitated to other perceived dangers, nor did it clarify the repressed trauma that might prove to be at the root of my anxiety.

As things stood, I was committed to enter the air force upon graduating in June. Robinson pointed out that as a psychiatric patient I could qualify for a deferment from military service. With a perhaps unseemly satisfaction I recognized that, relieved of a military obligation, I could proceed with graduate studies at BYU. During the middle of winter quarter, I approached the commander of the ROTC unit, doubting he would release me from my obligation to complete the program. His alacrity in dismissing me was almost insulting. As it turned out, I never had to invoke medical reasons for avoiding the draft. For the following seven years my draft board in Holbrook, Arizona, extended me an educational deferment. In those pre-Vietnam days, people praised rather than looked down on educational deferments.

During winter quarter I underwent several changes of behavior that indicated an increasing dilation of conscience on my part. I had rarely failed, during the four years since I had begun to think of myself as a disbeliever, to pray at my bedside every evening, reasoning that even if the Christian God did not exist, the creative force of the universe merited my respect and worship. Now, quite suddenly one evening, this archaic habit of saying a bedside prayer struck me as totally fatuous. Why should I abase myself by kneeling before an abstract principle that, having no personality, could neither hear nor care about my prayer? With that thought I went to bed without my customary prayer, nor would I ever again renew the habit of prayer.

Another change was my resumption of intentional masturbation, which at first was accompanied by considerable shame. I talked this guilty matter over with Robinson, who observed that masturbation is often a search for a release from tension. I asked him bluntly whether he masturbated. He said no. I asked why not. He said it would make him feel too guilty. His simple candor had a therapeutic effect on me. I accepted that masturbation was a matter to be settled with oneself and no one else. I will add that, from my present perspective, nothing seems more ludicrous than the notion that Deity concerns itself with whether human beings relieve their sexual tension in solitude.

A third change had to do with Schweitzer's principle of Reverence for Life. During the April rains I observed thousands of earthworms crawling from sodden lawns onto sidewalks where they died from desiccation as soon as the sidewalks dried. My impulse was, when a rain had stopped, to seize a broom and sweep as many earthworms as possible back onto the lawns where they could burrow into the sod. Several considerations held this impulse in check. Onlookers would have considered me insane. Furthermore, there were vastly more earthworms in need of rescue than I could save. Finally, my self-interest rebelled at the prospect of devoting myself to earthworms. I had more desirable things to do than save worms in distress or, for that matter, needy human beings. The ethic of devotion was unraveling among my feelings.

Leon and I graduated from BYU with a B.A. degree in English in June 1958. Leon and Gussie, who was pregnant, left for Snowflake immediately. Bound to Provo by my therapy sessions, I persuaded Mother to move to Provo for the summer—this to assuage the guilt I felt for having grown up and left her. We rented a small furnished apartment on north University Avenue. I slept on a bed that unfolded from a sofa in the living room, and Mother occupied the bedroom. It didn't occur to me that Althea might see this arrangement as evidence that I was as far as ever from making up my mind about getting married. Going home to Lakewood for a couple of weeks, she replied only once to my abundant letters. I fretted about her silence till Mother said, with some exasperation, "Why don't you marry her?" On our first evening together after she returned from Lakewood, I asked Althea to marry me. She said she would. We agreed that the ceremony should be at the end of the summer. The marvelous thing for me was how completely decided I felt.

During spring quarter I took a part-time job with BYU on a project to develop a large farm near Spanish Fork. I plowed, harrowed, and furrowed a large field with a tractor, taking pleasure in the open sky, the looming mountains, the pastures with grazing livestock, ancient orchards where magpies nested, and brushy fences where I might see a pheasant or a cottontail. By the time school was out, the farm had become a busy place. Drilling holes with a tractor-mounted auger, one crew planted 5,000 apple saplings. Another crew set out 15,000 watermelon seedlings. Yet another crew constructed sheds for 150 dairy cows. My job, which had now become full-time, was to level a half-dozen adjacent fields with a crawler tractor and an earthmover, amalgamating them into a couple of large fields amenable to a single sprinkling system. Sweating under a blazing summer sun, I worked ten hours a day, six days a week, for one dollar an hour, only half the rate of my previous summer's work. A national recession was afoot, and I did not have the fortitude to ask for a higher wage. Because the work engaged only a fraction of my mind, I had time to brood and suffer through alternating fits of anxiety, depression, and anger.

One day the boss instructed me to fetch a three-wheeled alfalfa swather from the far side of the farm. The machine, which I had never operated, was parked in a triangular plot surrounded on two sides by a ditch and on a third side by a field of ripe wheat. Because the ditch was deep, I concluded the usual operator had brought the machine through the wheat. The fact there were no visible tracks argued that the flattened wheat had sprung up again. So I took the machine through the wheat. Only after I looked back on three tracks of smashed wheat stalks did I realize how unintelligent my conclusion had been. Obviously the usual operator had the skill to cross the ditch. My boss threatened to fire me for ruining so much wheat. I made no reply but smoldered with the injustice of having been sent to retrieve a machine that I knew little about. The experience wasn't without value, for it made me more tolerant of other people's unintelligent decisions.

It was my displeasure to become intimately acquainted with seagulls that summer. Every day flocks of them flew from Utah Lake to feed on the grubs, worms, and insects uncovered by my earthmover. My dislike for the gulls was not entirely rational. I was

irritated by their fluttering and squawking and unnecessary peck-
ing of one another and by their pompous appearance while they
stood at repose, cocking their heads this way or that. One day
while I made cuts close to a patch of pebbled soil, a female killdeer
fled before my tractor, feigning a broken wing. Surmising she had
eggs on the pebbled patch, I worked elsewhere in the field for a
few days. Watching her comings and goings, I located the eggs and
inspected them during one of her absences. They were beautiful
speckled things. But, as I expected, within a day or two a seagull
found the eggs, and after that the killdeer disappeared.

I became familiar that summer with the locally famous Dream
Mine. At the base of the mountain a couple of miles south of the
farm, an imposing structure of white concrete stood over the main
shaft of the mine. Around 1900, a bishop from a nearby town had
a vision of Nephite gold buried in the mountain. Raising capital
through stock sales, the bishop's followers drove several shafts into
the mountain. One Sunday afternoon Althea and I visited the now
inactive mine, where a self-appointed watchman, who lived in a
nearby house, told us that the Nephite gold would someday be
found. In the oak brush above the mine Althea and I found two
monuments marking the precise locations where angels had visited
the visionary bishop, who was eventually excommunicated from
the Mormon Church. There is, I realized, a deep and unruly impulse among the Mormons to translate hope and desire into other-
worldly visions.

Althea and I were together every evening that summer. We went
on walks and drives, swam a few times in the Provo municipal
pool, and enrolled in an evening class at BYU in modern poetry.
On Sunday mornings we accompanied my mother to church.

Mother set up a quilting frame in her bedroom and stitched a
quilt for Althea and me. For most of the summer she had to crawl
under the frame to get into her bed. Though our relationship was
as affectionate and respectful as it had always been, this was a difficult, tense period for both of us. Mother was set on Althea's becoming a Mormon before we married. Over and over she pointed
out that Althea already lived the sober, decent life of a Mormon.
Sometimes she proposed that we delay the wedding for a year so
that we could be married in the temple. It was crucial, in Mother's

estimation, that her children marry "within the Covenant," as she called the temple ceremony. Otherwise they would be lost in eternity, not only to her but also to the spouse whom they had wed for time only. I met my mother's daily importunings with a steadfast refusal. My identity seemed at stake. I talked all this over with Robinson during my weekly therapy session. He saw my disbelief itself as an act of resistance to my mother and predicted that once I had purged my repressed anger, I would return to the faith. I did not reject this possibility out of hand, sometimes referring to it usefully to make Mother and my other relatives feel more hopeful about me.

Althea and I were married on Sunday morning, August 31, 1958, in Charles and Betty's home in Orem. It was a happy day, and I think of it often with satisfaction. Althea made her own wedding dress with a hem at midcalf. I bought a tweed suit and a narrow rust tie. Althea's parents were present, as was my mother. Althea's former roommate Kathy Merrill was there. Leon and Gussie and Marion and Lenora came from Arizona. At the conclusion of the ceremony, which had been conducted by a Mormon bishop, Althea and I exchanged simple gold wedding bands. She had not asked for and I had not offered to buy a diamond engagement ring. Afterward, we had a luncheon in the backyard with a wedding cake, and a few amateur photographs were taken.

We stayed the first night in a motel in Richfield where the condition of heightened lust in which I had existed for so long was at last alleviated. The next night, having naively equipped ourselves for camping, we put down a mattress and blankets in a campground at the north rim of the Grand Canyon. We saw, from the tents and trailers close around, that the pleasures of the previous evening were not to be repeated. The next evening, having toured the viewpoints of the north rim all day, we took a cabin. Almost immediately a dinner we had eaten at the main lodge struck us with diarrhea, and we spent the night hearing one another use the toilet through a thin plank wall. So again there were no erotic pleasures.

The next day, mercifully recovered, we drove on to Snowflake where Mother had arranged an open house in our honor. We were touched by the violin playing of Snowflake's music master, Rufus Crandall. His rendition of a plaintive old song that my older siblings had sung while I was a child, "The Last Rose of Summer," is still vivid in my memory. Late that night we retired to a bedroom in Mother's house. Althea gave the rattling bedsprings a push, and I knew once again there would be no lovemaking. In a few days we returned to Provo and took up domicile in our own basement apartment at 757 East 620 North where, I am happy to report, we made up for the deprivations of our honeymoon.

··· 12

Nebo by Moonlight

ALTHEA AND I SETTLED QUICKLY into a comfortable domesticity. Without discussion we divided prerogatives and duties between us. We shared the checkbook and the automobile. I took out the garbage, maintained the automobile, and paid the bills. She did the shopping, cooked dinner, and did the dishes, often with my help. As I recall, I was as likely as she to get out the vacuum and clean the floors. She proved a frugal shopper and an excellent cook. She bought powdered milk in fifty-pound sacks and potatoes, onions, and apples in bulk, and cheddar cheese by the brick. She could make liver palatable by sautéing it in tomato sauce and onions. Sometimes I myself baked a vanilla cake for dinner. About once a week we shared a single large Coke or a milk shake at a drive-in.

I enrolled in graduate courses and taught two sections of freshman English at BYU during fall quarter 1958. I was called a graduate assistant, a misnomer because I had full responsibility for the two courses. Althea found a job as secretary of the freshman English program, so I saw her two or three times during the day. We bought three-speed bicycles and pedaled to campus each day. Althea was a pretty sight, pedaling in her high heels and full woolen skirts.

At an evening social of the English faculty and graduate students, Althea and I were approached by P. A. Christensen, who congratulated us on our marriage. Standing tall, seeming to glare through his thick lenses, with his hair bristling in its wonted crew cut, he said in his grand hoarse voice, "You are both so sane!" His judgment was based, I assume, on classes we had taken from him as undergraduates. Neither of us have ever again felt so honored.

I was enthusiastic about my teaching. I liked my students and they liked me. One day, leading a discussion while seated, I fell over backward in my chair and the class roared. I could only laugh with them. I was of course learning much more about writing than they were. I formed habits of sentence structure and punctuation that I observe to this day. Before the year was out I had arrived at a sense of what makes a good freshman theme, thereby gaining confidence in the crucial business of grading papers.

One afternoon while crossing campus I saw the plate-glass windows of the science building ripple like the surface of a pond. This, the effect of a minor earthquake, was a manifestation of the wild, a reminder that the crust of the earth is vibrant with untamed motion. Another adventure occurred one evening while I pedaled my bicycle to a nearby grocery store. Two policemen in a squad car stopped and interrogated me. They had received a complaint of a Peeping Tom riding a bicycle and wearing a coat like mine. They returned with me to our apartment and asked Althea to verify my recent whereabouts.

During winter quarter 1959, I took a seminar from Edward Hart on British literature of the eighteenth century. I was interested in this era because of Albert Schweitzer's admiration for its rationalism. In a letter to friends, I waxed enthusiastic over the synthesis of the logical, ethical, and religious faculties that this age believed it had achieved, saying, "it must have been a great experience, even thrilling, to have conceived the universe as orderly, and to have felt that the same reason which could perceive this, also very plainly dictated a religious ethic to men." In my seminar paper I interpreted Jonathan Swift as one who yearned to believe in this synthesis but ultimately saw too much contradiction in the actual behavior of human beings. Hence in *Gulliver's Travels* it is the talking horses who embody ideal reason while creatures who look like human beings, the Yahoos, are utter brutes. In the letter to our friends, I admitted that I, like Swift, was no true rationalist: "I feel a great want in my outlook on life. I believe I am rational, but I have no basis for my morality (although I am moral), nor do I have any real religious conviction."[1]

During spring quarter of 1959 I took a course in the modern English novel from Bruce Clark, who delivered well-organized lectures in a compelling and melodious voice. Here I read Hardy, Galsworthy, Joyce, Maugham, and Lawrence and became interested in the novel as a genre. Hardy's *Jude the Obscure,* one of the most powerful novels I had ever read, struck me as the essence of tragedy. I realized that for me tragedy does not require a noble or highborn protagonist possessed of a so-called tragic flaw; tragedy requires only that I identify deeply with any sort of protagonist who comes to inconsolable loss, rousing in me pity, fear, and a paradoxical enhancement in my own esteem of whatever human qualities the protagonist displays. I was also attracted to the sexual candor of D. H. Lawrence and chose to do my term paper on the erotic in some of his short stories. Clark liked my paper but chided me for having gone on too long with a defense of sexual imagery in fiction. From these two, author and professor, I gathered that the sexually explicit has its own proportionate and unapologetic place in literature. I also wrote a paper on Melville's *Moby-Dick* under the direction of Bryant Jacobs that quarter. I was fascinated by the epic grandeur of Captain Ahab and found a resonance among my own feelings with his indignation against God for being the author of evil as well as of good.

During winter quarter Leon wrote from Tucson, where he had entered a graduate program in English at the University of Arizona, proposing that he, Charles, Roald, and I take homesteads in Alaska. I was not attracted by Alaska. I do recall a recurring fantasy about taking a summer job as a sheepherder in Utah. More realistically, Althea and I gathered gear for a summer of camping. We bought cheap sleeping bags and a Coleman stove at a grocery store, and Althea's mother used her horde of S&H green stamps to give us a cooking kit and a light Hudson's Bay ax. Our first camp was in a grove of aspens on the Skyline Drive along the Wasatch Plateau. Our sleeping bags, spread on top of cots, were cold. They were, as we realized later, designed for indoor slumber parties. Furthermore, we had no idea that the air beneath a cot is colder than the ground. We got up, put on all the clothes we had, and placed some newspapers between the cots and sleeping bags. We still spent an uncomfortable night. On later campouts we reinforced the bags with blankets and heated rocks wrapped in newspaper at our feet. Camping doesn't come easy. You have to learn how to do it.

I also took up fishing that summer, though not very successfully. I caught my first trout at Mirror Lake in the Uintas while
Althea and I camped with friends. This was our introduction to a
mountain range, which, above all others, would enter our emotions. On our second day in the Uintas, I developed an altitude
headache that mere aspirin wouldn't touch. Luckily Althea introduced me to Anacin, which quickly relieved the pain.

During the 1959–1960 school year I shared an office with
George Bennion, a former high school teacher with numerous children, who was homesteading a hay ranch at a remote place called
River Bed in Utah's west desert. I don't know yet how George managed to work on the ranch, teach freshman English, and take graduate courses. For a few weeks in the fall, while he hunted for a
house for his family, he had dinner with Althea and me and slept in
a sleeping bag on the floor of our office. Althea and I visited his
ranch, which consisted of two or three shacks, four or five fields of
alfalfa watered by a diesel pump, and about eighty head of Here-
ford cattle. George's father, Glynn Bennion, lived on the ranch year-
round. Wry, ribald, and widely read, Glynn became for me a study
in the spirit of homesteading, for even as he grew old he refused to
retreat to the city where his lovely and gracious wife, Lucille, lived.

Althea and I first saw Ingmar Bergman's movie *The Seventh
Seal* during fall quarter 1959. We went back to see it several times
before it left Provo. In time it would become our most-viewed
movie ever. I was prepared by a seminar in medieval literature that
I was taking to appreciate Bergman's allegory of a Swedish knight
who plays chess with the black-robed figure of Death. The knight's
haunted search for evidence of God, carried on amid his running
game of chess with Death, seemed close to my own.

Early autumn of 1959 was beautiful—frosty nights, sunny days,
mountainsides ablaze with scarlet and yellow. Setting aside the
scruples against killing I had acquired from Albert Schweitzer, I
made plans for hunting deer. With a revived affection, I oiled and
polished my rifle and fondled a host of gleaming brass cartridges. I
recruited Althea, my nephews Woody (Elwood) and Dwain, and
Woody's bride, Beth Bunnell, for a hunt in Pole Canyon, where I
had shot three deer during my early college years. Before dawn on
opening day we clambered up a narrow defile in a side canyon and

took positions on knobs and ridges. Again I rejoiced in the re-
sounding gunfire at dawn and, with running deer in my sights, experienced again an irrepressible bloodlust. In its wake, I again
experienced regret and disgust as I set about the bloody business of
gutting the fallen game.

We dragged the four does we had shot to the bottom of the canyon and loaded them into our car. The next evening Woody and
Beth came to our apartment, and we skinned the carcasses, split
them with a wood saw, and cut the meat from the bones. With
much hilarity, we worked till two in the morning, wrapping roasts,
steaks, chops, and hand-ground burger in freezer paper and writing
whimsical names on the outside to identify contents. The next day
we deposited the packaged meat in a rented cold storage locker. Althea and I had many other sociable exchanges that year with Woody
and Beth, with whom we played Rook almost very weekend.

During winter quarter 1960, I took a course in American transcendentalism from Marden Clark, who generated excellent class
discussions. I wrote a paper on the correspondence between ideas
and objects in Emerson's thought; for Emerson, an analogy—the
mind's recognition of a similarity between two objects—was evidence of an actual rather than a merely abstract connection. I wrote
another paper on *Walden,* pointing out Christian-like touches of
guilt and gloom in Thoreau's generally optimistic narrative. I
longed for something to worship, and the transcendentalists informed me that nature was eminently worthy of my worship. Rip-
ened by now to a complete disbelief in Christianity, I was willing to
test whether Emerson and Thoreau might not, after all, offer something real to me. One Sunday afternoon in February Althea and I
took a drive up the right fork of Hobble Creek Canyon near Spring-
ville. Sun glistened on the snowy woods and fields that lined the
road, offering a cheerful relief from the prevailing gloom of the
Utah winter.

Fresh from reading the transcendentalists, I was in a mood to
accept their premises. Near a farm, however, we encountered a
contradictory sight. A dog came limping down the middle of the
pavement before us, forcing us to stop and let it pass. It dragged
one of its front paws, which made, as I realized after I had rolled
down a window, an eerie clicking sound. With horror I realized the

paw had been stripped of its flesh some time ago, probably by a trap, exposing to view now blackened, jointed bones two or three inches long. With this I realized that transcendentalism took far too little recognition of evil. Evil for Emerson was privative, that is, it was simply the absence of good. For Thoreau, death was benign because new life feeds upon life that has died. Like Ahab, I was no transcendentalist. I could not be reconciled to death nor to its precursors, suffering and debilitation.

In general weekends were hard for me to get through. On school days, teaching, class attendance, study, and paper grading helped keep up my spirits. I went on with a weekly therapy session with Burton Robinson off campus. Two afternoons of each week I also met on campus with a free student therapy group that Robinson had organized. During one of these sessions, a young man whose depression kept him in bed two and three days at a time suggested that he and I go to the gymnasium and work out our frustrations by boxing. I told him boxing would bring me no relief. He taunted me, asking whether I was afraid of him. Rage seized me. He sat across the table from me; I shouted, leaped up, and tilted the table till it threatened to topple on him and those sitting beside him. I sat down trembling and he broke into sobs. During my next private evening session, Robinson probed my anger, which I related to the humiliation I had suffered from bullies in high school. At one point, rage seized me again, and I leaped up and struck the door to Robinson's office with a clenched fist. For a moment terror showed on his face. We did not explore my anger further that evening.

I sympathized with the plight of a gay student in our therapy group, who said that whenever he conceptualized a woman's vagina, he saw teeth in it. Because of him I concluded that homosexuality lies beyond volition and those who possess it are not to be blamed or reviled. I also developed some feeling for a young woman in the group, who, though not remarkably attractive, conveyed a subtle magnetism. One day while she and I conversed outside following our therapy session, I realized I could fall in love with her. As we finished our conversation, I decided to be less forward with her. Thereafter, my attraction subsided. This demonstrates not only my complete distrust of romantic love but, more important, my loyalty toward Althea. Being true to her had become a central part of my conscience.

I couldn't discern romantic love among the emotions that bonded Althea and me. If you had asked me whether I was "in love" with her, I would have said no. Furthermore, I would have said I had reason to believe she wasn't "in love" with me. Yet I would have also said we loved each other. I made a distinction between being in love and loving. I discerned affection, mutual dependence, and a healthy lust in both of us. We liked to be with each other, each feeling comfortable and reassured when the other was present. Our attachment was deep and from all appearances permanent. Although I believed myself unhappy for many reasons, Althea was not one of them. Tranquil, tolerant, and agreeable, she was fundamental, indispensable even, to such happiness as I could admit to. So I say we loved each other in many ways, the multifarious word *love* describing a family of emotions. However, we never spoke of loving each other. Perhaps her reticence derived from mine. Certainly mine was strong. I couldn't tell my mother that I loved her, nor my siblings, nor, as I now saw, my wife. I could write it in letters but not speak it. However, it wasn't a matter that worried me. I trusted that Althea could intuit my feelings from my behavior, just as I intuited hers.

During the winter of 1960 I applied for doctoral programs at seven or eight western universities for the following academic year. I received offers for a teaching assistantship at the University of Utah and the University of Washington and for a fellowship at the University of California at Berkeley. I could not refuse this last offer—a stipend of two thousand dollars allowing full-time study and a waiver of out-of-state fees. I was especially attracted to Berkeley because my father had studied anthropology there almost sixty years before.

My graduation with a master's degree in June was a happy triumph. Attending were Althea, Stella and Arvid, Leon and Gussie, and Mother. The next day Roald came from Ogden, where he and Luana were visiting her father, and he took me to a sporting goods store in Provo and bought me a Colt frontier-style .22 revolver, my first and only handgun, which I soon learned was not an accurate shooting instrument. That afternoon Althea and I loaded our camping gear into our car and joined Charles and Leon and their wives at Scofield Reservoir near Soldier Summit. Chunky twelve- and thirteen-inch rainbow trout responded eagerly to our bait and, toward evening, to flies trailed behind casting bubbles. That night we made an impromptu camp in a grove of aspens a mile or two up the canyon from the reservoir. Overhead glowed a benign, star-studded sky.

Because a doctorate in English from Berkeley required two modern languages and one classical language, I enrolled in German and Latin at BYU for the summer of 1960. I studied hard and scored at the top of my classes. In early September Althea and I loaded our belongings into our automobile and a rented U-Haul trailer and drove to California. On our first night, we set up our cots beside the highway in eastern Nevada and went to sleep. We were awakened at dawn by a car rolling to a quiet stop on the other side of our car. Two men got out and walked around the end of our trailer. It seemed an ominous moment, yet I could not bring myself to reach for the revolver under my pillow. As it turned out, they had run out of gas and coasted to a stop by our car, wanting to ride with us to the next town.

We stayed for a few days with my nephew Marion Hansen Jr. and his wife, Maline, near San Jose while we hunted for an apartment in Berkeley. Rent seemed high in Berkeley. We finally found a studio apartment for seventy-five dollars a month at 2813 Shattuck Boulevard. Marion and I spent a pleasant Saturday attempting to quiet the knocking engine rods in my Chevy, practicing, as I now judge, amateur auto repair of the rankest sort. We removed the oil pan, filed the rod caps, positioned shims between them, and bolted them back together. We started the engine and it seemed to run fine. The next day Althea and I headed for Berkeley. When we had barely got onto the freeway, the engine rattled horribly and froze tight. That was the end of the black Chevy. A member of Marion's ward sold us an old Plymouth for seventy-five dollars, assuring us it used only a little oil. On our first drive to Berkeley, the Plymouth burned more than two quarts. We parked it at our apartment and got along without a car for a while. We eventually paid a salvage yard ten dollars to tow it away.

I registered for lecture courses in Chaucer and Shakespeare and for a crash course in Ph.D. German. I was pleased to make an A in the Chaucer course, conducted by a brilliant lecturer, Charles Muscatine. I had no such luck with the Shakespeare course, where I spent enormous time preparing exams and papers and still drew a B. I also passed my reading exams in both French and German. Althea found a secretarial job on campus with the Department and Museum of Paleontology. I often dropped by her office and found a fascinating litter of fossils and artifacts in nearby halls and rooms. Althea disliked her job intensely, being pulled between two female supervisors with blurred lines of authority. Our apartment was a mile from campus, a distance we easily walked or, more often, rode on our bicycles. The campus was a pleasant place with large dignified buildings of brick and stone, wide curving walks, and towering redwood trees. I was assigned a carrel in the stacks of the main library and spent much of my time there.

I got into an evening therapy group at a private clinic under the direction of an undistinguished psychologist whose name I have forgotten. None of the other members of the group were Mormon, but their miseries were familiar enough. I had my church membership records moved to a ward in Berkeley and accepted positions as leader of the Explorer Scouts and teacher of a Sunday-school class of teenagers. Familiar Mormon practices irritated me much less here than they had in Utah. Althea rarely went to church with me. She said going to any church made her feel guilty. She liked me to say a blessing on our food before we ate. I asked her why. She said because it didn't hurt to express gratitude for life and well-being. This is a practice we have followed all our married lives, an exception, obviously, to my earlier assertion that I had stopped praying. I continued to wear the underwear with sacred marks required of those who have had their endowment in a temple, another practice I have followed to the latest moment. I am not sure why. At any rate, Althea has never objected.

I soon acquired a distaste for California that I have never overcome in all the years since. I felt oppressed by the congestion. Only rarely in that temperate but rainy climate did we see a liberating expanse of blue sky. On such sunny days as there were, we saw, from the balcony of our apartment, the blue sparkling bay and the gleaming buildings of San Francisco. The cityscape seemed to go on interminably. If we were willing to cross the Bay Bridge, make our way through San Francisco, and cross the Golden Gate Bridge, as we sometimes did on a Sunday afternoon, we could find a public beach that was not crowded with people. We clambered down a steep trail to a boulder-studded coast and looked out upon an angry surf. Here I recognized the wild and for some little time forgot the congestion that lay behind me.

At Thanksgiving Althea and I bought a new cherry-red Volkswagen Beetle for a little less than seventeen hundred dollars, a sum borrowed from the university credit union, to which Althea belonged. Within a few hours of taking possession of the vehicle, we headed south to Lakewood for the holiday. Looking over the snub nose of our Beetle's front-situated trunk, we felt as if we were perched on the very road. The vehicle steered easily, and its four-cylinder, air-cooled engine made thirty miles to the gallon. It slowed dramatically on hills, making us wonder at first whether there was something wrong with it. At Lakewood we played Hearts at night with Arvid and Stella, who were cagey players. Stella and I went fishing at a public wharf in Long Beach, where no license was required, and filled a large bucket with what she called rock cod. I caught a sixteen-inch flounder, whose eyes had already migrated to its flat, gray upper side. I tried to pry open its mouth with my thumb, as I had learned to do with trout, in order to extract the hook. The result was a bloody rim of teeth marks on my thumb.

We visited both Lakewood and Snowflake during the Christmas vacation. After returning to Berkeley, I wrote the first draft of the story published many years later as "Road to Damascus." In this story a non-Mormon husband is shown in the process of a painful conversion to his wife's faith through a series of encounters with ghostlike visionary figures. I had been reading Chaucer and, impressed by his use of allegory, conceived of these visionary figures as allegorical symbolizations of the internal psychic forces that might lead to a resistant husband's conversion. In Snowflake at Christmas I had learned of the conversion of a cousin's husband, and I had begun to consider the psychology of conversion. I wrote this early draft in something of an ecstatic amplification of Faulkner's style, which I would later judge to be, if compelling and grand for Faulkner, a matter of sheer affectation for me. Ambitiously, I sent the story to *Atlantic,* whose editors rejected it with this comment, "You write with a facility which has held our attention."

I enrolled for spring semester 1961 in a seminar in nineteenth-century American literature from James D. Hart, author of the *Oxford Companion to American Literature*. This was one of the most bracing educational experiences of my life. Hart said it was his intent to have precisely ten students in the seminar. Twelve were enrolled. He asked which of us had not yet passed at least one of our required foreign languages. Two raised their hands and were dismissed. My first assignment was to research the background of an unpublished letter by William Cullen Bryant regarding the construction of his house. Among the abundant resources of the university library I found myself entirely absorbed by this seemingly trivial task. A second, much more extensive assignment was to explicate Melville's novel *Redburn* in terms of the economic, social, and literary forces of the decade in which it had been published. Again the resources of the library made this an intriguing task. I went without much sleep for three nights in a row in order to draft my fifty-page paper. Throughout the last night, Althea typed final pages on her portable typewriter as I revised them in ink from the rough draft. At dawn we had an hour's sleep before we went to campus. My grade in the seminar was an A.

My adviser at Berkeley was Ian Watt, an Englishman and author of a prestigious study of the beginnings of the English novel in the eighteenth century. I met with Watt three or four times in his office while he gulped a piece of stale pie for lunch. My Mormon background did not impress him. "I'm not sure you know enough about suffering to do well in our doctoral program," he told me on one visit. It seemed useless to tell him I knew a good deal about suffering.

Watt urged me to proceed with the requirement that students with a master's degree from elsewhere take that department's master's examination. Transfer students were notorious for putting off this exam, and advisers were under pressure to hasten us forward. I obediently scheduled myself for an exam around the first of March. Watt, thinking to be helpful, warned me not to neglect the Scottish Chaucerians in my preparation. So I duly read up on that minor school of late-medieval poets.

I was examined for about an hour by three senior English professors. I candidly replied, "I don't know," to many of their questions. Nonetheless, I was not prepared to be called back into their presence after the exam and informed that I had failed. The purpose of the exam had been to see, first, whether I had read widely and, second, whether I could reason upon what I had read. My scant attainments in the first, one of the professors said, made it impossible to assess the second. All seemed astonished that I had presented myself for the exam. One of them called it "reckless." The Scottish Chaucerians had not been mentioned. Even if they had been, they would not have begun to salvage the exam for me.

On the day after the exam I sought out a group of teaching assistants in an office they shared in common. They heard my story and shook their heads. "You don't try the master's exam until you are almost ready for your doctoral prelims," one of them told me. Others described the biases and favorite questions of the very professors who had examined me. These students had, as I saw, an extensive, carefully marshaled lore regarding the comprehensive exams at both the master's and the doctoral levels. I felt isolated, foolish, and cheated.

The question now was whether I should prepare to take the exam again, as I was permitted to do, or transfer to the University of Utah. There is no question that failing the exam had undermined my confidence. Furthermore, I doubted that my grades, equally proportioned between A and B, were high enough for renewing my fellowship. During the Easter break, Althea and I drove to Utah to explore the possibility of transferring. We retraced the route of our September migration through Nevada, crossing an endless succession of north- and south-running ranges of desert mountains and their intervening valleys. I reveled in the wild, open country, being particularly touched near the end of our journey by the sight of Mount Nebo, the southernmost peak of the Wasatch Range and one of the most imposing. I described the day in a letter to Roald:

> A recent snow storm had topped all the mountains with snow. The day hovered white and blue—the white mountains in all directions, continuously arising, one after another, the broad grey, sage-brush valleys, and the blue, blue sky. And in the moonlight night in Utah, driving down off the mountain from

Eureka I suddenly saw old Nebo, vast, white, and brooding in the half darkness....It was a comfort to me and a coming-home to see Nebo.[2]

Arriving in Provo at midnight, we could not rouse Woody and Beth by knocking and had to enter their unlocked door and make our way to their bedroom. We stayed this and the next night with them in their squalid basement apartment. They were living on a tight budget. Both mornings we shared pancakes made with a single egg, a frugality that Woody highly recommended. On the first day, a Thursday, we visited BYU and the University of Utah. The next day we attended something of a family reunion in Price, where Charles, now a history instructor at Carbon Junior College, had moved with his family. Leon and Gussie also arrived from Arizona with Mother and our sister Mary. On Saturday we had a picnic at the Wedge on the San Rafael Swell. It was my first view of the gorges, cliffs, and slickrock expanses of that country. On Saturday night, as I wrote Roald in the letter cited above, we had a long discussion "of culture and provincialism, most of us agreeing, Charles rather vehemently, that we were really a provincial family. We find more comfort in the old way of life, a way admittedly local and narrow, than in an espousal of sophisticated or cultural living." On Sunday morning, after a breakfast of Scofield trout from Betty's freezer, Althea and I departed for Berkeley, where we arrived some nineteen hours later.

Within a week or two, I was informing family and friends of our decision to transfer to the University of Utah. The decision was based not only on the negative matter of the failed examination but also on the positive matter of a renewed appreciation for Utah. Old Nebo in the moonlight had worked its charm. Our trip to Utah had confirmed for both Althea and me that we had bonded with its farms, pastures, and ranges; its deserts, plains, plateaus, and canyons; its sage, juniper, and pines; its fish and wildlife. Ever since then, both of us have felt that Utah is home.

There were things besides my classes to be finished before we left California. I now completed research into my father's connection with the University of California. Believing my father a man of extraordinary stature, I had decided to write a biography of him.

I was pleased to apply the techniques of historical research that I had mastered in Hart's seminar to a topic so close to my own feelings. My father had enrolled at the University of California in 1903 and 1904, returning to Arizona in the fall of 1904 for reasons of health. The registrar's office allowed me to copy his registration documents and grade reports, and the Lowrie Museum of Anthropology allowed me to copy his letters to A. L. Kroeber, founder of the university's Anthropology Department, and to inspect the Indian skeletons and artifacts that my father had excavated in Arizona and shipped to Berkeley under Kroeber's direction. I felt my father's presence while I viewed the bones, pottery, grinding stones, axes, and spearheads he had collected, then felt keenly this irony, that the man who had retrieved these artifacts from the obscurity of the ground was himself a fit subject for archaeological study, having now moldered in the ground for close to eighteen years.

For all our eagerness to depart Berkeley, Althea and I felt nostalgia for a few good friends and regret for a few things left undone in San Francisco. Though we had attended a production of Archibald MacLeish's new play, *J. B.,* we had put off attending the symphony and opera, thinking we had time. Ironically we had made time to visit a strip joint with friends, a smokey little tavern where aging women did their bump and grind while young marines pounded beer mugs on the tables. My fascination with the dancers' jostling breasts was quickly replaced by pity for their seeming fatigue and utter indifference to what was going on among their audience.

After school was out in June I took four of my Explorer Scouts on a backpack trip in Yosemite. We had prepared for this by constructing our own pack frames from thin strips of oak and canvas straps from a war surplus store. We camped a couple of nights in a campground crowded "at the rate of one camp—two to twelve people—to every rod," as I said in a letter. During the day I took the boys to Glacier Point, where we saw a panorama of the Yosemite Valley, and later hiked with them to the Nevada and Vernal Falls on the Merced, where we viewed "cascades of pure white water tumbling and spraying and spewing for hundreds of feet down the sheer cliffs."[3] On the third day, we broke camp, drove to Tuolumne Meadows, donned our backpacks, and trudged six miles down the Tuolumne River to a little canyon nook called Glen Aulen.

After we had eaten a sparse supper cooked over a smokey pitch-pine fire, one of the boys looked around and wished, most ardently, that we were back in the public camp grounds where there were girls. At dawn, after a cold and uncomfortable night on the ground, I climbed a gigantic slickrock slope with one of the boys and looked over the country.

> To our right was a tremendous amphitheater of solid granite which had been carved into a concave shape by an ancient glacier, as we could tell by the deposits of glacial boulders all around and by the polished surface of the rock mass. I measured the length of this concave piece of rock and found it to be 360 yards from bottom (where the Tuolomne River roared) to its top. It was about the same distance in width. Everywhere the gray granite protrudes in that country, and in the distance I could see mysterious juttings of high Sierra peaks—a beautiful sight. I was satisfied we had come to Glen Aulen.[4]

This was my initiation into backpacking, a sport that admittedly involves a great deal of hardship and little of what is called entertainment. I had seen photos of backpackers in magazines and felt an instinctive attraction to the idea of entering the wild with an entire sustenance on my back. Nor was I disillusioned by this first experience.

Around the first of July Althea and I shipped our books by parcel post to Charles and Betty in Price; loaded the trunk, back seat, and top rack of our Volkswagen with our remaining effects (including two bicycles and a broom); and drove to Long Beach for a two-week visit with Althea's parents. This would be our last visit to Lakewood. Althea's father had decided to retire at the astonishing age of seventy-four, and he and Stella were making plans to sell their house and return to Arvid's hometown of Stanton, Iowa. Stella and I went fishing from a pier in Long Beach almost every day. It was by this pier that I saw, in a vending box, a newspaper announcing the suicide of Hemingway by means of a shotgun. "Did you see today," I wrote Leon, "that old Ernest Hemingway went down the dark river? Shotguns frighten me."[5]

In mid-July Althea and I drove on to Price where, at Charles and Betty's house, a heroic safari assembled. Charles had persuaded a number of his relatives to drive cross-country to Maine, where Roald was stationed at Loring Air Force Base. Charles and Betty would make this a part of their annual summer trek to visit Betty's parents in Delaware. The company of fifteen included Charles and Betty and their four children in a Chevrolet sedan; Leon and Gussie and their two children in a Volkswagen Beetle; Althea, my sister Lenora, her son, and I in our Beetle; and Mother, who rode in each car every third day. We camped along the way, finding a motel room for Mother every third night so that she could care for her colostomy in a bathroom. Our route to Maine passed through Wyoming, Montana, North Dakota, Minnesota, Wisconsin, Michigan, Ontario, and Quebec. Returning, we crossed Ohio, Indiana, Illinois, Iowa, Nebraska, and Colorado.

In Maine Roald educated us further in the realities of the cold war. Through a chain-link fence we saw rows of giant, droop-winged B-52 bombers. Armed with nuclear bombs, some of these were in the air at all times, ready to turn toward the Soviet Union at a moment's notice. When our brief visit was over, Charles and Betty left for Delaware while the rest of us toured the upper East. We took in the Book of Mormon pageant at Palmyra, New York. A vast crowd, seated on folding chairs, viewed this impressive dramatization of the final wars between the Lamanites and Nephites and the recovery of the Golden Plates by Joseph Smith. Before following the other members of our party from the parking lot to the pageant site, I made my way into the thick, briary woods and defecated, burying my feces in the boggy ground by means of a folding camp shovel. I did this because I was not certain sanitary accommodations would be provided at the pageant site. When I arrived there, I saw, to my great mortification, banks of commodious, clean, brightly lit restrooms. Again I had demonstrated my ability to act on unintelligent premises.

The next morning, a Sunday, we attended a testimony meeting in the Sacred Grove, where Joseph Smith said God the Father and God the Son had first appeared to him. The trees were tall with bare trunks and leafy tops. Shafts of sunlight came through the shade. A hushed reverence rested upon those around me. I could not help sharing it, and I saw a glimmering of why I, a disbeliever, could not abandon Mormonism.

Driving on, we saw the House of the Seven Gables in Salem, clambered over the decks of the USS *Constitution* in Boston Harbor, and visited Longfellow's house in Cambridge. We drove to Concord, inspected the bridge where testy colonists had started the Revolution, and visited Walden Pond, which by western standards was no pond at all, but a lake. In New York City, we rented hotel rooms for two nights at a price amounting to about a third of the cost of the entire trip for Althea and me. The grim, littered streets of this city struck me as the essence of ugly. We went to a play and visited the Metropolitan Museum of Art. Rejoining Charles and Betty at the home of Betty's parents, we visited Betty's favorite beach on the Atlantic. The gray ocean rolled in with a solemn, relentless surf beneath a generally cloudy sky. I would remember this scene upon reading Steven Crane's "Open Boat," where the gray Atlantic symbolizes the indifference of nature to human desire.

Within a day or two, we drove on to Washington, D.C., where we sat in the gallery of the Senate and toured the Smithsonian. Returning cross-country, we paused in Stanton, Iowa, to visit Althea's parents, who were staying there while trying to decide where to buy a house or condominium. Stanton, the Swedish farming community where Althea had passed the first six years of her life, seemed a sleepy place. Vegetable gardens grew in backyards, and lawns had a shaggy, untrimmed look. A large white frame Lutheran church with a spire stood on the town's most prominent hill. Arvid and Stella and their friends gathered around our caravan and were regaled by Charles's and Leon's good-natured joshing. The day was humid and hot. Local lore had it that at night in such weather you could hear the crackling and popping of the growing corn.

Later that day we paused at the Mormon immigrant cemetery at Florence, Nebraska, near Omaha, where we saw the names of some of our ancestors inscribed on a monument dedicated to Mormon pioneers who had died in the encampments on the Iowa and eastern Nebraska prairies. Among the names was Polly Haynes, my mother's great-grandmother. Weeping, my mother recounted Polly's life. My mother believed she had a calling to preserve, enlarge, and pass on family history. In 1961 she had only recently retired from teaching and had devoted herself to genealogical research. Thanks to her, I was intimately aware that in our return journey across the United States we retraced an ancestral path.

We separated in the Rocky Mountains of Colorado, Charles and Betty and their children going on home to Price while the rest of us drove to Snowflake. It was a sad separation. There had been tensions, especially between some of the children. But overall, our love for each other had been cemented even more firmly by our epic, never-to-be-repeated journey. Althea and I stayed with Mother for a week before driving to Utah. I asked at the high school for records about my father and was delighted to receive original manuscripts of some of his pageants. Althea and I visited Lakeside and took a photo of the ranch house, which was destined to burn before we would return. I was happy throughout the week yet troubled by a shift in my loyalties. Home was no longer here. My future lay in Utah, and I was eager to get on with it.

··· 13

A Grasshopper's Way of Life

IN SEPTEMBER 1961 ALTHEA AND I RENTED a small house in Salt Lake City, which we furnished with furniture lent us by Althea's parents. I enrolled in graduate courses at the University of Utah and was unexpectedly hired to teach a section of Freshman English. Althea secured a job as the secretary of an economics research office on campus. She began immediately to make plans to pursue a master's degree in English. After Christmas we moved into Stadium Village, on-campus housing for married students in converted military barracks. Rent was forty-three dollars a month, water and heat included. Our Volkswagen was paid for and ran a long way on a tank of gasoline, which cost about twenty-five cents a gallon. All told, we lived very inexpensively.

My mother lived in Salt Lake during that winter, doing genealogical research. In the spring she went home to raise a garden. Around Thanksgiving, Althea's parents gave up their plans to relocate in Stanton, Iowa, and moved to Salt Lake. My mother invited us to dinner each week, and so did Althea's mother. We took them on rides and phoned them often.

For a doctorate, I was required to complete forty quarter hours of course work and afterward take a comprehensive examination and write a dissertation. I hoped I could do this within two years. I took four. The examination was called a preliminary examination (or prelims, for short) from the fact that students were not considered candidates for the Ph.D. till they had passed it. I was determined to be prepared for this exam as I had not been for the master's exam at Berkeley. From my first day on campus, I began to ask questions about it.

My instructor in the eighteenth-century novel during fall quarter was the frail, aging Edward Chapman, who had the habit of closing his eyes and rolling his eyeballs upward while lecturing. Sometimes he opened his eyes and stared fixedly at a corner of the ceiling. He rarely glanced at his notes, which, reputedly, he had not changed in many years. Nonetheless, I found his lectures highly informative, and I took abundant notes on them. When he underwent emergency surgery during the following quarter, I contributed a pint of blood, for which I received a note of such heartfelt gratitude that I was ashamed of all the times I had joined other students in deriding his mannerisms.

I took a course on the Victorian poet Gerard Manley Hopkins from Brewster Ghiselin, himself a poet of considerable reputation. Everybody mentioned that he had known D. H. Lawrence personally. Ghiselin was unimpressed by my interpretation of Hopkins and gave me a B in the course. I judge myself to have learned far more than my grade reflected. I was fascinated by the sheer musicality of Hopkins's verse, whose complexities forced me into a study of prosody. What I learned of my own initiative about imagery, metaphor, alliteration, meter, and so on would prove invaluable in my career as a teacher.

While studying or grading papers at my desk, I ate an abstemious lunch of baking powder biscuits left over from breakfast, yellow cheese, and runty apples, which Althea and I bought by the bushel from roadside stands. I left one of these apples on my desk for many months. When it became dark and shriveled, I told the other graduate assistants that it was a memento mori, a reminder of death that kept me from becoming excessively attached to things of this world. Once they took note of the apple, keeping it became a point of obstinacy with me. Who can explain why I had kept it to that point? I do recall developing something of an affection for it.

It was easy to make friends—very different from Berkeley where the few students with whom Althea and I fraternized had been known to us at BYU. One morning a ruddy-faced, red-haired student from Chapman's class hailed me as I walked toward the union building. This was George Leonard Bird, called Red, one of the most amiable and gregarious human beings who ever lived. Red and his wife, Barbara, and son, David, resided in housing for married students built off campus. David had a gerbil that bit me when I foolishly stuck a finger into its cage. At a Saturday-night party at Red's apartment I met Candadai Seshachari, a small, bald, utterly affable Hindu who had recently passed his prelims. Eager for clues as to my own future experience, I queried Sesh closely while he squatted against a wall nursing a beer in the half-darkened room. I had no idea that eight years later Sesh would return from India as my colleague at Weber State College, where he would become one of my dearest and most loyal friends.

Althea and I took Mother to Snowflake for Christmas. We found my niece Gale and her children visiting her parents, Marion and Lenora. One bright, frosty morning we went ice skating on a cow watering tank in the junipers. Marion, the only one with skates, pulled children on a wide-pan scoop shovel. Althea and I conversed casually with Gale while we watched. Gale and I had shared a fervent intimacy when we were little children. I have often regretted the mere cordiality into which we grew from our teen years forward. By way of being pleasant I asked her on that frosty morning by the watering tank whether she intended someday to move back home to Snowflake. She said very quietly, "Solomon is my home now." While Althea and I were at Berkeley, Gale's eldest son, a boy of six or seven, had died from burns suffered when spilled tile cement had exploded in their house. I thought now of the boy buried in Solomon, a farming community in southern Arizona, and knew why she no longer thought of Snowflake as her home. I felt renewed in that fervent intimacy we had shared as children.

Throughout most of my first year at the University of Utah I considered myself happy. I thought it possible that my three years of therapy with Burton Robinson had cured me of the pathological emotions that had afflicted me in the past. However, near the end of spring quarter 1962, those pathological emotions returned in full force. One morning in the library an eccentrically dressed man seated himself opposite me at a study table and solemnly opened a folded seat pad from an automobile as if it were a briefcase and extracted scraps of paper, which he scrutinized from all angles, including upside down. He struck me as going through the motions of study as a little child might have. With this display of what I considered psychosis, I was suddenly overwhelmed by the all too familiar surge of terror and almost uncontrollable impulse to run. For a day or two I hoped my hysterical mood would dissipate, but it didn't. As before, despair and grief accompanied the anxiety. The two sections of Freshman English I was teaching seemed to relieve rather than heighten my anxiety. My anxiety was most acute while I sat in my graduate courses. I recall an informative lecture by Harold Folland in a course on the late Victorian novel. It seemed to require an enormous energy not to bolt from my seat and dash from the room. Between surges of anxiety I went on taking notes as best I could.

I soon sought out the university counseling service, where I was offered, without charge, either two therapy sessions a week with an intern or one session a week with a psychiatrist. It says something of my emotional disorder that I chose frequency of contact with the intern over the advanced training of the psychiatrist. The intern was an unmarried woman of about thirty-five named Helen Ratcliff. She wore suits and spoke with cautious circumspection, and our relationship remained formal. I never called her anything except Miss Ratcliff. Though I felt my dependency on her to be demeaning, I continued in therapy with her till the end of my stay at the University of Utah. I doubt I could have finished my doctorate without the support I drew from her. I recognize with gratitude that individuals and institutions made many contributions to my education that I did not earn or pay for. Miss Ratcliff's services rank high among these.

Like Robinson, Miss Ratcliff concentrated on my relationship with my mother. She said my current breakdown had likely been triggered by my mother's leaving Salt Lake for the summer. That wasn't a helpful idea at this moment. I could see no pattern in the initial circumstances of the breakdowns I had suffered over the past eight years. I could admit a childlike dependency on Miss Ratcliff. I couldn't see any such dependency on my mother.

I grieved for my mother, that was certain. I grieved because she had lost my brother Alma, who died five years before I was born. I grieved because she had lost me, who had grown up and gone away. Sometimes I felt as if there had been no difference between Alma and me in my mother's feelings. Sometimes I wondered whether, even as she had suckled me, she had regarded me as a tiny cadaver in her arms, dead and perpetually mourned. When I first had that insight I was excited. I thought it might be the Big One, the insight into a trauma or devastating experience that would heal me quickly and completely. It wasn't. My unhappiness was a jig-saw puzzle of many pieces. My mother's grief over the death of Alma was one of those pieces. I couldn't tell how big and intricate a piece it might prove to be.

I didn't take or teach classes during the summer of 1962. Instead, I planned to read extensively in preparation for my prelims, which were always in my thoughts. Immobilized by anxiety and depression, I did very little reading. My accomplishments that summer were more along the line of vagabonding, or, as I would later term it, grasshoppering. Althea and I went fishing, explored back roads, visited family and friends, and initiated ourselves into serious backpacking. Most notably, we made our first excursions into the interior of the Uintas, whose bare rocky crest, terraced basins, tumbling streams, placid lakes, and solemn pine forests we quickly learned to cherish.

Our backpacking gear was of mixed quality. We ordered expensive down sleeping bags from Eddie Bauer; these were not mummy bags but had tapered bottoms. We bought a cheap tent with wood poles and no floor, flimsy plastic air mattresses that often deflated during the night, and leaky ponchos from a war surplus store. We had no stove. Instead, I carried our light Hudson's Bay ax and built fires, both for cooking and for keeping us company at night. Nowadays low-impact backpacking prohibits campfires. You have to crawl into your sleeping bag and tent early just to keep warm. But in those days our campfires gave us an evening. The glowing coals opened interior vistas of thought. From time to time we turned away from the fire, accustomed our eyes to the dark, and viewed the vast arch of the sky crowded with brilliant stars.

I will not pretend backpacking was an unmitigated pleasure. It required almost more tolerance for discomfort than I had to give. From the start it seemed an endurance test of aching shoulders, unpalatable food, sleepless nights, and altitude headaches to be countered by quantities of Anacin. If it hadn't been for the good fishing I doubt we would have done much backpacking. After watching my success on a trip or two, Althea bought a spinning outfit and began to fish. During the day, with sun on the water, we fished with worms; at evening we trailed a fly behind a casting bubble across a tranquil surface dimpled by rising trout. We fished for food as well as sport, releasing only the fish too small to eat. We caught brook and cutthroat trout, less often rainbow trout. Once, at a very high lake, we caught several arctic grayling. Many Uinta lakes had no fish in them in primitive times and were first stocked by canisters of fingerlings transported by packhorse. That summer of 1962 we saw a low-flying airplane release a shower of tiny fish into a lake. Technically, you domesticate a lake when you stock it with fish. Some people favor returning the Uinta lakes to their fishless pristine condition. As for me, I would *feel* a Uinta lake to be less wild without fish.

Our companions in the Uintas during the summer of 1962 were Robert and Francine Bennion. Francine, a gifted pianist and a college dormmate of Althea, was gracious and cultivated. Bob was amiable and well stocked with anecdotes from his ranching youth. An assistant professor of psychology at BYU, he was a brother to George Bennion, whose hay ranch in the west desert Althea and I continued to visit. I had much in common with Bob, including an acquaintance with northeastern Arizona, where he had served a mission. Unfortunately, I felt myself to be on an unequal footing with him because of his status as a clinical psychologist. Understandably, Bob liked to talk about the psychology of maladjustment, which was, however, a topic that made me anxious, particularly when he discussed the problems confronting persons of same-sex attraction. From puberty on, I had feared that I might find homosexual impulses in myself, often wondering whether the antipathy I felt toward physical contact with males was only a facade. What if, down deep, I was repressing my true nature?

In early September Althea and I backpacked with Bob in Glacier National Park while Francine, newly pregnant, visited her parents in nearby Lethbridge, Alberta. We were struck by a blizzard in the middle of the night some eight or ten miles from a trailhead. Of necessity, Bob, who carried no shelter, crowded into our tiny tent, and in a state of sleepless anxiety I lay tightly wedged between him and Althea for the rest of the night. My anxiety, focused on this enforced proximity to a male, now struck me as evidence of an evasion. Could it be true that I suffered from a latent homosexuality? Oddly, something like a hysterical ecstasy accompanied this thought. Maybe this was the Big One, the grand and mysterious key to my puzzling pathology. Maybe if I confronted a tendency toward homosexuality bravely, I would be healed of my chronic anxiety and depression.

For some weeks I attempted to peer behind the aversion I felt toward genital contact with men to see whether there was an attraction as well, my distrust of my own psyche being such that I was unwilling to categorically dismiss the possibility. In the meantime, Miss Ratcliff said she could see no evidence I was gay. I continued to make love to my wife every night and to enjoy the sight of a shapely female body wherever I met one. At last, with a busy fall schedule of graduate courses and two sections of Freshman English to instruct, I simply forgot to worry about the matter.

In retrospect, I attribute much of my anxiety to Bob's status as a clinical psychologist, which made him one on whom I wanted to depend, as a child depends on a parent. But he accepted me as a full peer, sharing his views on psychology as a colleague, not as a therapist, and that, as I would later come to understand, engaged my pathology. I will add that Bob and Francine remain our close friends these forty years later.

During this period Althea and I have acquired many homosexual friends, whose experiences have reinforced our belief that sexual orientation is not a matter of choice but a given of nature. As for my anxiety regarding my own sexuality, I discern a similar anxiety in many men of heterosexual orientation. It appears to afflict women as well. It is, I judge, the root of homophobia, which results, in its least-injurious form, in repressive laws and, in its most injurious, in brutal violence. Those who repress and injure persons of same-sex attraction in the name of morality practice a perversion of morality. Like racial prejudice, the fear of homosexuality is an uncivilized impulse to be reined in and mitigated by humane values.

At the beginning of fall quarter Althea quit her job as secretary and began studies leading to a master's degree in English. We paid tuition, rent, groceries, and incidental costs quite comfortably from my modest stipend as a graduate assistant. Like other Americans, we followed the Cuban missile crisis anxiously in December 1962. When the crisis was over, Roald wrote about waiting for orders to fly his B-52 bomber toward a Soviet target. While on alert, he made me a Christmas gift of a wide leather belt embossed by coyote tracks. I attached this belt to a large chrome-plated oval buckle decorated with the figure of a bucking horse. For many years I wore this belt through the loops of the Levi's in which I dressed at home or among friends. I had also begun to wear black Wellington boots on all occasions, even when dressed in slacks, coat, and tie for teaching. These boots, I fancied, said something of my western identity.

During my first year at the University of Utah I had decided I would write my dissertation on western American literature. Accordingly, during fall quarter of 1962 I enrolled in a course in the American novel from Don D. Walker, director of the American Studies program and scholar of western literature. Following a pre-conceived plan, I wrote a term paper on Edward Abbey's *Brave Cowboy* and, when Walker gave the paper an A, asked him to chair my dissertation, a proposition to which he agreed.

All through the dreary winter of 1963, while studying in my library carrel or grading papers at my graduate-assistant desk, I re-membered sunny lakes and beckoning trails in the Uintas. Preparing for summer, Althea and I bought open-faced Garcia Mitchell spinning reels, fly rods and reels, materials for making our own metal lures, and a fly-tying outfit. The lures I assembled and painted caught very few fish during the following summer. The flies I tied similarly failed to convince fish—with the exception of a slender-bodied nymph with a short hackle, which proved effective when trailed behind a casting bubble on Uinta lakes. If trailing a fly be-hind a bubble may be called fly-fishing, I have done a great deal of fly-fishing in my day. As for fly-fishing on a stream, I never gave it a proper test. What little I did entangled my leader in overhanging branches, convincing me that I had little instinct for casting.

My mother returned to Salt Lake City for genealogical research during that fall and winter. Near the end of winter, Althea and I took her to visit her brother Parley Savage and his wife, Leone, in Tooele. Parley had a thick, crooked nose, heavy jowls, and a broad, bald pate rimmed by close-cropped hair. Each morning he hacked up lumps of phlegm and spit them into the living room wastebasket. At meals he extracted his false teeth, placed them in his shirt pocket, and gummed his food vigorously. He preferred to spoon potatoes and gravy into his mouth with the flat blade of a table knife. His conversation was not for the impatient. He lumbered circuitously through interminable stories, sometimes asking to be reminded what his original point had been and demonstrating a testy annoyance with anyone who attempted a new line of conversation during one of his lengthy pauses. His favorite topic was the injustice done him and his mother, Nora, by his father and his father's other wife, Adeline. As he remembered it, he had been sent to work in the fields day after day while Adeline's boys played. He remembered that Adeline had a piano while his mother had none, also that she was usually abed from a mysterious ailment, requiring his mother to keep her house and tend her children.

My mother listened uneasily to Parley's grievances. Sometimes, with a pinch on his arm, she declared he had exceeded the truth. Parley admitted that his resentment was less than Christlike. Only lately, he said, had he managed to pray for the power to forgive Adeline. It struck me as tragic that a seventy-five-year-old man was struggling to forgive offenses that had occurred so long ago. I had grown up on my mother's affectionate reminiscences of the mingling of her father's two families. Parley's bitterness was a corrective. I saw that Mormon polygamy had magnified the rivalries and resentments that afflict nonpolygamous households. Although I would not be alive if it were not for Mormon polygamy, it is not an institution that I can respect.

I took three influential courses during spring quarter 1963. One was a seminar in American literary criticism from William Mulder, an urbane and well-informed professor. For my paper I made a survey of the literary criticism of the western—the cowboy novel, as it is often called. Another course was on the writings of Henry Adams, taught by Don Walker. Walker's lectures, delivered in a deep, resonant voice that I never tired of hearing, were well organized and cogent. As in Mulder's course, I turned my paper toward my own interests by studying Adams's attitude toward the American frontier. The third course, informative though unpleasant, was on the history of the trans-Mississippi West. It was taught by the aging and bilious Leland Creer, who had the distinction of being the most insulting, demeaning teacher I have encountered in more than sixty years as a student and teacher. Creer regularly paused during lecture to stare balefully at some hapless student and say scornfully, "I suppose you think you are going to pass this course without studying." One day a girl was clipping her fingernails. He asked her name, found her class card, and tore it up. "Get out," he said. "You are no longer enrolled in this class." He emphasized important points by repeating key words with a rising crescendo of fury as if the failure of earlier students to reproduce these concepts in examinations had convinced him of the indefensible sloth of all students. Very early I saw that his belligerent gaze almost never swung to his far right. Sitting there, near the back of the class, I escaped being a target for his ire.

I took one course and taught another during the summer of 1963. This was a happy summer, for my chronic anxiety had largely disappeared. I considered giving up therapy but did not have the courage to do so. I enjoyed conversations with Charles, who, having decided on a Ph.D. in history, had enrolled in summer school and was sleeping on our sofa weeknights and driving home to Price on weekends. Althea and I backpacked on weekends without other companions. Wearily shouldering my pack at the beginning of each trip, I asked myself again why I did this in the name of recreation. In Naturalist Basin we escaped the Boy Scouts who camped on its lower lakes by toiling up a final steep quarter mile of trail to Morat Lake, where we camped in isolation. A small waterfall tumbled into this lake, and a talus field of boulders from Mount Agassiz formed a third of its shoreline. Fishing from these boulders at noon one day, Althea and I discovered that a worm, towed into place behind a half-filled casting bubble and allowed to sink next to the shadowy crevice of a submerged boulder, often drew out an impulsive trout. It was satisfying to look down on this drama through the noonlit water. From each venture we carried home enough trout for two or three dinners for us and Charles.

One day at Morat we saw a marten, a large weasel-like predator, making a nervous, zigzag path across these boulders in search of pikas. Its intended prey, a small furry relative of the rabbit with rounded ears, sometimes scolded Althea and me with shrill squeaks while we fished along the boulders. On the grassy eastern and southern shores grew columbines, Indian paintbrush, and ground-hugging marsh marigolds. Back from the shoreline stood thickets of lodgepole pine. At night we conversed around the glowing embers of our campfire. At bedtime, I doused the fire with urine and water. Overhead an incredible umbrella of stars winked and glimmered. At dawn, needing to relieve myself, I sauntered through the trees to the edge of the terrace on which Morat lay. I dug a small hole with a plastic trowel, and while I squatted over it, I looked across a twenty-mile expanse of forest encircled by high, barren, rocky ridges. Utterly at peace, I knew the strenuous labor of back-packing was entirely worthwhile. No other activity reminded me so forcefully that, for all the civilized clutter of my mind, in a deep and fundamental sense I belonged to the wild.

My experiences with the wild figured in my search for a dissertation topic. Western literature was about the frontier, and the frontier was where Euro-Americans had met wilderness. In actuality, the people who settled the frontier viewed wilderness as an antagonist whose dangers were to be neutralized and whose wealth was to be plundered. But in literature, which is the domain of myth as well as of history, wilderness could also appear as a benign presence to be cherished for its own sake. Among the values consistently associated with wilderness in fiction, poetry, and oratory was freedom, which meant, as I began to think on the matter, freedom from social restraints. Perhaps it was because I myself felt hedged in by a thousand civilized protocols that I was attracted to the study of freedom and restraint. But as this summer of 1963 came to an end, I was beginning to realize how complicated my topic would prove. Obviously wilderness imposes its own kind of restraint on human beings, and, conversely, civilization offers a kind of freedom not found in the wild.

This insight was reinforced by a working visit to George Bennion's ranch in mid-September. George's hired hand had gone on a drinking binge, and bales of alfalfa sat in the fields. For three days Althea drove a tractor while George and I walked along on either side, throwing the seventy-pound bales onto a trailer. At the stack yard, George threw bales from the trailer onto a motorized escalator, and Althea and I placed the bales on a growing stack. We began soon after dawn and worked till dusk with an hour off for lunch. The sun was hot, and dust and leaves clung to our sweaty skin. Our pay was in friendship rather than money, for, as we knew, George teetered constantly on the edge of insolvency (and in fact eventually lost the ranch to foreclosure).

George's father, Glynn, who lived on the ranch year-round, irrigated the cleared fields with clear, cold water that gushed from a diesel-driven pump. Glynn wore rubber boots, bib overalls, a dark chambray shirt, and a battered narrow-brim Stetson. A grizzled stubble dusted his leathery, sun-browned face. He fed baled hay to seventy Herefords in a feedlot and affectionately scratched their backs. At mealtime he compensated for lonely months on the ranch by holding forth in long, rambling monologues. We took our meals in the one-room shack where he lived. Half his cot was covered with stacks of paperback westerns. On a table sat an unwashed plate with a visible grease ring around its center. He boasted that after each use he wiped the plate clean with a morsel of bread, washing it only after the grease ring grew to its edge. This occurred about four times a year. As for the dirt on the floor, he said that he refused to panic and sweep it out because over the long haul his boots carried out as much as they carried in. While I was at the ranch on an earlier working visit, Glynn took a .30-30 onto the porch of his shack and shot at a group of antelope feeding in a field. "It's a rare freedom," I commented, "to be able to shoot at antelope from your own porch." "Yes," he replied, "and it's also a rare freedom to be able to pee off your porch at night instead of going out back to the privy."

I could understand why Glynn preferred to live on the ranch. I projected readily into its rhythms of watering, baling, and feeding. I valued his freedom from housekeeping and fashionable dress. I valued the stark beauties of the desert—the pastel coloration of dawn and dusk and the clear star-crowded sky of night. But I suffered as well from the tedium of repetitive labor; the loneliness of vast, vacant distances; the monotony of a sparse, drab vegetation; the grim press of summer heat. I wanted a shower, white sheets on my bed, the books in my carrel, more people to talk to. All of this, as I say, was on my mind as I sharpened the focus of my dissertation. I could see that in my examination of western literature I would have to look past the simplistic myth of an all-sufficient freedom in the wild and seek patterns of ambivalence, complexity, and even contradiction arising from the fact that wilderness imposes its own kind of restraint and civilization offers its own kind of freedom.

In October 1963, I passed my minor prelims in American and British history, having devoted fifteen days to full-time preparation. I enrolled in a course on Hawthorne from Kenneth Eble but did not teach any classes because I had been awarded a university research grant of two thousand dollars. Althea, who went on working on a master's degree, supplemented my grant by teaching a section of Freshman English.

On opening day of deer season I hunted on Mount Nebo with Steven Tanner, a mild-mannered undergraduate from Ogden. After we had hunted separately for a while, Steve showed up saying he had wounded a fawn and needed my rifle to finish it off. Later he explained what had happened. After wounding the fawn, he had shoved a new cartridge into the firing chamber of his rifle but found that the bolt would not close on it, which meant that he could neither fire nor extract it. He tried to push the cartridge out by inserting a long, brittle stick down the barrel. As might be expected, the stick broke off in the barrel, leaving Steve with an absurd if not dangerous situation. He later took the rifle to a gunsmith who solved the problem by forcing the bolt to close on the cartridge, something Steve and I could have done had we had the courage.

After passing my prelims in history, I began research on an article on the development of livestock law in territorial Utah. I was persuaded to this digression from preparing for my prelims in English by Don Walker, who had agreed to serve as guest editor of an issue of the *Utah Historical Quarterly* on the history of the cattle trade in early Utah. Walker also recruited articles from two other graduate students who had become my close friends, Neal Lambert and Richard Cracroft. The article I wrote was my first scholarly publication.[1] The pleasure I took in writing on this inherently dull topic shows that I had been transformed into that quaint social type known as the scholar.

In November, near the time of John Kennedy's assassination, Althea and I bought cheap skis, boots, and poles and took up Utah's most famous winter sport. Conventional wisdom in those days dictated long skis; accordingly, the tips of our skis came to the wrist of a raised arm. Such skis were actually more adapted to speed than to carving out christies, as parallel turns were then called. Unable to afford fashionable ski attire, we skied in Levi's. We shared a single ten-ride pass, and when it was used up, we quit for the day. We couldn't afford lessons. For technique we read library books on skiing and sought advice from friends. We quickly lost any hope of acquiring the grace and freedom we admired so much in advanced skiers. Yet skiing was an absorbing activity that erased all other matters from our minds. One day while skiing I pulled my left hand from its mitten and found my wedding band missing. I have never replaced it, not from disaffection from my marriage but from an inherent dislike of jewelry.

My mother's face fell when I told her we had bought skis. She accurately predicted they would lead us to further violations of the Sabbath. Furthermore, they seemed another sign that Althea and I, childless after five years of marriage, would go on evading the duty of parenthood. On the same grounds she objected to my applying for another research grant for the following year. Now in the fourth year beyond my master's degree, I admitted that, had I known my doctoral studies would take so long, I would not have begun them. But at this point Althea and I agreed it would be an enormous waste not to persevere. In the meantime, I made light of our dilatory way of life by calling us grasshoppers in some of my letters— this with reference to the fable in which an industrious ant survives a winter while a frolicking grasshopper perishes. I went on to pretend that the grasshopper's way of life was actually virtuous. "According to the gospel of grasshopperism," I wrote in a family newsletter, "herein is righteousness. For every hour spent on earth at grasshoppering, a millennium shall be returned in the hereafter."[2] However dubiously this doctrine may have struck my relatives, it shows that Althea and I had achieved a kind of contentment in graduate school and did not mind putting off for another year the troublesome question of what to do with the rest of our lives.

Soon after passing my history prelims in October, I set up a schedule of methodical preparation for my prelims in English. As winter quarter 1964 began, I settled into an uninterrupted observance of the schedule, sufficiently motivated by fear to spend ten to fourteen hours a day in study. Following directions from the English Department, I prepared to translate passages from the Anglo-Saxon *Chronicles* and *Beowulf* and to respond to questions, either in writing or orally, on fourteen specified authors, on the development of the novel, and on the rudiments of bibliography and research. In addition, I understood myself to be responsible for a survey-depth knowledge of all the periods of English and American literature and, to a lesser degree, the literature of ancient Greece and Rome. Adhering meticulously to my schedule, I reviewed all these subjects, refreshing what I had learned in previous courses and filling in, as best I could, the blanks left by my prior neglect.

In February my brother Earland, fifty-seven, died unexpectedly of intestinal bleeding brought on by chronic colitis. He had been principal of Snowflake elementary school for some years. Althea and I drove to Snowflake with Mother, Charles, Roald, and our nephew Dwain, all of whom were living in the Salt Lake area that winter. More than five hundred people attended the service in Snowflake. At the grave in Lakeside cemetery, a double male quartet sang "Come, Lay His Books and Papers By," the hymn composed for the funeral of Mormon pioneer educator Karl Maeser and sung at my father's funeral as well. Our brother Elwood told and retold a sad story: informed at the hospital that a colostomy would save his life, Earland had groaned and—so Elwood asserted—chosen to die. Peering into the coffin at the viewing, Joe Hansen—the eight-year-old son of my sister Lenora—uttered an eerie animal wail. Dwain discussed colitis in clinical detail, saying it was the disease of passive men and he himself was afflicted with it. (He would in fact die of it, following an emergency colostomy, eighteen years later.) For my part, I regretted how little I had ever known of Earland. I was comforted, however, by the eager conversation in which the assembled Petersons engaged. It was as if we took license from Earland's death to reinforce a hold on life for the rest of us.

As my prelims approached near the end of April, my anxiety intensified. It was difficult to distinguish between this perhaps normal anxiety and my recurrent pathological anxiety. I began to feel I had not spent enough time in preparation. I was confident that my examiners would be kind and fair, yet the sheer magnitude of the subject matter—the entire canon of English and American literature—loomed before me. I myself could devise countless questions I couldn't answer. About a week before the exam, I asked Don Walker whether I shouldn't postpone it. He said that was a decision I would have to make. I inferred a subtle encouragement from his tone of voice and left the date unchanged. After a couple of sleepless nights I secured sleeping pills from the student health service. I took one pill but felt so groggy and incoherent the next morning that I threw the rest of the pills into the garbage.

I went to the first session of the exam in a half stupor. When I saw the topics, a steady adrenaline-fed energy came over me. I wrote for two hours both morning and afternoon on Monday, Tuesday, and Wednesday, maintaining my composure even after leaving blank some thirty out of a hundred items on an identification section. (I found out later that my examiners considered my score high.) On Thursday I researched and prepared an oral presentation on a topic given on Wednesday. On Friday I began a three-hour oral test with five examiners. After my prepared presentation, the exam went forward with a wide variety of questions. By and large I felt I was doing well. I recall being asked by Harold Folland whether I had read Shakespeare's *Henry V*. When I said I had, he asked a question about it. I said I had not reread the play recently and could answer the question in better detail if I could apply it to *Richard III* or *Henry IV,* part 1, which were fresh on my mind. Folland agreed and I went on with my discussion.

After the exam had ended, I waited in a corridor, at first feeling confident that I had passed. However, as long minutes ticked away and no one emerged from the examination room, I began to worry. Obviously my examiners were engaged in a debate, which did not bode well for me. At last the door opened, and Walker came out with a smile. "We have decided to pass you with distinction," he said, launching me, who had not known that such a ranking was possible, into a state of incredulous euphoria. That night Althea and I celebrated with a dinner at a Chinese restaurant. We had planned on including Charles and Betty, but at the moment we were dining, Betty was being delivered of their fifth child, whose birthday, April 24, 1964, is easy for me to remember.

··· 14

A Silvery Tinkling Laughter

FEW PEOPLE KNOW THAT I ONCE HAD A POLITICAL CAREER. During the summer of 1964, I campaigned for a seat in the Utah House of Representatives. I had served as Democratic chairman of the voting district comprising Stadium Village since the spring of 1962. Early in 1964, urged by the chairman of the legislative district and with no other contender from the Democratic Party in view, I filed for the seat. Two days before the end of the filing period, a psychiatrist also filed as a Democrat. As the primary election approached in August, my opponent made handsome mailings, which I couldn't afford. My total expenditure was seventy-five dollars for five hundred calling cards with my name, photo, and several high-sounding phrases about my position on government. I spent afternoons and evenings knocking on doors and handing out these cards. I lost by 416 to 867 votes. My opponent won the seat in the general election, which turned out to be a landslide for the Democratic Party. One of my professors, Harold Folland, congratulated me on my loss, reminding me that service in the legislature would have seriously impeded work on my dissertation.

I inherited from my parents the idea that the Democratic Party stood for helping the unendowed masses to achieve a more prosperous life, whereas the Republican Party stood for conserving wealth in the hands of those who already had it. In his 1964 campaign for the presidency, Republican Barry Goldwater emphasized the virtue of relying on yourself rather than on the social services of government. Goldwater's followers made a moral issue of the matter. One of their campaign slogans said: *In your heart you know he's right.* One problem for me was Goldwater's wealth. His zeal for principles that preserved his own riches struck me as

hypocritical. A larger problem was that I couldn't believe in conservative economics. I could see that the competition inherent in
free enterprise implied inevitable losers. Self-reliance paid off only
for the winners. If government didn't look out for the losers, who
would? Certainly not the Goldwater conservatives. So I cheerfully
voted for Lyndon Johnson.

It may seem odd that I was surprised when, in mid-August,
Althea told me she was pregnant. We had in fact made love without contraception a few times some weeks earlier. This was not
something we had talked over or planned, and I can account for it
only as a not entirely conscious recognition on our part that, with
my Ph.D. appearing certain within a year or less, we had no legitimate excuse for postponing our family. That duteous impulse
toward procreation quickly passed, and we resumed our usual pre-
cautions. I more or less forgot we had ever abandoned them until
one startling day weeks later Althea told me our grasshopper life
would soon be over.

In the fall, Althea enrolled in more graduate courses while I settled down to uninterrupted labor on my dissertation. I had decided
to limit my topic, freedom and restraint in western literature, to fifteen or twenty recent novels that treated the frontier experience
with realism and some sophistication of style and structure. To assemble my list I drew shamelessly on Don Walker's wide reading. I
was always impressed by the novels he recommended. For a while
I read and took notes at the rate of a novel every two or three days.
By November I had begun to write early chapters on Althea's portable Smith-Corona. To solace my labor I played country-western
records borrowed from Roald on a portable hi-fi borrowed from
Leon and Gussie.

During November I inquired about a faculty position in English
for the following year at twelve western colleges and universities—
institutions no farther away than a long day's drive from Salt Lake
City. Most of these institutions said they didn't need a person of
my qualifications. I applied finally only at BYU and Weber State
College in Ogden. Both offered me an assistant professorship.
Among a number of reasons for preferring BYU was the fact there
was no prospect for teaching graduate courses at Weber State, a
four-year college with a student body of fifty-two hundred. I went

so far as to begin to attend church regularly, testing whether I could tolerate the full Mormon regimen required of BYU faculty members. I even accepted a position as instructor of my elder's quorum, which I held till I graduated. Nonetheless, at the new year I accepted the offer from Weber State. The sticking point finally was not church attendance or payment of a tithe. It was the restriction BYU would have imposed upon what I could write and say. Even after I had decided on Weber State, Althea urged me to continue attending church. She believed a church—almost any church—was necessary for the moral nurture of our child. She said our child would fit better into the multitudinous Peterson family if that church happened to be Mormon. I agreed. However, I was ill at ease in church. My disbelief being complete, I felt myself an observer with no investment in Mormon doctrine or practice.

By the beginning of 1965, Althea appeared very pregnant, being a woman of short torso. During autumn her pregnancy had worked as an aphrodisiac on me. It seemed I made love more vigorously and with greater pleasure than ever before. However, with the new year I became more and more anxious about the fetus that grew inside her. I began to dread the stirrings that I sometimes felt while lying beside her at night. Sometimes her distorted belly seemed monstrous. One night a couple of weeks before the birth I distinctly sensed the fetus as a presence, and my remaining composure gave way to total fright and an overwhelming compulsion to run. My pathological syndrome had returned at its most virulent. It appeared after seven years of therapy I had made no advance whatsoever upon my crippling anxiety. This was very enigmatic, as well as discouraging, for I could think of no reason I should be terrified of the infant soon to be born.

Althea went into labor on a snowy Saturday night in early April, and I drove her to the LDS Hospital. By morning it had become evident that her cervix was not dilating properly, and the obstetrician ordered an intravenous medication for forcing dilation. All day Althea grimly endured the recurrent pains without a murmur. By afternoon my determination to be courageous had evaporated. I phoned and asked my mother and Althea's mother to come to the hospital. This was for my sake, Althea being indifferent to their presence. In the early evening, some eighteen hours after we had come to the hospital, the obstetrician decided on a C-section. About a half hour later, on this evening of April 11, 1965, I was given a brief glimpse of our daughter before she was rolled away to the nursery on a cart. She had fat cheeks and thick, unruly black hair. A nurse filling out a birth certificate asked for her name. Although we had found a couple of names Althea liked in a book of Peterson genealogy—Bengt Earland for a boy, Karrin for a girl— there had been no firm agreement between us. Assuming I had to respond to the nurse's request instantly, I blurted out "Karrin." It was just as well. I am not sure we would have chosen any other name even if we had dithered over the matter at greater length. We pronounced it *Car-un*. When she got to school and found it necessary to correct its pronunciation, our daughter began to dislike her name. She has seemed reconciled to it as an adult. As for myself, I have always been glad we named her Karrin.

After leaving the hospital on that first night, I asked my mother to let me sleep at her apartment. She kindly gave me her bed and slept on the sofa while I lay rigidly awake all night in a state of shock. The four days Althea was in the hospital following delivery were very difficult for me. At Miss Ratcliff's suggestion I asked Stella and Arvid for permission to spend the days with them. I set up a card table in their living room and went on attempting to draft a chapter of my dissertation. I found myself unable to concentrate for more than two or three hours a day and spent much time staring at the typewriter in a stupor of misery. In other matters Miss Ratcliff was less than sympathetic. She wanted to know why I was not being more supportive of Althea, who had undergone the trauma of an extended labor and surgery. She suggested I give Althea a gift. That evening I dutifully went downtown, bought a candleholder, and took it to Althea. I could see it didn't mean anything to her. Neither of us has ever attached much importance to gifts.

On one of my evening visits at the hospital I did a very shameful thing. I asked Althea whether she would consider giving Karrin up for adoption by someone else. She said, quite simply and without any display of emotion, that she wouldn't. For more than thirty years nothing more was said on this matter, which has loomed in my own conscience as the most incredible and unredeemable thing

I have ever done. I recognize, too, that it would have been a practical as well as moral error. No influence toward emotional stability would prove greater in my later life than the presence of an affectionate and competent daughter.

There is something to be said for silence between spouses. Althea's taciturn response to my recurrent emotional crises was, I judge, exactly right. She didn't exhort, accuse, or lament. She surely must have felt like doing so. If she herself was depressed or anxious, she didn't let me know. Instead, she remained a calm, predictable presence on whom I relied. My reluctance to speak of intimate feelings kept me from expressing my gratitude directly. But I think she intuited, then and later, that I was grateful.

I took Althea and Karrin home from the hospital on a hot Friday afternoon. For a week or two Stella came during the day to help out. At night I changed Karrin's diaper and got up to bring her to Althea for nursing. In the vastness of my misery I failed to take full account of the comfort I found in holding that tiny bundle in my arms. In retrospect, I recognize Karrin began to project herself among my deepest affections from the day we brought her home. After Stella stopped coming, I helped Althea give Karrin her bath in a dishpan in the kitchen sink. Sometimes in the evening when we couldn't quiet Karrin's crying by other means, we went for a car ride. Lulled by the vibrations of the car, she went to sleep. A number of my relatives gathered from out of town for Karrin's blessing at my ward. After the ceremony Stella and Arvid had us all to dinner. There is a photo of me holding Karrin in the lacy dress she wore at the blessing. She is squalling and I look stolidly unhappy. Nonetheless, I could recognize in myself a growing dependency on my infant daughter. I developed the habit of kissing her fat cheeks whenever I held her. One day when she was about three months old, the moving shadows of the elm branches outside the window triggered a silvery tinkling laughter from her. It was a most melodious, delightful sound.

On many Sundays during the summer of 1965 Dwain brought his three-year-old daughter, Megan, to visit Karrin. Dwain was in the process of a divorce from Marge Egbert and was living alone in an apartment. The apparent issue between them was his abandonment of the Mormon faith. The subtle, more fundamental issue I judged to be Dwain's revolt against his own passivity. One day when he had outpatient surgery on his sinuses, I picked him up at a clinic and brought him to our apartment. I recall looking up from my typewriter from time to time while he lay recuperating on our sofa with his eyes closed. It strengthened me to see that, for all my own distress, I could help provide a refuge for this dear companion from my boyhood.

For perhaps a month following Karrin's birth, I doubted whether I would finish my dissertation. Eventually I found myself able to concentrate for longer periods. Drudging on without inspiration, I finished a draft of my final chapter by the end of June. Luckily my reading committee was in a mood to push forward with a critique of my chapters. Don Walker read each of my chapters closely, penciling in many specific suggestions for improvement, while Kenneth Eble and Henry Webb offered more general criticism. The chapters were also reviewed by Harold Folland, the chairman of the department, who offered the most serious challenge to my work by objecting to my extensive use of the term *alienation*.

I had given my dissertation the ponderous title of "The Ambivalence of Alienation: The Debate over Frontier Freedom in the Quality Novel of the Twentieth Century." By *freedom* I meant an escape from such ordinary social restraints as marriage, respect for law, good manners, sobriety, and so on. I examined this escape in fourteen novels, devoting a chapter to each. While reading these works, I had been impressed by their differences of attitude. Some of the novels clearly celebrated the frontiersman's bachelorhood, violence, and prodigality as heroic, whereas others portrayed these values in a negative light and still others with ambivalence. Hence, as my title suggested, my overarching insight was that western fiction of the twentieth century had been a vehicle of a debate within the collective American psyche over the worth of the freedom allowed by wilderness. I was disappointed not to have arrived at a grander, more astonishing conclusion. It was the best I could come up with, and it did serve to unify the disparate parts of my dissertation.

Alienation was a word with wide currency while I was in graduate school. I heard it in lectures and ran into it in scholarly articles. Critics applied it to the characters of the best novelists of the twentieth century—Dreiser, Hemingway, Faulkner, Dos Passos, and Fitzgerald, among others. Early in my study it had struck me that the supposed freedom of the frontiersman was actually a form of alienation from society. Before long the term had become a synonym for frontier freedom in my thinking—and, unfortunately, in my writing. In chapter after chapter I wove the term into the fabric of my analysis. The problem lay with the novels that depicted the frontiersman's removal from society as blissful and fulfilling. Alienation simply wasn't accurate when applied to happy characters.

I was in Folland's office when he challenged the term. I agreed to do something about it and went home. Within an hour or two I realized it would take at least a month to make an adequate revision. I had about a week if I intended to graduate in August. I returned to Folland's office the next morning and argued for keeping the term. He shrugged his shoulders and left the matter in my hands.

While I was still making minor revisions to my last chapters, Althea began to type the first chapters onto multilith mats with a rented IBM Selectric typewriter. The typing went on for days. Often Stella was present to care for Karrin. Sometimes Althea propped the baby carrier beside the typewriter, and Karrin seemed lulled by the clattering of the machine. Eventually I delivered the mats to a printer, and he in turn delivered the printed pages to a bindery. Three or four copies of my dissertation were bound in bright-red leather and a half dozen more in paper. I gave the latter to Stella, my mother, and several siblings, a dubious gift, as I now recognize. No one reads a scholarly work for pleasure.

There being fees to pay, I went to the cashier's office in the basement of the Park Building on the day before the formal defense of my dissertation. While standing in line I experienced a renewal of the stark terror and impulse to run that had visited me for some weeks before and after Karrin's birth. Now my terror centered on the circumstances of the defense. I would be asked questions, and I would be expected to return coherent answers immediately. In its presently virulent stage my surging anxiety seemed certain to paralyze my thought processes. I would be unable to speak. I had functioned coherently in oral examinations before; I could not tell why I was so sure now of my inability to perform. While waiting to pay my fees, I also considered the teaching career that would open before me if by some miracle I did manage to succeed in the defense of my dissertation. I would be expected to lecture three or four hours a day. Suddenly I was terribly frightened of becoming a teacher. The pleasure I had always derived from teaching, the self-assurance I had always felt in front of students, was of no effect now. It seemed certain that this same boundless anxiety would recur over and over in the classroom, emptying my mind, paralyzing my tongue.

When I got back to our apartment, I told Althea that I doubted my ability to function during the defense. I said it was likely I would not get the Ph.D. I spent a sleepless night and the next morning sat at my desk trying to steady my erratic thoughts. After lunch Althea asked whether it would help if she and Karrin accompanied me as far as the building where the defense was to be held. I said it would. I put on a white shirt, tie, and jacket. Althea put on a nice dress and put something pretty on Karrin. She placed Karrin in the stroller, and the three of us went slowly across campus.

Don Walker had said the defense would be a mere formality. So it proved. My examiners were supportive and kind. The instant I entered their presence I felt calm and composed. Their questions, concentrating on the dissertation, seemed easy to answer. Folland brought up the impropriety of the term *alienation*, saying the day would come when I would regret having used it. Otherwise he made no issue of the matter. After an hour or so I was invited to step into the hall. It seemed only seconds before Walker emerged and, smiling, said, "Congratulations, Dr. Peterson." The long ordeal of pursuing a degree was over. I walked out into the summer sunshine, a reprieved man. But only temporarily. My anxiety was now fixed on the teaching career that awaited me. It seemed certain I would be unable to function in the classroom.

Joseph Peterson at Berkeley, 1903

The ranch house at Lakeside, shortly before it burned, 1962

The new composite family, 1924. *Back:* Elwood Peterson, Earland Peterson, Lydia Peterson, and Joseph Peterson. *Front:* Mary Peterson, Lenora Peterson, and Wanda Peterson.

Alma Peterson,
age two, 1927

Christmas Day 1934: Levi Peterson, Leon Peterson, Roald Peterson, and Charles Peterson

Levi Peterson, Roald Peterson, Leon Peterson, and Charles Peterson, 1940

Joseph and Lydia Peterson, 1940

Levi Peterson, near the time of graduation from the eighth grade, May 1947

Levi Peterson,
Christmas Eve 1949

Levi Peterson, missionary in
Switzerland at the time of the
dedication of the Swiss Temple,
August 1955

Levi Peterson, missionary in Switzerland, formal portrait, June 1955

Althea Sand, at Brigham
Young University, 1956

Wedding day, August 31, 1958. *Left to right:* Arvid Sand, Stella Sand,
Althea Peterson, Levi Peterson, and Lydia Peterson.

Levi and Althea Peterson, Lakewood, California, summer 1959. Levi grew his first beard that summer.

Levi Peterson, Althea Peterson, Stella Sand, and Arvid Sand, Lakewood, California, Thanksgiving 1960

Levi Peterson, Althea Peterson, and Karrin Peterson getting ready for graduation, University of Utah, August 1965

Althea Peterson, Karrin Peterson, and Levi Peterson at Hardware Ranch, Utah, winter 1967

The house on Twenty-fifth Street, Ogden, Utah, March 1971

Levi Peterson
planting his annual
garden at the
Twenty-fifth Street
house, Ogden, Utah,
early 1970s

Levi Peterson in the study of the Twenty-fifth Street house, sitting at the two-sided desk he built, early 1970s

Lydia Peterson's house in Snowflake, Arizona, summer 1971

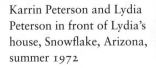

Karrin Peterson and Lydia Peterson in front of Lydia's house, Snowflake, Arizona, summer 1972

Peterson family reunion, Flag Hollow, Lakeside, Arizona, June 1986. *Standing, left to right:* Charles Peterson, Betty Peterson, Waldo Ray, Mary Ray, Lewis Tenney, Wanda Tenney, Levi Peterson, Althea Peterson, Roald Peterson, Lenora Hansen, Marion Hansen, Gussie Peterson, and Leon Peterson. *Seated, left to right:* Coral Peterson, Arley Peterson, Leora Peterson and Lucilia Peterson.

Peterson siblings and spouses at Karrin's and Mark's wedding, 1993. *Left to right:* Marion and Lenora Hansen, Lewis and Wanda Tenney, Charles and Betty Peterson, Roald and Luana Peterson, Leon and Gussie Peterson, and Levi and Althea Peterson.

Levi Peterson on the trail to Mount Timpanogos, Utah, Memorial Day weekend, 1994

Roald Peterson and Levi Peterson searching for wild horses in the Cedar Mountains, Utah, May 1992

A collage of books by Levi Peterson

Lars and Hans Boettcher,
autumn 2001

Levi Peterson, 1981

Cedar City, Utah, summer 2004. *Back row, left to right:* Levi and Althea Peterson, Karrin Peterson and Mark Boettcher, and Charles and May Peterson. *Front row, left to right:* Lars Boettcher and Cameron Beals (May's grandson).

Althea and Levi Peterson on Levi's seventieth birthday, 2003. Friends brought a cake and a first edition of *The Virginian*.

··· 15

An Entire Landscape of Possibilities

ALTHEA AND I MOVED TO OGDEN soon after my graduation in August 1965. We rented a small house on Lake Street, not far from the looming cliffs of Mount Ogden, about two miles from the Weber State campus. We were followed immediately by Althea's parents, who rented an apartment a mile or two away. We bought three-speed bicycles, and I cycled to campus as long as the weather stayed good. At that moment I held the only doctorate in the English Department except for that held by Leland Monson, dean of the arts and humanities division, who rarely taught English courses. During fall quarter, I taught three sections of freshman composition and an American literature course for general education students. Some students belittled Weber State, calling it Harrison High (the campus being on Harrison Boulevard). I made sure my students had no cause to believe they were still in high school. At the end of the quarter I wrote my mother that I had given one A among my seventy-five composition students. Most of my students received a C. Such rigorous grading, I opined, would help raise academic standards at Weber State, which had made the transition from junior college status only a couple of years before I hired on.

For a while I thought I might keep my fright within tolerable boundaries, but as the quarter wore on, the nightmare I had predicted at the time of defending my dissertation materialized. Fearing a total paralysis of my thoughts, I wrote each lecture in complete sentences, a daily labor of many hours even though I padded the lectures by reading illustrative passages from the text. I entered each class with dread, and increasingly, as the quarter wore on, I suffered multiple seizures of anxiety during which I continued to read my lecture like an automaton. There was no comfort whatsoever in the fact I had survived the anxiety of a previous day with no break in my coherence.

As fall quarter opened, I entered therapy with an Ogden psychiatrist, Blaine Belnap, whom Miss Ratcliff had recommended. I would continue to have weekly sessions with Belnap for nearly eleven years. With considerable hope I began to take a tranquilizer that he prescribed. In the dosage he allowed, it did nothing discernible for my anxiety. Nonetheless, it symbolized help, and I went on taking it for several years. More immediately helpful was another tranquilizer that allowed me to sleep soundly and wake without feeling groggy or befuddled.

Belnap always wore a suit and tie and spoke in a quiet, tentative way. He wrote on a yellow notepad while I talked, sometimes asking questions or making cautious suggestions. He said it was obvious my pathology was roused by situations that forced me to recognize myself as an independent adult. If that was true, I asked, why had I been able to teach college classes without distress when I was a graduate assistant? He said status made the difference. I myself had been a student then. Now I had a Ph.D. and a tenure-track position. What he said made sense. It seemed to fit the recurrence of anxiety I experienced while a missionary, which, as I recalled, intensified after I had been made a senior companion. Being a senior companion implied I was one of the grown-ups.

Almost any interpretation of a person's unconscious is hypothetical. Even the concept of an unconscious mind with its own weird rules of logic is hypothetical. I had been sympathetic to my therapists' views from the start. I was willing to consider any possibility that might relieve the symptoms of my pathology. One day Miss Ratcliff pointed out that I felt helpless most of the time. I heard her as saying I felt hopeless. I agreed. I could readily recognize my despair and depression; they were always with me. She corrected me, reminding me she had said helpless. I could recognize feeling helpless about my phobia. I needed somebody to help keep that terrifying impulse to run in check. But I couldn't see that I felt helpless and vulnerable in all things, like a very small child who needs a loving caretaker nearby at all times. That was a crazy idea. It didn't make sense. However, as I later came to accept, a crazy idea is precisely what is required to explain a pathology as crippling as mine. Right or wrong, I function today on the assumption that as a little child I internalized some terribly dysfunctional attitude that forbade me ever to grow up and that ordained that I would experience a small child's hysterical impulse to run from an overwhelming danger whenever I was forced to recognize I had taken another step toward adult competence. This dysfunctional attitude, I will point out, coexists with a strong determination to be a competent adult.

The winter of 1966 was snowy and grim, and I was in the midst of what I judge, nearly forty years later, to be the lowest, most critical period of my life. Crippling anxiety continued to afflict me in every class. Out of class, despair plagued me. During the final examination period in March, my mother came to visit us. One morning, too anxious to go to my office, I tried to grade essay exams at a table in our bedroom. Althea, Karrin, and Mother were in the living room and kitchen. My emotions were so distraught that I could not grade a single paper. I started over and over, admitting after a paragraph or two of a particular essay that I simply could not make meaning emerge from the written lines. I stayed at the table all morning. I believed myself finished as a teacher.

For weeks I had considered resigning my position. I didn't know what I would do for a living. I thought of pumping gas in a service station. I don't know why I thought I might feel better with that kind of a job. To gather funds for the transition, I stopped paying our rent. That was the only time of my life I ever intentionally failed to pay bills promptly. So my inability to grade essays that morning seemed a culmination. I wasn't thinking of taking another job, however. I was thinking of suicide. I have always feared the appeal of suicide. It is an easy way out. Althea called me to lunch at noon. I gazed at the sandwich on my plate for a minute or two, then suddenly burst into sobs. Althea and Mother exchanged startled glances. Karrin, seated in her high chair, stared. I don't remember what I said by way of explanation.

A month or two before this incident, Mother wrote that she had dreamed about me as a little child. I was tied by a rope to a baby's crib, and she was trying to untie me. "You do not have to write me every week," she wrote. "Do not let the strings of your childhood curtail you more."[1] But I remembered my senile grandmother's pitiful inquiry, every day when anyone came from the post office, whether there was a letter from her son Parley, and there never was. For that reason, if no other, I couldn't stop writing to Mother regularly.

After I had broken into sobs during lunch, we took a ride up Weber Canyon, and I felt a little better. That evening I discovered I could grade papers again. So that part of the crisis was over. On my next visit, Belnap prescribed antidepressant pills. These took two or three weeks to kick in. But they did kick in. It was one of the miracles of my life. All of a sudden I felt much better. Winter ended and warm, sunny days came on. We had a pack frame designed for carrying a child. One bright afternoon I shouldered Karrin in that frame, and Althea and I walked to a convenience store for a Dr. Pepper. I remember how intensely I loved Karrin that day. She was a year old, and I was happy to be her father. I couldn't imagine anything better. My love for other persons tended to be subterranean. It left signs of itself, so I knew it was there. But my love for Karrin was as palpable and kinesthetic as the sensation of kissing her fat little cheeks or running my hand over her silky hair.

Satisfying routines soon emerged at home. Returning from campus at five, I interacted with Karrin while Althea prepared dinner. We almost always took a ride after dinner. We got into the habit of going to a hamburger place called Sir Basil's and ordering Cokes for Althea and me and a small ice cream cone for Karrin. Karrin soon learned to mimic Althea's request for a ten-cent Coke, saying cutely, "Sen sent soke." Back home, we read to Karrin on the sofa, and then I would sing her to sleep. After Karrin learned to read, we substituted games for reading together. After we had played games, Karrin would munch Cheerios and read a while on her bed. Then I would come in and sing songs to her, and she would go to sleep. I sang to her till she was nine or ten.

During that first spring Althea and I traded our Beetle in on a white Volkswagen van. For a while I was charmed by this spacious vehicle. Later I realized it was cold in winter and amplified road noise like a sound chamber. It had double side doors and removable middle and back seats. I quickly converted it to a rudimentary camper with a platform for our sleeping bags and a nook on the floor for Karrin's pad. We acquired a Coleman lantern, stove, and oven, and I began to cook elaborate outdoor meals. We often took Stella out for an evening picnic in the nearby mountains. Arvid, who got ill on curving mountain roads, usually declined to go. Midsummer we backpacked with Karrin overnight to Kamas Lake in the Uintas. One Friday afternoon, while Stella and Arvid kept Karrin, Althea and I drove to Cedar City and attended our first Shakespeare play. We camped that night in a nearby canyon and returned to Ogden the next morning.

I taught summer school for extra pay. I joshed amiably with the students in my accelerated freshman composition course, and they demonstrated their affection by decorating the spokes and handle bars of my bicycle with crepe paper as if I were going to participate in a children's parade. The extra money made us itch for a house of our own. During the fall of 1966 we looked at a lot of houses. I didn't think we could afford anything except a very small tract house. Althea didn't want a tract house because that was what her parents had owned in California. Our real estate agent showed us a two-story, all-brick house within the boundaries of our ward that had been built around 1900. It had a large lot, a full basement good for storage but not for living, and a hot-water radiator system fired by an ancient coal furnace converted to gas. Althea and I inspected the house for perhaps twenty minutes one evening and agreed to buy it. That was how we came to 1561 Twenty-fifth Street in Ogden.

We moved in around November 1. From the start, Althea liked the house better than I did. Our friends congratulated us, reminding us that builders just don't make houses as sound as they used to. That was one myth I was quickly disabused of. In the attic the rafters were lightly braced and spaced at alarming widths. The walls were covered by painted layers of wallpaper. Aged, broken linoleum covered the stairs and the kitchen and bathroom floors. In other rooms, worn carpets covered equally worn hardwood floors. The kitchen range dated from the 1930s. The kitchen cabinets and counters, the latter composed of a tan concrete, probably dated from the 1920s or earlier. There were only three electrical circuits in the house, and these were old-fashioned knob-and-tube wiring. There were no wall outlets in the basement and only three on the first floor and two on the second. In short, we had a worn-out house on our hands.

My pathology reasserted itself after our move. Belnap said that was to be expected since owning a house is another step into adulthood. However, I was angry as well as anxious and depressed. I had hated grimy walls and worn-out fixtures since my missionary days. There was something in me that said I deserved no better than that, which I resisted angrily. I told Belnap the old place was a shit house. He drove by and told me later it didn't look like a shit house to him. One evening soon after moving in, we invited Roald and Luana and Charles and Betty to dinner. My shame over having them see what a decrepit place we had saddled ourselves with grew while I vacuumed and helped tidy up. In a fit of anger I kicked a toy mailbox from the kitchen floor, and it struck the top of the kitchen door. Althea turned from the sink and deliberately dropped one of our treasured plates to the floor, where it shattered. Anger begets anger.

By December I had resigned myself to fixing up the old house. We conjectured, accurately as it turned out, that it would take ten years. Using coarse sandpaper, we scratched the paint on the walls and ceilings of two upstairs rooms, rented a steamer, and removed many layers of paper. The uncovered plaster showed dozens of cracks, some of them very long. Having washed the surfaces and filled the fissures, I cut untextured vinyl wallpaper into strips and pasted it over the cracks. Using a trowel I buried the strips under thin layers of drywall mud, feathering them into the surrounding surfaces as smoothly as I could. After sanding, we painted the walls and ceilings with primer and a white finish coat. They looked good.

In the meantime Althea was refinishing an antique oak dining table and set of chairs. She had the patience for this kind of work, first applying paint remover, then sanding the tiny crevices for hours, then applying walnut stain—which suited our taste better than oak stain—and two layers of varnish. Later she would remove the ivory paint from the handsome mantel around our fireplace and find it was of oak. This too she refinished with walnut stain and varnish.

During winter quarter 1967, Althea and I took an evening course in woodworking at Clearfield High School with Roald and Luana, who had bought a house in nearby West Point only weeks before we bought our house. Althea turned a couple of tall candlesticks on a lathe, and I constructed the drawers for a desk. Here began my ambition to have a workshop of my own full of woodworking tools. One night at home I realized there was space for a workbench and a wall of tools in one of our basement rooms. To this point our basement had seemed an inconvenient fright of radiator piping and low, open joists made grimy by the coal smoke of earlier years. For the first time I rejoiced in the ownership of this old house. It seemed a fine thing for a man to have his own workshop.

Tall maples grew on our parking strip, and even taller poplars surrounded the house, littering our lot with leaves in the fall. A tangled brush patch grew in the middle of the backyard. The first summer I rented a tiller and turned an uncultivated back corner of the lot into a garden. I planted peas, onions, lettuce, zucchinis, acorn squash, corn, and tomatoes. The corn and tomatoes were especially good. We felt rich while they lasted. I built a couple of hutches and began to raise rabbits. A city inspector showed up one day and gave me a week to get rid of the rabbits. I suppose a neighbor had reported me. That was all right. I had slaughtered one of the fryers for our table but couldn't bring myself to kill another.

Everything about the house and lot was enabling. I dared make changes, dared to experiment. If I ruined something, I had only myself to answer to. I won't say I ever truly liked the house. I did like the lot. It was always brushy and a little wild and unkempt and comfortably close to the looming cliffs of Mount Ogden. Throughout the thirty-five years that we owned it, the house would remain an adversary for me, always in need of renovation and repair. For Althea, the house was always a comforting sanctuary. Leaving it would be far more difficult for her than me. Nonetheless, the house began to glow with nostalgia for me after Karrin had grown up and moved away. It was her childhood home, and its rooms resonated with her presence even when she was living elsewhere.

I began to expand professionally during my second year at Weber State. I proposed an upper-division elective course in western American literature that was approved by the college curriculum committee. I also proposed a library collection of the popular western or, as it is often called, the cowboy novel. The director of the library funded the project. For a couple of years I solicited westerns from used book dealers, and our library ordered some thirty-five hundred titles dating from 1885 to 1965, paying as little as two and three dollars apiece. It was my intention eventually to use this collection for a scholarly study of the western. Though my interests have turned elsewhere, I do not discount the possibility that I will yet write an article or chapter based on this collection.

During the spring of 1967 I condensed my dissertation into an article and read it at the meetings of the Utah Academy of Science, Arts, and Letters. Golden Taylor, now a professor of English at Utah State University and editor of the journal of the newly founded Western Literature Association, asked to publish it.[2] In June I participated in a workshop on western literature organized by Don Walker at the University of Utah. Three of my papers were based on chapters from my dissertation. The fourth paper was based on fresh reading I had done in Mormon fiction. This was my first serious consideration of Mormon literature, and it taught me how thoroughly western, how thoroughly of the American frontier, Mormonism is.

Many refuse to consider Mormon literature a species of western literature. There seems little affinity between the popular western and Mormon literature; the literature of the Mormon pioneer celebrates endurance rather than heroic violence. Mormon literature is generally indifferent to the romantic themes of the purity and divinity of nature. Yet it was precisely the social vacancy of the frontier that allowed Mormonism to establish its distinctive identity. The very existence of Mormonism is a frontier—and therefore a western—phenomenon.

By 1967 the rhythms of my teaching had begun to repeat themselves. Thereafter, I had little to distinguish one quarter from another or, for that matter, one year from another. I considered myself happy. I judge myself to have been assertive yet good-humored in the classroom. I had stopped writing out my lectures, although I was still wary of a paralyzing accession of anxiety. I had begun to make many friends in the English Department and on campus generally. One of the older faculty members from the junior college era, Cluster Nilsen, took a liking to me. Cluster was bald and rotund and pursued a hobby of buying worthless horses at auctions. He had close to twenty-five of these nondescript animals in corrals and pastures around the Ogden area. In the summer, he roamed

Ogden and its suburbs in his battered Ford pickup, collecting grass clippings for his horses. He began to take me on rides once a month or so.

On our excursions, Cluster and I developed the habit of stopping for breakfast at restaurants of the greasy-spoon variety where I learned, from Cluster's evil example, to drink coffee. I still have this bad habit. I do not think I am a serious caffeine addict. I like coffee mostly because it is a convenient sin. It is a very handy, inexpensive way to stay out of harmony with your church. As for Cluster, I don't think I exerted any counterinfluence on him. He marveled at the number of themes I assigned and meticulously graded in freshman composition. "You really believe writing can be taught!" he said, shaking his head in wonder. A cynic on the matter, he taught spelling and little else. One day I saw him carrying a set of themes back to class in a waste can. I recognized the difficulty of measuring progress on the part of students in basic writing courses. Nonetheless, I went on assigning and grading abundant themes in my freshman courses. I couldn't quite accept that my serious intentions didn't count for something in this world.

For a while Cluster kept a stallion. Eventually he had the stallion castrated and asked my help in transporting him from the vet. The poor creature's emptied scrotum was swollen big as a balloon. We turned him into a pasture full of mixed horses, expecting him to be docile. The former stallion didn't recognize he was a gelding and savagely attacked the other geldings. Somehow I felt good about that.

At the end of winter quarter 1970, Cluster had surgery for an enlarged prostate. When I went to the hospital to visit him, the receptionist told me he had already gone home. I said it was too early. All she knew was that his room had just been vacated. She phoned around and discovered he had died of a heart attack in his room about an hour before I came. I was one of the pallbearers at his funeral. At the burial I recognized that his death had given me a hold on Ogden. You start to feel like the place where your friends are buried is home.

During my second year at Weber State I shared an office with Robert Mikkelsen. Bob was six feet six inches tall and very articulate and witty. He said no one had dared smoke openly on campus in junior college times, and it would surprise you whose faces you might see in the dark recesses of the campus heat tunnel at noon when someone struck a match to light another cigarette. Bob bought a large gray gelding named Sam from Cluster. One day while Bob hunted deer on Mount Ogden from Sam's back, a buck ran headlong into them on a trail. Sam wheeled so fast that Bob's rifle flew out of its scabbard and clattered to the ground. Another day when I rode Sam, he shied so violently that I nearly fell off. The only foreign object anywhere around was a soda bottle cap on the ground. Maybe the sun had glinted off it. Who knows? At any rate, my esteem for the intelligence of horses went down.

During my third year at Weber State, Bob became chairman of the English Department, and he made me director of Freshman English. That released me from a fourth of a teaching load. I used the time for scholarship as well as for administrative duties. I was routinely promoted to associate professor as of July 1968, and granted early tenure as of July 1969. The latter was a pleasant surprise. Bob had recommended me, as policy allowed in those days. In 1968 I was appointed a member of the college curriculum committee, and in 1969 I became its chairman. I underwent something of a change in academic values while on this committee. At first, like many of my colleagues in the humanities and sciences, I believed Weber State should be chiefly a liberal arts college, an attitude reinforced by the fact that all the disciplines traditionally associated with a liberal education were organized into the large School of Arts, Letters, and Sciences ably administered by a single dean, Dello Dayton. Our flourishing School of Vocational Technology struck me, as it did many others, as archaic, a holdover from junior college days.

I remember opposing a proposal from the Department of Electronic Technology on the grounds that the new course would be taught by instructors holding only bachelor degrees. The next day I visited the department and talked to some of the faculty members for the purpose of strengthening my opposition. To my surprise, the head of the department praised me at the next meeting of the committee for having come personally into their terrain. Slowly I began to sympathize with the aims of vocational education, and by the time my service on the curriculum committee ended, I had accepted Weber State as what is called a comprehensive college, an institution of multiple purposes.

As chairman of the curriculum committee, I discovered I had a knack for making groups function efficiently. I could tell when discussion had reached the point of useless repetition, and I found myself able to predict the outcome of most votes. It always amazed me how many of my colleagues, if allowed to, would go on endlessly repeating their arguments without seizing the initiative by making a motion favorable to their position. They seemed to be waiting for someone else to empower them. I judge that, generally speaking, the academic mentality does not allow for an aggressive stance in committee dynamics.

In 1967 a former German tank officer, Helmut Hofmann, was appointed academic vice president. Almost immediately William Miller, college president, suffered a crippling heart attack, and Hofmann, a forceful personality, became the chief decision maker on campus. Hofmann said the English Department could not go on adding full-time instructors to meet the phenomenal increase in enrollment at the college. Accordingly I collaborated with colleagues in designing sections of beginning composition seating 125 students each, five times the usual number. I taught one of these giant sections for a couple of quarters and recruited and trained noninstructional graders for the students' weekly essays. The students didn't like being graded by persons whom they never saw, and I didn't like assigning final grades for writing I had not read. After two quarters we dropped this experiment. However, Hofmann was accurate in his prediction that the legislature would not continue to fund instruction of large multisection courses by tenure-track faculty. Before long, two-thirds of Weber State's composition courses were being taught by adjunct instructors paid at low part-time rates.

On Thanksgiving Day 1968, I flew to Milwaukee to attend the annual conference of the National Council of Teachers of English (NCTE). This was my first flight in a commercial jet. Gazing out a window on takeoff, I was suddenly seized by my old nemesis, the hysterical impulse to run, and my anxiety continued at a pathological level until the return jet touched down in Salt Lake City three days later and I saw Althea and Karrin waiting for me at the passenger unloading gate. This induced an important insight. I owed my general tranquillity to my relationship with my now three-year-old daughter. I could be on either side of a stable parent-child relationship and feel secure. As my mother's child, as my daughter's appropriately functioning father, either way I was okay. I was ashamed of this subtle, indirect dependency on my daughter, but I couldn't simply will it away. So I ignored my shame and went on being generally happy. I wondered, of course, what would happen when Karrin grew up and left home. I could see already I would be in trouble again.

What I saw at the NCTE conference in Milwaukee was astonishing. Teachers from colleges and universities all over the nation were frightened of their students beyond any conception I had been able to form from the news media in Utah. I had been aware of student demonstrations, seized buildings, and radical changes in policy and curriculum on many campuses—fortunately not on my own. What startled me most was that the shattered professors whom I met at the conference appeared to agree with the heady self-confidence of the student rebels. The keynote speaker at a banquet claimed that these young people really were the smartest and wisest the world had ever known; the reforms they were inciting really were going to remedy the ills of society at large.

A professor who sat by me on the plane out of Milwaukee asked what I was reading. I showed him a manual on house wiring I had recently bought. He said that was strange reading for a professor. That didn't matter. In March 1969, I took out a permit from Ogden City and began one of the great adventures of my life, the total rewiring of our old house. The basement, having no ceiling, was easy to wire. On the first floor I ran Romex cable up from the basement. On the second floor I ran it down from the attic. I became proficient at fishing the cable from the interior of the lath-and-plaster walls, but when it hit a header, I had to open the wall. By the time I was finished at the end of the summer, there were gaping holes all over the house. That didn't worry me. I knew I could make the walls look good again. I wired in something like twenty-five circuits, ran twelve hundred feet of cable, and installed ninety-five outlets. The Ogden City inspector said I had done a better job than many licensed contractors. Only once did I make a mistake.

I flipped the switch to the dining room lights and the kitchen lights came on.

Early in 1969 I bought a four-inch jointer and a table saw with a nine-inch blade, both of industrial quality. I had acquired a textbook on woodworking and cabinetmaking, and I practiced the craft by making intricate stands for these new tools. In February we bought a used sedan, a Plymouth Satellite with a small, fairly efficient V-8 engine, our only vehicle ever with an automatic transmission. During the summer I negotiated the sale of my five-acre plot of pines in Lakeside and used the money to buy a new Ford pickup with a gas-gulping V-8 engine. We sold the Volkswagen van, and in the fall I bought a small used camper for the pickup, which I renovated the next spring. With battery-run lights and a butane stove, the camper took much of the clutter and inconvenience out of overnight trips.

I see in myself a compulsion to eat my share at the trough of consumer civilization. How can I otherwise account for exchanging the land at Lakeside, an inheritance from my father, for a pickup and camper? Or account for the new bathrooms I would soon be installing in our house or, later, the kitchen with fine oak cabinetry, new refrigerator, oven, cooktop, dishwasher, and garbage disposal? Why didn't I have spirit enough to make a virtue of simplicity and poverty? I failed in that because I associated simplicity and poverty with an arbitrary exclusion from happiness. I didn't think about poverty when I was a boy because everyone else in town was poor too. Yet our poverty had its own subtle implications. Not only did I not have material things when I was a boy; I felt that I shouldn't have them. A vague destiny refused to authorize them. Inarticulate cosmic rules forbade them. I resented all that by the time I had an income to dispose of. I wanted what other people had. Getting and spending, having and using, empowered me. Wisely or not, I was entered fully upon the force track of consumer civilization with little incentive to get off.

In July 1970 I became chairman of the English Department. Autumn quarter was harried, for I continued to serve as chairman of the college curriculum committee. College enrollments had been increasing rapidly, and the English faculty numbered more than twenty full-time faculty and almost that many part-time faculty, making ours by far the largest department on campus. I thought of myself as a prompt and efficient administrator. I met deadlines, replied to memos, made schedules, and managed the budget meticulously. I tried to adjudicate student complaints against teachers with fairness and tact. This was not easy to do because a chairperson has far less power over the faculty than students imagine. I pursued the interests of the department vigorously. For example, when plans were scuttled to provide a home for the department in a new wing of the library, I made myself unpleasant in the higher councils of the college until we were allotted offices in the new Social Science building, where the department is still housed more than three decades later.

I had an ambition to make the department known for both good teaching and scholarship. It troubled me that some of my colleagues taught in a monotone voice, meandered illogically during lectures, or failed to meet classes consistently. Weber State, like many other institutions, had recently established formal student evaluations of faculty—a result of the nationwide student revolt. Using these, I set in motion tenure evaluations that resulted in the immediate resignation of one recently hired faculty member and the eventual termination, following appeals and protests, of another. My ambition was for nothing less than an entire department of master teachers.

Perhaps my most important contribution to the English Department was to settle the controversy over who would teach upper-division courses. We all had to teach at least two sections of basic composition every quarter. We were all scheduled at least one section of literature for general education. Upper-division courses, not nearly so abundant, were at a premium because they were for our majors and minors, advanced students who took their studies seriously. A chairperson could have scheduled them democratically, giving each teacher a turn. My predecessors had not done this, nor did I intend to. What was needed, however, was a clear understanding as to who had a right to teach these courses. By now, four or five of our faculty held doctorates (including Candadai Seshachari, whom Bob had hired from India in 1969). Six or seven others had doctorates in progress. Following open discussions in the department, I assigned each of those having or pursuing doctorates a proprietary interest in an upper-division course. The result, I hoped, would be the development of specialists in all the periods of British and American literature—medieval, Renaissance, neoclassical, romantic, Victorian, and so on—and in linguistics, the theory of composition, and the teaching of English in high schools. I hoped these favored persons would eventually publish articles in their fields. They would have to do so, I recognized, largely from personal pride because the college allowed them no relief from the teaching load of twelve quarter hours required of all faculty. This policy did not make friends for me among the faculty members who were not pursuing doctorates. I have often thought the matter would have generated less resentment had I carried it out silently, without open discussions in the department.

In October 1970, on the evening before leaving for a conference in Idaho, I developed a toothache. Our dentist, Clyde Field—the father of my sister-in-law Luana—met me at his office at dawn and opened the tooth. He gave me a small vial of a tarlike substance that he claimed was sheep dip, used to treat sheep for scabies and other diseases of the hide. Following his instructions, I kept a bit of cotton soaked in this substance packed in my tooth till I returned from the trip. I smelled like a railroad tie treated with creosote.

Clyde gave his patients novocaine if they asked for it. I never asked. Once he did a partial root canal on me without numbing my jaw. He said my jumps let him know when he had got down to the healthy part of the root. There was less trauma for the tooth that way. Of course, there was more trauma for the rest of me. After Clyde had died and his practice had been sold to another dentist, I began asking for novocaine. A root canal or crown prep with novocaine was nothing. I could sometimes go to sleep in the dentist's chair.

The conference I attended in October 1970, at Sun Valley, Idaho, was a joint meeting of the Rocky Mountain Modern Language Association (RMMLA) and the Western Literature Association (WLA). Ernest Hemingway's widow Mary and his son John spoke to a plenary session of the RMMLA, and we made a tour to the nearby Ketchum cemetery to view Hemingway's grave. In a session of the WLA, I read a paper on A. B. Guthrie's book *The Big*

Sky, a novel about the mountain man's destruction of his wilderness paradise. This was my first experience of intuiting the rapt attention of an audience. I liked the feeling. I said that as a region the West has a distinctive sense of tragedy, arising from the loss of wilderness, and that *The Big Sky* is the best expression of that regional sense of tragedy. Golden Taylor liked the paper and published it in *Western American Literature.*[3] Later another scholar published a paper refuting my assertion that *The Big Sky* has the qualities of literary tragedy. I haven't had a lot of luck in persuading other people that any work of literature that makes you feel an inconsolable loss is a tragedy. Most people who have any ideas on the matter insist on a noble protagonist with a tragic flaw, a formulation that fits *Hamlet* or *Macbeth* but not *The Big Sky.*

The trip to Sun Valley energized me. Yellowing aspens, vast sagebrush plains, and crossings of the Snake River evoked the mystical West among my emotions. The day after returning, I wrote Leon a long letter expressing my excitement. I said I could see the pattern my life would take for the foreseeable future. It was my destiny to record in whatever form given me—essays, fiction, perhaps even photography—the beauty of the western ethos I had inherited. The beauty in which my regional identity was rooted was complex and various. There was the vague and unutterable beauty of the vanished continental wilderness. There was the beauty of the frontier epic—the doings of those heroic sufferers, the pioneers, who had made the modern West. There was the beauty of the present landscape, the small cities, the farms and pastures, the residual wilderness. Finally, there was the beauty of "a natural human being living out his allotment of life in the particular locale we call the West"—here I was referring to the beauty of my own life.[4] I had traveled in the East, had lived in Europe. I was of the West, and in the West I intended to stay.

As fall quarter of 1970 began, I had completed five years at Weber State. In that period my life had taken a definite turn for the better. I considered myself generally happy. I was growing in many directions. At home I was becoming something of a handyman. I aspired to more than that, intending eventually to master the craft of making fine furniture. At school I wanted to be not only a good teacher and a respectable scholar but also an administrator who helped his colleagues be good teachers and respectable scholars. And for an avocation, as I have indicated above, I aspired to express the beauty of my native region. I wasn't sure how—through writing, likely, but writing what? At any rate, it seemed that in following my life's trail I had come out on a commanding ridge and before me stretched an entire landscape of possibilities.

··· 16

A Wilderness Journal

I KEPT A HANDWRITTEN WILDERNESS JOURNAL from 1969 to 1975. It was chiefly about my excursions into wild places near the Wasatch Front and in the Uinta Mountains. Sometimes I went farther afield to Wyoming, southwestern Utah, or northern Arizona. I amplified some of my entries for the *Possible Sack*, an informal organ published by Don Walker at the University of Utah. I present a sampling of these published entries here. I have resisted the impulse to revise them. They are as I wrote them in the early 1970s.

Entries on Natural Religion

FEBRUARY 22, 1970. Today was a warm winter Sunday. Althea, Karrin, and I took Grandmother Sand on a drive up Lost Creek. Karrin and I climbed a hill from which the snow had melted. While Karrin collected bleached snail shells from beneath the sagebrush, I sat warm in the sun, listening to the wind in the junipers.

I had some yearning on this Sunday afternoon for people—and for church. I often remember an old anxiety when I am in wilderness, an old compulsion to find paternal reassurance there. At times I want the canyons and creeks to be simply a cloak for God, and I want to pull that cloak aside and find Providence. It warms me to imagine that some great, unseen hand makes my way straight and assures me of survival. But when I look steadily at the grey sage and dark junipers, I cannot discern divine personality. I cannot strain my vision past the world I see and make out a God possessing perfect traits of human knowledge, power, love, and justice. I know nothing of what I cannot perceive.

At times I feel that with such seditious thoughts, I have no right to religious emotion. I suffer a touch of shame, as if only those who believe in divine personality have a right to worship. Despite such doubts today, I felt reverence for the trees and brush and the wide, cloud-blown sky. If I stir myself, I do not really believe that religion is the monopoly of those who interpret God anthropomorphically. God is as free and unpreempted as air. He is not defined by concepts corresponding to a particular character in the unseen portion of the universe; religion does not have to depend upon God's possessing any particular character. God is whatever I worship. He is defined by those responses in me of reverence and awe for the world I perceive.

• • •

JUNE 27, 1970. This late afternoon, Althea, Karrin, and I hiked up Taylor Canyon, directly east of our section of Ogden. The canyon stream rushed, the air was warm, and the mountain-sides glowed with the rich yellow-green of full summer. As we returned, I picked a cluster of flowers—small trumpet shapes in mingled colors of lavender and pink. I felt a surge of wonder at the genetic impulse that had produced among its endless variations these fragile blossoms hidden, like Emerson's Rhodora, from the human eye. That surge of wonder was intensely pleasant to me, and I immediately recognized it as religious. It was a feeling affirmative of me and immensely fulfilling.

Tonight as I think about that feeling and the flowers that evoked it, I believe I recognize words that will express what it is that I discern in wilderness. The flowers brought freshly upon me the recognition of being and of the impulse to be.

All of the world that I perceive is expressed in one word—being. I recognize being everywhere—myself, other persons, animals, rocks, earth, everything that fills void, everything that is. And that unperceived dimension of being that some call God, or cause, or essence, or natural law, I best discern as the impulse to be.

Any naming of the intuited and imperceptible must at best be done by analogy with something tangible. Within myself I find impulse. The best explanation I have for the multifarious being about me is by analogy with that impulse within me. Brook and rock, fish and man—in us all is the impulse to be. Being and the impulse to be—these are all and everything. Together they are nature.

• • •

APRIL 24, 1971. Last week end, Althea, Karrin, and I kept our custom of celebrating the full arrival of spring by driving to Flaming Gorge. On our pick-up, we carried the little camper I bought last fall and renovated during March. In it, we gave up our pioneer fortitude and tasted the novelty of camping with the compact convenience of sink, stove, and indoor beds.

The best moment of the trip was at noon at Dowd Mountain overlook. Several thousand feet below, Flaming Gorge Reservoir reached off through a multitude of canyons, opening wide at one moment and at another disappearing from view behind the ridges and escarpments that the serpentine Green River has left behind in its leveling course. Chimney buttes shimmered to the north where the Firehole River joins the Green. To the east and south, strange snow-covered mountains rose and fused with the sky on an opaque horizon.

I was filled with awe and reverence. I was once again touched by the perennial mystery of wilderness. My experience at such times is complex and variable, but at this particular moment, it seemed to me that my emotions were drawn to being. The far reaches of ridge and mountain suggested the impulse or collocation of impulses that has produced the earth. Alternately shadowed by wind-blown clouds and relit by the noon-day sun, the land before me spoke of the forces that, unplanned, unbidden, unpremeditated, have grown into mountains, forests, and me. Reverence for this natural process is my religion.

• • •

JUNE 16, 1971. I sat on the screen porch this late afternoon, reading a book on the evolution of life while I waited for sunset. How awesome is the quixotic and unpredictable sort of matter that we call life. Who could have guessed the countless forms, the intricate balancings, the complex adaptations living matter has come to? It is useful for a predator fish living at lightless depths of the ocean to have a light for attracting victims. Its living tissues oblige; the fish evolves, on a rod dangling out over its massive jaws, a faint electrical glow. The impulse within living tissue seems to have no limit to the forms it will take or the purposes it will meet if only its environment is encouraging.

I am impressed by this evidence for design and intelligence in the universe. But I am equally impressed by the unintelligent raising of mountains that are only to be leveled again, and by the waste and cruelty of creating admirable species only to give them as prey to more aggressive species. Nature is the most impenetrable of mysteries.

Albert Schweitzer speaks somewhere of being burdened throughout his life with the sense that the universe is inexplicably mysterious. So I feel. Being is unfathomable. I have no explanations why things exist. But along with puzzling, I also marvel. Being is an ultimate good and a cause of profound wonder.

Entries on Wilderness as the Symbol for Infinity

JUNE 22, 1970. Althea, Karrin, and I have returned from a two-week visit with my mother in Snowflake, Arizona. I am always startled, when revisiting the terrain of my childhood, to see how open and sky-filled it is. I felt this recurring surprise one morning when Althea and I left Karrin in the care of Grandmother Peterson and drove to Four Mile Knoll. This knoll took its importance in the pioneer days of Snowflake as a mile-post on the road that crosses the rolling plain lying between Snowflake and the railroad at Holbrook. Four Mile Knoll and a dozen other knolls dot this plain, remnants of ancient strata of earth and rock that now for the most part have been carried down the washes and gullies leading to the Little Colorado River. The sides of Four Mile Knoll are steep and are littered with boulders that have broken away from the overlying grey sandstone as water and wind have eaten out the red earth beneath them.

When Althea and I climbed the knoll, it was nine o'clock, and the sun was well into the sky. Already the center of the sky had taken on the intense blue of full day, while its distant edges shimmered with a dense luminescence. The morning breeze, almost absorbed in the tranquility of a hot Arizona day, at moments brushed our faces with hints of a fresh and cool dawn, while the new heat aroused a rich and pungent odor from the junipers that dot the sides of the knoll. At the top, Althea and I slowly walked the circumference of the knoll. Wherever we stopped, we could see into immensity. In all directions, the plains of the Little Colorado stretched into distant tranquility. During long months in Utah, I forget how completely Arizona is a land of horizon. In its own way, Utah is also a land of a big sky. The same mountains that at times restrict and obscure the horizon, at other times give the viewer the elevation he needs to see the place where land and sky fuse. But in Utah, the horizon is almost always a half horizon, a semi-circle. On Four Mile Knoll, I was reminded that in Arizona, land and sky reach out to each other in full circle. The sky was not impeded or diminished by looming cliffs, ridges or peaks. The open, rolling land gave accent to the arch of the sky. But this land also has projections and irregularities that give character to its horizon and preserve it from that sterile imperceptibility of an ocean horizon. From Four Mile Knoll, I could see on the horizon the long igneous ridge that local people call the Point of the Mountain. I could see Mesa Redondo, the White Mountains, the Mogollon Rim, the San Francisco Peaks, the mesas and knolls of Navajoland, the upthrust lava peak of the Woodruff Butte. If at times these features made the horizon seem closer, they also made it seem more tangible, more real and discernible.

Standing there, absorbing grass and juniper, rock, sun, and sky, I became aware of the horizon's meaning. Horizon is more than the place where land and sky meet, more than the place where the earth forms a rim or where land disappears. Horizon symbolizes immensity. It tells me that immensity has no measure. As a human being, I am accustomed to standards of measurement that are known and familiar, that allow me to scale every new thing against something proximate to myself. It is easy to suppose that my street, my city, my particular range of mountains confine all space and being. But the horizon teaches me differently. A horizon is not an end or a border beyond which space and being cease. A horizon suggests movement without cessation, distance without terminal, space without boundaries. A horizon suggests infinity. That is what I could discern as I stood on Four Mile Knoll looking into the shimmering edges of a hot June day.

• • •

AUGUST 25, 1971. Last week, Althea and I backpacked with Bob Mikkelsen and a few of his friends over Rocky Sea Pass in the Uinta Mountains. We camped at a lake in Rock Creek Basin. On the second morning, Althea and I resisted the enticements of Bob for a day of fishing and hiked off to explore the mystery of a distant unnamed pass on the main Uinta ridge at the head of Rock Creek Basin. The morning sparkled with sun as we made our way through thickets of lodge pole pines, across lush meadows drained by clear streams, and along the borders of limpid Uinta lakes. By noon we were climbing sharply toward the pass. As we approached timberline, Rock Creek Basin opened southward to our view. The creek had furrowed a narrow gorge in the center of the basin, from which the land rose in broad terraces rimmed by minor cliffs and covered by forests of lodge pole pine and fir, which were occasionally broken by lakes and meadows. On either side of the pass toward which we climbed, peaks rose into mounding spheres of barren rock, skirted by weather-beaten shrubbery and talus slopes composed of boulders as large as automobiles. As we topped the pass, we were startled. Without warning, we were looking over cliffs that fell away for a thousand feet. The peaks, we could see, were spherical only on their southern half; on their northern side, they were cut away abruptly, as if a giant cleaver had sheared them, leaving behind upright walls of unbroken rock measuring thousands of acres.

Our map gave the basin into which we looked the iterative name of the Left Fork of the East Fork of the Bear River. There was a satisfaction, a sense of a completed circle, for Althea and me in recognizing that the Bear River, which drains into the Great Salt Lake scarcely more than twenty miles from our home in Ogden, here has its beginning. Like other Uinta north slope basins, this basin was more narrow than its southward draining counterpart. But like Rock Creek Basin, this basin had a floor composed of terraces rimmed by minor cliffs and covered by timber and meadow. There were two lakes in the basin. One of them was a shimmering, delicate amethyst.

Althea and I stayed on the pass for perhaps an hour and a half, a scant time for absorbing an inexhaustible mass of detail, of line, color, and configuration. As we sat, the weather changed. The wind was quickening, and drifts of rain cloud were filling the sky. Out over the basins we could see alternating movements of sun and shadow. Standing like gods on Olympus, we could see a drifting thunderstorm flashing and rumbling over the western wall of Rock Creek Basin. North and south, in the distant reaches of the basins, mist and dust put into strange relief the receding ranks of ridges that fell away one behind another. Far away, on the plains that lie on either flank of the Uinta range, the horizon was lost in the ambiguities of conflicting sun and storm.

With a single sweep of my eyes, I could comprehend cliff, forest, lake, sun, and sky. The world was magnificent and immense. I could see and feel infinity. In our fevers and dreams, infinity terrifies us. We see ourselves on the verge of the Miltonic abyss, confronting darkness and the void. The terror of infinity adds to our compulsion to cling to the domestic. For there, in a world that we ourselves have constructed, behind fences that we have erected, we can imagine that we are in a universe with meted boundaries and a comforting familiarity. But on this high pass, there was no way to deny that space and being are without limit. I was by moments depressed, but there was also pleasure in my recognition of infinity. The pleasure arose, I could recognize, from the fact that the scene before me, with its tangible infinitude, fed the hunger of my ego for immensity and magnitude, for girth and greatness. By my ineluctable human tendency to project myself into whatever person or thing or scene that I encounter, by the irrational, compelling act of imaginatively taking on the identity of what is before me, I had taken on immensity. Like the child in Whitman's poem who went forth and became what he saw, I had become the vast cliffs, the broad basins, the shimmering lakes, the dark forests, the sweeping drift of sun and cloud. Within me is a boundless thirst for being, a desire for magnitude and immensity, a childlike impulse to fill the universe with my own being, to shout out with a mighty clamor the worth and dignity of a living thing. For that moment, in that high place, my deep thirst was slaked, my hunger fed, and I was happy.

Entries on Wilderness as the Symbol for Immortality

MAY 16, 1970. Last week I was at Kelton, an extinct town on the old transcontinental railroad north of the Great Salt Lake. No house stands now at Kelton. The town site is marked by an attenuated cottonwood tree, the old grade of the railroad, bricks and boards half buried among the sage brush, and a small cemetery. The cemetery contains several small grave plots, enclosed by weathered, dilapidated picket fences, in which a few wood and stone markers memorialize lives that came to an end ninety years ago. Wilderness is fast reclaiming this last remnant of the town, aided by unthinking hunters. A metal sign, which, in the name of the sheriff of Box Elder County, sternly forbids the molestation of graves, has been riddled by defiant blasts from shotguns. Ominous excavations within the burial plots indicate that, in the opinion of some modern curio collector, these century old bones are as legitimately susceptible to harvest and display as the fossil bones to be found in a million year old Australopithecine site.

The leveled town and the corroding cemetery are at one with wilderness. On the day of my visit, the sky was hot and wide and blue, and a restless wind eddied and roiled into dust devils that spun columns of dust at a furious pace across the sage-covered plain. The fading remains of a permanent human presence here only enhanced my sense of wilderness.

My recognition that the town had returned to wilderness left me ambivalent. I was depressed by the undeniable evidence of my own brevity and mortality. I was forced to recognize that those wild and natural events within my own body—that passionate beating of my heart, that rhythmical heaving of my lungs—are revolutions of a wheel rolling toward death. Two little graves, marked by marble lambs, fixed my attention. The faded wording upon the stones told me that sibling babies were buried here. They undoubtedly had for a time a kind of immortality in the grieved memories of those who buried them. Now, almost a hundred years later, those other lives, who had conceived and nurtured these little lives and who had buried them here and for a time remembered them, those lives too were at rest in some faraway quiet place. These little lives had no more relevance now that the hot wind crooning in the nearby cottonwood tree. I was stifled and still, knowing that someday, somewhere, the wind will blow across the scene of my irrelevance, too.

Confronting this fact at Kelton, I was depressed. But I was surprised to discover within myself a contrary reaction, a paradoxical exhilaration, a sense of uplift and enhancement. These graves spoke promise and comfort to me. In their presence, I recognized not only what I am, but what I wish to be. If in actuality, I am brief, in desire I am eternal. I find no relenting within myself, no compromises on the issue of living. There is the steady throb, the constant rush of blood, the insatiable appetite, the desire to drink deeply and then ever more deeply. I do not often feel my will to live in its full intensity. My feelings are like impounded water, latent with energy, awaiting only the opening of floodgates to flow. This hot, wide sky, this wind-roused land, this weathered little cemetery unlocked my desire for life and being. From the intensity of that desire, a joy arose. It was a paradox that I did not understand and will bear explaining. Out of the recognition of death came an affirmation of life.

◆ ◆ ◆

MARCH 15, 1971. I walked along a dike at the Bear River migratory bird refuge on this sunny afternoon. I saw tasseled reeds waving in the wind. I sensed brotherhood with them and felt strongly the wish to live forever.

◆ ◆ ◆

JULY 18, 1971. Yesterday I sat a while on a rim of the Granddaddy Basin of the Uinta Mountains. My wife and daughter and my brother and his family were in camp at Betsy Lake, from which I had wandered, following no trail until I emerged upon a rim of minor cliffs overlooking an immense and unbroken forest. As I sat, I was utterly peaceful. I found myself fervently wishing that the forest would live forever. I felt a close and warm kinship with it, and, as my feelings progressed, I found myself almost believing that the forest would live without cessation. This feeling puzzled me, because forests, like men, do not live forever. In some compelling way, this forest symbolized eternity for me.

It may be that my sense of the forest's immortality arose from its collective longevity. Individual trees are split by lightning, or infested by wood borers, or uprooted by spring winds, but the forest goes on for millennia. Or it may be that this forest stood as a forceful symbol for eternity because, as wilderness, it stands for all being. This forest has emerged from the incomprehensible process that we call nature. It is an expression of the great impulse to be, and even though this forest shall cease to be, there are other forests in other places and there will be other forests in other times. And if there are no forests, there will be rocks and oceans, or planets, stars, and cosmic dust. There is no end to being. Being is beyond time. It is eternal.

I am comforted that being is beyond time, for time is a destroyer. I do not know how to define time. To give some poor accounting of what time is, I have to use linguistic tenses of was and is and will be and to coin indefinable words such as past, present, and future. Time is that inner mystery when I awaken to discover that actuality had fled into memory, and that the future has become a new actuality. All that I know with certitude is that for being, time is flux and change. Its motion leaves nothing static and unaltered. Elements radiate into other elements. Substances combine into a new substance. Life flourishes by generation. Individuals grow and die, and species evolve into other species. Time is beginning and ending, growth and decay, consciousness and annihilation. I am in time, and I am bound over to death.

If I am evanescent and brief in fact, I am not so in desire. In desire I am eternal. Eternity, I think, is time without its beginnings and endings. I would be without beginnings and endings. I would escape my fated march toward death, I would evade annihilation. I would see myself in the dawn forever. I would smell fresh air and see suns rise. I would hoe my garden and sit with my friends tomorrow as today, and the day after that, and then always the day after that. My will to be is endless.

As I sat yesterday on the rim overlooking the Uinta forest, I lived as one who lives timelessly. I was filled with tranquility, and my thoughts of time and brevity and death did not disturb me. I borrowed and put on the eternity that I sensed the forest to have and that I have sensed wilderness in many places to have. This forest evoked my will to live forever, to be endlessly. And there in its presence, and in the presence of the open sky and the fresh wind, I sat with the calm assurance of the immortal. I lived beyond time, beyond beginnings and endings. I was one whose being was forever.

Becoming a Writer

DURING THE SUMMER OF 1970 a skunk took up residence under our garage and began to raid our corn patch. It would pull down a ripe ear, strip back the husk, take two or three bites, and move on to another ear. I phoned the local office of the state department of wildlife resources and also the city animal control department. Both informed me that the skunk was my problem.

One evening I set a jaw trap attached to a long pole at the back of the garage. I had read in a trapping magazine while a boy that you could carry a trapped skunk by a long pole to a tub of water and drown it without causing it to stink. The next morning a skunk was in the trap. It looked very large and the pole very short. I got my .22 rifle and shot it in the head, killing it instantly. A wall of nauseating stench drifted across the neighborhood, and the old German next door, Carl Guertler, shook a finger at me across the fence, saying, "Brother Peterson, you haf broken the law. You haf fired a weapon within the city limits." I put the dead skunk in a box and transported it to the county landfill in the back of my pickup. At the intersection of Twenty-fourth and Washington, two young men waiting in an open Jeep for the red light to turn sniffed the air and looked around. You can never tell where you will smell a skunk in Utah.

Carl Guertler's wife died that fall. They had no children and only a few relatives in the United States. To that point we had been merely cordial. Carl was meticulous and orderly, keeping an immaculate rose garden and raking leaves from his lawn twice a day. Such a personality was bound to disapprove of my negligent way of keeping a yard. I let our lawns go two or three weeks without mowing, and I never edged them. After Carl's wife died, we began to have him over to dinner every Tuesday night just because we could guess how lonely his life had become. I don't recall whether it was Althea's idea or mine to have Carl over. It doesn't matter. We were entirely united on such things, and Althea thoughtfully tailored her menus to the diabetes with which Carl was afflicted. She became something of a surrogate daughter to Carl, who distinctly preferred her personality over mine. We continued the weekly dinners till he died more than ten years later. We soon expanded the Tuesday evening to include an hour of 35mm slides from his extensive collection, which he had taken while on vacation in Germany and western America over a period of many years. I admired his photographs and began to ask him questions about photography. In the spring of 1971 he told me there was a used camera like his for sale downtown—a primitive single-lens reflex Exa, a little brother to the more sophisticated Exacta.

That is how I got into photography. With a sense of happy self-indulgence, I read up on shutter speed, aperture size, and film sensitivity. For months I documented each shot I took, recording camera settings and light conditions in a notebook and comparing results when I had retrieved my finished slides. Over the next thirteen years I acquired two other cameras and accumulated more than five thousand slides. Photography doubled my interest in my surroundings. At first I thought all of my slides were beautiful. Going over my slides now I am puzzled by my unpredictable fits of zeal. I find multiple shots—with few discernible differences—of a certain cloud formation or of a berry-laden juniper bough or of a person in a given background. At any rate, the aspects of my life amenable to photography are amply documented from 1971 to about 1984. After that, I got tired of taking pictures and quit.

It struck my fancy during the summer of 1971 to express my western identity through the clothes I wore. I bought a pair of ranch Wellingtons—plain black boots with a half-high walking heel. I shopped around for a modest silver narrow-brim Stetson with a stockman's crown. The only narrow-brim Stetson with a stockman's crown in Weber County was black. After several trips back to the store to ponder, I bought this hat. The first day I wore my boots and hat on campus, I met a professor from across campus. He broke into loud laughter and, without a word, went his way shaking his head. That ended my attempt to look western on campus.

I helped replace the shingles on my mother's house during the summer of 1971. For some years Althea and I had been extending our summer visits to two weeks or more, during which I applied to Mother's house some of the handyman skills I was acquiring by working on our house in Ogden. I repaired cupboards, installed new screen doors, made new window screens, and laid vinyl floor tile in the kitchen. I was happy to please Mother with these projects because I had disappointed her in so many other ways. My most heroic project was the shingling of her house during the summer of 1971. I call it my project only because I initiated it. For more than a week, Leon and Marion worked side by side with me from dawn till dark, replacing weathered wood shingles with green asphalt shingles. We relied on Marion's know-how because neither Leon nor I had ever roofed a house before.

One morning while we were on the roof, my brother Elwood stopped on his way to the post office and talked to us from the street. I never saw him alive again because he died from a rare kind of cancer in April 1972. At Elwood's funeral Althea and I left Karrin in the child-care room. After the assembled Petersons had marched into the chapel, I regretted having left Karrin. I left the service, got her, and returned to a couple of empty seats on the side. As I ordinarily do during funerals, I wept abundantly, and Karrin took note of the tears streaming down my face. That is how a gift for grief is handed on from one generation to the next.

After Elwood had died in a Phoenix hospital, his son Woody inspected coffins at a mortuary and became angry at the cost. He drove the two hundred miles to Snowflake, went to work in his shop, and by the time of the funeral three days later had built and varnished a handsome coffin of birch. Elwood was buried at Lakeside where my father and many of his descendants are interred. After the dedication of the grave, a mortician instructed family members to leave so that cemetery workers could fill the grave. Theo Peterson, a son of my father's brother Hyrum, said, "I'll be damned if I leave this job unfinished." He seized a shovel and started throwing dirt, and others joined him. The Peterson family, it would seem, had not adapted to the funerary customs of a commercial age.

Visiting Snowflake during the summer of 1972, Althea and I found a heated dispute in progress over the whereabouts of the graves of Stott, Scott, and Wilson, suspected horse thieves lynched on the Mogollon Rim in 1888. Snowflake's chief of police, a classmate of mine in public school, said the graves were in one canyon. The town's nonunion barber, maybe ten years older than I, said the graves were in another. A cavalcade of cars, ours at the end, drove seventy miles of rough gravel road to settle the matter. There were three granite gravestones of recent vintage in the canyon that my classmate favored. The barber said that didn't matter. In 1940 he had helped dig up the graves of the lynched men in another canyon. It was possible, he said, the county had moved the graves while constructing a new road. My classmate, wearing his badge and pistol, began digging in one of the graves. When he was thigh deep, someone said, "Isn't it against the law to dig up graves?" He stopped digging and thought a while. Then a look of enlightenment came over his face. "I am the law," he said and went on digging. He found a few bones that a high school biology teacher identified as human. My classmate buried the bones but not before his cousin had surreptitiously pocketed one of them.

A year or so later the barber got into legal difficulty over his appropriation of some stray sheep. Not long afterward, he appeared on a float in Snowflake's Pioneer Day parade, which Althea and I witnessed. The float was a wagon with a live sheep strapped into a barber's chair. Dressed in his white tunic, the barber stood behind the chair with shears in his hand. It was an act of sheer genius in social dynamics. The crowd along the street clapped and cheered, assuring the culprit that all was forgiven. This barber was a complete libertarian. He refused to buy a business license and gave haircuts for a dollar when union shops were charging five or six. Eventually a union barber forced the law to shut him down. I got a haircut from him every time I went to Snowflake during the 1970s. He listened patiently while I told him what kind of haircut I wanted, then gave me the same two-minute haircut he gave everybody else.

I went on during 1971 and 1972 performing my duties as chairman of the English Department. I put a lot of effort into developing our department as an influence with the teachers of English in junior and senior high schools in northern Utah. I helped organize workshops for English teachers and sometimes participated in them as a self-styled expert on the assignment and grading of student writing. I continued to pay attention to the acquisition of doctorates by our faculty. When one of my colleagues angrily rejected an opportunity to retake his failed prelims at the University of Utah, I told him he would lose his assigned upper-division teaching specialty if he didn't acquire the doctorate. He wept and insisted he wouldn't take the exam again. But pretty soon he did, and he passed it.

During the winter of 1972 college president William Miller announced his retirement, and a search for a new president began. Faculty anxiety was high and rumors flew madly. The Academic Council, as our Faculty Senate was then known, declared a special meeting of the entire faculty. I spoke passionately in favor of an elected faculty screening committee. Within a few days the Board of Trustees had ordained such a committee, and I found myself elected to be its chairman. This was a heady experience, and for the next two years I seriously considered fixing my ambition upon an administrative career. I thought ultimately, even, of the presidency of a college or university.

I might have taken warning from my failure to influence other members of the screening committee. I favored a candidate who exemplified the ideals of a liberal education. My colleagues on the committee favored Joseph Bishop, a candidate grounded in current management theory. I met Bishop at the airport and on our drive to Ogden judged his questions to be so uninformed and his discourse so lacking in substance that my colleagues would write him off immediately. That evening another committee member, Jerald Storey, and I took Bishop to dinner. From the moment we were seated, Storey and Bishop began an intense, excited dialogue that excluded me entirely. Both were MBO enthusiasts. MBO stood for Management By Objectives, the first of a number of high-sounding management theories I have seen come and go at Weber State. Bishop's current position was as a consultant in MBO for a consortium of junior colleges in several states. Although his experience as an academic administrator was not extensive, other committee members were also impressed by his ability to hold forth on MBO, and his name was advanced, along with the names of two other applicants, to the Board of Trustees. I will not attempt to dissect the politics of the Board of Trustees except to say that the strong support of the faculty screening committee told in Bishop's favor. He became the president of Weber State College as of July 1, 1972, and soon afterward appointed Jerald Storey his academic vice president.

Returning from Snowflake in August 1972, I noticed that I couldn't see whether the road ahead was clear for safe passing. I had been wearing reading glasses for three or four years—horn-rimmed things that seemed to suit my masculine personality. Now an ophthalmologist diagnosed tiny cataracts, a clouding of my natural lenses. He had no explanation for their appearance in an otherwise healthy man of thirty-eight years. Half my genes are Swedish. Maybe the strong Arizona sun of my boyhood was too much for my Nordic eyes. The cataracts developed quickly, and by the end of spring quarter 1973, I was grading student papers with a magnifying glass. I had surgery for the removal of the clouded lens in my right eye in early July. Cataract surgery wasn't a simple outpatient process in those days—though it was much advanced over the era when you had to lie with your head immobilized by sandbags. For six weeks I followed a restrictive regimen—no reading, no lifting, no bending over, a shield over my eye at night. The enforced inactivity was tough, and there was always the anxiety that I would break the sutures by doing something stupid.

As I expected, my pathological emotions kicked in. I came out of the surgery in a claustrophobic mood. The anesthesiologist claimed I was out during the entire operation. I remembered waking over and over and finding my arms strapped tight. On the following nights, I dreamed of baying hounds, a pool of blood, and a disemboweled child. One Sunday I went to church with Althea. While the deacons were passing the sacrament, I began to cry and couldn't stop. Althea whispered that we should leave. She drove me up Weber Canyon and I felt better.

Eventually I was fitted with a contact lens that gave me normal distance vision. Ordinary glasses gave me additional correction for reading. At bedtime I took off the contact lens and used thick glasses with a narrow field of vision for getting about the house. It was a miracle to see again, and my spirits immediately rose. I was astonished to make out the trees on the distant ridges of the Wasatch. I had forgotten they were there. I went for three years with one good eye before gathering enough courage to have surgery on the other eye. One eye is not as good as two, but it is infinitely better than none.

During the spring of 1973 I was reappointed chairman of the English Department. However, before I began my second term, the position of director of the college Honors Program opened suddenly. Jerald Storey suggested that I apply. I did and was appointed. I was still thinking of an administrative career, and this new position seemed a step in that direction.

An honors curriculum existed at that moment, and that was about all. I hired a secretary, Marilyn Diamond, and for the first year she and I occupied small side-by-side faculty offices. After that, I occupied a spacious administrative office, and she shared a large nearby office with the secretaries from two other programs. There was never, during my nine-year period as director, a lounge where honors students could meet or a dedicated classroom where special honors courses could be taught. There was no honors faculty. My parsimonious budget required that I hire instructors from existing departments on an overload basis. I could either pay them directly or transfer the money to their department chairperson, who released them from lower-division courses by hiring adjunct instructors with the transferred money. It was never easy to find instructors. By default, I usually taught at least one honors course each quarter.

I became aware during the 1970s of a proclivity for laboring in behalf of causes in which I had only an indirect interest. In addition to teaching, directing the Honors Program, and writing, I carried on considerable miscellaneous activity, attending meetings, joining clubs, accepting membership on committees, speaking to groups, and so on.

Among the many professional organizations that I joined was the Western Literature Association, on whose executive council I served during the early 1970s. In 1973, Golden Taylor, who edited the association's journal at Colorado State University, proposed that the journal be transferred to Utah State University with his son-in-law Tom Lyon as editor—an arrangement that Golden, who also served as the association's sometimes irascible and high-handed executive secretary, negotiated without prior consultation with the executive council.

As we assembled in October 1973 in Austin, Texas, for the annual conference of the association, it was by no means certain that we would endorse this proposition. However, before the council met, Max Westbrook, a Texan and, like Golden, one of the founding figures of WLA, took me aside and pointed out that Utah State's offer to provide an office, an editorial assistant, and released time for an editor of the journal was not likely to be duplicated elsewhere. Max must have lobbied the other council members too, because all of us voted in favor of the proposal. Nonetheless, the council appointed a committee to rewrite the WLA constitution and bylaws with an eye to roping in Golden a little. I served on that committee, penning various drafts for my colleagues' consideration over a period of nearly six months. Although we debated abolishing the position of executive secretary, in the end we left it intact. We had all agreed you can't cashier a founding father. I will add that the soft-spoken Tom Lyon would prove to be a capable, highly respected editor of the journal.

While in Austin, I talked pleasantly with Golden one evening at Max's home. I asked him why he had left the Mormon Church. He said because the church had required him to stifle his own thinking. Elder Spencer W. Kimball, whose wife, Camilla, was a sister to Golden's wife, Ethyl, had tried to dissuade him. Recounting that story to me, Golden blazed into anger, struck a fist against a palm, and said, "By God, I insist on an untrammeled mind!" Yet, only moments later, while he spoke of informing his elderly father of his decision to leave the church, tears filled his eyes and his voice broke.

Another organization to which I devoted much time and energy was the Utah Academy of Science, Arts, and Letters. As chairperson of the Letters Division of the academy from 1973 to 1975, I was on its board when the question arose whether the academy should, like the recently defunct Utah Conference on Higher Education, shut itself down. Those who favored closing the academy pointed out that scientists and scholars of national aspiration rarely presented papers at its meetings. I argued in favor of keeping the academy alive. I also volunteered to become the editor of a re-vamped journal for the academy, which hitherto had, without peer review, published any article read in an academy meeting whose author would pay for the costs of publication. Committing the academy to pay full publication costs, the board ordained peer review for its semiannual journal and appointed me its unpaid editor. Casting about for a more appropriate title than *Proceedings,* I came up with *Encyclia.* Reasoning that the academy embraced all branches of knowledge, I coined this neologism by association with *encyclopedia,* which refers to a comprehensive compendium of knowledge.

I served as the entire staff of *Encyclia,* being in effect editor in chief, managing editor, overseer of peer review, copy editor, proof-reader, layout editor, marketing specialist, and shipping clerk. I had no released time from my customary duties in the classroom and office of the Honors Program, my superiors at Weber State assuming that my schedule included spare time for extracurricular activities. It was therefore perhaps fated that the first issue of *Encyclia* would prove disastrous. I will not go into the details of this error-ridden issue, which sits today on library shelves, a glaring testimony to my inexperience. I will at least credit myself with learning my lesson. I became much more attentive, much more insistent, with every stage of the journal's production. Judging that my major mistake had been to allow an Ogden printing firm to also handle the typesetting and layout of the journal, I sought out a typesetter in Orem, a somewhat impoverished fellow who worked in a back room of his small, child-worn house. At least once during the production of each issue, I drove the seventy-five miles to Orem and worked till late at night, checking final proofs and supervising lay-out. One evening I shared the family's dinner, a giant bowl of taco salad and copious flasks of orange juice. It was heart wringing to see the eager joy with which the five children attacked the taco salad. My workplace was a table in a tiny bedroom where two of the boys slept. One night, the six year old came in with a fistful of M&Ms and, fully clothed, lay on his bunk. After a while I became aware that he had gone to sleep. I removed M&Ms from his fist, took off his shoes, and pulled a cover over him before going on with my work.

Althea and I gave Karrin a puppy for Christmas in 1973, a black and white cross between a Chihuahua and a fox terrier. Karrin named her Peppermint Patty. We called her Peppermint and, later, Dingus. She was friendly and affectionate and bonded readily with all of us. She liked to sit on our laps while we read or studied or drove a car. We had her spayed at six months and around the same time succeeded in getting her housebroken. One day I had the good luck of apprehending her in the act of defecating just inside the front door. I caught her up with a roar, thrust her muzzle close to the excrement, and tossed her out-of-doors. With that she understood what I was after. From then on she barked to go outside when she need to relieve herself. In general, she was a great nuisance. Outdoors she rolled in carrion and ate the excrement of other dogs. Indoors she shed hair constantly. As she got older, she developed warts and became utterly unlovely. Still we cared for her scrupulously. The very vulnerability of a dog, the fact you can legally take it to the vet's on any day and have it killed, invokes the parenting instinct in human beings.

I reacted with alarm to the oil embargo of late 1973. Following the agreement of the OPEC nations to reduce production, prices doubled overnight and lines of automobiles began to form at service stations in many parts of the nation. Congress legislated a fifty-five-mile-an-hour speed limit on the nation's freeways and ordained—futilely, as it turned out—a new generation of smaller automobiles with gas-conserving engines. The national media were suddenly full of talk about the ultimate depletion not just of petroleum but of many other natural resources as well.

In early 1974 I traded in our Plymouth sedan on a Volkswagen Superbeetle, a vehicle with slightly more trunk space than our first Beetle but otherwise identical to it. I soon sold the pickup and camper at a price greatly to the buyer's advantage. Time would show my haste in disposing of extravagant automobiles was foolish. The big car has not disappeared from the American scene. It has proliferated anew in the sports utility vehicle that suburban housewives insist upon in increasing numbers. The day will come when the natural resources on which an ever-expanding consumer civilization relies will be exhausted. I have no idea when that will happen. That it will happen is certain. In the meantime, my personal willingness to conserve is meaningless against the vast collective impulse of modern world civilization to consume at a high rate. A consumer civilization will conserve only when it has run out of resources. It is impossible even to imagine the suffering and anguish and civil warfare that will then ensue.

We spent the cash from the sale of the pickup on sporting gear. We bought a tent of medium size for car camping. We bought skis, bindings, boots, and down jackets for the three of us, also pack frames and down mummy bags for backpacking. I bought a chestnut-colored Schwinn ten-speed bicycle, which I considered beautiful. I rode it between home and campus in good weather for five or six years. Then it was stolen, the thief cutting the cable that secured it to a rack on campus. That broke my will for cycling. I bought a battered used ten-speed, thinking a thief wouldn't want to steal it, but I never rode it and eventually gave it away.

During the summer of 1974 I decided to get on with becoming a writer. From the moment of declaring myself an English major at eighteen, I had coveted fame as a writer. Now I was forty. Turning forty was psychologically harder for me than turning fifty and sixty would prove to be. It seemed incredible that I had arrived at the threshold of middle age. I would have to act soon if I were ever to become a writer. Yet I had also recently acquired a taste for administration. I fancied I had the intelligence and social skills to work up through administrative ranks to the presidency of a college or possibly even a university. Quite fortuitously, events in the summer of 1974 helped me abandon this unrealistic ambition.

From the moment of his installation Joseph Bishop had planned to create a separate school of general education with its own faculty and curriculum. He drew his plan from the example of a large community college in Florida, where it may well have been a workable idea. A community college typically does not offer majors and minors and does not require a highly specialized faculty. At Weber State, a large four-year institution, fully half of the academic departments could field a faculty large enough to service their majors and minors only by virtue of having general education courses with which their faculty could fill out their required teaching load. Depriving them of general education courses, as Bishop planned to do, would seriously diminish, if not kill, their major and minor programs.

In 1974 Bishop broke the large School of Arts, Letters, and Sciences into three smaller schools; moved its dean, Dello Dayton, into a meaningless position; and sacked the deans of three other schools. He hoped the six new deans would help implement his as yet unrealized plan. Instead he had set in motion events that made the faculty of Weber State into the most militant and intractable of any institution in Utah. In the spring of 1976 a meeting of professors, department chairpersons, and even some of the recently appointed deans voted to call openly for Bishop's resignation. The Board of Trustees supported Bishop, and in the late summer of 1976 a compromise was reached that allowed Bishop to continue as president of the college. He was required, however, to abandon his plan for a separate school of general education and to accept the demoted dean, Dello Dayton, as his academic vice president. Bishop went on under this settlement until, early in 1978, he resigned to accept a call from the Mormon Church to serve as a mission president. In my judgment, he had never grasped how to lead a faculty by aligning himself with its predominant interests.

I confess that I viewed the sacking of the deans in 1974 as an opportunity for me. I had written speeches for Bishop, including his inaugural address. As chairman of the English Department I had duly applied the principles of MBO to the English faculty. Hoping that my success with the Honors Program would recommend me, I applied for the deanship of the new School of Humanities. But nothing was certain, and I decided to let events determine my ambition. If I were appointed dean, I would concentrate on rising through the administrative ranks. If I were not, I would concentrate on writing. In early summer, my good friend Bob Mikkelsen was appointed dean, and the matter was settled. I did not think of myself, even at this point, as becoming *only* a writer. For the moment I was both a teacher and a petty administrator. I knew that over the long haul I would remain a teacher. My writing might complement my teaching but not supplant it.

Althea, Karrin, and I skied with dedicated zeal during the winter of 1974–1975. For three months we took to the slopes on both Saturday and Sunday. Althea and I had a few lessons. Karrin completed a full beginner's course with the Miller Ski School at Snowbasin. By the end of the season Althea and I could do parallel skiing under ideal conditions. The snow had to be packed yet soft and forgiving, and the sun had to be out. Cloudy days were hellish. Some skiers can adapt to terrain by kinesthetic feeling. We couldn't. We had to be able to see where we were going. Sometimes I experienced the wild while skiing. I would stop at a boundary and look out across undisturbed, pristine snow. More than once I saw grouse perched in a fir tree. On an ideal day, carving good turns, I felt something close to wild freedom in the rushing air and hissing snow. I was glad to be out-of-doors, glad to be alive.

The next winter we bought season passes at Snowbasin. In early February 1976, Karrin severed a tendon on a shard of glass while sliding on her knees in the snow near our house. Her lower leg swung like dead weight while I carried her into the emergency room of the hospital. Later that evening an orthopedic surgeon sutured the tendon and put a cast on her leg. While that was going on, Althea and I watched the Winter Olympics in the waiting room. Skiing the next weekend, I took a tumble in order to miss a tree and wrenched my knee. The orthopedist said I could either wear a cast on my knee or walk as if I had a cast on it. So I walked with a stiff leg for six weeks. Althea skied with friends a few more times. We figured we had skied enough to make back our investment in season passes, but we never bought season passes again. I will say this for season passes: they relieve the pressure to buy half-day passes and ski every available minute. While we had them, we skied only during the best part of the day, starting at ten and quitting soon after two.

By the mid-1970s, Karrin was a veteran backpacker, who could handle a spinning rod with finesse and bait a hook and gut a trout. We made three or four excursions into the Uintas each summer. Once we backpacked with Charles and Betty and their children in the Uintas. We backpacked with Leon and Gussie and their children in the White Mountains of Arizona and, on two occasions, in the San Juans of Colorado. On another memorable trip with Leon and his family, we climbed King's Peak, the highest point in Utah.

Peppermint came along on most of our trips. She slept at night inside my mummy bag in the crook of my knees. An unsavory odor filled my nostrils if I pulled the hood of the bag over my face. Peppermint ran herself to exhaustion on our excursions and refused to eat the dried dog food I carried for her. One day we came out of the Uintas in a thunderstorm. A cold wind blew and hail covered the ground. Looking back, I couldn't see Peppermint. I called and she wobbled onto the trail and ran forward a few steps. Then she tumbled and lay still, unconscious from hypothermia. I carried her under my poncho and she soon revived. I was glad she was a little dog. We met a lot of people in the Uintas with big dogs, which were never on a leash. Typically I scooped up Peppermint and said, "This is so my dog won't tear your dog to pieces." Quite often the people with the big dogs wouldn't laugh. They just looked scornful. A dog the size of Peppermint was no better than a pissant in their eyes.

We never had any serious accidents while backpacking, but once I thought we might. We were hiking up Smith's Fork on the north slope of the Uintas. It's a beautiful trail, gaining elevation gradually and giving dramatic views of Red Castle Peak. Near our destination, a lake at the base of the peak, the trail crossed a creek that rushed and tumbled into Smith's Fork only yards below the crossing. Using a staff, I helped Althea and Karrin across and returned for my pack and the dog. Only when we were all safe on the other side did I admit to myself how foolish I had been to attempt the crossing. Had we stumbled or slipped we would have been swept irretrievably down the torrent. I worried all night about our return. About noon the next day we broke camp, shouldered our packs, and went up the creek. Near a place where it narrowed between deep banks, I saw two fallen lodgepole pines. Cutting them from their half-buried roots with my small ax, I shoved them across the creek, one a little lower and offset from the other. The idea was to sit on the upper trunk with your feet on the lower and scoot across, a butt-width at a time. Karrin went first. As she climbed onto the opposite bank, she exulted, "That makes me feel triumphant!" The word *triumphant* surprised me. It wasn't a word kids typically use.

Speaking of Karrin and unusual words, once when she was eight or nine, she saw me under the kitchen sink trying to remove a clogged gooseneck. She asked me to let her do it. Concentrating on an unyielding slip nut, I growled at her. She stamped her foot and said, "You make me feel womanish!" I came out and handed her the wrench. I don't remember what happened after that. I just remember that word *womanish*. I don't know where she learned it.

Early in the summer of 1976 I had the cataract in my left eye removed. I was in a much better mood than after my first operation and spent my time creating a short story by using two tape recorders. I spoke a first version into one recorder, then, playing it back, revised it with the second. I went back and forth between oral drafts until I had a long and complicated version of my story "The Confessions of Augustine." Later, with my vision restored, I made such drastic changes on the typewriter that I lost my confidence in the oral composition of fiction. I for one am a visual writer. At any rate, I count the summer of 1976 as the beginning of my fiction writing. Like the character Fremont in my story, I was forty-two.

Late in the summer I undertook the renovation of our kitchen. I had already built oak cabinets for a cooktop and an oven. Despairing of time, we ordered the remaining cabinetry custom built to our specifications by Anderson's Milling Company. When it came, sanded but otherwise unfinished, it filled our entrance hall and living room. I mounted it over a period of weeks, and Althea and I together stained and varnished it. I laid Formica on the counters, installed a sink, and wired in the cooktop, oven, and dishwasher. We had been working on our house for ten years. We now considered it finished.

During spring break of 1977 we went to Snowflake and returned with Mother, who planned to stay with us a while. Mother was suffering from tic douloureux, a neuralgia that sent jolts of pain through her face. To keep her warm we bundled her in a sleeping bag in the front passenger seat of our Volkswagen. Althea and I took turns driving, otherwise sharing the back seat with Karrin and Peppermint. Returned to Ogden Althea announced her lower leg was swollen. It had been hurting for days, but she hadn't said anything. As it turned out, she had deep vein thrombosis in her left calf, made worse by the long, cramped ride in the Volkswagen. It was at this point that she told me she was pregnant. She had been asking to have another baby since Karrin was a little girl. Only as I could see Karrin approaching her teens did I concede. We had been making love for more than a year without contraception. The pregnancy, so the doctor informed us, had induced the blood clots in her leg.

Mother went to stay with Charles and Betty, and Althea was hospitalized for twelve days, then came home to continue taking a mild anticoagulant that would not harm the fetus. The physicians advised an abortion, warning us that only a more forceful anticoagulant would help dissolve the blood clot in her leg. Althea refused. After a couple of days at home, she had a natural miscarriage. She wept but we were both relieved. She returned to the hospital for thirteen more days. The veins of her lower leg suffered permanent damage, and she had to wear a support stocking and keep her leg up when she wasn't walking or otherwise being active. After that, neither of us had the courage to try for another child.

Karrin wishes she had a brother or sister. Obviously, Althea and I also wish she had one. My pathological emotions stood in the way. Though I believed I would learn to love a second child as intensely as I loved Karrin, I couldn't master my fear of another accession of the crippling terror I had felt during the final weeks of Althea's pregnancy. By the time I had grown beyond that fear, it was too late. I don't know whether I would have agreed to try for a second child earlier if Althea had been more insistent. It wasn't like her to insist on anything. Althea has made many concessions to me over the years. I grant that I have made many concessions to her. I could wish that mine equaled hers, but I fear they don't.

Turning twelve in April 1977, Karrin took a hunter's safety course and began to hunt small game during the following autumn. I bought her a single-shot .410 shotgun and bought myself a pump-action twelve gauge. We typically had poor luck. We shot a few grouse in the mountains and a few coots in the marshes. We hunted on Sundays a good deal. Later, in junior high school, Karrin fell in with a group of Mormon kids and began attending seminary. After that, we gave up hunting and skiing on Sunday. I was grateful for the three or four autumns that we hunted together. I was able to bond with the new person she was growing into.

One Thanksgiving morning we went duck hunting. Before dawn we set up a blind and put out our decoys. No ducks appeared. The sun came up bright and warm, and we found ourselves the only hunters out. Everybody else knew something about ducks we didn't. Driving along a dike we saw a solitary hen mallard that paddled to safety under a culvert. As we passed over the culvert,

Karrin told me to let her out and then keep driving. The unsuspecting duck came out of the culvert, and Karrin shot it on the water. We went home in great triumph and had Althea photograph us on the leaf-littered back lawn. In the photo we wear our thigh-high wading boots and hold our shotguns, and the mallard dangles from Karrin's fist.

Late in the fall of 1977 our Superbeetle broke down, and the Volkswagen dealership predicted three weeks for ordering the necessary part. With a thousand-dollar loan from Althea's mother, I bought a Toyota pickup with a five-speed manual transmission and a cab-high aluminum canopy over the bed. I was so ambivalent about buying it that I offered the salesman a ridiculously low sum. He told me the offer wouldn't fly with his boss. When he returned with a counteroffer, I said it had to be my first offer or nothing. He came back saying if I would just come up a hundred we could have a deal. I said my offer had become a matter of principle and they could take it or leave it. They sold me the pickup. This was the only time I ever won at the little game car retailers play with buyers.

I loved this economical little truck. In fact, I berated myself for not buying one earlier. I installed a water pump and sleeping pad in the back, and we slept in it instead of a tent when we went car camping. I hauled some memorable loads in it. One summer my mother gave her piano to one of Leon's daughters. When we visited her, she said she missed the piano. Although she had become quite deaf, she had been playing the piano some. She said if she could find another one at a reasonable price, she would buy it. I took the canopy off my pickup and drove to Showlow and asked a used furniture dealer for a cheap piano. He showed me a piano on which the tuning screw for a crucial key was stripped and couldn't be adjusted. I said that didn't matter. The piano looked good, and my mother was deaf and wouldn't know the difference. He sold it to me for seventy-five dollars. I hauled it back to Snowflake and got a couple of nephews to help me unload it. It pleased my mother greatly.

One winter we took my mother home to Snowflake in this truck. We had bought her a new sofa, which we loaded into the back. Mother sat next to the passenger's window, Karrin sat in the middle, and Althea and I took turns driving and crawling into a

sleeping bag on the sofa, where, our noses only a few inches beneath the canopy, we slept away the miles. Peppermint alternated
between riding in the cab and snoozing in the sleeping bag. Going
through Richfield I stopped to buy a Coke. I asked my mother if
she wanted something to drink. She said no. When I returned with
my Coke, she asked what it was. I said root beer because she disapproved of caffeinated drinks. She asked if she could have a little in
a spare cup. I gave it to her. She drank it without comment. Almost
instantly she became energized and talked volubly for more than
an hour and a half. I think that was the only caffeine she ever had
in her entire life.

In 1978 I saw some return on my efforts to become a writer. I
had acquired a copy of *The Writer's Market* and had been submitting stories to magazines. After many submissions, "The Confessions of Augustine" found a publisher in the *Denver Quarterly,*
which paid me $105. My story "Road to Damascus," much re-
vised from a draft I had written at Berkeley in 1961, was published
by *Dialogue: A Journal of Mormon Thought.*[1] At the end of 1978,
the Association for Mormon Letters (AML) gave me its fiction
prize for these stories. I had also submitted these stories and eight
others in the Utah State Division of Fine Arts writing contest for
1978. Entitled *The Confessions of Augustine,* my collection won
the first prize of $1,000 in its category.

My prize attracted the attention of Lavina Fielding Anderson,
an associate editor of *Ensign,* the official magazine of the Mormon
Church, who asked me to let her read the collection. Soon she arranged to have me read to a small group at her home on a Saturday
evening in June 1978. I read a chapter that, vastly revised, would
appear later in *The Backslider.* The small audience listened with
rapt attention. In retrospect, it is hard to overestimate the importance of their pleasure as an influence upon my later writing. Although I didn't realize it at the moment, they strongly reinforced
my impulse to write with a tough realism about Mormons in sin
and turmoil. For the first time in many years, I had begun to feel
like an insider among the Mormons.

18

Putting a Pathology to Use

WHEN I DECIDED TO GET ON with becoming a writer in 1974, I had in mind there would be at least four books in my future: a collection of short stories, a novel, a wilderness journal, and a scholarly study of western literature. I had in fact been working on my wilderness journal for a couple of years, and when I laid it aside unfinished in 1975, I intended to return to it sooner or later.

I laid it aside, as I now see, because it had gone in an unmanageable direction. It had started on a positive, optimistic note, which may be accurately sampled, I think, in the extracts I have included in Chapter 16. Toward the end, however, I began to talk about my pathological emotions. My final entry, an essay of some nineteen pages, attempted to explain these emotions by reference to unhappy childhood experiences involving my mother. I submitted this entry and several others to Don Walker for the *Possible Sack* in June 1975.

Don took the title of his publication from the belt bag in which Rocky Mountain trappers carried their "possibles"—minor items of clothing and gear. Edited and partly written by Don, this informal journal was typed, multilithed, and mailed from the English Department at the University of Utah. When it first appeared in 1971, I was keeping a handwritten wilderness journal on an irregular basis. The entries were anything but finished. Don's willingness to publish a selection of finished entries in successive issues of the *Possible Sack* proved crucial to their creation. I had an incentive and a recurring deadline for writing. I did most of my writing after putting Karrin to bed in the late evening during winter months. I sat in our study at a desk I myself had built and clattered away on a manual Royal typewriter. This labor helped hone my style. I wasn't in a rush. Night after night I worked on sentences until they seemed just right.

Don and Marjorie Walker were by now among our closest friends. Two or three times a year we got together with them and some of Don's former students for dinner and conversation about western literature. At least once a year Don organized a camping trip for a motley collection of professors and students, past and present, whom he called the Wild Bunch after Butch Cassidy's gang. We engaged in frontier Olympics on these outings, seeing who could toss dried cow patties the farthest or who could chop through a limb the fastest. Sometimes we assembled at the Walkers' hideaway ranch in Millard County. They had built a simple cabin and spent their summers there, reading and writing. Althea and I have never known more literate people than Don and Marjorie. They read world-class philosophy, history, biography, and fiction. Marjorie liked to talk with me about Snowflake. Her father, Charles Flake, who was killed by a sniper's bullet a few weeks before her birth, had grown up in Snowflake. Moreover, my mother had had a crush on him during her first year of high school at the Snowflake academy.

I didn't know that the entries from my wilderness journal that I submitted in 1975 were to be the last. For a couple of years Don kept saying he was about ready to do another issue of the *Possible Sack* in which my entries would appear. Then he said he had decided to shut it down altogether. Much later he told me my long final entry had something to do with his decision to abandon the *Possible Sack*. He believed it would injure my mother deeply. It probably would have. It wasn't a good essay anyhow. I don't think a wilderness journal is a good format for untangling pathological emotions. And in the meantime I had begun to write stories, which make a very good format for untangling a pathology.

Could I use a better word than *pathology* here? *Insanity,* perhaps. My condition was surely insane. I knew that as early as 1954. But *insanity* is a harsh word. *Neurosis* is gentler. Back when I started therapy, insanity broke into two kinds, *neurosis* being supposedly less crippling and socially more respectable than psychosis. I feared I might become psychotic plenty of times. So I clung to that word *neurosis*. However, it isn't used much now. So why not call it my pathology? Technically, pathology is the scientific study of disease. My dictionary also says it is the manifestation of a disease. As far as I am concerned, that is what my affliction adds up to: a disease. A serious disease.

Why did I want to explore this condition in a wilderness journal? My journal was my chief intellectual preoccupation for four or five years. My relationship with wilderness was always on my mind. But my pathology was always on my mind too. From my first recognition of it in the early 1950s, it was inescapable. Even in my good moods, I kept trying to figure it out, hoping that my next bad mood wouldn't be quite as bad as the last. Inevitably I began to think about how wilderness reflected all of my moods, good and bad.

In that last long entry that helped kill the *Possible Sack* I said wilderness evoked and reinforced my adult identity. In wilderness I felt independent and competent. I was speaking, of course, of the benign, happy side of the wild. That entry began with a clear, starry night at a campground in the Uintas. I had recovered from my first eye surgery and could see again. Althea and Karrin were asleep inside the camper, and I loitered outdoors for a long time.

In earlier entries I dealt, more profoundly I think, with some of the ways the not-so-benign wilderness evoked my pathology. I went deer hunting alone one bright October day. It was the last day of the season, and I didn't meet another hunter anywhere. Midafternoon the sky turned dark and gloomy. I panicked and wanted to run. I restrained myself and continued to hunt till nearly dark. I said, when I wrote about this experience in my wilderness journal, "Whatever mood lurks within me—the morbid as well as the cheerful—wilderness has in its immense variety some circumstance, some environment that will evoke that mood."[1]

I left psychotherapy in early 1976 and never returned. My years in psychotherapy added up to seventeen. The last ten and a half were with Blaine Belnap. I broke off with him reluctantly. I think he had decided I was cured. During 1975 he raised his fee and, even more decisive for me, began to show signs of being bored with my case.

I didn't feel cured. It is true that my moods were preponderantly confident and eager. Even in my bad moods I could forget my misery while preparing lectures or conferring with students. Yet I had to admit that I didn't trust my sense of well-being and competence to last. If I consulted my feelings on my most positive day, I could discern a glimmer of my old nemesis, anxiety. While teaching I suffered a constant dread that a slight memory block would trigger a paralyzing anxiety—a dread exacerbated by the fact I had given up writing out my lectures and had only notes to fall back on should that paralysis occur.

I understood that at the center of my pathology was a hysterical anxiety over becoming independently competent. My need for a parent was fixed and inveterate. Even though I was an adult, I felt like a little child, helpless and vulnerable, unable to figure out the world for myself. All little children feel helpless and vulnerable and want a parent nearby. That feeling is supposed to evaporate when they grow up. In my case, it didn't.

I was aware that my good moods, the periods when I felt competent and secure, were dependent upon circumstances subject to change. Stable routines on campus, an abundant social life with friends and relatives, and above all the steady presence of my wife and daughter, especially my daughter, kept me happy. There was an inexplicable chemistry in the small, tight relationship that circumscribed Karrin and me. I could satisfy my need to act as an adult by caring for her as a father should. At the same time I could feed my insatiable need to be a child by meeting her child needs— a curious instance of vicarious or sublimated satisfaction of appetite and need.

By the 1970s I was achieving other uncanny insights into my pathology. I had been practicing introspection for many years. Early morning seemed the best time for introspection. It was as if my unconscious mind had been open all night and had only just now closed, and if I tried hard I could still catch glimpses of what it contained. During the three or four periods a year when my pathological emotions were uppermost, I often awoke with an image of myself lashing my own bare buttocks with a willow or cane. Accompanying the image was a kinesthetic impulse in my arm muscles to carry out the action. I associated this image with whippings my mother gave me when I was a child, and I concluded that I had internalized my mother's desire to punish me and applied it to myself.

I could remember my mother requiring me to go outside to the tamarisk patch by our house and break off a switch. Then she made me go into the bathroom and bare my buttocks and she whipped me with the switch. Rage accompanied this memory, a rage so strong that I could believe I had wanted to kill my mother. My first therapist had been of the opinion that my anger toward my mother made me an unbeliever. I couldn't kill her, but I could kill her God. Anger, I will note, was the most positive of my pathological emotions. It invigorated me, whereas anxiety and despair drained my energy. At some point in the early 1970s I confronted my mother with the foregoing memory. She contested its accuracy. She agreed she had probably sent me out to the tamarisk patch for a switch but was sure she would have let that threat of punishment suffice. She wouldn't have whipped me. I knew better than to insist upon my version of the incident. I already knew that memory is constructed of both fact and fiction. Furthermore, as I spoke with my eighty-year-old mother on the matter, I felt pity instead of rage. She seemed so aged and frail and needy, and we were both vastly beyond the circumstances that had given rise to my uncertain memory.

Another bizarre image that began to occur to me during the early 1970s was of crisscross marks on some kind of a wood surface. I would have attached no significance to this image had it not recurred, morning after morning, while I shaved. In time I began to see bloody feathers mashed into the crisscross marks. At this point I recognized the image as a memory of the chopping block we had used for cutting off the heads of chickens destined for Sunday dinner. Soon this more elaborate image began to evoke another image: the bloody neck of a decapitated chicken, rising above a collar of feathers and skin. This image, too, recurred over and over. At first I resisted what it suggested to me, which was my own cut-off penis. At last the association seemed inevitable, and I accepted that during my early childhood I had feared the cutting off of my penis. My memory of having been whipped in the bathroom with my pants down now took on new meaning. I could discern among my remembered emotions an anxiety that my penis might be the object of my mother's attack.

I knew as a child that my mother wanted me to be a girl. She liked to tell me that it took her three days after my birth to accept that I was a boy. She always ended the story by assuring me how happy she was with me as a boy. Yet she teased me when I was small by calling me Levida. Her teasing made me angry. It was as if I feared a girl's name would turn me into a girl.

This matter became even more complicated after I sorted out another image that came to me spontaneously in vacant moods. I remembered standing beside a pine tree while men filled my father's grave—an authentic memory. What I couldn't account for was that I saw myself throwing something into my father's grave. I was certain I had not actually thrown anything into my father's grave while it was being filled. Yet the clarity—and persistence—of the image persuaded me that I had wanted, very badly, to throw something into the grave.

In time I understood it was my penis and testicles I wished to throw in. It was an offer on my part. The clatter of gravel on the wood box that held my father's coffin brought home the finality of his death. It staggered me. They really were burying him! As I said earlier, I was destined to have nightmares about being buried alive for a long time. My father died from cancer that had metastasized to his lungs. I didn't know anything about cancer. For all I knew, it was my own recalcitrance that had killed him. Watching the dirt cover his coffin, I was ready to deal. I would give up my masculinity if he would come back from the grave.

This interpretation of the recurring image of throwing something into my father's grave was another crazy idea. It defied my adult understanding of my father's meaning in my life. He had stood as a positive masculine role model. I had consciously wanted to be a man like him. I could think of nothing he ever said or did to suggest he might want me to be a girl. Yet it seems so certain that it was my penis and testicles I wanted to throw into his grave that I have been led to this conclusion: my parents had always appeared united on matters regarding my character and conduct, and I had no way of knowing only one of them wanted me to be a girl.

I became aware of the foregoing images independently of Blaine Belnap. I was in fact going many weeks between visits with him while I was reconstructing these images. He reinforced them by not dismissing their importance when I told him about them. He didn't suggest meanings. I gradually came to those on my own. But of course he encouraged me to believe they had meanings. I am grateful for his calm and rational assistance.

As I say, I left therapy in 1976 and haven't been back. I may yet go back. I am aware that certain eventualities could trigger my pathology, the most obvious of which would be the death or serious debility of my wife or daughter. I fervently hope to die before either of them.

Is there anything positive to be said about my pathology?

It has made me introspective and probably more thoughtful than I would have been without it. It has made something of a psychologist of me. I believe, loosely speaking, in the id, the ego, and superego and in fixation, repression, internalization, and sublimation. It has made me willing to believe that human beings suffer much more than they make known to one another. My adviser at Berkeley, Ian Watt, told me he was not sure I knew enough about suffering to do well in their doctoral program. I must have looked bland and happy to him. He for his part certainly looked morose. If you search for trouble and misery in the lives of those who appear happy, you will find them. It isn't human to be consistently joyful. For most people, perhaps for all, the seasons of joy are brief, sure to be replaced by seasons of pain.

Perhaps the most positive thing to be said about my pathology is that it has fueled my writing of fiction. I can point out its subtle influence in all my fiction. In some of my fiction its influence has been more than subtle. Nowhere is it more evident than in my character Jeremy from *The Backslider*, who at college age emasculates himself and insists ever after that he is a little girl named Alice.

The Backslider was published in 1986. I created the version of Jeremy who appears in it no earlier than 1983. My first version of Jeremy appeared in a story I read at Lavina Fielding Anderson's house in 1978, of which I spoke in my last chapter. I had actually been thinking about a character like Jeremy as early as 1975 or 1976. I recall walking home from campus on gloomy winter afternoons seeking relief from my pathological emotions by creating a character who would carry out in fiction the horrifying deed that I had wanted, as a boy, to carry out in actuality. I knew from the start that I would portray the deed graphically. My motives for making it graphic were complex. Perhaps most important was my feeling that you can't express the horrifying through euphemisms and abstractions. Readers won't really feel the horror—if that is the effect you are after. A related motive, I admit, was to shock and startle my readers, whomever they might prove to be, because I felt angry over the bind my mother had put me into. It could be called writing for revenge. It could also be called a case of displaced aggression—taking out on humanity at large a grudge I had with a single individual. People do that kind of thing all the time.

The story I read at Lavina's wasn't a good one. For one thing, the plot was static. The narrator, the character who would evolve into Frank in *The Backslider,* looked back across several decades at his brother's self-emasculation. For another, I hadn't yet gotten over a propensity for heavy-handed symbolism. In the present moment of the story, perhaps twenty years after his self-emasculation, Jeremy is shown digging a giant terraced pit with a horse-drawn scraper. His brother finds an illustrated edition of Dante's *Inferno* in the house and realizes Jeremy is constructing the pit of hell. The point of the symbolism is that Jeremy's life has been hell and he awaits rescue from it. In the version that became *The Backslider,* Jeremy—only months after his self-emasculation—more plausibly digs a trench with one terrace in it, and the narrator doesn't interpret its meaning. It's just another crazy incident in the life of this psychotic youth, who thinks he is a little girl named Alice.

Though the story wasn't a good one, the audience at Lavina's listened intently. As I said in the last chapter, I think the tough realism with which I was depicting faithful Mormons had caught their attention. It was something they hadn't seen before.

Creating the character of Jeremy was good therapy for me. Whether it ultimately made good fiction others will have to judge. The further I went with Jeremy, refining his personality through extensive revision, the further he got from the actualities of my life. Other characters and events influenced my concept of Jeremy. Long before I had finished writing the novel, Jeremy's psychosis and self-emasculation had become secondary interests. For that reason, perhaps I shouldn't say my pathology has fueled my fiction. Instead, I should perhaps say it has helped to ignite it. I have had to find the fuel elsewhere.

19

The Canyons of Grace

ALTHEA'S FATHER DIED ON MARCH 5, 1979, at the age of ninety-one. He had shrunk into a very small silvery-haired man whose lower right leg was bent like a bow from malnutrition suffered during his childhood in Stanton, Iowa. Arvid had followed quiet routines of reading and watching television for many years. His face lighted whenever he saw Karrin. He called her Snookie and gave her five-dollar bills. A year or two after his death Karrin wrote a poem likening his silvery hair to the white irises growing along the alley in our backyard.

At the end of the summer of 1979 Althea, Karrin, and I made a monthlong tour of Europe. Arming ourselves with passports, Eurail passes, youth hostel cards, and a book called *Europe on Fifteen Dollars a Day*, we traveled in Germany, Belgium, Denmark, Sweden, France, Spain, Italy, and Switzerland. For a while we tried to gain time by traveling at night. The clack of the rails kept us awake, and after a bout of exhaustion in Madrid, we traveled only by day.

Among the art museums we visited were the Louvre, Prado, and Uffizi. In the basement of the Louvre stood unfinished statues by Michelangelo of slaves struggling to be free. The partially cut stone was alive with emergent hope and anguished impotence, which the fourteen-year-old Karrin felt as acutely as either Althea or I. In the Prado we came upon Picasso's *Guernica* and Bosch's *Garden of Earthly Delights* and in the Uffizi Botticelli's *Birth of Venus*. It is hard to explain the astonishment I felt upon discovering that my perambulations upon the face of the earth had brought me into the presence of such famous paintings. My most prized insight into the nature of painting occurred in a small museum dedicated to Picasso in Barcelona. On display were a half dozen or more of Picasso's abstract renditions of *Las Meninas,* a well-known representational painting by Velázquez that we had recently viewed in the Prado. Obviously Picasso had seen a variety of abstract outlines in Velázquez's design. For the first time in my life I could see what an abstract painter was after.

Upon our return from Europe, we learned that Althea's mother had inherited the estate of her childless sister, Althea, an irony because the two had been estranged for many years, owing, my wife thinks, to her aunt's reneging on a promise to pay for her college tuition if Stella would name her Althea. In early 1980 Stella used part of her unexpected inheritance as a down payment on a house at 1571 Twenty-fifth Street, just two doors above ours. We quickly evolved the custom of having her to dinner every evening. She generously used some of her inheritance to buy us a new Toyota Corolla. Stella was an intensely Christian woman, although by 1980, offended by a display of dancers clad in leotards during a worship service, she no longer attended the local Methodist church. But she contributed substantially to the Ogden Rescue Mission and read from the Bible and prayed daily.

In January 1980 I received a letter from Ann Lowry Weir, senior editor at the University of Illinois Press, saying she had been expecting me to mail a collection of short stories. The press published four collections each year in its short fiction series. I had sent Weir a story months before—"The Confessions of Augustine," I believe. Her reply had seemed so perfunctory that I let the matter drop. Now, assured of her interest, I mailed a hastily assembled collection of ten stories. Thus began a period of intense concentration upon the writing of short fiction, a period having strong religious as well as literary implications for me. It was already clear that my inevitable subject matter was Mormons in sin and turmoil, which I hoped to render with the eye of a realist. I didn't like to read fantasy, much less write it. Nor did I want to treat the ideal— a subject matter for sermons, not fiction. My plots and characters had to reflect the probable and the ordinary as I understood them. The only society I felt I knew well enough to treat realistically was Mormon. Furthermore, I was compulsively attracted to conflicts between belief and disbelief and between sexual impulse and conscience. I had long discerned such tensions among my fellow Mormons, who are, after all, entirely human despite their aspiration toward a more celestial condition.

Nonetheless, at that moment I thought of myself as writing for an American rather than a strictly Mormon audience. I didn't hope for a best-seller. I have never in my life allowed myself to fantasize about making money, being utterly doubtful of my ability to do so. What I did hope to do, subtly, almost subconsciously, was to please readers of a highly developed taste—English professors, perhaps, or doctors, lawyers, and businesspeople with literary interests. An enduring fame—that is what I fantasized about. I hoped to be remembered over the long haul as authors like Hardy and Steinbeck were remembered.

About a month after I had mailed my stories, Weir returned a referee's evaluation. Six of the stories, the referee judged, were mere sketches and should be forthwith abandoned. The other four had possibilities but would require considerable revision. These included the "The Confessions of Augustine" and "Road to Damascus" and early versions of "The Shriveprice" and "The Canyons of Grace." Whether I was capable of writing finished stories was doubtful, said the referee; certainly I stood in need of editorial help. Weir said simply that she looked forward to my resubmission and left the matter at that.

I have rarely felt so challenged. Though I had been teaching students how to analyze stories for decades, it was obvious I didn't know how to write one. I borrowed handbooks on writing fiction from the library and found them useless. I wrote to several prominent schools of creative writing, whose directors said their curriculum could do little for a writer at my stage of development. Reluctantly I accepted the fact that I would either teach myself or never learn. I began to read Barth's *Locked in the Funhouse* and Malamud's *Magic Barrel* simply because they were handy. Quite immediately I saw that I could do what was being done in those stories. The most important thing I saw was how they established a conflict in a character and then enlarged it through an advancing action. By May 1980 I had begun to revise the story that would become "The Shriveprice" and had started a new story, "The Gift." At some point during the summer I began a draft of "The Christianizing of Coburn Heights." I continued to hone myself on the techniques of fiction, a topic on which I thought constantly as the following passage from a midsummer letter to Don Walker will show. In a good story, I said,

> incident grows out of incident, all moving to a resolution or revelation;....the components—dialogue, description, act, interpretation—should be mixed and mingled and come proportionately to each other;....style should have a simple, workable modernity about it during much of the story but should become lyrical, intense, profound at rare, strategic moments....I am revising and revising; if there is any hope at all that I can write good stories it will be because I invent by trial and error, I overcreate and then pick out what seems good, I spill off dozens and dozens of scenes and passages and see over a period of many weeks something emerging that strikes at least my critical sense as good.[1]

Althea, Karrin, and I gathered with family and friends in many contexts during the summer of 1980, an association that, for all its pleasures, also heightened my concern over the subject matter of my writing. In June, we spent two weeks in Snowflake. On the second weekend we attended a reunion of the descendants of my father and his brother Hyrum at Lakeside. By 1980 this annual event was being held at Flag Hollow, a secluded glen in the pines transected by a tiny stream lined with wild irises on the eighty-acre homestead that had been the heart of my father and Amanda's ranch. The reunion featured a potluck dinner in the evening, a variety show of sorts at the campfire with children presenting inaudible songs and incomprehensible skits, overnight camping for those who wished it, a Dutch oven breakfast in the morning, a brief business meeting, and general visiting under the shady pines.

Several of my nieces, hearing me speak of my two recently published stories at the reunion, asked me to mail copies to them. At least one of these nieces, Mary's daughter Joan Washburn, found the stories troubling. During the fall of 1980 Joan wrote a tactful remonstrance to the stories. "What I object to is the picture I think they may be painting of you...which seems in variance with the great & good man you are in my eyes. The shocker is not to my sensibilities (I've read worse) but rather that one I think so highly of should delve his mind in subjects which I am sure are not reflective of his self in action." I am quite sure that Joan shared her opinion with my mother because near Thanksgiving of 1980, while I was busily putting my collection into its final shape, my mother wrote me: "Are your stories wholesome? Do they uphold true and honest principles? I hope no child of mine will write poor stories—or bad stories. There are so many good people in the world—so many true, honest hearted people—surely we should portray the good side of this lovely world of ours."[2]

Anticipating such criticism, I had already tried to add balance to the collection by writing a couple of positive stories, "The Gift" and "The Christianizing of Coburn Heights." I also toned down passages of graphic description of sex and violence and reduced obscenities in dialogue in my other stories. Furthermore, I decided to strike a preemptive blow against a charge of immorality by writing the preface to an anthology of Mormon stories that would eventually be published as *Greening Wheat*.

Greening Wheat had its origin early in January 1980 when, following a lecture, I spoke with Peggy Fletcher and Allen Roberts, who had recently assumed responsibility for *Sunstone* magazine, about gathering a dozen or more Mormon short stories of high quality and publishing them as a collection. I would gather and edit the stories and write an introductory essay, and *Sunstone* would finance the printing. Peggy and Allen liked the idea. They had on hand more good stories than their magazine could publish, which they would turn over to me. I thought in terms of a liberal Mormon audience and hoped, as I specified in a letter, to achieve variety and balance: "comedy, tragedy, heroism, romance, reverence, problems, disillusionment in theme; in treatment, conventional narrative, but also hopefully some experimentation and some evidence of high sophistication in technique and craftsmanship."[3] Peggy and Allen gave me, as I recall, ten or twelve manuscripts. In addition, I asked literary friends, academic and otherwise, for titles of published stories they liked, and I published a call for submissions. By the summer of 1980 I had gathered some forty stories of such quality that I was satisfied I could compile a creditable collection.

My composition of the preface was hastened when Edward Geary, professor of English at BYU and president-elect of the

Association for Mormon Letters, reported a dearth of submissions for that organization's annual symposium. Along with being in charge of local arrangements for the symposium, I volunteered to read my preface as an essay in one of the sessions. In this preface I granted that literature had a duty to be moral as well as artistic but insisted that morality was served not by excluding a depiction of the problematic but by achieving "breadth, balance, and proportion."

> An explicit treatment of sex, violence, or other disorderly impulse is not of itself immoral. Immorality exists—pornography exists—whenever these qualities are given in such unrelieved, completely amassed detail that they become the single large effect of a work. But when any of them is balanced proportionately with other qualities and appears as a part, rather than the entirety, of experience, it is valuable and appropriate. Nothing human should be excluded from literature; neither should any single aspect of experience—cheerful or dark—monopolize it.[4]

During the fall of 1980, I settled into a period of intense, uninterrupted writing. I had fortunately been granted a sabbatical leave at full salary for fall quarter for the express purpose of finishing a collection of short stories. Relieved of the duties of directing the Honors Program and teaching, I wrote in my campus office for ten or twelve hours a day and sometimes went on writing at home in the evening. On campus, I wrote on a Royal manual typewriter dating from the 1950s, at home on a Royal manual from the 1970s. Both had a light, rapid key action that I liked because it allowed my fingers to speed along closely behind my thoughts. All in all, I worked with a concentration that amazes me now. It was not difficult for me to achieve that concentration. I didn't chafe and wish I was elsewhere. I didn't pine for recreation. What I was doing was recreation enough.

Something of my creative process may be seen in the genesis of "Trinity," the idea for which came to me during a boring sacrament meeting in September 1980. In the Louvre in 1979 I had seen three early paintings entitled *Trinity*. In each, God the Father, a bearded, thick-haired patriarch, stood heroically erect, holding in his arms the collapsed, dangling body of the Son, ivory in hue, naked except for a loincloth, and showing the bloody wounds of the crucifixion. Above them hovered a dove encircled by a nimbus of glory. In one of the paintings, the face of God the Father showed a grim vengeance; in another, an utter tranquillity; in the third, a vast, poignant grief. This last struck me forcefully, causing me to go back and forth between the paintings a number of times. It suggested that Deity can be touched by human tragedy, that God can suffer as his children suffer, that God pities us in our mortal condition. In sacrament meeting a year later, I saw a way to duplicate in fiction what I supposed the painter had been trying to do with oils. Within a week I had written a substantial draft. None of the other stories had come anywhere near so easily. In this story I brought two sufferers—a male missionary who has admitted his homosexuality, a female missionary who has undergone an abortion—before the very painting I had viewed. Predictably, the brief story does not end cheerfully, yet it suggests that there is solace in the idea that God suffers when humanity suffers.

The longer I worked on the collection, the stronger became my conviction that my believing friends and relatives could not read it without concluding that, although I remained on the rolls of the church, I was no Mormon in any way that mattered—and the stronger became my need to be forthright about the incongruity between us. For that reason I decided to place the title story, "The Canyons of Grace," last in the collection. In this story, set at an archaeological dig in the canyons of southeastern Utah, a young Mormon woman first defies God through deliberate sexual transgression and then symbolically kills him by ceasing to believe in him, a spiritual progression that, to my view, mirrored my own. I placed this story last because, rightly or wrongly, I judged it would resonate more forcefully in the minds of my readers from that position, thereby serving as a kind of manifesto declaring my liberation from Mormonism.

During the last few days of 1980 I mailed a completed manuscript to the University of Illinois Press. It included seven stories. It was the culmination of a nine-month period of improvement in technique and statement. Reading Barth, Malamud, and others, thinking constantly about the nature of fiction, writing and rewriting endlessly, I had grasped, at least to my own satisfaction, what had been wrong with my earlier stories. I believed I had developed an instinct for structure, intuiting how to weave the aspects of fiction—event, introspection, dialogue, description—into an organic whole. I believed I could see how to link plot and character, making the development of a conflict a matter of growth, or at least of change, in a character. I didn't doubt I had much more to learn. For the moment, however, I had done all I could see to do with the stories. The important thing, as far as my future was concerned, was that the stories, all except "The Gift," would prove acceptable to the University of Illinois Press. Their publication in 1982 as *The Canyons of Grace* would encourage me to continue writing fiction.

My life went on happily enough throughout 1981. On campus I taught classes, managed the Honors Program, and pursued the multiple quaint causes that I have always engaged in. Karrin turned sixteen in April and received her driver's license. From then on, our Corolla became chiefly her car while Althea and I shared the Toyota pickup. The three of us skied in the winter and backpacked in the summer. Late summer we attended the Shakespeare festival in Cedar City and spent two weeks in England. During the early summer we awaited, with the rest of the Peterson family, news of my brother Leon's monthlong ascent to the summit of Mount McKinley in Alaska. I esteem his successful climb as one of the highest achievements by any member of my extended family.

One evening near the end of March 1981, I received a phone call at home from a stranger who identified himself as Daniel Curley, one of the readers of my stories submitted to the University of Illinois Press. He said he would give an enthusiastic endorsement of my stories to the press. His purpose for calling was to ask my permission to publish two of the stories, "Trinity" and "The Canyons of Grace," in *Ascent,* a magazine devoted strictly to short fiction that he edited. I was ecstatic. A few days later Ann Lowry Weir forwarded his written report. I spent as much time as I could find during the next two months revising yet again the six stories that would eventually appear in the published collection. I withdrew a seventh story, "The Gift," because Curley spoke against it. In June I resubmitted the six, and when a second reader had endorsed them, Weir informed me that she regarded them as finished. In mid-October she phoned me the good news that they would be published during the early fall of 1982.

For a couple of months in the spring of 1981 we kept my aged mother, who was not so senile as to forget to actively proselytize Althea. Because she was quite deaf and could not join in the conversation with Stella and Karrin at the dinner table, I took breakfast and lunch alone with her, allowing her to reminisce upon her past, particularly upon her first marriage, which, prodded by my curiosity, she unfolded in great detail. One day at lunch she told me she was a visionary woman. I asked how so. She reminded me of a dream she once had of Lenora and Mary in a bed; Mary was weeping and Lenora was trying to comfort her. She had decided this meant that Waldo would die and leave Mary a widow. She said she had recently had another dream. She saw her own name, Lydia, embossed in golden letters. Then she saw a hall full of chairs, two of which were empty. She knew one was hers, the other was Waldo's. She wondered how Mary could survive the loss. A little later that same day, while I worked in the study, I heard Mother muttering in her bedroom, "There was a little dog named Rover. When he died, he died all over." After a silence she said, "When I die, I hope I die all over."

Younger persons than Waldo were fated to die during the next year. Just before Thanksgiving 1981, an automobile accident killed my high school friend Howard Ramsey and his wife, Clare, sister of my sister-in-law Gussie. Dwain phoned me the news of the accident. Within two months, Dwain himself was dead. At Christmas he came to Salt Lake to visit his daughter Megan. On Christmas Day Megan phoned that he had undergone an emergency colostomy for bleeding from his colon, the result of chronic colitis. For fifteen days he showed improvement each time I visited him. Then one day he was hooked to a dialysis machine because his kidneys had stopped functioning. For the next fifteen days he looked worse each time I visited. At the end of January 1982, he died, a little short of forty-eight.

At the viewing in Snowflake, his body was dressed in temple robes—a great comfort to his mother and siblings. I read a sketch of his life at his funeral, saying we should take consolation from the fact that he had lived nearly a half century and had done the essential things of a normal life. He was buried in the Snowflake cemetery, scarcely a hundred yards from his brother Woody's house. The next day, still in Snowflake, I wrote a letter to Charles about the funeral. Many family members had come, I said, "instinctively knowing, inarticulately, tacitly knowing, that a funeral is a time for celebrating life, for gathering in such numbers that the collective presence of the family overshadows death. There is among the Petersons a vibrant family mystique; cousinship is comforting, sustaining, unquestionably meaningful."[5] That's one view of what a funeral achieves.

I found less consolation in the deaths of younger relatives. Attending Dwain's funeral was my niece Amanda Tenney Nikolaus, Wanda's daughter, who suffered from an inoperable brain tumor. Two months later Amanda died. Her little son, informed that his mother had gone into the sky, looked for her there. It wrenched my heart to hear that story. Earlier deaths had been just as sad. In 1970, a nephew backed a truck over his tiny daughter. That same year, at twenty, my niece Carol, Earland's daughter, was killed when her car went off a curve on a graveled road. Leon wrote me about that funeral, which I was unable to attend. "Our mortality was sitting upon us starkly," he said. "The effort to comfort each other seemed so futile when it was so apparent that we were all dying. The years furiously running together have left us wrecked on the sideway."[6] That's another, equally valid, view of what a funeral achieves.

Returning to literary matters, I proposed the formation of a writing group during the fall of 1981. I had come to know and respect three other aspiring Mormon writers, Bruce Jorgensen, Linda Sillitoe, and Dennis Clark, through the Association for Mormon Letters. By New Year's 1982 we were already well under way with establishing a routine of meeting once a month for dinner at the home of the writer whose turn it was to have previously mailed a manuscript for our critique. Needless to say, our spouses were fully engaged in all our discussions. Our gatherings required considerable travel, Bruce and Donna living in Provo, Dennis and Valerie in Orem, and Linda and John in Salt Lake City. (John spelled his last name as Sillito whereas Linda, disliking the mispronunciation strangers were likely to give it, added an *e* to her spelling.) Althea and I soon regarded these three couples as dear and intimate friends with whom we felt utterly comfortable.

In January 1982, having served as president of the Association for Mormon Letters during the previous year, I delivered the customary presidential address at that organization's annual symposium. My address, published later by *Sunstone* magazine, was entitled "The Civilizing of Mormondom: The Indispensable Role of the Intellectual." In terms of defining my own relationship to Mormonism, I have written nothing more important than this essay.

I defined civilization, at least in its benign aspects, as a dynamic process in which one culture adopts a desirable improvement or change for the better from another. The Mormon Church, I pointed out, is a part of this large dynamic process, its members commingling with the members of sister cultures on a daily basis, influencing and being influenced by them. Because the collective, worldwide process of civilization is incomplete, no particular culture has as yet arrived at a perfect fulfillment of it. Like all other cultures, the Mormon Church stands in need of continual change for the better. Those Mormons best suited to propose that the Mormon Church adopt developments and changes occurring in other cultures are its intellectuals, who by virtue of wide reading and a curious, rational mind "are instinctively attracted to the expanding edge of civilization, where the old is constantly transformed into the new in science, art, morality, and dozens of other categories."[7]

If, while completing my stories only a year earlier, I had sensed my distance from Mormonism acutely, I by now admitted to an impulse to intensify my involvement with it. I had long recognized that I was no anti-Mormon, having no wish to see Mormonism dwindle and die away. But I did wish to see it liberalize itself, becoming more humane, more adaptable to change, and less at odds with science and learning, and I saw therein an active role for people like me. My mood now, for various reasons, was such that I wished to take up that role. This essay, while defining the role, was also a step toward realizing it. Almost everything I have written or said within a Mormon context ever since has been done with an eye toward realizing it further.

I had defined myself as a liberal Mormon because a small, nascent community of liberal Mormons, centered chiefly along the Wasatch Front, appeared to have accepted me as such. I encountered these amiable, tolerant people on the editorial staffs of

Dialogue and *Sunstone,* among the regular attendees at the annual Sunstone symposium, and among my fellow workers on the board of the Association for Mormon Letters, to say nothing of the three writers and their spouses with whom Althea and I had begun to meet once a month as a writing group. All these people had two large qualities in common. They fit my definition of an intellectual, being broad-minded, widely read, and acceptive of change. And they were believers. As far as I could tell, they worshiped with sincere faith. Most of them were fully active in their home wards and attended temple sessions. I admired them greatly and believed I did well to add my effort to the cause of making the Mormon Church a comfortable home for such worshipers as they.

In September 1982 I returned to full-time teaching at Weber State, having, after nine years of service, resigned as director of the Honors Program. I had also resigned as editor of *Encyclia,* although I was committed to edit another issue before I could lay down my duties. My teaching load consisted of two freshman composition courses, a lower-division course in general education literature, and an upper-division course in literature for majors and minors. This would be my typical teaching load for many years to follow. I did not mind teaching the comp and general education courses, which required little preparation on my part, leaving me some time for my own writing. I was pleased that my new quarters, a small faculty office on the second floor of the Social Science building, had a window looking westward over Ogden and the Great Salt Lake.

In late September 1982, I received my first copy of *The Canyons of Grace.* A couple of weeks later a bundle of free author's copies arrived. The book of 135 pages existed in hardbound and paperback versions. My photo appeared on both. I show a graying mustache and sideburns and a short-brimmed hat. Although I was happy to hold the book in my hands, it would be several months before I had a sense that its appearance was a significant event.

The winter and spring of 1983 were exceptionally wet, with results that fascinated me, given my interest in how the wild and the civilized impinge upon each other. Water from melting snow ran between banks made of sandbags on downtown streets in Salt Lake City. Mud slides along the Wasatch Front engulfed several neighborhoods. In Spanish Fork Canyon an entire mountainside gave way, damming the Spanish Fork River and inundating the hamlet of Thistle. The first concern was to breach this natural dam so that impounded water did not rise to the bursting point. After that, Highway 6 and the track of the Denver Rio Grande Railroad had to be rerouted at a higher level. I felt a curious intimacy with this landslide. I wrote my mother: "I have been going into our TV room every evening lately at ten p.m. to see the news....It is almost as if the slide has an inner musculature, a lateral impulse to move sidewise as well as down. [It] teaches us all over again (as do the rising waters of Utah Lake and the Great Salt Lake) that human construction and technology do not measure up to unusual exertions of nature."[8]

In March 1983 my project for publishing a collection of Mormon short stories by various authors, which had languished for lack of funds, was suddenly alive again. Scott Kenney, formerly chief editor of *Sunstone* and now in charge at Signature Books, proposed to take on the venture and with considerable expedition saw *Greening Wheat* through to publication during the fall of 1983. Scott called for a shorter collection than I had previously planned. At his urging, I also decided to include one of my own stories, "The Gift." I therefore had the unpleasant task of informing a few authors whose stories I had previously accepted that their stories would not appear in the collection.

By the spring of 1983, *The Canyons of Grace* had established a modest public presence. It had been reviewed by a number of periodicals beyond Utah, including *Publisher's Weekly*, the *Los Angeles Examiner*, and the *Chicago Tribune*. Within Utah, some bookstores were selling out and reordering—though, as I became aware, they didn't order large quantities. Friends mentioned having read the reviews in the local newspapers. A few of them apologized for having borrowed the book rather than buying it. I was happy to have them read it, not having expected to make money in the first place. One day a woman from rural Idaho, visiting in Ogden, phoned me to complain about the image of missionaries that my story "Trinity" might leave with Gentile readers. Our conversation went on for forty-five minutes. A Catholic woman in Brooklyn, Marylee Mitcham, descended from lapsed Mormons, wrote me that she had picked up the book in a used bookstore. Marylee and I would correspond with considerable candor throughout the following decade. Eventually she would convert to the Mormonism that her ancestors had abandoned.

As for my relatives, their reaction to *The Canyons of Grace* was mixed. I felt it proper to mail an inscribed copy to my mother and each of my siblings. My eldest sister, Leora, was impressed by the book and congratulated me for it. She surprised me by identifying with Arabella of the title story, saying that she, who like Arabella had been unmarried at thirty, understood perfectly Arabella's desire for sexual experience. However, she took exception to the book's erotic descriptions and obscenities: "Cut down on the dirty words and minute details of the sex act. They add nothing to the story, but are an offense and embarrassment to many readers. A reader's imagination can supply them if he craves titillation or dirt."[9]

Predictably, I had misgivings about sending the book to my mother. On a brief visit to Snowflake at Christmas, I had warned her of parts that might offend her, specifying the passage in "The Christianizing of Coburn Heights" where the demented little lady deposits her own fresh excrement upon the stake president's porch. A few days after I had returned to Ogden, Mother wrote a frantic letter, pleading with me to recall the entire printing of the book and have that dishonorable passage excised from it. "As I sat here crocheting I thought of that filthy ending you said you were going to give one of your stories. Please, I plead with you not to dishonor the name you bear by so doing. You will not prosper if you do. No matter the cost of recalling it, please do not have the part in any book or paper. I have not taught you to think or act this way. Please, please, please."[10]

Nonetheless, Mother later asked me to live up to my promise to mail her a copy. I replied that I would but asked her, a little peevishly, I fear, to brace herself for a good many passages that would likely offend her. Soon I received a gentle remonstrance from my sister Mary, with whom Mother was staying in Mesa that winter. "Mother says you are sending her your book. Leon told her not to read it. Roald said for me to intercept it. Lenora says she must not read it. All these filtered in to me unsolicited. Also that Joan thinks

I might be disturbed by it. My goodness! What a commotion! And
in the midst of it Mama is crying about the story you let her read."[11]
Mary went on to say that she would intercept the book if she could
manage to be at home when the postman delivered it. I replied with
a friendly letter, acquiescing in her decision. She succeeded in inter-
cepting the book. I do not remember what she did with it, nor do I
remember what she did with the copy I inscribed to her. Judging
Greening Wheat to be less offensive to conservative Mormon taste,
I sent Mother an inscribed copy when it appeared during the fall of
1983. I doubt that she read it. Even when she was younger, she
didn't read fiction.

Despite such minor squalls within the family, on the whole, as
I have said, my stories made me feel more, rather than less, a Mormon. Certainly the alienation that I had anticipated as I placed the
title story at the end of my collection did not occur. My sense of belonging extended not only to my friends on the liberal Mormon circuit but also to the members of Thirty-third Ward where I attended
church—though I continued to express my belonging in an unconventional way, feeling quite unable, for example, to respond to
Mary's request in 1982 that I prepare myself for attending the
temple. I weighed the possibility for a month before replying to
Mary. Temple attendance implied a full tithe, attendance at a multitude of meetings, Sabbaths with no active work, frank confes-
sionals with my bishop, and church jobs requiring much time and
tedium. My desire to belong simply couldn't take me that far. "I
can't explain my inability to be a total active Mormon," I wrote
Mary. "I have had a central core of personality to which nonconformity, resistance, rebellion have seemed absolutely vital and indispensable."[12]

Yet, as I also told Mary, I was more happily involved in my
ward than I had been at any time since my boyhood. I attended
church meetings with considerable regularity. I continued to carry
out my duties as a home teacher. I lent a hand at ward dinners and
quorum socials. I paid modest sums by way of fast offerings and
building maintenance. Once my mother wrote a check for one hundred dollars to be paid as tithing on my behalf. She gave it to Karrin, and Karrin gave it to me. I returned it to my mother and paid a
few dollars of tithing so that I could tell her I was a partial tithe

payer. Karrin had by now become a totally active member, and I was happy to sit by her in sacrament meeting. Once in a while Althea and her mother attended. Stella, though a Methodist in conviction, liked to partake of the sacrament. I asked our bishop's approval, and he said she could.

Somewhere around 1983, as I was turning fifty, I was asked to attend the high priests' group in our ward. I did so briefly but found the older brethren so somnolent that I soon went back to the elder's quorum. No one scolded me for this disobedience. After a year or two, there being no one else of my age among the elders, I returned to the high priests' group and have continued there ever since. I have never been ordained a high priest because of unworthiness. Once I saw a ward record that listed me as a high priest. I concluded it was a computer that had ordained me. A computer isn't likely to be sensitive on moral issues.

Ironically, it was around this time that I became president of the Sunday-school class that I attended most frequently. This class was taught by Myrene Brewer, the gracious, silvery-haired widow of J. W. Brewer, whose tire stores are spread across Utah and surrounding states. In the beginning, Myrene looked worried when I raised a hand to ask a question. Later, I think she realized that my questions induced discussion among the class that made her task easier. In time, she domesticated me to her purposes by declaring me president of the class. As such it was my duty to see that the roll was taken and to designate persons to open and close each session with prayer. I recall a summer afternoon when Althea and I went early to Myrene's cabin on the south fork of the Ogden River and helped her prepare a party for class members. Properly speaking, Myrene didn't have the authority to make me president of the class, that being the prerogative of the ward bishopric. However, they didn't protest. Myrene carried a lot of weight in that ward. When *The Canyons of Grace* appeared, she bought a copy. She used to tell people, "When I want a fling, I just read one of Levi's stories." With such an amiable, eminently decent human being as Myrene thinking I was an acceptable Mormon, how could I feel otherwise?

··· 20

The Backslider

IN HER OLD AGE MY MOTHER CROCHETED colorful afghan covers every day except Sunday. Crocheting was a sufficient diversion, making her weekday life tolerable. Sundays, when she couldn't do it, were hellish. She went to church, but that still left a lot of the day with nothing to do. She became restless and irritable and hobbled around the house, muttering. I had ample opportunity to observe this phenomenon because every spring between 1980 and 1985 she stayed in Utah for a couple of months, sharing the time between our house and that of Charles and Betty in Logan. When she was at our house, I frequently went into her room to say goodnight. She was always asleep, having dozed off on her bed as she read or crocheted. She did not mind being awakened, since she went off again easily. I clasped her hands, and she murmured that she loved me with a fervor that left no doubt. This ritual assuaged my guilt and brought a sense of reparation for my old crime of having grown up and left her. Nonetheless, I found her irritability on Sunday distressing. I told her God probably wouldn't care if an old woman crocheted a little on the Sabbath. She wasn't to be talked out of it. The Sabbath was ordained for rest from weekday business, and crocheting was her weekday business.

I wasn't dealing with anything new in my mother. I perceived at an early age that the deity she worshiped sold his rewards and protections for a stiff price. That may account for my compulsion to calculate the price—to measure the pain and frustration—of Christian worship in my fiction. Writing the stories in *The Canyons of Grace* did not purge my fascination with the topic. Having mailed the stories, I went on with it in my novel *The Backslider*, on which I had been working intermittently for half a dozen years. Moreover, encouraged by good prospects for my stories, I was eager to apply to a novel what the stories had taught me about writing fiction.

I have mentioned an early chapter of *The Backslider* that I read to a group at the home of Lavina Fielding Anderson in June 1978. By that date I had already been thinking about at least two of its main characters for three or four years—Jeremy, destined to rename himself Alice, and his older brother Frank, witness to Jeremy's self-emasculation and interpreter of its significance. However, not until early 1982 had I conceived of a plot resembling that of the novel to be published in 1986. By then Frank had supplanted Jeremy as my center of interest. He was no longer a mature, self-aware city dweller but a nineteen-year-old cowboy working on a remote ranch. A dedicated rebel at the beginning, he was quickly catapulted into a monklike repentance by Jeremy's self-mutilation.

During a session of our writing group in March 1982, Linda Sillitoe protested, with an edge of humor, what she called "Levi's God." She didn't doubt the verisimilitude of Frank's dilemma; she simply hoped he could make his way to believing in a kinder, more forgiving deity. After the session, I wrote Linda that "I want the book to be about redemption, and I want Frank to find redemption....For Frank in his penitential moods, there is no salvation, no forgiveness, for those who laugh, eat, and copulate. Salvation comes only for those who cut away joy. But from what I hope are authentic pains, authentic brutalities, comes at least a hope for the salvation of this man who cannot finally do otherwise than laugh, eat, and copulate."[1] The phrase "at least a hope for salvation" doesn't convey much conviction on my part. The truth is I had a hard time believing that a fulfillment of appetite and a sense of salvation could exist in the same person. How I was to make Frank's redemption credible would remain an unsolved problem till I had almost finished the final chapter during the summer of 1984.

By mid-1983 another problem was plaguing me. I had completed four chapters. Before me lay four or five more chapters elaborating upon Frank's ever-intensifying dissatisfaction over his inability to live austerely, leading him finally to consider the ultimate penance, the shedding of his own blood. I regarded my plot as promising and was determined to see it written. Yet it had turned into a depressing story and appeared destined to remain depressing for many pages to come.

In June 1983, Althea, Karrin, and I took my mother to Snowflake following her two-month stay in Utah and stayed a week with her in her house. One morning after breakfast, I sat at the dining table making notes for my next chapter. Quite suddenly the impulse to create a comic Frank struck me, and I began to write a chapter that chronologically preceded all I had written so far. In it Frank had become comic, and his story was rendered in a new narrative voice, still in the third person, but cast in a simple, colloquial style close to Frank's manner of speaking and thinking. My relish for writing had returned. It was fun to write about this Frank.

Finishing the chapter when I got back to Ogden, I read it to the writing group at a retreat we held at a cabin on the upper Weber River. Linda had suggested we hold the weekend retreat, an arrangement we would repeat each summer for the next five or six years, and Bruce had secured the cabin, free of cost, through the generosity of Gene and Charlotte England, who at that moment did not belong to the group. My colleagues approving of the chapter, I decided to include it as the first in my novel. After revising it, I would recast the existing four chapters in a simpler, more colloquial style reflecting a Frank who had the seeds of both comedy and anguish within him. I determined to do this on the confidence that I would somehow be able to harmonize these elements, a confidence in which I would waver from time to time.

In September 1983, Karrin moved to Provo to attend BYU, where she had a scholarship. As she prepared to leave, I wondered whether I could adapt to her absence from our home. I still needed her to complete the circle of parent and child that I found so essential to my emotional stability. Luckily, frequent phone calls and weekend visits sufficed. Karrin was eighteen, the age when, as I had always told her, she would be free to make her own decisions. Actually, she had been making her own decisions for four or five years. Fortunately, they were sensible. She took along our Corolla, while Althea and I made do with the Toyota pickup. She roomed with a cousin, Leon and Gussie's daughter Jane. Jane got married at Christmas, with the consequence that Karrin liked BYU less. At the end of spring semester 1984, she moved home and the next fall entered Weber State, where she would complete a bachelor's degree with majors in English and psychology. Needless to say, Althea and I were happy to have her home.

On the weekend Karrin left for Provo in September 1983, Althea and I made a field trip to Garfield County, the general locale of *The Backslider*. We camped on a broad, grassy plain south of Escalante, sleeping in the back of our pickup, which was enclosed by a canopy. Far to the north a bank of clouds hovering over Boulder Mountain flashed with lightning much of the night. Although we couldn't hear the thunder, our dog, Peppermint, could, and she trembled and shook in the cab. Not far from where we camped, at a place where the road passed through a flat bottom, I said to Althea, "Right here is the ranch where Frank works." The ranch, of course, existed only in my imagination. Back in Escalante the next morning, we visited the high school, church house, and two small general stores. In the novel, Marianne attends that high school, and Frank shops in the stores. Later, we explored back roads emanating from the town. Following Alvey Wash, we passed through a declivity so narrow that I could almost touch the vertical walls through my open window—another setting that would appear in the novel. Frank and Marianne pull their horse trailer through that defile on the day they ride to Canaan Peak, and a flood down Alvey Wash forces them to spend a night huddled in Frank's pickup, providing the occasion of their first fornication.

This wasn't our first exploration of Garfield County, nor would it be the last. I like a real place for a setting for my fiction. Almost as soon as I first began thinking about this novel, I selected Panguitch as Frank and Jeremy's hometown because on my many drives between Snowflake and the Wasatch Front I had passed through it and wished that I had grown up there. Almost any little Utah town makes me wish I had grown up there; having lived in Snowflake, I intuit its social rhythms, its pleasures and promises, its comforting predictability. In the late 1970s, Althea, Karrin, and I spent a night in a Panguitch motel. I poked around town and went to a Saturday-evening priesthood meeting in the North Ward church house. Soon I had expanded my interest to the surrounding Garfield County, which was large, thinly populated, and remarkably scenic. Within its boundaries were high aspen-covered plateaus, Bryce Canyon, the Henry Mountains, and the intricate slickrock erosions approaching the north shore of Lake Powell. I read histories of the county, studied maps, and for more than five years subscribed to *Garfield County News,* a weekly newspaper rarely counting more than six pages. On all our visits to the county, I paused to talk to local residents.

One day in the tiny town of Tropic, we saw a man and a boy digging a trench behind Bryce Valley High School. I got out and chatted a while. The man worked as janitor and school bus driver. Though he said he was second counselor in the local bishopric, he used mild swearwords comfortably. He also said he was a professional cougar-hunting guide, presently unemployed because wildlife officials had suspended his license for killing a female cougar outside his appointed territory. He said his dogs had jumped the animal within his legal territory but had treed it outside. Arriving to call them off, he saw a trap dangling from one of its paws. Hoping to remove the trap, he roped the animal, threw the end of the rope over a higher limb, and stretched the lion so that it couldn't claw him as he climbed the tree. Unfortunately, the limb the animal was perched on broke, and as it plummeted, the jerk of the rope broke its neck. Being a good Mormon, he reported the death. The wildlife officers rejected his story, fined him, and took away his license. "That'll teach me to be honest," he said. I knew instantly that I would use this man and his story in my novel.

I took great pleasure in researching Garfield County. Imagining my characters' lives in a realistic setting gave me a sense of myself living a second existence. It is a commonplace that fiction gives its reader a vicarious second life. Less well known, perhaps, is the fact that it also gives its writer a vicarious second existence, an experience far more profound and vivid, in my judgment, than that of a reader.

At the beginning of fall quarter 1983, I was distracted from my writing by the necessity of learning how to compose on a computer. I had publicly opposed computers on campus, more because the unbridled enthusiasm of some of my colleagues annoyed me than because I doubted the utility of computers. As fall quarter opened, Sherwin Howard, dean of the School of Arts and Humanities, cagily silenced my opposition by assigning me a new Commodore 8032, which had, as I recall, thirty-two kilobytes of memory, barely enough to store seven or eight pages of single-spaced typing. Nonetheless, it was an expensive, extravagant device, and I would have felt guilty had I failed to master its use. Predictably, it influenced my mode of composition greatly. I could type faster because mistakes were easily corrected. I could revise instantly, inserting sentences into existing text or rewriting whole passages without affecting what went before or after. With a typewriter, I had been able to track my revisions. Not so with a computer. Revisions evaporated into cyberspace. Predictably, my conversion to writing with a computer made me notorious on campus, as I explained to Karrin in a letter: "Many people come by my office, since I generally leave the door open, to marvel, query, and jeer. They say, 'I told you you'd get hooked.' I say, 'Of course. I knew I could write faster on it. But my real purpose in having this infernal machine is to fathom its weaknesses as only an insider can fathom them. I am preparing a definitive speech against computers.' They laugh in disbelief and go on."[2]

All my writing since June had been in Frank's simple, colloquial style—a style that often seemed to exclude me from the novel. Sometimes a situation seemed to call for a lyrical or poetic, rather than a colloquial, treatment or, at other times, to invite a complex or subtle commentary foreign to Frank. Often, too, I found myself disliking the staccato effect of unrelieved simple sentences. However, my reservations were allayed when, in the early fall, I read *Summerfire*, an accomplished novel by Douglas Thayer, with whom I had attended classes while we were undergraduates at BYU. This novel is about a callow Mormon youth from Provo whose innocence is tested, though not destroyed, by a summer on a Nevada hay ranch. What struck me most forcefully was the utter absence of complexity from its style. Simple sentences abounded; diction was rigorously concrete. Suddenly, short, elliptical sentences sounded totally right in my own writing. They seemed to line up, one after another, without dissonance. Frank's colloquial processes— the language patterns I had grown up with and that I still encountered in freshman themes—became my unquestioned medium. I rejoiced in my freedom from standard style and found pleasure in trying to render my narrative through the earthy metaphor and colorful idiom of ranch country. It seemed to me now I had found some compensation for the exclusion of my own educated sensibility from the narrative, as I explained in a letter to Leora in January 1984:

The simpler language of common people has its own subtle beauties and metaphors and originalities, and I am having some pleasure in discovering them. I am working intuitively toward a word selection and a sentence structure that is I hope both colloquially expressive (in the manner of common speech in southern Utah) and simply beautiful. I say "intuitively" because I do not know beforehand what I am working toward. I begin by trying to imitate the speech of everyday people in Utah, especially country people, and then I move from there toward rearrangements that strike me as effective, moving, perhaps even elevating. In a sense the sentence structure of common speech frees me. It takes liberties that correct English doesn't dare, it is willing to make loose connections, oblique and slanting references which the grammarian finds too ambiguous or untraditional.[3]

In November 1983, I had an inquiry from an associate editor of W. W. Norton in New York, who had read the review of *The Canyons of Grace* in *Publisher's Weekly*. She said she would like to see some of my work in progress. I was elated. In mid-December, I sent her the new first chapter of my novel. In late February 1984, she invited me to send more. Near the end of May, I mailed the next four chapters. In mid-July she rejected the novel, saying its religious conflict "wears thin." She spoke of the "inanity" of the dialogue and the "lengthy descriptions of chores around the ranch." "It just didn't work for me in the end," she concluded.[4] Nonetheless, my appetite for a publisher of national scope was whetted by the experience. It had been a mistake, I decided, to send only part of the novel. I would finish the work and try another New York publisher.

My chief business during the summer of 1984 was writing. I ordinarily I went to my office every morning, seven days a week. On Saturday and Sunday I came home at noon. On weekdays, when I stayed till evening, I had Althea drop me off in the morning and I walked home. At home I gardened and mowed and watered the lawn in my usual negligent manner. Once in a while Althea, Karrin, and I did a day hike in the Uintas.

In July, the writing group held another weekend retreat at the cabin on the upper Weber. Althea and I were assigned to provide breakfast for Saturday morning. The duty of preparing it fell upon me because Althea stayed at home Friday night to care for Stella, who had fallen ill. However, Althea went shopping with me on Friday afternoon for the necessary supplies. At one point she put a bottle of maple syrup into our shopping cart. I protested that imitation maple syrup was less expensive. She dismissed my suggestion with a wave of her hand and went around to the next aisle. I quietly replaced the true maple syrup with the imitation and followed her with the cart. I did this on the assumption that the obligation to prepare the meal gave me authority over its planning. The next morning, as I served breakfast, I couldn't resist telling our friends about switching the bottles. "I knew Bruce and Dennis couldn't tell the difference between the real syrup and this imitation stuff," I said. Unluckily, the story was repeated for Althea when she arrived just before lunch. Never before, never after, have I seen her angrier. She doesn't take deceit lightly.

In August 1984 Althea, Karrin, and I took a two-week vacation in England. We covered much the same terrain that we had covered during August 1981, driving across southern England to Cornwall in the southwest, then north through Wales and the Lake District, and into Scotland. On both trips, we devoted a single daytime visit to London. On both trips, the British vacation season was in full progress, and masses of people were on holiday, as they called it. This meant some standing in line at the popular tourist sites and occasional difficulty finding lodging, but it also meant many satisfying conversations with the natives in unexpected places.

The British seemed a polite, patient, good-humored people. It struck me that they distributed their collective wealth more evenly than did Americans. They seemed less extravagant, less obsessive about shopping, more concerned to conserve the remnants of natural beauty among their crowded surroundings. English shops were smaller and more specialized than in the United States, less efficient yet friendlier. Motorways, as their freeways were called, were few. Their typical semi was a ten-wheeler. Petrol was expensive, and automobiles were compact. On the whole, the British made me feel better about the long-term prospects for civilization than did my fellow Americans. They showed human beings could pursue a decent, creative way of life without extravagance and waste.

We met the past on every hand. We saw the Elgin marbles in the British Museum and the mystical romantic paintings of William Blake in the Tate Gallery. We saw a model of a primitive steam engine two stories high, used to pump water from the coal mines of Cornwall during the early nineteenth century, on exhibit in a museum in Truro. We saw a breach in a wall of Berkeley Castle in Gloucestershire, made by the cannons of Oliver Cromwell during the English Civil War, permission for the rebuilding of which would require, even today, an act of Parliament. We watched a medieval morality play, acted in the open air of the ruined Coventry Cathedral, bombed by the Germans in 1940. We generally avoided cities and sought the unspoiled countryside. There were pastures grazed by cattle and sheep and tilled fields yellow with grain ready for harvest, outlined in their irregular dimensions by hedges or rock walls, highly picturesque when viewed across a valley. I was reinforced in a perception I had come to long before: that the rural, when uncorrupted by the encroachments of suburbia, has much the same emotional effect upon me as does the untouched wild.

On both trips we visited Hawkhurst, a village in Kent from which Althea's maternal grandmother derived. On our second trip, the rector of the parish church directed us to the home of Betty Clark, as he called her, keeper of the parish records. This amiable woman obliged Althea with the vital statistics for a number of her ancestors. Included was the fact that Althea's great-grandmother had been born out of wedlock—information Stella would receive with dismay, while Althea found it merely curious. More remarkable was the fact that when I had asked after Betty Clark at the door, the doughty housekeeper who had answered our knock drew herself up in full dignity and declared that she would inform Miss Elizabeth Clark of our desire to speak to her. Clearly a stranger was not to presume upon the familiarity of a nickname here.

That fall Althea began study for a master's degree in Spanish at the University of Utah. Though she had acquired enough course credits for a master's degree in English before we left the U in 1965, she had digressed into the study of foreign languages at Weber State, slowly acquiring majors in French and Spanish and a minor in German. In 1984 she applied for and received an assistantship in teaching first-year Spanish, the language that she favored, at the University of Utah. She drove between Ogden and Salt Lake City five days a week for the next three years. At New Year's 1985, we bought a Toyota Tercel station wagon whose four-wheel-drive feature would prove useful to Althea on more than one snowy morning. We also bought her an Apple MacIntosh computer, to which she and Karrin adapted readily.

As 1984 waned, I was finishing *The Backslider* in what I considered a hybrid style. While revising the nearly completed draft, I succumbed to the impulse to infuse the narrative with words and sentences that Frank would never have used. I quickly realized that while some passages invited this somewhat more formal expression, others were best left entirely in their original colloquial style. The result was a dissonance that took me some time to feel comfortable with, as I explained in a letter to the writing group.

> At first this disparate quality weighed on me; like a window without a shade it seemed to let strangers stare in on the incongruities of my novel. I am no longer worried. Rather abruptly, perhaps, it has come to me that consistency is not important, that duality and ambivalence of character are utterly human, that style can be dialectical, can proceed from incongruities into harmony. Complexity means variety. So as I proceed with my revision, I believe and hope that standard style, with excursions into eloquence, and colloquial style, with wry, satirical implications, will become a single larger style.[5]

I had also become comfortable with the even stronger disparity that lay between the comic elements of the novel and its serious statement about penitence. In a sense, its serious statement about penitence can itself be viewed as comic if the comic is allowed to include unlaughing satire. I grant that the ideals of celibacy and poverty that Frank espouses midnovel have an alien ring to the ordinary Mormon. They are of course extrapolated from the larger Christian tradition, seen today in the celibate priesthood and residual monasticism of the Catholic Church. The spirit of asceticism and self-denial that they imply appeared plentifully among the founding fathers of Protestantism, and their overtones may be heard today in the preaching of born-again evangelists. So it was a conscious allusion on my part to have Frank engage in an act of medieval-like self-flagellation. He has married the pregnant Marianne with an understanding that they will not have sexual intercourse but will treat one another as brother and sister. Though this resolve predictably breaks down, Frank disciplines himself to making love to his wife only on Friday nights. On Saturday mornings, he retreats to a shed and tabulates his good and bad deeds for the week, finding that the bad far outweigh the good. Thereupon, he gives himself ten slashes with a leather strap cut from an old harness. "They were nothing at all, a token, a sign of what he would do if he was free to please God."

I was of course chiefly interested in making a comment on Mormon varieties of penitence. As the final chapter opens, after they have decided to remain married, Frank and Marianne are found trying to live by Frank's stringent standards, companionable, ascetic, and committed to having sex with each other only when they are ready to have another child. To prevent himself from masturbating in his sleep, Frank has sewn a pair of leather gloves together and attached thongs, with which, at his command, Marianne ties his hands at night as they go to bed.

How did I come up with this contraption? While I was writing the novel, a list of ways to avoid masturbation circulated among disapproving liberal Mormons, supposedly written by a modern apostle, whose name I have forgotten. I recognized that the authorship of the list could well be specious, yet its instructions were undeniably the sort young men regularly received—and still receive—from their bishops and mission presidents. One item called for restraint of the hands during sleep. Recalling that I myself had regularly masturbated in my sleep during my early college and missionary years, I came up with the contraption described above, which, had I been so unfortunate as to have thought of it in those days, might have effectively cut off all release of my sexual tension.

In my novel, the contraption fails its intended purpose when Frank awakens one night, requires Marianne to release him, and—obviously in a sleep-altered state of mind—forces her to have sexual intercourse with him. In the aftermath of this relapse, Frank seizes a vegetable grater from the kitchen counter and scrapes skin and flesh from the back of his hand. While the stunned Marianne bandages his hand and prepares breakfast, he admits his ingrained anger against God and declares that he has lost his will to struggle against his carnal appetites. Both he and Marianne recognize a looming catastrophe. A couple of days later, she tells him she knows he is bent on emasculating himself as Jeremy has done. He has in fact decided on the deed. The difference will be that Frank will make sure no one is present to rescue him as he has rescued Jeremy. He intends to bleed to death—this to carry out that most stark of Mormon varieties of penitence, blood atonement.

Many Mormons have never heard of blood atonement. I was in my twenties before I encountered the doctrine, which holds that certain unspecified sins cannot be forgiven by simple repentance. Only the shedding of the sinner's own blood will suffice. Sermons preached by Brigham Young and Jedediah M. Grant during the mid-1850s promulgated the doctrine. Historians favorable to Mormonism claim it was never practiced. Even as mere pulpit rhetoric, it is astonishing. I recall how incredulous I was when I first heard of it, yet I sensed its resonance with the deity of my mother and her ancestors. It helped persuade me that they were not alone in their stern belief. The early Mormons were a penitential people.

How was Frank to be rescued from the looming catastrophe? The precise nature of his rescue was a crucial matter, being a climax on whose success the rest of the novel would depend. I had decided quite early that it would be an epiphany, an appearance of a celestial being to Frank, rather than some motion of his own self-corrective psyche. This was in keeping with Frank's mentality— and with the Mormon mentality at large. Although they do not often experience them, Mormons believe in epiphanies, or visions, as they call them. Mormonism began with the appearance of God the Father and Jesus Christ to Joseph Smith, who described them as personages of transcendent brilliance hovering in the air above him. The tendency in Frank's family toward visions and spiritual manifestations is therefore, while exceptional, not unheard of among the Mormons. Frank is turned from a backslider into an ascetic monk by two visions, one of God targeting him through the scope of a high-powered rifle, another of his own hands manacled to a post. These visions occur in such circumstances, I trust, that my reader accepts them as realistic characterizations. Visions having placed Frank into irreconcilable conflict with his appetites, it seemed appropriate to allow a vision to extricate him from it.

But what sort of vision? The epiphany that I finally created for Frank did not occur to me till I was well into the composition of the final chapter of the novel during the summer of 1984. Everything I had thought of before that moment seemed wrong. The hovering transcendent beings reported by Joseph Smith are frequently depicted in Mormon paintings. Their image struck me as entirely alien to my novel. Behind Frank's epiphany, preparing for it, perhaps even causing it, is his Gentile wife, Marianne, healthy, hearty, decent, and comfortable with her appetites. Throughout the novel, she serves as a quiet countervoice to Frank. (Just as my Gentile wife has served as a quiet countervoice to my emotional excesses. Although they are unlike in appearance, temperament, and personal history, Althea and Marianne have in common a sanity and good sense that eventually rubbed off on their men. It is no coincidence that *The Backslider* is dedicated to Althea.) Marianne senses early that, although Frank believes in the atonement of Christ, he doesn't feel atoned. When at last he accompanies her to a Lutheran service, where she partakes of the Holy Communion, she returns to his side in a pew and whispers, "Why can't you let his blood be enough? Why do you have to shed yours too?" Though at the moment he seems not to understand her meaning, in the vision that finally saves him the Jesus who appears on a horse and in the clothes of a cowboy echoes Marianne's question: "Why can't you let my blood be enough? Why do you have to shed yours too?"

This Jesus enters my novel in the first chapter where Marianne, barely introduced to Frank, informs him of a pleasant daydream she indulges in, in which she fancies she is lost among trees somewhere and a cowboy Jesus appears. "He has a beard and he looks like there isn't anybody in the whole world he can't love. He says, I found you; you were lost, but I found you." I had no idea at the moment of creating that passage that it would recur later in the novel. It was merely a way of establishing the nature of Marianne's piety. In the final chapter where Marianne is shown trying hard to adopt Frank's severe way of life, she brings up her daydream of the cowboy Jesus in order to refute its validity. The real Jesus, she insists, will be the rider of the white horse of the Apocalypse, whose eyes are "as a flame of fire" and who wears "a vesture dipped in blood." But as Frank departs on a long truck haul with a bandage on the hand from which he has scraped the skin, Marianne recants, calling after him from the doorway, "No matter what you say, Frank, Jesus is kind. I can't believe in no other Jesus."

It was only as I created the foregoing scene that I thought of the cowboy Jesus as the center of Frank's saving vision. From that moment to the very latest, it has continued to seem just right despite involving several details that some Mormon readers have found not merely offensive but blasphemous. One such detail is the setting of the vision, which occurs to Frank at a urinal, prompting my friend and good-humored critic Richard Cracroft, professor of English at BYU, to call it the "Vision of Our Lord of the Urinal." Another offensive detail is the cigarette that the cowboy Jesus lights. For many Mormons, Jesus is the epitome of obedience; he wouldn't break even a small Commandment. Frank's Jesus distinguishes between the important and the unimportant. Smoking is unimportant. The important thing is that he induces Frank to reinterpret the idea of redemption. "Jesus is kind, just like you always said," Frank tells Marianne in the closing moments of the novel, unable to say more for fear of losing his composure. Marianne's casual, comforting fantasy has become Frank's epiphany.

This, then, was the novel that, by November 1984, I considered finished and ready for submission. Hoping it might appeal to a national audience, I continued my attempt to place it in New York. In early November, I submitted a draft of some six hundred pages to Houghton Mifflin. This firm rejected it with a printed form. In late December, I mailed it to Doubleday and Company. This firm returned it in March 1985 with respectful commentary. I next submitted it to a New York agent recommended by the editor from Norton who had reviewed and rejected the work. In late April this agent said, while granting the novel was well written, that it had poor prospects in her market. In June the manuscript was awarded a second-place prize in the annual writing competition of the Utah Arts Council. On the strength of this prize a local publisher, Gibbs Smith, proprietor of Peregrine Smith Books of Layton, Utah, asked to see the manuscript. Discouraged with the prospects for publication, I allowed his staff to sit on the manuscript for six months without inquiry. Retrieving the manuscript in January 1986, I mailed it to another literary agent in New York City who, on the basis of my story "Trinity," had invited me to submit something for his consideration. In early May he informed me by telephone that he had spent a weekend reading the manuscript. He doubted he could market it. "You are a good writer," he said, "but this isn't a terribly interesting or exciting story."[6] I believed I had given the New York market a full test. What I had written did not appeal to the broad national readership served by the New York publishing industry.

In early 1986, Signature Books asked to see the manuscript. That small Salt Lake–based firm specialized in history and literature appealing to a liberal Mormon audience. It had published my anthology *Greening Wheat* and had done a reprint of *The Canyons of Grace* with a new cover. This reprint, I will note, put far more copies into circulation than had the modest first printing done by the University of Illinois Press. By 1986 Signature Books was under the direction of Gary Bergera and Ron Priddis. Gary, in charge of manuscript selection and production, and Ron, in charge of marketing, functioned as harmonious equals. At Gary's request, I submitted the manuscript of *The Backslider* to Signature board member Lavina Fielding Anderson, who in late April recommended its publication. By June Gary had accepted the manuscript and scheduled it for a pre-Christmas publication.

I revised the manuscript a final time before Signature Books turned it over to their copy editor. It had been more than a year and a half since I had worked on the manuscript. Time and distance had proved salutary. Devoting a long day to the revision of each of the ten chapters, I reduced the length of the work by 10 or 15 percent. At the request of Gary and Ron, who took me to lunch for the sole purpose of bringing up the matter, I excised some of the graphic erotic passages and some of the obscenities spoken by my characters, retaining such touches as the backsliding Frank's reference to God as "the Big Son of a Bitch in the Sky" and his assertion that magpies are as "as common as horseshit at a rodeo," a term I picked up from a friend. I made many other stylistic changes of a subtle and tonal sort, but indispensable, as I judge, for giving the work a luster that pleases me still.

Momentous changes had occurred in my life between 1984 and 1986, which I will elaborate upon in greater detail in later chapters. By June 1985 I had taken on the writing of the biography of

Juanita Brooks as my major intellectual endeavor. In December, my mother died and with her my sense that I had a home in Snowflake. Eight months later, in July 1986, my sister Leora died.

Leora's death meant one less sympathetic reader of *The Backslider* among my relatives. When it appeared in early November 1986, clad in a slick blue cover on which the photo of a cattle drive was superimposed, I sent inscribed copies to my immediate brothers, Leon, Roald, and Charles; to my sister Lenora; and to several nieces. I did not send it to my other surviving siblings, Arley, Wanda, and Mary, believing, without rancor, that it would offend them. I expected no response from Lenora, anticipating that she would be displeased but would say nothing adverse. She did respond, however, quickly and with a quiet affirmation that touched me deeply. "Through all its problems," she wrote, "I find an underlying compassion in the people. I had to smile at your ending—such a washing away and final gentleness."[7] Affirmative responses—and occasionally distressed ones—began to arrive, two or three a week. Within a year of its appearance I would conclude that, regardless of what I might write later, *The Backslider* was likely to remain my most important book.

The word *important* must be qualified. In terms of copies printed and revenue generated, its success was exceedingly modest. Ron Priddis ran newspaper ads and arranged a series of signings for me, some of them in the company of Pat Bagley, whose book of cartoons, *Treasures of Half-Truth*, Signature had just published. The signings proved unproductive, especially for me. For example, in the Crossroads Mall of Salt Lake City, Bagley signed fifteen copies of his book while I signed three of mine. The main outlet for Deseret Bookstore refused to display my novel openly, though for a while it carried a small stock in the back for those who might ask for it. Nonetheless, about half the original printing sold within a year of its appearance. By 1990 that printing had been exhausted, and Signature published an inexpensive mass-market paperback version, which, interestingly enough, sold nearly fifteen hundred copies within a few months. This version of the book remains in print as of 2006.

I wasn't concerned with revenue. I made my living by teaching, not by writing. What counted was that from the start I knew I had enthusiastic readers. They spoke to me in person, wrote letters, or called on the phone with a sufficient frequency to keep me believing in the worth of my novel and encouraged in my ambition to write other things. I was invited with some frequency to read before university classes, clubs, associations, and informal groups of friends. I read, for example, before the Algie Ballif Forum in Provo, the B. H. Roberts Society in Salt Lake, and the Writers at Work writing workshop in Park City. Invited to speak on the same program with Wallace Stegner at the luncheon of the Intermountain Booksellers Association in September 1987, I chose to discuss *The Backslider*.

When, soon after the novel appeared, I did a signing at the BYU bookstore, my second cousin Matt Hilton, a lawyer, bought copies for himself and his father. Knowing they were conservative Mormons, I feared they might feel cheated. A couple of months later, I unexpectedly met Matt at the entrance of the federal courthouse in Salt Lake City. To my surprise he told me he and his father were using the novel to reactivate a lapsing friend. Since then, numerous people have told me that my book has helped them remain a Mormon. My other books and my many essays and public addresses on Mormon topics have supported my avocation as a worker for the liberalization of Mormonism. But none, I think, bolsters that role as distinctly as *The Backslider*. At a party one night, a woman told me the novel had helped allay her fears that her father, a suicide, would be damned. One day a cashier at a grocery store, a young man, said he had read the book. "What it means," he said, "is that God is no enemy of human appetites." I couldn't have said it better myself.

I am very glad to have written *The Backslider*. There was great pleasure in creating it and a palpable disappointment when, during the fall of 1984, I regarded it as at last finished and I put Frank and Marianne from my thoughts, where they had been dwelling night and day for many years. It had provided, all in all, a positive, spirit-elevating topic for my thoughts during many a bad mood. It has continued to please me since its publication. The work has taken root among my affections. I like to reread it from time to time. It holds up well, and I have little impulse to change it. If I ever made anything beautiful, it is this book. In my feelings, it is a gravestone, a monument left behind to testify that I have lived. Granted it is a fragile monument. The paper it is printed on will slowly disintegrate as it ages. It is vulnerable at any time to fire and water. And like many a gravestone, it may soon stand unvisited by anyone. Still, given the general anonymity of death, even a fragile and temporary monument is better than none.

My Mother's House

In AUGUST 1985 I PARTICIPATED at the annual Sunstone symposium on a panel discussing the now infamous salamander letter, which supported the claim that the youthful Joseph Smith had engaged in magic while searching for buried Spanish treasure in upstate New York. The letter, which conservative Mormons dismissed out of hand, troubled liberal Mormons, who generally accepted it as authentic. In my presentation on the panel, I proposed that Joseph Smith had advanced into an authentic prophetic role through hesitant and sometimes undignified stages. His had been a "tentative revelation and experimental prophecy," I said, an interpretation that I hoped, rightly or wrongly, would help my liberal friends remain Mormon.

I publicly supported the prophetic character of Joseph Smith because I regarded my liberal friends, most of whom believed in him, as crucial agents in the civilizing of Mormondom. In any event, the issue raised by the salamander letter quickly became moot when, early in the fall of 1985, two persons were murdered and a third one injured by homemade bombs in Salt Lake City. It was soon evident that the injured person, a vendor of historical Mormon documents named Mark Hofmann, had himself perpetrated the bombings in order to cover his forgery of many of the documents he had offered for sale, including the salamander letter.

In early September 1985, Althea, Karrin, and I spent a week with my mother in Snowflake. On our first evening in town I met a boyhood friend, who surprised me by referring to my recent appearance at Sunstone and by hinting that therein lay a reason that I should have a talk with his cousin. The next day we met at noon in an office at the school where his cousin taught. Setting some religious books on the desk before him, the cousin began to proselytize me with an eloquent fervor—as I quickly realized—to the cause of Mormon fundamentalism. The error into which the modern church had fallen by abandoning polygamy, the cousin asserted, was to be corrected by the appearance of "One Great and Mighty." The cousin modestly granted that he did not think of himself as that promised reformer. Throughout nearly an hour of preachment, my friend sat in silent admiration of his charismatic cousin while I, for the first time in my life, recognized myself to be in the presence of the leader of a cult, albeit a very small one—a personality who obsessively gathered lesser personalities in tight orbit about him.

I agreed to meet with them again, and they called at my mother's house on the last night of our stay in Snowflake. Taking the initiative, I said that I was a liberal, not a fundamentalist, and therefore on the opposite pole from the center of the church. I reported that I had that morning asked a woman in the grocery store whether the town was troubled by fundamentalists. "She named both of you," I said. The cousin wanted to know whether I intended to inform against them. I said certainly not, being no agent of the church. My concern was with my friend. Turning to him, I said something like the following: "If you keep flirting with fundamentalism, nothing is more certain than that you will be excommunicated. Knowing who you are, knowing your ancestors, knowing their loyalty to the church, I can't imagine you can survive excommunication. It will tear you to pieces." His face drained of its color.

As I write these many years later, my friend still attends church in Snowflake. I don't flatter myself that my warning had much to do with this eventuality. The importance of my warning lies in what it shows about me. At Sunstone, I admonished liberals; in my mother's living room, I admonished fundamentalists. I was indifferent to making Mormons of persons who were not Mormon. But if I met a wavering person whose identity was deeply Mormon, I had an impulse to help that person remain in the fellowship of the church.

An even more significant event occurred during that week at my mother's house, for which some background will be required.

Several years earlier, while my mother and I were seated in her living room, she had remarked that there was nothing erotic about the temple ceremony. In a reflective mood, she went on immediately to inform me that in 1929 she and my father had completed a part of their second temple blessing at home. I was astonished that in nearly fifty years of association she had never mentioned that she and my father had been recipients of the rare (and now entirely discontinued) second temple blessing. And of course I was instantly curious as to what the home part of the ceremony had consisted of if not something erotic. But she would divulge nothing further, seeming, in fact, to be ashamed of revealing as much as she had. In the months that followed I asked friends for details about the second temple blessing. None of them knew anything; many of them didn't know such a ceremony had ever existed. On later visits my mother at least obliged me by telling me that she and my father had engaged in the temple portion of the ceremony while attending General Conference in Salt Lake City in April 1929, but had delayed the portion performed at home until June because it was then they moved into the house they had bought in Snowflake. They wanted the ceremony to serve as a dedication of the house in which their children would grow up.

We had brought my mother to the house in September 1985 expressly to satisfy her longing to be in it. On earlier visits she had cooked and cleaned with something like her former vigor. But now, while Althea and I prepared meals, vacuumed floors, and ran mice-soiled bedding through the washer, she shuffled a few papers at the dining table or sat quietly on the sofa next to the table with her hands folded in her lap.

On perhaps the second morning, she said something that riveted my attention. From the sofa, she looked toward the door entering the kitchen. "Right there," she said, "was where your father and I completed the ceremony for our second blessing."

"Right where?"

"There. In the doorway to the kitchen. He sat in a chair. I cried. He thought it was because I was humiliated. It wasn't that at all. I cried because it was so sacred."

I was frantic to know more. I dug, I pried, I pleaded, but she refused to tell more. During the following days, I thought of the matter constantly. Helping in the house, taking walks, shopping for groceries, I concentrated intently upon the facts at my command. The ceremony had gone forward in the doorway. My father had sat in a chair; my mother therefore had not been in a chair. But she had not been inert. She had done something that made her weep, and my father had reason to believe she wept from humiliation.

And then, on the next to the last day of our stay, it came to me: she had washed his feet! Christ washed the feet of the ancient apostles. Sometimes the president of the church, it is said, washes the feet of modern apostles. So my mother had washed my father's feet. Nothing she said indicated that he had in turn washed hers.

Early on the morning of our last full day at the house, I loaded garbage cans in the back of our car and took my mother for a drive to the county landfill. Junipers stood thick upon the hills, and the sky was immense, utterly blue, and afloat with clouds of silvery white. As we left the landfill, I launched a deceit, pretending that I knew from other sources the full ritual of the second blessing. I said to my mother, "It's a lovely ceremony, the washing of the feet that follows the second blessing in the temple." My ruse worked. Disarmed by this evidence that I knew, she confirmed my surmise. She spoke of kneeling, of placing my father's feet in a basin of water, of drying them, of weeping.

The next morning, we said good-bye. Mary came to take Mother to her house. Althea, Karrin, and I departed for California where I would spend a week at research on the life of Juanita Brooks, whose biography I had undertaken to write. Our good-bye was the last we would ever say to my mother, who died on December 10, 1985, a few days short of ninety-three.

We spent December 13, my fifty-second birthday, traveling by automobile from Ogden to Snowflake to attend the funeral. I slept that night for the last time in my mother's house. We held the funeral the next morning in Snowflake's yellow rock church in which I had attended meetings during most of my childhood. At the viewing before the funeral, I merely glanced at my mother in her coffin, fearing to lose my composure if I did more. She lay in a beautifully finished birch coffin, which my nephew Woody, who had recently undergone open-heart surgery, had made for himself. After the funeral, we followed the hearse to Lakeside, where my mother was buried in a plot with Alma, Amanda, and my father. As the coffin was lowered into the grave, Leon remembered that he had promised Woody that he would remove the expensive brass handles from the coffin. He got a screwdriver and climbed into the grave. I understood his reasons and approved entirely. I was also grateful for the comic relief this touch of frugality gave an otherwise sad event.

In the late afternoon, Althea and I assembled with my siblings at the house. In a brief council we agreed that, rather than see this structure, incommodious at its best and now very deteriorated, fall into the hands of strangers, we would donate the land on which it stood to the local school district on the condition that the district raze the house. As we left town that night, I sealed off my emotions, ignoring as best I could the enormity of my loss.

We returned to Snowflake in July 1986 to attend the funeral of my sister Leora, who had died of a massive stroke. On the way we paused in Cedar City to attend the Shakespeare festival, having reserved tickets months in advance. We were joined by a considerable retinue of relatives, who included Lenora and Marion. From the latter we learned the details of our mother's death. She had collapsed in their house in Mesa. From the moment she fell to the floor, it was evident she was dead. Marion knelt beside her and dedicated her to God. Shortly the paramedics arrived and attempted to resuscitate her. Luckily our mother was beyond them. I have wondered whether Marion's prayer helped frustrate the well-intentioned but, in this case, misguided efforts of the paramedics to revive an old, worn-out woman who was ready to die. The dedication of the dying to God is a folk ritual among the Mormons, often practiced but not officially defined. What wrung Lenora's heart was that she had scolded our mother that very morning for one thing or another. "Poor little Mother," Lenora muttered over and over while she recounted the incident. "If I had just told her how much I love her."

Of a lesser dignity was an incident that had actually occurred at the preceding year's Shakespeare festival but that I had managed to utterly repress from my memory till I was reminded of it at the festival of 1986. We were seated on a grassy hillock, taking in the preliminary green show, a medley of Elizabethan song and dance performed on a small outdoor stage. I found myself seated beside a small sapling, which caused me to remember, as I later wrote in a letter to Marcella, who had divorced my nephew Dwain shortly before his death, that at precisely that same spot a dog had urinated on me at the festival of 1985, an event so bizarre that I wondered how I could have forgotten it for an entire year.

> He was a three legged animal; he had had one of his hind legs amputated. He came lurching along quite ably, approaching the little tree. I sat nearby with a tart in one hand and cup of coffee in the other. I thought, What a well adjusted cripple that dog is. Just then he paused on the other side of the tree from me and with horror I suddenly realized what he intended to do. He elevated what was left of his leg and marked off his territory, throwing a fine trajectory of urine directly toward me. I made a desperate lunge backward and spilled some of my coffee. Worst of all, I was not absolutely sure that drops had not fallen on my tart. Such is the sense of deprivation which anyone has who grows up in Snowflake that I ate it anyway.[1]

Following the festival of 1986, we drove on to Snowflake, where we found lodging with my niece Joan Washburn, whose home would become our headquarters in Snowflake for a decade to come. A little later on the evening of our arrival, Althea and I walked past my mother's house, which stood dark and empty, awaiting imminent destruction. As we went by it, the shock of my mother's death came over me. It was as if I had managed to evade its meaning till this moment. She was gone. Simply, totally, irrevocably gone. My view of the house that Sunday night was my last. I couldn't bear to go back and inspect it by daylight.

At Leora's viewing the next day, I spent only a few seconds before the open coffin. The cosmetically arranged corpse didn't seem like Leora at all. During the funeral, I distracted myself by recalling that the bishop who conducted the service had once upon a time, when we were both young loggers, deposited a pile of excrement upon a rock next to my lunch box. Leora was buried in the Lakeside cemetery among the growing accumulation of Peterson graves. Of all our parents' children, she loved Lakeside the most except perhaps for Andelin. She had built a cabin near the shore of the lake and spent the summers of her later years there. After the burial, a hardy neighbor fielded the traditional Mormon funeral dinner in her house across the road from the cemetery, where I was comforted by a thick gathering of brothers, sisters, nephews, nieces, and cousins. The vitality of this milling, chattering group obscured the mournful silence of our dead in the cemetery just across the road. I am happy to add that Althea and I had taken up the custom of calling on Leora at her cabin during our summer visits to Snowflake. I corresponded a good deal with her, too, often about my writing. Her last letter to me, a few weeks before she died, expressed her satisfaction with the fact that Signature Books had required me to clean up my language in *The Backslider*.

I have said little of Althea's response to the passing of my mother and Leora. I suppose that is because it seemed so manifest that we grieved equally. From almost the very beginning of our relationship, Althea began to feel herself a full, affectionate part of my extended family. I was aware, as early as her second visit to Snowflake at Thanksgiving of 1957, that my family was an important, perhaps even crucial, factor in her commitment to me. Althea wept only a little at viewings and funerals, and like me she rarely talked about her grief. But at candid, confessional moments she revealed, months after the deaths of my mother and Leora, that she continued to weep for them in private.

Soon after our return to Utah after Leora's funeral, I carried out an unusual church assignment. My bishop, a colleague from the History Department at Weber State, asked me to provide a load of split wood for the summer encampment of girls from our ward at Camp Bartlett in Idaho, some 120 miles from Ogden. As an afterthought, he asked me to stay a night at the camp, it being church policy to have men holding the priesthood nearby for giving blessings, assisting in getting injured girls to town, and fending off vandals. Policy required two men, but my bishop failed to come up with a companion. Loading sawed wood from the pile back of my garage, I set out alone on a Monday morning in a Toyota pickup we had recently bought for Karrin. The camp was aswarm with more than six hundred women and girls from many wards in northern Utah. I briefly spoke to two other men as I arrived, the last I would see. I split the wood, ate dinner with the girls from our ward and their leaders, and accompanied them to a campfire program,

the only man among a multitude of females. I have rarely felt more
out of place. Though the ladies from our ward suggested that I
sleep in what they called "the priesthood tent" at the periphery of
the camp, I told them I would spend the night in the back of the
pickup in the parking lot, where they could find me if they needed
assistance. I spent the night being either too hot or too cold, fighting mosquitoes, and sliding toward the back of the pickup because
it was parked on a slope. Around two, it rained briefly. By three,
the sky was clear and my bag had dried out. At five, I gratefully got
up, shaved with cold water, and departed, feeling that "truly," as I
wrote to Don and Marjorie Walker, "I was the camp eunuch."[2]

The academic year of 1986–1987 was unusual in that I taught
a half load at Weber State and devoted the other half of my time to
the duties of editor of *Western American Literature*. Utah State
University, where the journal was housed, had negotiated to buy
half my time from Weber State so that the regular editor, Tom Lyon,
could take a sabbatical leave for writing a book. This transaction
had no impact on my salary, which Weber State continued to pay.

I remember this year as one of the most pleasant of my adult
life. I taught a half load at Weber State and worked steadily on the
biography of Juanita Brooks. *The Backslider* appeared in November, and I was diverted by letters, reviews, and readings related to
it. Althea began her final year of graduate study and teaching in
Spanish at the University of Utah. Karrin moved into an apartment
of her own and worked part-time in a bookstore. Having scored
well on the LSAT exam, she applied for acceptance into a half-
dozen law schools for the following year. Once or twice a week she
came by my office at Weber State, and we went off together for a
submarine sandwich.

I spent two days a week at Utah State University, housed on the
top floor of Old Main next door to the office where Charles edited
the *Western Historical Quarterly*. He and I rarely failed to spend
ten or fifteen minutes chatting with each other. From time to time
we sauntered across campus to the university's dairy outlet for an
ice cream cone. In early October I attended the annual conference
of the Western Literature Association in Durango, Colorado. As
acting editor of the association's journal, I loitered in the hotel
corridors and had, as I wrote Leon, "innumerable conversations
that educated and edified me in the ways of scholarship in Western

literature."[3] I had arrived early in order to hear an address by Louis L'Amour, best-selling author of cowboy Westerns, but found the event canceled because L'Amour was ill. On my way to breakfast the next morning, I met Frederick Manfred, the Minnesota-dwelling author of *Lord Grizzly,* one of the best mountain-man novels. Manfred, a congenial, blue-eyed giant of Frisian descent, had also come early to hear L'Amour. To pass the vacant evening, he had bought one of L'Amour's novels and tried to read it. "After heavily editing the first two pages, I stopped reading," Manfred said, making a consummate if succinct judgment upon the literary merits of L'Amour.

At Utah State, I shared a spacious office with Charlotte Wright, Tom Lyon's capable editorial assistant, who had informed me upon our first meeting that she was not a secretary. Accordingly, I wrote a multitude of letters to referees and authors, many of them long and detailed, on a manual typewriter. My duties also included copy editing and helping Charlotte with proofreading and mailing. Charlotte, for her part, oversaw book reviews, typesetting, and layout. I enjoyed Charlotte greatly. She had a caustic wit and was highly suspicious of piety. Born of a large, ardently conservative Mormon family, she had gotten herself excommunicated in "the fun way," as she described it. She scolded me repeatedly for the fact that, between sips, I hid my daily cup of coffee in my desk drawer so that Charles would not see it if he happened to stroll in. She laughed vindictively one day when I discovered, following a visit from Charles, that he had stood conversing at the side of my desk while looking down upon the drawer I had forgotten to close.

In early June 1987, with my year as acting editor of the journal nearing its end, Althea, Karrin, and I attended the Peterson reunion in Lakeside. We stayed at night at Joan's house in Snowflake, as did a number of other relatives. As for my mother's house, it was gone, and the lot it had occupied had been turned into a graveled parking lot. We routed our homeward journey via Mesa, staying with Mary and Waldo, who had driven home from the reunion expressly for our convenience. My primary purpose for this detour was to visit my brother Arley, who had not attended the reunion.

Althea and Karrin dropped me off at Arley's house and drove on to Mary's. At eighty-eight, Arley was frail and so slumped that while he sat his chin almost touched his knees. He dabbed at his tearing eyes and runny nose throughout the evening. Coral, in an early stage of senility, seemed energized by my visit. Both of them laughed hard at some of my stories—Arley with so much vigor that I feared he would fall out of his chair. Becoming serious, I concluded by telling them how I had wrested from my mother forbidden detail about the ritual of the second temple blessing in which she and our father had participated. Arley and Coral listened with rapt attention, as I expected they would. Then I hugged them both, told them I loved them, and set out afoot in the dark for Mary's house.

Along my way the Mormon temple glowed with reflected light, reminding me that a temple is an utterly sacred place for Mormons. People don't joke or talk about trifling things in a temple, and those who are called to officiate there take on a new sobriety in their everyday lives. But, as I was now thinking, sacred experiences occur elsewhere too, at births, deaths, marriages—and at moments of saying good-bye, especially when there is reason to suspect they might be the last. I had recognized something profoundly sacred, timeless, and transcendent between Arley and Coral and me as we hugged each other and said good-bye. Our good-bye had been made holy by the ripe possibility that I would not see one or the other alive again. Was it prescience on my part? I had indeed seen Arley alive for the last time. He would die the next April, and I would observe a baffled, senile Coral sitting beside his coffin at the viewing, patting his cold folded hands and saying over and over, "I love you, honey. I love you, honey."

I told Mary when I got to her house that people can experience the sacred in places other than the temple. She agreed. The matter remained on my mind while we drove the seven hundred miles home to Ogden the next day, and on the following day I wrote her a letter explaining why I had brought it up that evening. Mary had once told me about hearing a divine voice in the temple. I had been astonished that she would confide that sacred experience to me, a doubter, because she is a quiet, vulnerable person. I did not dispute or reject her account yet now felt moved to conclude my letter by writing: "I wanted to tell you about my sacred experiences so that you would know that I have them." Mary replied, "I'm grateful you had a sweet experience too, and thank you for telling me."[4]

I had attributed her telling me about hearing a divine voice to a concern for my salvation: she hoped it would help me believe. I felt honored and loved—but also condescended to. From the outset of my disbelief I have felt an impulse to concede spiritual superiority to my believing loved ones. There has seemed no logical place in my impersonal cosmos for the sacred. Yet over and over I had found myself projecting upon a particular place, person, or circumstance an emotion for which I had no other word than *holy, sacred,* or *hallowed*. With time, having become tolerant of my inconsistencies and lack of a coherent worldview, I accepted the validity of my experience of the sacred. I shared this fact with Mary because I wanted her to know my spiritual life was as rich as hers. I wanted her not to grieve for me. I wanted her to be more hopeful about my chances on Judgment Day, if there was to be such a thing.

The letter I sent Mary on the day after arriving home in Ogden anticipates remarkably an essay I wrote about my parents' second temple blessing during the fall of 1990. I wrote the essay, "My Mother's House," quickly, needing something to submit to my writing group. Two days after the writing group had critiqued the essay, I mailed it to *Dialogue*. A week later, the new editors of that journal, Ross and Mary Kay Peterson, accepted it for publication.[5] Like my story "Trinity," this essay had emerged without travail. At that time, I couldn't remember precisely when I had arrived at the insights it expressed. But the letters I have reviewed for writing the present chapter—especially the letter to Mary—remind me that not until my return to Arizona for the Peterson reunion of June 1987 had I fully engaged in the grieving process over my mother's death— a process reinforced and quickened by Leora's death and by my visit to a frail and ailing Arley. By then, a number of crucial associations had coalesced in my mind. The house I grew up in, my grief over my mother's death, my sense of the sacred, my understanding of the nature of good-byes, and my parents' second temple blessing had all become a single pattern of meaning.

I had come to understand that the house represented the family my mother had nurtured in it. Three children and two grandchildren were born in the house. Her husband and her mother died in it. Her children grew up and left it. The house remained. Its rooms resounded with departed laughter. Presences were in every corner.

Comfort and reassurance emanated from its walls. She ignored its inconveniences—windows that seeped dust during spring winds, pipes that froze every winter, mice that dwelled in its hidden spaces. It was *her* house, the only house she ever had. It provided what was necessary and thereby became sacred. Throughout my childhood, she often spoke of its sacred character. *Hallowed* was the word she consistently applied to its births, deaths, and extraordinary manifestations of love. I intuited a definition of that word from her while very young. I intuited at an early age that births, deaths, and extraordinary manifestations of love sanctify.

When I had put myself to the task of ferreting out the full story of my parents' second temple blessing, I had unknowingly put myself on track for one of my most intense encounters with the sacred. When my mother had confirmed that she had washed my father's feet, I imagined the scene in extraordinary detail. I saw a sturdy white chair familiar to my childhood placed near if not precisely in the doorway. My father was seated upon it. His feet were bare. My mother knelt before him, a towel draped over her lap. A basin of water sat between them. She lifted one of his feet, immersed it, set it upon her lap, and dried it, then lifted the other. Handling his bare feet overwhelmed her with a sensuousness light-years beyond the merely sexual. Tears streamed down her cheeks. My father was chagrined in the extreme, believing her humiliated. He disliked ostentation and self-vaunting, and it seemed to him the ceremony placed him in the exalted position. He didn't recognize that, according to the allegory inherent in the ceremony, my mother represented Christ while he represented the apostles. For the moment, the ceremony being in progress, he said nothing; later he would apologize. But there was nothing to apologize for. The sacred had descended upon her house, replete with assurance that the happy things destined to transpire there would, after the house had finished its mission and had been swept away into the oblivion of the past, continue in a faraway and eternal realm.

My siblings sometimes murmur their disapproval of my probing of family secrets. Certainly I feel ambivalent about my drive to know and to talk about everything. Nonetheless, from the moment of first securing the secret of my parents' second temple blessing, I have felt a deep propriety about it. Later events have made it appear even more fitting. It has seemed uncanny, fated even, that the episode should have culminated during the last week my mother ever dwelled in her house; that within hours of her burial her children should agree upon the destruction of the house; that upon viewing the parking lot where the house had once stood, I should have experienced a bewildering sense that my childhood had not happened there but elsewhere in a lost and unapproachable terrain.

In light of these eventualities, the episode whereby I learned the completion of my parents' second temple blessing seemed a private ritual between my mother and me, a sacrament performed for sanctifying our last good-bye and for solemnly releasing the house from its dedicated purpose of sheltering a family. I rejoiced in my good fortune, unanticipated, perhaps undeserved, to have shared such an intimate secret with my mother on the threshold of her death. It was as if our final good-bye had followed an ancient and dimly understood protocol, an emergence from an uncanny and unknowable repository of the divine.

Juanita Brooks

I KNEW ABOUT THE SIGNIFICANCE of the Mountain Meadows massacre and its historian, Juanita Brooks, as early as 1958. However, it was not until 1973 that I was motivated to read Juanita's account of the massacre. I heard her speak that year at a small assembly in the special collections room of the Weber State library. A lifelong resident of Dixie, as Utah's hot, arid southwestern corner is called, she seemed the essence of the rural. She was seventy-five. Her face was plain, her dress and adornment simple, her demeanor utterly unpretentious. But her resonant voice had a mesmerizing effect, and by the end of the session her sincerity and spunk had captivated me.

Shortly after her visit of 1973, I read both *The Mountain Meadows Massacre* (1950) and *John Doyle Lee: Zealot, Pioneer Builder, Scapegoat* (1961). Immediately I felt that both works were tragedies in the same sense that *King Lear* and *Othello* are tragedies—the first because the Mormon militiamen who, assisted by Indians, massacred more than one hundred non-Mormon men, women, and children in 1857 were fundamentally good and decent men, and the second because the conviction and execution of John D. Lee, the only participant in the massacre to be punished, were scapegoating that, as far as Mormons are concerned, deepened, rather than alleviated, the dark hue of the massacre.

Accordingly, in April 1976, I read an essay entitled "Juanita Brooks: The Mormon Historian as Tragedian" at a session of the annual conference of the Mormon History Association.[1] Althea, Karrin, and I joined four busloads of other residents from the Wasatch Front for a four-day tour that included, beside the principal activities in St. George, an initial meeting in the historic pioneer church in Parowan, a visit to the site of the massacre, and a visit to the polygamist colony at Colorado City just across the border in Arizona. While reading my essay at the initial meeting in Parowan, I sensed that the large audience listened with rapt attention, so I was not surprised that their applause was long and loud. We met Juanita in person the next evening at a barbecue in a St. George park. The eleven-year-old Karrin procured Juanita's autograph on a paper towel from a lavatory, a document still in my possession.

On the basis of my essay, two editors from the University of Utah Press, Norma Mikkelsen and Trudy McMurrin, at different moments suggested that I write a biography of Juanita. By June 1985, humbled in my aspirations for my fiction and encouraged by a likely acceptance by the University of Utah Press, I agreed to undertake the task. Juanita's voluminous letters and manuscripts, which she had donated to the Utah Historical Society, had by now been conveniently cataloged. Furthermore, I was pleased to make use of the training in historiography I had received in my doctoral program at the University of Utah—biography being, after all, a species of history. Finally, I was attracted to the idea of assessing another person's life from beginning to end, especially one for whom I felt a deep affinity, born of my recognition that both she and I were dissenters from Mormon conformity who derived from a Mormon village and who remained affectionately attached to a numerous swarm of Mormon relatives.

Researching the biography was much more enjoyable than writing it. I tackled this first phase of the project with verve and energy. During the summer of 1985, I drove each weekday for almost two months to Salt Lake City where I examined the Juanita Brooks Collection in the archives of the Utah Historical Society, which occupied some seventeen linear feet of shelf space. I arrived at eight in the morning, took twenty minutes at noon for a homemade sandwich washed down with a cola purchased from a machine, and stayed on till the archives closed at five, eventually making several thousand photocopies for my working files. I also examined materials in other libraries and archives, some of them far beyond the Wasatch Front. In September 1985 I spent a week in California, making interviews and researching files at the Stanford University Press, which had published the first edition of Juanita's history of the massacre. Armed with a tape recorder, I held interviews in St. George at Christmas 1985, and again at spring break 1986. During my spring visit, Juanita's sister Eva took me to the nursing home, where I briefly viewed Juanita, who, by now in the advanced stages of Alzheimer's disease, lay on her side asleep, curled more or less into a fetal position.

By the summer of 1986 I had settled into writing a first draft—an utter grind, as I had known it would be. For me, writing at this early stage is fraught with tension and frustration. My ideas are not fully connected to each other till I have written them, and groping for those ideas and seeking to make them emerge into the clarity of full consciousness is an enervating business. Though I taught no classes during the summer of 1986, I distracted myself with a great many things other than the biography, revising *The Backslider* a final time for Signature Books, attending my sister Leora's funeral, and beginning the yearlong stint as acting editor of the journal of the Western Literature Association at Utah State University. During the following school year, I worked on the biography at least a few hours every day. On the days I did not drive to Logan, late afternoons found me behind the shut door of my office, getting in four or five hours on the biography before trudging home in the twilight. The result was that, despite all the distractions, I completed a draft totaling nine hundred double-spaced pages by midsummer of 1987. I marvel even now that I had the gumption to stick with it. That gumption came, I suppose, from my mother, whose life was defined by tedious labor.

I had, fortunately, a great mass of facts about Juanita from which to draw. I selected facts according to two aims. The most important was to elucidate the basis of her fame, which derived from her history of the massacre and her resolute demonstration of loyal dissent. A secondary aim was to reconstruct the other aspects of her life: her daily doings, her personality, her virtues, her foibles, her relationships with family and community. These secondary facts interested me a great deal, so much so that several reviewers of my book would assert that I had overweighted my account of Juanita's life with mundane facts. I tried to select details with color and a touch of novelty—with some success, if I judge from those readers who later informed me that they liked reading about Juanita's *whole* life. In any event, my chief motive for providing an abundance of domestic detail was to demonstrate how her achievement had been crowded into the complex and busy life of a wife, mother, and teacher.

As for the facts elucidating her fame, they added drama and suspense to my narrative, much like the central conflict of an absorbing novel. The most notable among these was the controversy surrounding the posthumous reinstatement of the disgraced John D. Lee into the Mormon Church. When the First Presidency informed Lee's descendants of their ancestor's reinstatement in the spring of 1961, Juanita's biography of the scapegoated pioneer was in the process of publication. Juanita eagerly sought permission to announce the reinstatement in her book. Elder Delbert Stapley sternly denied the permission, informing her that church president David O. McKay had threatened to rescind the reinstatement if she disobeyed. Furthermore, a squadron of John D. Lee's descendants, fully believing that President McKay would carry out his threat, had her fly to Phoenix and pled with her throughout a long, harrowing day not to proceed. It was typical of Juanita that she did proceed.

Fortunately, she was not excommunicated, and her conviction that President McKay would not rescind the reinstatement proved sound. Furthermore, reviewers of the biography, many of them non-Mormon, congratulated the church for its restitution of Lee's former status. This episode covers five pages in my biography. "If there was a single summit year in Juanita's life, it was 1961," I wrote at the end of the chapter. "If there were summit moments in that year, they occurred on June 13 and July 8 when she courageously confronted Elder Stapley and the assembled Lees."[2] It was a triumph for Juanita, the reinstatement being a tacit recognition by the church of the injustice done Lee by the covert bargain that had ensured his conviction.

I completed the biography at the end of October 1987. On the day I walked into the office of the University of Utah Press with the final draft in hand, the subeditor who had been assigned to work with me, a young woman, embraced me with surprised delight. I had, I took it, exceeded her expectations by finishing the work within the time I had promised. The document consisted of

12 chapters, 525 double-spaced pages of text, 1,485 endnotes, and 14 pages of bibliography. Included was a packet of photographs from which 21 would be selected for the printed work. The manuscript was quickly refereed and accepted, and in December, I made a variety of improvements suggested by the referees. Thereafter, I had little to do with the biography, which was published in October 1988.

I taught a course in the writing of biography at Weber State during the spring of 1987 and a section on that topic at a writers' workshop at Utah State during the summer. I continued to be active on the liberal Mormon circuit throughout 1987, doing many readings from *The Backslider* and speaking at a dinner celebrating the twentieth anniversary of *Dialogue* in August. I amplified my tribute to this important liberal Mormon journal with a description of a secure method for sleeping in church:

> I plant my feet with toes turned outward, and I twine my arms and hook my thumbs in my belt. This maneuver keeps me from lolling sideways onto my neighbor while I am unconscious. Next I bow my head, pressing my chin upon my breast. This keeps my mouth closed and muffles the distracting snorting and snuffling common to sleepers. Then I close my eyes and give myself over to slumber. Some forty or fifty minutes later I awaken to the sounds of the closing hymn, much edified and enormously refreshed. No longer do I resent the fact that no one has reported hearing a new idea in a Mormon sermon since the death of Brigham Young.[3]

I was not exaggerating much on my actual practice. I had in late years developed my mother's enviable ability to sleep in church and had found, truly, that church attendance had become much more tolerable. I have repeated the foregoing description many times elsewhere, provoking invariable laughter and reinforcing my perception that my tone of friendly irreverence does as much as my ideas to attract listeners on the liberal Mormon circuit.

In September 1987, Karrin entered law school at the University of Utah. She rented an apartment near campus in Salt Lake City, and I helped her haul furniture in her pickup. She was also an ensign in the navy reserve, her interest in the military having been roused by dating airmen from Hill Air Force Base. Althea and I attended her swearing in at Fort Douglas in Salt Lake City where she—a tall, lithe, dark-haired young woman—appeared in handsome navy whites. Althea had by now completed all the course work toward a master's degree in Spanish at the University of Utah. She put off writing a thesis, however, and did not receive the degree. That didn't seem to matter for her purposes. She was hired at Weber State as a part-time adjunct instructor in first-year Spanish, a position she would fill with much satisfaction and an enormous dedication till we both retired from Weber State in the year 2000. She used the earliest proceeds from her teaching to have a large satellite dish erected in our backyard, with which she could follow daily TV soap operas in Spanish broadcast from Mexico and Los Angeles. Her assiduous attention to pronunciation and idiom in the colloquial language of the TV dramas gave her, over a three- or four-year period, an intonation and fluency in Spanish ordinarily acquired only by persons residing in a Spanish-speaking country.

I pursued my usual quota of quaint causes throughout 1988. In February I agreed to become a member of the board of trustees of the Weber County Library, a position I would hold for nearly ten years, serving for one year as chair of the board. In April 1988 I found myself obliged to a second term as president of the Association for Mormon Letters. Discouraged by the poor results of a call for papers, the existing officers had decided to dispense with the annual symposium featuring scholarly discussions of Mormon literature. I joined a number of objecting friends in a plan to revive the symposium for the following year—a plan that required that some of us accept positions on the board of the faltering organization. Accordingly, for the second time I became president-elect of the AML for 1988. After I had rotated through the offices of president and past president, I remained on the board as editor of the AML newsletter until I retired from teaching in 2000. My newsletters were plain, brief, and not always punctual. I supported the AML because, selfishly, I believed its encouragement of a high quality in Mormon writing would help create a readership favorable to my own writing and because, less selfishly, I believed that such a readership would help liberalize Mormondom. I am pleased that at its symposium in February 2000, the organization made me an honorary life member.

Early in 1988 Roald was appointed president of the West Point, Utah, Stake. Althea and I felt honored that he would ask us to share what he called his "special moment" by attending the stake conference at which he was installed. It was truly a significant achievement, the highest church position attained by any of our parents' children. Roald would remain in the position for nine years, a dedicated and benign pastor to the people of his stake. In July, he invited me to attend a special priesthood session in the Salt Lake tabernacle, for which he had secured passes. Despite the hard, narrow benches, I considered it a privilege to be present in the historic building, sitting in close view of the frail, aged prophet Ezra Taft Benson. We saw him again about a month later when Roald and Luana took Althea and me to an outdoor pageant in Clarkston, a small town in Cache Valley. The pageant was about Martin Harris, one of the early intimates of Joseph Smith, who by the vagaries of pioneer migration was buried in Clarkston. After a dinner of roast beef and corn on the cob served in the recreation hall of the church, we took seats near sunset in bleachers on a hillside from which we could see not only the stage below us but also the towns and fields of the valley beyond, gleaming with a slanting light. At dusk, while latecomers filled the final seats, a collective murmur suddenly rose from the crowd. Before us the aged prophet and his wife were being assisted to seats. Spontaneously, with no accompaniment and no central direction, the crowd broke into a hymn, "We Thank Thee, O God, for a Prophet." The pageant that ensued was interesting, but for me what made this event memorable, like my visit to the tabernacle, was the grand spectacle of Mormon ethnicity in full expression.

Another notable event of the summer of 1988 was the death of our dog, Peppermint Patty, who died peacefully on a pillow on our kitchen floor. Nearly fifteen years old, she had become so thoroughly covered by warts that we generally petted only her belly. After she died, I dug a pit behind our garage, and with tear-blurred eyes Althea and I buried a dear friend.

That summer, exceptionally dry, was also the occasion of the great Yellowstone fire, which we followed, like the rest of the nation, on our TV. There were fires everywhere in the West, including a considerable conflagration in Taylor Canyon on Mount Ogden, visible from our bedroom window. That fire swept upward through a lateral canyon, torching the oak and fir on the adjacent slopes and subsiding only when the updraft of wind died at the top. For many years since then, I have monitored the regeneration of plants in the lateral canyon. Today, black, skeletal fir trunks protrude from a flourishing green undergrowth. Such fires are appropriately called wildfires even when human beings set them. Watching the fire in Taylor Canyon, scarcely a mile from my house, I appreciated again how closely the wild impinges upon my domesticated being.

Early in the summer of 1988, the organizers of the annual Sunstone symposium in Salt Lake City, scheduled for mid-August, invited me to deliver an address in a plenary session called "Pillars of My Faith." It made good sense to decline the invitation. How could I reveal even to a liberal Mormon audience the depth of my disbelief? I already played an ambiguous role as a known dissenter whom people troubled by doubt sought out. Sometimes strangers phoned me or came to my office. One woman, who did not name herself, wanted to discuss a novel she planned to write about a faithful Mormon wife and mother who had discovered she was a lesbian. On her last visit the woman told me she was abandoning the project. It seemed too likely, she said, that her family and friends, on reading the novel, would know she herself was such a person. Occasionally, students would call at my office and discuss their doubts. I didn't express my views on religious matters in the classroom, yet sensitive students inferred doubt from the tenor of my lectures on religious and philosophical movements pertaining to literature. I recall an anguished student asking how he could adjust to a universe without God. I said, "The human spirit has resources of its own," and he went away with some degree of comfort.

Given the ambiguities I discerned in my status as a doubter, I recognized the prudence of declining the invitation to deliver a "Pillars of My Faith" address. However, my appetite for being at the center of attention overcame prudence, and I accepted the invitation. I set out with my preparation determined to go as far as I could with harmonizing my own integrity and my listeners' need for an affirmation of Mormonism. Predictably, I was dogged by uncertainty. I recall weighing the probable response of my writing group to my address while Althea and I backpacked with the

Jorgensens and Clarks over Rocky Sea Pass and camped in Rock Creek Basin of the Uinta Mountains. We had got into the custom of hiking or camping a half-dozen times a year with these friends. On this occasion we camped on a small lake near which a hidden spring, as a ranger had told us, was still flowing during this dry summer. One evening, casting a bubble trailing a fly, I pulled six trout in quick succession from the lake; minutes later they were frying in butter on our camp stoves. On our return hike Bruce and Dennis disrobed and waded into a pond along the trail, their bare buttocks gleaming, while Donna, Valerie, and Althea retreated behind a screen of fir shrubs. A little later, Bruce pulled Pascal's *Pensées* from his pack and discoursed on selections while we trudged along the trail. In the meanwhile, I was preoccupied with the reaction of these dear friends to the address I had been drafting. I often felt that they accepted me because they interpreted my doubt as tentative or in some manner mistaken. It was as if they were convinced a believer lurked inside me, awaiting unusual circumstances to be evoked. Rarely had the precise wording of my writing struck me as so important. Somehow I had to affirm and validate their faith without sharing it.

The six weeks during which the essay took shape were a period of renewed thinking about myself. In rereading the published essay, I see that while I admitted my doubt candidly, I couched it in the most positive terms I could think of. I tried to distance myself tactfully from the particulars of Mormon theology, giving emphasis to the central doctrine of generic Christianity that appealed to me, the immortality of the soul. My longing for immortality, I said, was my bond with Christianity. "I am a Christian by yearning. Opposed to my doubt and perversity is a longing that the gospel be true. Christians are made, said the apostle Paul, of faith, hope, and charity. Though I have little charity and less faith, perhaps I have hope in some abundance."[4]

I read the essay before a crowded hall in the Hotel Utah. It was brief, taking, I suppose, no more than twenty minutes. From the start, I intuited the audience's rapt attention. The applause was the warmest and most sustained of any I have ever experienced from an audience, before or after. For these liberal Mormons, it seemed I had struck the right chord in explaining my doubt. The published essay, appearing in *Sunstone* magazine a few months later, generated a similar warm, affirmative response from other friends and relatives. Leon phoned his compliments, quoting Gussie, who had always been forward in protesting my trifling and impious conversation, as saying, "Well, at last I understand him." Tracie Lamb, a former honors student at Weber State, now married and living in Seattle, wrote, "I guess I was surprised that you could be reverent. I didn't really doubt that there was more to you. I just had never seen it myself."[5]

In September 1988, while my biography of Juanita was in the late stages of production, I was informed that the manuscript had placed among the finalists of the annual David W. and Beatrice C. Evans Biography Award administered by the Mountain West Center for Regional Studies at Utah State University. The first prize was ten thousand dollars. I was not to expect this prize, as my good friend and director of the center, Ross Peterson, informed me, but I could rely on a consolation prize of one thousand dollars. The award dinner was an elegant affair—a plum-colored program, cut carnations as centerpieces, starched linen napkins, and wine goblets filled with pink lemonade (this being Utah). After introductions of the Evans family and several speeches, the awarding of the first prize proceeded, to which I listened in the comfortable expectation that I was not its recipient. To my utter astonishment and subsequent wordlessness, I heard my own name announced. Ross was that kind of fellow. He enjoyed benign deceits.

Although I am sure the high esteem in which Juanita Brooks was held generated considerable interest in my book, I also believe that the award won it a prominence along the Wasatch Front that it would never have achieved otherwise. Congratulations for the award arrived by mail, telephone, and office visits. Don Walker wrote: "A warm congratulations, Levi! This morning I found a tiny news note about a major happening. $10,000 bucks! You don't have to tell what you're going to do with all that loot. The prize is what matters. In the context of western letters, it's damn near like winning the Nobel Prize."[6] That was effusive praise from the normally reticent Don. When the hardbound book appeared in late October, the Mountain West Center promoted it with a vigor never before nor after applied to anything I have written. There were many announcements, and elegant, well-attended receptions were staged in Salt Lake City and Ogden. On both occasions I was far too busy signing books to sample the copious buffet.

Sales were brisk, even a little breathtaking, though the modest dimensions of my success soon became apparent. Impressed by the fact that the first printing of two thousand copies had sold out by Christmas, I was baffled by the director's decision to do a second printing of only one thousand. When it took more than a year for that printing to exhaust itself, I appreciated his foresight. Obviously the market had been saturated. I was pleased when, a year or two later, the press decided to do a large printing of a softbound edition, which would be available for a decade.

The upright Juanita Brooks being the subject of my book, I had felt free to dedicate it to my parents and, once it had appeared, to mail inscribed copies to all my surviving siblings, including Wanda and Mary, both of whom replied with kind, appreciative remarks. The major newspapers of Salt Lake City and Ogden reviewed the book favorably, as did a number of magazines and journals. Other awards followed. Although as an officer of the Association for Mormon Letters I had explicitly forbidden my colleagues on the board to enter my biography into consideration for an AML award, they nonetheless gave it a special award in biography at the annual symposium held during the winter of 1989. In May the Mormon History Association granted it their Best Book of the Year award, which included a check for five hundred dollars. Moreover, I was frequently invited to speak about Juanita or the massacre, on which, without intending it, I had become known as something of an expert. I spoke twice from the pulpit of the St. George tabernacle, from which, according to local legend, all the presidents of the Mormon Church except Joseph Smith had at one time or another preached. My last address from that pulpit was at Juanita's funeral following her death on August 26, 1989, about nine months after my biography had appeared. I felt deeply honored that Juanita's children would ask me to speak. I felt comforted and somehow fully initiated into the inner circle of those who claimed Juanita as their own.

Juanita influenced me in countless ways. She reinforced my affinity with rural Mormons and with my own large and loving family. I admired her indefatigable energy and spunk. I regarded her as an authentic hero, all the more believable because of her ordinary ways. From her I took solace for the increasingly evident fact that my own writing was restricted in its appeal, regional at best and perhaps limited to a liberal Mormon readership. From Juanita's habit of conserving a record of her life, I became even more meticulous about documenting my own. For example, I began to keep a diary in 1988. (I continue this practice at present, writing while in the bathroom early every morning; regularity counts in diary keeping as well as in personal hygiene.) From Juanita's account of the massacre, I was reinforced in my perception of the dark side of Mormonism and felt even more justified for having treated its penitential impulse in my fiction. Finally—and most important—I was impressed by the model of loyal dissent Juanita presented.

The reinstatement of John D. Lee to his former membership and temple blessings was one proof that Juanita's stubborn insistence upon recounting the saga of the massacre influenced the Mormon Church. As I write this chapter, some fifteen years following the publication of my biography, I am able to report another proof, the church's purchase of the site of massacre and renovation of the deteriorating monument that had previously stood there. In 1990, no less a person than Gordon B. Hinckley, then first counselor in the First Presidency and soon to become president of the church, encouraged the construction of a second monument on a hill overlooking the site of the massacre. By 1998, embarrassed by the deterioration of the original monument, President Hinckley committed the church to its renovation, which he personally dedicated on September 11, 1999, the 142nd anniversary of the massacre.

The renovated monument is an impressive structure. In its center is a cairn of rocks set in mortar. Surrounding the cairn is a low stone wall whose base and cap are composed of polished coral sandstone. Two plaques are affixed to the wall. One summarizes the massacre, making it clear that Mormon men had a greater responsibility than their Indian cohorts. The other says that the monument is on property owned and maintained by the Church of Jesus Christ of Latter-day Saints. A handsome picket fence of wrought iron surrounds the monument. Nearby an American flag waves on a pole.

If, upon the publication of her history of the massacre, you had told Juanita that fifty years later the prophet and president of the church would initiate and dedicate a beautiful monument to the slain emigrants, she would not have believed you. But it has happened. The forces of liberalization have brought the Latter-day Saints to the point where they can admit rather than angrily and punitively deny that old collective sin. This fact has enormous implications. It shows that loyal dissent works. Juanita's example lives on, encouraging those who wish to see Mormonism change in a positive, progressive way.

··· 23

Night Soil

IN NOVEMBER 1989 I DELIVERED THE MANUSCRIPT for *Night Soil,* a collection of seven short stories, to Signature Books—a much delayed project that I had begun almost precisely five years earlier. I will therefore backtrack to account for it.

Finishing *The Backslider* in late 1984, I launched into a story in the spirit of my novel, creating a rural derelict named Pickett, who on a Sunday morning straps on his artificial leg and, beset by sinful distractions and a heart full of self-incrimination, makes his way to the cemetery to visit the grave of his amputated leg, which at his insistence has been given a Christian burial. Like one of the thieves crucified with Jesus, who asks to be remembered when Jesus returns with his Kingdom, Pickett pleads, "Lord, don't forget old Pickett."[1] I first named the story "The Good Thief," later "Night Soil." The story was slanted toward Mormon readers, who I hoped would sympathize with the religious yearnings of this compulsive sinner if for no other reason than that the Jesus of the Gospels forgives the sinful readily.

In early 1985, I began a story inspired by my reading of *A Vagabond for Beauty,* the letters of Everett Reuss, an adolescent artist from California who tramped the wilds of southern Utah and northern Arizona with a pack-laden burro during the 1930s. Eventually Reuss vanished from a camp in the canyons south of Escalante, Utah, leaving behind on a rock the Latin inscription *Nemo,* meaning No Man or Nobody. His somber letters made it seem entirely possible that, tired of living, he had simply walked off a cliff. By the time I had finished the story, which I named "Sunswath," my emphasis had shifted from the suicidal dweller of the canyon country to the common-law wife who keeps him alive by the exercise of her will. Pregnant with their second child, she finds strength to sustain her morose husband through her private—and heretical—administration of the sacrament of the Lord's Last Supper.

I turned the story in this direction as a gesture of respect for the ill-fated feminist movement in the Mormon Church. By 1985 the open aspiration of women for an active role in ritual and governance had been thoroughly discredited among the large mass of Mormons. That aspiration had been made immediate and palpable to me by association with the likes of Linda Sillitoe and Lavina Fielding Anderson, both of whom would within a few years find themselves outside the church, Linda by choice, Lavina by way of discipline from an angry stake president. Though they did not know it, my story was dedicated to them. It is, I will add, the most carefully crafted story I have ever written. In it, so I believe, a wide variety of fictional elements mesh in succinct and efficient harmony.

During the winter and spring of 1985 I also worked extensively on another story, "Petroglyphs," inspired by a startling pictograph of a wooly rhinoceros, done in pigment on a cliff, which Althea and I had viewed on a field trip sponsored by the College of Eastern Utah in Price during September 1984. Our guide believed the pictograph authentic. If it was, it meant that Homo sapiens had inhabited Utah far earlier than hitherto suspected because the wooly rhinoceros it depicted had become extinct with the ending of the last ice age some ten or twelve thousand years ago. I for one believed it a forgery, though the only conceivable way the spurious artist could have placed the pictograph in its high position would have been by rappelling from the top of the cliff.

As my thinking about the story advanced, the forgery waned in importance, becoming a minor incident carried out by a secondary character, a cynical art professor. The story concentrates upon the recovery of a graduate student in history from the disillusionment he suffers when he discovers that his much admired major professor, a woman married to an invalid, is conducting an affair with the art professor. Dissatisfied with this story, I set it aside unfinished when I began research for the biography of Juanita Brooks in June 1985 and did not resume work on it until 1989.

I did not entirely suspend work on the collection while writing the biography of Juanita Brooks, taking time during the winter of 1985–1986 to write "The Third Nephite." This story derives from the attempt of a friend and his charismatic cousin to convert me to fundamentalism on the occasion of my last visit with my mother in Snowflake in September 1985. I drove away from Snowflake already planning a comic story about a rural Mormon who is saved from the enticements of a persuasive fundamentalist by the intervention of one of the Three Nephites, immortal figures from Book of Mormon times believed to be still roaming the earth carrying out heroic deeds on behalf of needy Latter-day Saints. I had contemplated making a character of one of the Three Nephites for years without finding a satisfactory place for him in my fiction. In my finished story as in my earlier conjectures, he is an unlikely candidate for the office of mythical hero, being "a runty fellow: hollow chest; scrofulous neck; Adam's apple big as somebody's elbow; yellow mustache running from nose to ears like a shaggy hedgerow dividing his face into plowed, pitted properties; bleary eyes with gummy corners."[2]

The idea for "The Newsboy" came to me a few weeks before I finished writing the biography during the fall of 1987. I awoke one night from a happy dream about apple blossoms in my mother's yard. For reasons I do not understand I began recalling experiences from my years of delivering newspapers in Snowflake. By the time I got up, I was forming a plot consolidating widely separated experiences into a single day. Like me, the newsboy of my story rides a horse that tries to bite him and defecates on sidewalks and other unacceptable places. Like me, the newsboy encounters an adult world full of problems and failures from which he is protected by the filter of innocence and inexperience. For example, when a childless spinster from whom he collects the monthly subscription offers him an extra dollar for allowing her to hold him on her lap, he complies briefly and goes his way untroubled. Nothing of that sort ever happened to me. However, along my newspaper route were several old maids, as they were uncharitably called in Snowflake, one of whom was so gaunt, unkempt, and visibly solitary that even as a boy I pitied her. It was she that I selected as a model for the spinster who vents her child hunger upon my character.

People warmed to this story from my first reading of it. It was dramatized and presented in a theater in the round at Utah State University in 1988. I attended a production, laughing shamelessly at its funny lines. I positioned the story at the beginning of my collection in hopes that its unflappable good cheer would entice readers. A few years after the collection appeared, the story was reprinted in an anthology of stories prepared for schoolchildren in California.[3]

Finishing a draft of "The Newsboy" by December 1987, I began "The Goats of Timpanogos." As the title suggests, this story was inspired by a hike to the summit of Mount Timpanogos where Althea and I saw wild goats close at hand. The mountain and its wild goats relate to the conflict and theme of the story quite indirectly, providing the setting in which a grieving widower—precluded from being sealed in eternal marriage to his dead wife by his smoking habit—surrenders himself at last to the love of a New Age woman who is devoted to psychic communication and a belief in reincarnation. This is yet another of my stories rubbing against the Mormon grain, this one by showing disregard for the institution of eternal marriage and for the monopoly of the righteous upon grace and divine approval.

I began thinking about another story during the summer of 1988 while Althea and I drove through Wayne County, a lightly populated area bordering the sculptured canyons and cliffs of Capitol Reef National Park. The immediate stimulus for "A Wayne County Romance," which I wrote during the winter of 1989, was an abandoned sawmill on the outskirts of Bicknell. As we drove by it, I began to think of a character modeled on my high school friend Howard Ramsey, who, before he and his wife were killed by an auto accident in 1981, had acquired a fleet of logging trucks operating in the White Mountains of Arizona. For years I had been impressed by Howard's entrepreneurial spirit. On our last visit I was also impressed by the intelligence with which he—though of little formal education beyond high school—discussed works of art he had viewed in the Louvre while attending an international conference on forest products.

Like Howard, my character Wallace prospers through the production of lumber, is sensitive to the world beyond his native region, and keeps a pack of lion- and bear-hunting hounds. There the close resemblance stops. Wallace longs for formality, polish, and cultivation and surreptitiously reads romances, from which he concocts a protocol of gracious courtship—a protocol that Zelva, his good-hearted but matter-of-fact wife of forty years, neither expects nor desires. When a woman from the outside offers him an escape, he finds that a stubborn loyalty anchors him to Zelva, and he ruefully accepts that he will grow old and die in Wayne County.

It was with these seven stories either finished or well on the way to being finished that I let Gary Bergera of Signature Books know during the early months of 1989 that I was interested in placing a collection. Gary responded with encouraging interest. I did not submit the manuscript until early November 1989 because of my continuing dissatisfaction with "Petroglyphs," on which I worked until literally the eve of submitting. I remain dissatisfied with "Petroglyphs." The story strikes me as far too long and perhaps pretentious in dealing with the question whether knowledge ennobles those who pursue it or merely disabuses them of untenable ideals. Perhaps, too, there is an unnecessary unpleasantness about the art professor, who not only paints the forgery upon a cliff but, in an outburst of juvenile frenzy, also bedaubs a lesser surface with his own excrement and calls it art. Yet his scatological deed fits comfortably within the theme established by the title of the collection.

I had planned on calling the collection *Night Soil* almost as soon as I had finished the story of that title in early 1985. Because my writing group vehemently opposed that title, I submitted the collection as *The Uncankered Root* (a phrase taken from "Petroglyphs," which was at that moment also titled "The Uncankered Root"). Later my writing group vetoed that title too. For weeks I thought of alternatives. At one point I wrote a page of notes on the perplexity of selecting a title. "A title of a book should be poetic, metaphorical, attractive, evocative, suggestive, and, if possible, indicative of the book's contents. The problem for me is that in rereading the several stories I find no phrases of such qualities, nor am I able to generate a name from my unassisted thinking. I can't jump a high wire from a flat footed stance. Metaphors come to me in context, they come while I write."[4] At last, I reverted to *Night Soil,* this quaint synonym for human excrement striking me as an adequate metaphor for the derelicts, social failures, and backsliders who people most of my stories.

In the story that gives the collection its title, Pickett pauses on his way to visit the grave of his amputated leg for a visit with his girlfriend, Pansy. She shows him the privy in her backyard, destroyed when the brother with whom she lives took refuge there during a quarrel and she, in a fit of anger, split it apart with an ax. Later, after she and Pickett have made adulterous love, he muses on the contents of the exposed privy pit, declaring them to signify all the good meals she and her brother have eaten and all the joy that has accompanied those meals. "You left a bit of all that pleasure in that privy, didn't you?" he says. "It ain't a pit full of mire and mess. It's a picture album; it's a museum; it's your grandmother's trunk full of wonderful old things out of the past." When Pansy responds with disgust, Pickett exhorts her not to "begrudge poor things."[5] He speaks for the author, obliquely asking his readers not to disesteem the worship and longings for salvation of the unrighteous, the marginal, and the irregular.

A desire to be fair to potential buyers also influenced my preference for the title *Night Soil,* which, as I reasoned, would alert them to the considerable load of obscenities left in the text even after I had been persuaded to reduce their number. It would also alert them to my insistence upon describing the ungainly, sagging, overweight bodies of my characters.

Signature Books planned to publish the collection in November 1990 in time for the Christmas market. Eager to place the book in conventional LDS bookstores, Ron and Gary pressured me to sanitize my stories during the text-editing stage, an endeavor that Gary assured me at one moment was "challenging almost beyond words." I accepted many of the proposed elisions and substitutions. For example, their text editor substituted "you old pain in the butt" for "you old asshole" and "backside" for "anus." However, I rejected other proposed changes, and I responded to a second bout of changes appearing in the galleys—unmarked and discernible only by a close comparison between the galleys and my original manuscript—with the following note to myself: "I observe that text editors often wish to substitute their taste in style for that of an author. They should resist that impulse. Certainly they should exercise it with great circumspection. It is not the role of text editors to rewrite."[6] In retrospect, I judge that, generally speaking, text editors have enhanced all my writing. I think it especially important that in my fiction they have persuaded me to reduce the density of the obscenities I attribute to my characters in dialogue. I

will comment, however, that even a total cleansing of the obscenities from *Night Soil* would not have placed it on the shelves of conventional LDS bookstores, its essential conflicts and characters
being by and large unpalatable to Mormon readers.

Night Soil appeared as planned in mid-November 1990. It was
hardbound—the only book of mine done in a hard binding by Signature—and it had a pleasant light-orange cover showing a blue-
eyed, overall-clad Pickett against a looming bluff and a sickle
moon. Ron, in charge of marketing, scheduled what must be called,
by the standards of promotion I was accustomed to from Signature, a blitz of local advertising and signings. He scheduled radio
and TV interviews and bookstore signings and placed conspicuous
newspaper ads from Phoenix to Idaho Falls. For example, on a
Thursday morning I was interviewed on a Logan radio station.
That afternoon I flew to Phoenix where Ron had reserved rooms at
a hotel. The next morning I had a thirty-minute interview at the
TV Channel 5 studio, to be aired early on a Saturday morning. Toward noon Ron introduced me to fellow author Michael Fillerup,
a teacher from Flagstaff, Arizona, whose first collection of short
stories, *Visions,* was being published and promoted in tandem with
mine. Michael and I went on to an interview with a columnist from
the *Phoenix Gazette.* Midafternoon we sat through a poorly attended signing at a bookstore in Tempe. The next day we flew to
Utah, making appearances and radio interviews in Provo, Orem,
and Salt Lake City. A day or two later we made our way to Logan
and Idaho Falls. An interview I had in Salt Lake City with Vern
Anderson of the AP news service resulted in a respectful article that
would be published in both the *Salt Lake Tribune* and the *Mesa (AZ)
Tribune.* An interview with a reporter from the *Ogden Standard-
Examiner* resulted in an article about *Night Soil* that began: "Levi
Peterson, a Mormon, drinks coffee, sprinkles his speech with swear
words, and sleeps through Sunday church sermons."[7] I did not attend sacrament meeting on the Sunday the article appeared, believing I should give my fellow ward members a little time to forget it
before I reappeared among them.

The extraordinary vigor with which Ron promoted my book
did not pay off in sales. I fear we were pitching not to the wrong
market but rather to no market at all. After a fruitless signing at

the busy Layton Hills mall, I wrote in my diary: "Watching the crowd of people who are absolutely uninterested in my writing, I recognize what a minuscule niche I fill in the literary world."[8] A first printing of two thousand copies sold out in about six months. Ironically, more than fourteen hundred copies of the new inexpensive mass-market issue of The Backslider were sold during the same period. The considerable remnants of a second printing of Night Soil, which as I recall was also two thousand copies, were remaindered some seven or eight years later.

Nonetheless, I believe Night Soil enhanced my reputation as a writer. It was well received by the regional and liberal Mormon press, favorable reviews appearing in at least seven newspapers along the Wasatch Front and a variety of journals and magazines including Dialogue, Sunstone, and Western American Literature. Predictably, beyond the West, it was scarcely noticed. Publisher's Weekly ran a review that packed more dislike for my writing into 150 words than I had ever imagined possible. This was offset, I am happy to say, by another succinct review in Booklist, whose author liked my stories well enough to write me a letter praising them. A local reviewer whose praise I particularly valued was Eugene England, probably the most prominent of all liberal Mormons, who wrote: "His new collection has all the theological sophistication and seriousness of Canyons of Grace and the rich, healing humor and sense of how redemption works of The Backslider. But it has something more; it is suffused with heart-breaking mortal tenderness." In a more extensive review, Gene likened my fiction to that of Flannery O'Connor, asserting that I had "learned from O'Connor (and perhaps other Southern writers) the power of 'grotesques'— the physically or spiritually wounded and marginalized humans who paradoxically can be made to touch the very center of experience and feeling."[9] I am flattered by the association with O'Connor. I have, however, read very little of O'Connor, no more than four or five of her stories, all of them because they appeared in anthologies assigned to my students. If I have been influenced by any southern writer, it is William Faulkner, whom I read extensively during my graduate years at BYU. It is entirely possible that I unconsciously took permission from Faulkner to create characters far off from standard behavior and appearance.

In conclusion, I will report that I had only silence from a small group of readers whose esteem I would have valued greatly, my surviving siblings, to each of whom I mailed an inscribed copy of the collection. Regardless of their silence, it says something of my increased confidence in their general acceptance that I dedicated the book to my twelve brothers and sisters, living and dead.

··· 24

Our Compass Swings Northwest

THE YEAR DURING WHICH *Night Soil* appeared was one of major transition in my domestic life. In June 1990, Karrin graduated from the University of Utah law school and accepted a position with a law firm in Irvine at a salary as high as mine. Accordingly, she spent the first half of the summer preparing to take the California bar exam, which had a failure rate of 50 percent. Living in Salt Lake City, she often met Althea and me for a long day hike in the Uintas. On the Fourth of July, for example, we hiked from the Highline Trailhead to Four Lakes Basin, a round-trip of about eighteen miles. I retain a vivid image of the long-legged Karrin striding along the trail in front of her parents, assiduously memorizing the large ring of study cards that swung on her belt. On the drive home, we paused at Dick's in Kamas for our usual hamburger and strawberry shake.

Late in July Karrin drove to California with a load of furniture on her pickup. A week later, on the morning after she had finished the three-day bar exam, we met her in the Los Angeles airport and flew on together for a week in Hawaii. We spent the first three days in Oahu, visiting Waikiki Beach, the Polynesian Cultural Center, and Pearl Harbor. One of my most vivid experiences occurred when we came upon the footlong head of a needle-snouted fish on a beach at dusk; its body had been abruptly chewed off, evidence of marine predation that, curiously, made me feel connected with the wild. Another vivid experience was viewing a seat belt from a downed Japanese aircraft in the small museum at Pearl Harbor; constructed of coarse khaki fabric joined by a simple pronged buckle, this belt, again curiously, made the attack of December 7,

1941, seem immediate, as if the battle had finished only hours rather than decades ago.

On our third day we flew to the large island of Hawaii, where we were astonished to discover that the entire west side of the island was a stark desert fractured by vast, jumbled acres of ancient lava floes intermittently covered by yellow grass and giant prickly pear cactus. This was my first appreciation of the term *rain shadow*, the phenomenon that ordains that the leeward side of the mountains dividing these volcanic islands is as arid and barren as the windward side is lush and green. We rented a car and lodged in an isolated hotel on a palm-studded beach, grateful to have escaped the oppressive crowds of Oahu. We viewed a crater reeking with sulfuric fumes in Hawaii Volcanoes National Park, and later, on the coast east of the park, we stood on the still warm overcrust of an active lava floe, which, as we could see, produced a column of steam where it entered the sea, vivid evidence of how the Hawaiian Islands came into being in the first place. One evening we ate at the expensive fish and fruit buffet of our hotel, seated on an open terrace overlooking the beach and sea. Returning to our room, we saw that the maid had pulled back our bedcovers and placed lavender orchids on our pillows. "Elegant living indeed," I wrote in my diary, going on, however, to worry about the creep of extravagance into American life. "A surfeit of nice things. Some people can afford luxury on a daily basis; most of us scrimp for years and splurge in a glorious week of excess. The net result is that we want more, expect more. Air travel, luxurious hotels, abundant meals: we come to regard them as necessities."[1] It was nonetheless a happy time, marred only by my apprehension of the separation that loomed at its end, an apprehension increased by the fact that one morning at breakfast we read headlines announcing Iraq's invasion of Kuwait and President Bush's mobilization of U.S. forces. Karrin, by now, an experienced officer in the navy reserve, spoke excitedly—and with what I took to be an unfortunate eagerness—about the possibility that she would be called to active duty.

After her return from Hawaii, Karrin rented an apartment in Newport Beach, not far from her office in Irvine. Althea and I brought loads of clothing and furniture on a couple of weekend trips from Utah, giving ourselves some sense of Karrin's new locale. She drove to work on the interminably busy Jamboree Boulevard, jogged along the Newport estuary where water fowl and cottontail rabbits might be seen, and shopped in the posh Fashion Island mall, where, as I observed one evening in Nieman-Marcus, one could buy a green-dyed, close-shaved mink coat. Karrin flew home for brief visits at Labor Day and Thanksgiving. During the latter visit she learned she had passed the California bar exam. Nonetheless, she disliked southern California and decided to move to Seattle. During the Christmas vacation we helped her move home to Ogden, where she studied long hours for the Washington state bar exam, diverting herself by an occasional day on the ski slopes. Worrying over the advanced mileage of her pickup and our Tercel station wagon, I bought a new ice-blue Toyota Corolla sedan, in which, on February 20, 1991, at the age of twenty-five, Karrin departed for Seattle, ending her last extended stay in her childhood home.

At the turn of the year, Althea and I experienced another transition among our personal relationships in the recomposition of our writing group. On the last day of 1990 Linda Sillitoe wrote a letter announcing her withdrawal from the group—which implied her husband's withdrawal as well. She cited stress and lack of time to be herself as her reasons for retreating from what she called "the war zone," which meant, as she went on the explain, "investigating, writing, or speaking about Mormon issues, or anything particularly dark." Why should this require withdrawal from the group? "For one thing, the group lives within the war zone both in writing and real life."[2] I am pleased to say that Linda and John have remained our close friends to the latest moment.

At the first meeting of our reduced writing group in January 1991, Bruce Jorgensen suggested that we recruit John Bennion and his wife, Karla, as members of our group. John was a young assistant professor of English at BYU with a strong interest in writing fiction. A month later, Bruce suggested that we also invite Gene and Charlotte England to join the group, Gene having expressly asked to join. Predictably, we quickly learned to cherish the friendship of both the Bennions and the Englands.

I will note that on January 1, 1991, Weber State became a university, a change in name for which I had little enthusiasm because it was not accompanied by permission to offer graduate programs.

Nonetheless, calling itself a university has been good for Weber State, generating a new pride in faculty and students that has gradually improved the quality of the institution. Also, early during 1991, the Gulf War burst into full blaze. Uncharacteristically, I turned on our television set for a few minutes before departing for my office early every morning or paused midday in the foyer of the union building on campus to stare, along with a crowd of students and faculty members, at the latest footage of bombs exploding in Baghdad and oil wells burning in Kuwait.

At the end of winter quarter 1991, Althea and I paid Karrin a first visit in the Northwest. We drove the eight hundred miles between Ogden and Seattle under a sunny March sky, intrigued to observe the scenes that opened before us: widely separated towns; dreary sagebrush plains broken by oases of potato and beet farms in Idaho; the Blue Mountains of Oregon and Washington, serenely timbered with pine; beyond them, on either side of the Columbia, vast rolling hills planted as far as the eye could see with greening winter wheat; the orchards and hop fields of the Yakima Valley of Washington; and finally, the Cascade Range with sharp, craggy peaks and heavily timbered sides scarred by frequent clear-cuts. Although we viewed it for the first time, all this was a West familiar in its aridity and space; at Snoqualmie Pass, fifty miles east of Seattle, we crossed over into an unfamiliar West, a rainy land of tall trees and impenetrable understory and the inlets of the Puget Sound.

Our destination was Issaquah, a small city fifteen miles east of Seattle, where Karrin was staying with my niece Barbara (Mary's daughter) and her husband, Raymond Green. Recovering from a bout of flu, Karrin was discouraged by what had proved so far a fruitless search for a position with a law firm. Nonetheless, during the next couple of days, she cheerfully gave us an orientation to the Puget Sound—a drive through the tulip fields of the lower Skagit Valley, a picnic on a beach at Whidbey Island, a tour of Pike's Place Market and the piers of Elliott Bay, a crossing of the sound by ferry, and a two-hour hike along the Dungeness Spit, where the surf ceaselessly rattled the pebble beach. We departed from Karrin uneasily, comforted chiefly by the fact that Barbara had taken her in, for which I remain, even now, deeply grateful.

A long-term cancer patient, Barbara survived by undergoing, with uncomplaining equanimity, radical varieties of chemotherapy which repeatedly brought her back to periods of remission. She had resisted discouragement by setting survival goals. She had learned to fly, resolved to see her daughter, Amber, graduate from high school, and, having succeeded in that, resolved anew to see her graduate from college. As far as I could make out, Barbara was without religion of any kind. Belligerent in her independence from Mormonism, she demonstrated a cool reserve toward her believing relatives. As for me, I earned her trust by accepting a cup of coffee on our first morning in Issaquah. She forthwith relaxed in my presence, and we fell into a happy rumination upon the history of our family—and upon the personalities of its current members—that we would resume upon all my returns to the Northwest until Barbara's death on my birthday in 1994.

Within a month of our visit, Karrin found a position as public defender in the municipal court of Bremerton, across the sound from Seattle, and took an apartment in nearby Silverdale. She flew home from time to time, and we continued to make occasional journeys to the Northwest. Each good-bye was difficult, as I wrote in my diary in July: "Each departure from Karrin seems sharper and more definitive than the last."[3]

Karrin's departure from Utah threatened to break the magic circle of parent-child in which, as I have explained in earlier chapters, my pathological anxiety found its best surcease. It had remained intact as long as I could see her in person each week during her years of attending school in Provo and Salt Lake City. Now that she lived eight hundred miles away, I had to make do with telephone conversations. I reasoned that a weekly call could be justified by the nebulous rules that govern behavior between parents and their adult children. Nonetheless, I wanted—quite desperately—more than that. I therefore quickly fell into the habit of phoning her on Wednesday and Sunday nights, late enough, as I hoped, to catch her in from her day's activities yet still awake. Although Althea didn't share my urgency, she ordinarily picked up an extension and joined our conversations.

If Karrin wasn't in when I dialed on a Wednesday or Sunday evening, I was instantly anxious and continued to dial back every fifteen minutes or so till, as ordinarily happened, she arrived and answered the phone. Once in a great while the hour grew so late that I gave up dialing and went to bed, only to lie in a state of wakeful anxiety for much of the night. Aware that my anxiety would continue unabated till I heard her reassuring voice, I dialed again as she was getting up or after she had arrived at her office. Obviously I spoke with her only briefly on these occasions. I have no idea how much of my shameful dependence Karrin—or Althea, for that matter—intuited. It wasn't a topic I could discuss. Unfortunately, it was as compulsive as breathing. There was nothing to do about it except disguise it as best I could under the mantle of taking a fatherly interest in Karrin's welfare. That fatherly interest, of course, was sincere. The magic circle, though tenuously drawn and maintained chiefly by telephone, persisted. Karrin still stood ambiguously in my emotions as both my mother and my daughter and I as both her father and her son.

Toward the end of July 1991, Althea and I drove to Snowflake to participate in the forty-year reunion of my high school class, held in conjunction with the town's celebration of Pioneer Day. On a Saturday morning I joined more than thirty of my classmates from the class of '51 in front of the high school, where immediate emotional adjustments were required of me. Old enemies approached me with such evident pleasure that I instantly repressed the anger I had carefully nursed these forty years. I suffered other momentary uncertainties. As I wrote to a friend: "It was startling to look fervently into a face and say, 'Who *are* you?' Then came the familiar name and all was as it had been long ago. There is a certain trauma to abruptly restoring the past to the present across such an abyss of years."[4]

After our initial greetings, we took seats on a flatbed truck and found ourselves rolling into position among the horse riders, bands, floats, fire trucks, and shiny new semis composing the opening parade of the Pioneer Day celebration. I sat with my feet dangling off the truck bed, where I was soon joined by my niece Joan's ten-year-old son, Levi Washburn. Occasional shouts of "Hey, Levi!" from bystanders were directed, I soon realized, not toward me, but toward my nephew, who had achieved a certain stature of rascality about town. To vent my tensions—and confident that no one could make out what I was saying because of the general uproar—I began to shout at the bystanders, "Practice abstinence and take your vitamins, folks!" Curiously, this gave me a deeper sense of participating in the communal event of a parade.

At noon the class of '51 repaired to the recreation hall of a church for a Mexican meal and lengthy self-introductions. The tone of the event was entirely Mormon, those in charge being sweetly oblivious to the feelings of the few Gentile classmates among us. The seditious nature of my writing came up at the table where Althea and I sat. Barbara Jean Ellsworth said it was my old desire to attract attention that made me write books. Gussie Schneider, my sister-in-law, said that I took bad traits from many real-life persons and lumped them all into a single fictional character. Both those comments strike me as accurate. Prizes were distributed to Loral Decker for having the most children, nine; to my niece Gale Hansen for being the least changed; to me for having written the most books. Unquestionably the highest achiever among us was Coy Pettyjohn, formerly a brigadier general in the air force in command of intelligence throughout the entire Pacific, now retired and living in Las Vegas. In the parking lot after the luncheon, Coy and his wife got into a new Cadillac parked beside the aging Toyota pickup in which Althea and I had driven from Utah. Coy's Cadillac evoked the following reflection:

> Reunions are truly a moment of self assessment....[H]ere I am at 57, driving worn out Toyotas and living in an aging house still in need of renovations and on a lot shaggy with feral weeds. I used to think my books would salvage some significance for my life. I find little reason to exalt myself over my books any more, I suppose because I am so keenly aware of the enormous accretion of books in the civilized world. Still, in a sense, those books are for me the point of growth, of endeavor, of living fully, of realizing my childhood faith that the future held a grand eventuality for me.[5]

During the summer of 1991 I was hard at work on a collection of wilderness essays, as I shall detail in the next chapter. About a month after returning from the reunion, I diverted myself from that task by writing a short story about a man attending the forty-year reunion of his high school in rural Utah. The project quickly expanded into writing a novel, which I would name *Aspen Marooney*. In effect, I took an unplanned sabbatical from the wilderness essays, to which I returned in September 1992 after I had mailed a manuscript of the novel to a publisher.

Another event of great consequence in our lives was the death of Althea's mother on August 29, 1991, just a few weeks short of her ninety-third birthday. Unless we were out of town, Stella had taken dinner with us each evening for the more than eleven years she had lived near us on Twenty-fifth Street. During the past three or four years she had become more and more decrepit. Mornings Althea helped her get up, and evenings I helped her go to bed. She was in a condition of near emaciation, weighing scarcely seventy pounds. During the last six months of her life, she found it difficult to sit in any position that did not pain her back, and her congestive heart condition worsened until her lower legs swelled into unsightly trunks of such weight that she couldn't lift them into bed without my assistance. When her feet were down, water seeped steadily from small breaks in her skin. About a month before she died, we found a young internist who was willing to prescribe a diuretic aggressive enough to shrink her legs to normal size. She was delighted to see her ankles again.

On the evening of her death, as I prepared to help her into bed, she collapsed and fell to the floor at the side of the bed. Her eyes rolled strangely, and incoherent sounds emerged from her throat. I sat on the bed and pulled her into my arms and dialed for the paramedics and called to Althea. Althea got into the ambulance and rode with her to the McKay-Dee Hospital, while I followed in our car. By the time I arrived at the emergency ward, oxygen had been administered, and Stella was awake and coherent. We stayed a couple of hours until she was sleeping comfortably in a private room. Several hours later, about three o'clock, a nurse phoned us and advised us to come as quickly as possible. We sat perhaps a half hour beside her unconscious form watching the blips on the heart monitor decrease in frequency. We spent perhaps another half hour beside her after the doctor had said, "She's gone." We were grateful that the hospital staff gave us this uninterrupted time.

Sitting beside her tiny, silent form, I reflected on my more than thirty years' acquaintance with Stella. I had not only respected her but had enjoyed her company as well. Including her in our intimate lives had been no burden but a pleasure to me. I grant that I sometimes baited her by asserting that my relatives would have her vicariously baptized a Mormon following her death. But I couldn't forget how generously she had helped us with gifts of clothing and cash during our impoverished years in graduate school. I admired her for her devout daily reading from the Bible and for donating fifty dollars a month to the Ogden Rescue Mission from a meager social security stipend. I empathized with the orphan child that lurked in her at Christmas and Mother's Day. Her mother died on a Christmas Eve from an illegal abortion, leaving Stella, four, and her sister Althea, two, with a negligent father who parceled them out to a shifting variety of relatives and orphanages.

Stella died on a Thursday morning. The Labor Day weekend approached, and Karrin had an air ticket to Utah for a backpack trip into the Uintas with us. Accordingly, after having phoned Karrin, we made quick decisions about the funeral. We wrote an obituary and got it to the *Ogden Standard-Examiner* in time to make the evening paper, then phoned my close relatives and recruited them for songs, prayers, and a sermon.

Perhaps thirty persons, most of them my relatives, attended the funeral in a mortuary chapel at noon on Saturday. Charles prayed at the closing of the casket. Roald preached a gentle sermon. His daughters Kathy and Mignon, accompanying themselves on a guitar, sang hymns. His daughter Heidi read Stella's life history, and his daughter Erin read a long poem Karrin had written on the morning she had received word of her grandmother's death. Leon's daughter Britt and Roald's daughter Dawn offered the opening and ending prayers of the service. Charles's son John dedicated the grave at the cemetery. After the burial, my relatives and a few of Stella's friends gathered at our house for a dinner prepared by the good sisters of the Thirty-third Ward Relief Society. That's what a family is for, to back you up when you need a respectable number of mourners at a funeral.

Benign weather reigned throughout the early autumn of 1991. Our tomato plants continued to bear large, utterly delicious tomatoes until well into October. Weekdays, I taught my usual load of English classes and Althea her sections of beginning Spanish. Evenings and weekends, we emptied Stella's house and prepared it for sale. Outside we painted the eaves and window trim and hired a re-roofing job; inside, we painted three rooms and had a new carpet and linoleum installed. On the local market, real estate was in a severe slump. Stella had paid fifty-five thousand dollars for the house; we eventually sold it for forty thousand dollars. Half of that went to amortize Stella's remaining indebtedness and to pay for repairs and renovations.

After the sale of the house in January, Althea sent Karrin twelve thousand dollars from the proceeds for buying a new car. I hoped Karrin would buy something practical like a Corolla or Camry. However, assuming she would insist on something sporty, I counseled her to buy a Celica. She seemed amenable, so we were surprised when she phoned to say she had just bought a Toyota extended-cab pickup. She had, in fact, negotiated for a Celica to the point of preparing to sign a contract. Suddenly she paused and said, "I don't want a wussy car," and asked to look at the pickups. At the end of January, Althea and I flew on one-way tickets to Seattle for a weekend visit with Karrin and drove home in the Corolla, which, despite being a year old, seemed like a new car to us.

One morning near the end of winter quarter 1992, my colleagues Candadai Seshachari and Tom Burton came into my office and closed the door behind themselves, a sign that political maneuvering was imminent. Sesh was chair of the English Department and Tom chair of the Faculty Senate, both being among the most influential faculty members on campus. The present dean of Arts and Humanities was resigning, and an acting dean would be appointed for a year while a search would be conducted for a replacement. Sesh wanted to apply for the acting deanship with the idea that he would also apply for the permanent position. Someone was required to replace Sesh as chair of the department for at least a year. Tom and Sesh proposed that I make myself available. I demurred yet failed to say no definitively, and these two friends renewed their persuasions on our next sortie for pizza. I had gone to lunch once a week with Tom and Sesh from the early 1970s. A special chemistry existed among the three of us who had stood together in many a campus fracas. If one of us couldn't attend our appointed lunch, the other two were dispirited. When all three were present, we exchanged gossip and dissected campus events with gusto. Given such a relationship, it was fated that I would acquiesce to their latest proposal. I did so on the condition that if Sesh were not successful in his application for the permanent deanship, he would resume the chair of the department and let me return to full-time teaching. I will report, however, that he did not live up to his word on that score, and, when another person was appointed dean at the end of the following year, Tom and Sesh persuaded me to apply for a regular three-year term, to which I was appointed.

It was with some sense of history repeating itself that I returned to the office on the third floor of the Social Science building that I had been the first to occupy in 1971. My new duties, which included the teaching of one class each quarter, did not increase my time on campus, where it had long been my habit to spend nine or ten hours a day. Furthermore, I managed to keep writing, though on a less predictable schedule. Luckily, I have always been tolerant of interruptions while I write and able to take advantage of even an hour's free time. It was one of my pleasures to write while I ate a breakfast consisting, quite invariably, of an orange, a container of peach-flavored nonfat yogurt, a Texas doughnut that I bought at Smith's on my way to campus, and coffee that I brewed after arriving.

An enormous amount of traffic flowed through the departmental office, making for a pleasant social life. I bantered with the secretaries, exchanged anecdotes with faculty members, and chatted with students. In general I liked my duties and looked forward to each day with interest, existing on something of an adrenalin high. I could count on minor challenges—bracing rather than formidable—every day. My duties could range from approving a distilled water dispenser in the mail room for faculty members who esteemed city water polluted to investigating student complaints against teachers and, if the complaints proved well founded, as they sometimes did, negotiating an improvement in the offending instructors—a delicate matter for many reasons, not the least of which is that a chairperson has little power over established faculty members.

In addition to managing the department's current expense budget and hearing student complaints, I oriented new English majors and minors, certified the completion of requirements for the graduating majors and minors, evaluated credits for transfer students, and heard petitions for exceptions to university requirements regarding basic composition and general education literature. I recall granting the petition for credit from a Japanese student who spoke shy, painful English. Later my colleagues in the English as a Second Language section of the department told me that this student, finding himself locked out of a Baskin-Robbins ice cream store at closing time, had turned around, lowered his pants, and mooned the employees through the plate-glass window. Then he butted the window with his naked rear, broke the window, and cut his buttocks. Police arrested him but released him without charges after a friend showed up and paid Baskin-Robbins one thousand dollars for the window. (Well-heeled Japanese students were not uncommon on our campus at this moment of high prosperity in Japan.)

The complexity of my duties may be judged from my preparation of the quarterly schedule of classes, which had to be done months in advance. Because all students were required to take two writing courses and one general education literature course, our offering of courses was by far the largest in the university—as was our faculty, which consisted of close to thirty full-time faculty and thirty or forty part-time adjunct instructors. Most of the full-time faculty had proprietary rights over a favored course, usually upper division, which I had to respect. Most of them preferred to teach only during prime hours, that is, from eight to twelve in the morning. Furthermore, they grumbled if scheduled to teach more than two classes back-to-back without a break. I tried to honor these preferences but invariably found myself on the phone toward the end of making a schedule, renegotiating previous agreements with a number of my colleagues.

The adjunct faculty were not nearly so pampered. Their teaching was largely restricted to basic composition courses. In fact, they taught two-thirds of our large freshman English program. They were paid at about half the rate of a first-year assistant professor without the further enhancement of health and retirement benefits that the latter enjoyed. They had no job security, having a contract for a single quarter at a time. Furthermore, I alone reviewed their credentials and made the decision to hire them. Nonetheless, I saw no evidence that their instruction of basic composition was inferior to that of the tenure-track faculty. Some of them were among the best teachers in our department. With both guilt and gratitude, I recognize that my privileged status as a professor—and a writer—depended upon these, my exploited junior colleagues. Without the savings their instruction provided, our mutual employer, the State of Utah, couldn't have afforded my salary.

Turning to other matters, I made my one and only attempt to climb Mount Rainier during the summer of 1992. Karrin had by then joined the Mountaineers, a large Seattle-based climbing club, and had set her sights on climbing that notable peak. She recruited Leon, who had once climbed Rainier, to serve as her guide and invited me to come along. By way of preparation, I began to jog five miles a day and to take frequent hikes to Malan's Peak and Mount Ogden with a thirty- or forty-pound load of water-filled milk jugs in my pack. I persuaded a mountaineering colleague to teach me the rudiments of rappelling and of self-rescue from a crevasse. I found it hard to persuade myself to back over the lip of the cliff on my first rappel, but after I had done it, I found the experience exhilarating. On a later excursion with this colleague, I was accompanied by Brent Todd, a Salt Lake lawyer whom I recruited for the projected climb. Brent and his wife, Susan, were both former students of mine with whom Althea and I had fraternized closely for years.

In early August Leon flew to Utah and drove on to Silverdale with Althea and me. Unluckily, rain began that night, and we spent the next day, a Thursday, making marker wands from garden bamboo sticks and fluorescent highway tape. Having come near disaster on Denali while lost in a whiteout, Leon wanted to make sure we could find our route off Rainier in similar circumstances. At dawn on Friday, Leon, Karrin, and I met Brent at the Paradise ranger station, and we geared up and set off in a wind-driven rain, which as we ascended turned to snow. The storm, a ranger had told us, would continue until the next day.

My usual dread of the labor entailed by backpacking was compounded by the evident risks of our venture. The first problem, at least for me, was exhaustion. I had no confidence that I had the energy for making the top of the fifteen thousand–foot summit. Our packs bulged with ropes, crampons, ice axes, sleeping bags, body harnesses, food, headlamps, several changes of batteries, water-proof parkas, wind pants, fleece jackets, polypro underwear, and, ironically, drinking water for two strenuous days. The second problem was the storm. Presumably we could make Camp Muir and, if we could beat our competitors there, find an uncomfortable but dry berth in one of the shelters. But beyond Camp Muir, the route was tricky and dangerous. Leon hoped we could tag along behind a commercially guided party. He wasn't certain that we could, and he made no pretense at recalling the route from his use of it more than a decade earlier. As for finding it ourselves, we would be setting out at midnight, relying on headlamps, and, from all appearances, we would be in the thick of a snowstorm. We would be roped together in pairs, partners supposedly primed to save one another in event of a fall into a crevasse—with the likelihood that the fresh snow would make crevasses even harder to detect.

We toiled upward all morning, uncertain of our progress, there being around us only cloud, wind, wet driving snow, and, within the range of our limited visibility, a steep snowfield punctuated by protrusions of black rock. My apprehensions increased by the hour. I was therefore perhaps too ready to discern discouragement in my companions' talk. Leon said he hated making a wet camp, and Karrin said water was sloshing in her boots, funneled there by her wind pants, which she had tucked inside her gaiters. When we stopped for lunch at an outcropping of rock, I asked whether we should turn back. The others didn't dismiss the idea out of hand. Brent said he was willing if everyone else wanted to but favored going on. Leon and Karrin said they favored doing what everyone else wanted. I persisted, saying I thought it was prudent to turn back. That proved decisive. I felt guilty for aborting the climb until, three or four hours later in the parking lot, we discovered our sleeping bags and spare clothing were soaked. None of us, not even Leon, had known that lining a pack with a plastic garbage bag is standard procedure in the moist Northwest. I asked Leon how he had managed to keep his gear dry on Denali. He said it was so cold there the snow didn't melt. So ended my only attempt to make the summit of Rainier. I would manage to complete single day climbs to Camp Muir a couple of times in later years.

A new personality of great importance entered our lives on the

Labor Day weekend of 1992, when Karrin flew to Utah with Mark Boettcher, her instructor in a mountaineering first-aid class whom she had begun to date midsummer. I described Mark in my diary: "He is short, handsome, exceptionally well muscled, an accountant of German descent and dual German-Canadian citizenship who has nonetheless lived in Seattle since he was a few months old."[6] Mark's parents, now divorced, also lived in Seattle. According to prior plan, Althea and I met Karrin and Mark at the Salt Lake airport with gear for a backpack trip in the Uintas. However, an early snow there persuaded us to divert our trip to the dinosaur quarry near Vernal. Mark was impressed by the multitude of fossil dinosaur bones, great and small, that stood in half-excavated relief upon a high rock wall within the museum. As for me, I was impressed by his reverence for the sight. It seemed to me that he felt toward nature as I did.

Karrin and Mark flew to Utah again at Thanksgiving. We had Thanksgiving dinner at Roald's house, where Mark was introduced to Roald's large brood of offspring. The next day we drove to St. George to visit Charles and Betty and do a bit of sightseeing. On the following day we climbed to Angel's Landing in Zion National Park. An hour or so later, while I browsed at a book stand in the park visitors' center, Mark approached me privately and asked whether I objected to his asking Karrin to marry him. I said Althea and I would welcome him as a son-in-law. The next day, on our drive toward home, we paused while Karrin and Mark climbed a slickrock butte. When they returned to the car, Karrin said Mark had proposed while they climbed and she had accepted.

Althea and I drove to Silverdale for Christmas in the old pickup we had taken over from Karrin, enduring its discomforts in order to haul a load of furniture she had left behind. On Christmas Eve, we had dinner in Karrin's apartment with Mark and his father, Gerhard Boettcher. On Christmas Day we crossed the sound by ferry and, again with Mark and his father, had dinner with Barbara, who remained her cheerful self though she was visibly diminished. Her chemotherapy now dripped into her veins at home by means of a very small IV visible only as a bulge underneath her blouse.

The next day Karrin, Mark, and I went cross-country skiing in deep powder near the Paradise ranger station at Mount Rainier.

We followed a three-mile trail to a frozen lake amid a wind-driven snowfall. "A satisfying workout," I wrote. "The firs were weighted with a flocking of fresh snow, and all seemed wild in a most pristine way. We had hamburgers at a little restaurant outside the park. Life doesn't get any better."[7]

Because Snoqualmie Pass had been closed by the storm, Althea and I drove home via Portland, arriving in Ogden some sixteen hours and 920 miles after departing from Silverdale. As 1993 dawned, there was no question that my emotional compass—and Althea's too—had swung northwest.

··· 25

A Stillborn Book

AFTER FINISHING THE STORIES for *Night Soil,* I wanted to get on with my long-delayed book about wilderness. I intended to include the journal entries I had published in the *Possible Sack.* Otherwise it was to be a collection of essays on topics yet to be determined. With a typical vigor I began in late 1989 to read and make notes. For a year and a half I applied myself to the task with a full dedication. Thereafter, amid much interruption, I returned to it intermittently for a period of three or four years during which the project underwent a metamorphosis from wilderness essays to autobiography.

Along the way I finished a number of essays. Several were published in periodicals, and in my judgment several others deserve to be. But as an entity the collection never coalesced. My head swarmed with ideas, which in my confusion I stated and restated in several thousand manuscript pages. Following is a typical statement of purpose to be found among my multitudinous notes. It is an early one, written the day after I had submitted the manuscript for *Night Soil* to Signature Books. My intentions were admittedly vast—a lifetime project, as I now realize, at least for a person of my abilities and education:

> I wish to try my hand at the traditional task of describing, praising, and discerning the meanings of the external wilderness. I wish to delineate those aspects of civilization most threatening to, most propitious for that wilderness. I will endorse the frequently met argument that protecting wilderness affirms and provides for human survival since ultimately even an advanced technology has an ecological basis. I also wish to stalk into the thickets of the human psyche to substantiate, if possible,

the hypothesis that certain impulses within civilized persons remain wild, to both their advantage and disadvantage.[1]

During the first year I read extensively, making careful summaries of close to forty books and articles. By the fall of 1990, having little assurance that the ideas I was laboriously quoting and paraphrasing in my summaries would appear in a particular essay, I stopped my general reading, thereafter reading only in response to questions arising from essays on which I happened to be working. As for my writing, it was exceedingly tentative at first. Even after I had decided on a topic for an essay, I wrote many, many pages of exploratory notes. Presently these notes and early drafts, carefully dated and cast in sound, articulate sentences, fill a dozen or more thick files. Many passages have an eloquence and cogency that make me regret that more of them could not have found their way into a finished essay.

My first essay was a presentation at a conference at Weber State ambitiously called the "North American Interdisciplinary Wilderness Conference." This was in February 1990. Partly to clarify my own thinking, I made my presentation a defense of the kind of wilderness that I frequented and enjoyed, a terrain so close to cities that many would not consider it truly wild.

The frame of the essay was an excursion Althea and I made after firewood in the Wasatch-Cache National Forest about forty miles from our home. The account was actually a composite of excursions we had made after firewood three or four times each fall for nearly twenty-five years, it being one of our undeviating luxuries to have a blaze in our fireplace for a couple of hours on winter evenings. Both of us regarded these outings as a happy diversion from ordinary affairs. It was our habit to park the pickup in a shady spot, and while I sawed dead aspen trunks into fireplace lengths, Althea read novels or studied Spanish. When it was time to load our bounty, she joined me in conveying it to the pickup armful by armful. Then, seating ourselves against a tree at the edge of a ridge, we ate sandwiches and enjoyed the forested scenery.

Such a forest, as I admitted forthrightly in my essay, was not the place to go for a complete escape from domesticated things. I noted, for example, the pleasure I had from watching my chain saw chew its way through aspen trunks. Nonetheless, having felt the wild much more vividly than the domesticated in this setting, I proceeded to describe ways in which it impinged upon me. A stunning vista opened from the high Wasatch crest where I worked: "Caught in the midst of their autumnal change, the forested slopes flowed with green, gold, scarlet, and orange." I also contemplated at length my wild cousins, the ants, whose nests I disturbed while sawing up dead trunks. I followed the peregrinations of a particular ant up and down a bending stem of grass, supposing that the little creature was debating "whether this tubular pathway into the sky might not come at last to a cornucopia of formicidaean delectables." In conclusion, I articulated the hitherto unstated thesis of my essay. A place did not have to be as remote and inaccessible as the Brooks Range, the Himalayas, or the Atlantic Trench to qualify as wild. "I go by easier standards. One sees by my foray after wood and my companionable feelings toward ants how readily satisfied I am."[2] Already I felt that this essay or something even more elaborate would have to come at the beginning of my collection of essays, giving my potential readers due warning of what I meant by the word *wilderness*.

While I was preparing this essay for the wilderness conference, I received an invitation to speak on a topic of my choice at the Chicago Sunstone symposium, to be held in April 1990. Upon accepting the invitation, I decided to carry out a project that had been on my mind for a long time, to see what could be done about harmonizing the theory of organic evolution and Christianity with a Mormon audience in mind. The result was "A Mormon Evolutionist and the Wild God's Grace," which I read at a plenary session of the symposium and later published in *Sunstone* magazine.

I position myself in the essay by admitting that I am certain of only this about God, that he is the creative force inherent within natural law. But I go on to say that I *hope* he is more than that. For one thing, as I remind my listeners by alluding to my essay "A Christian by Yearning," I hope God is the ground for human immortality. For another, as I proceed to say in this essay, I hope he is also "a miraculous meta-law riding above and transcending Nature, mysteriously nudging it toward ends which may yet prove grand and moral."[3] My essay examines how these grand moral ends find expression in certain Christian tenets.

I allude in the essay to Pierre Teilhard de Chardin, a Jesuit pale-ontologist whose attempt to reconcile the Catholic faith with evolu-tion is justly famous. For Teilhard de Chardin, the entire creation, inorganic and organic alike, is infused with an impulse to evolve into something more orderly, complex, and divine. Evolution ceased to be merely corporeal and became spiritual as well with the ap-pearance of the human brain, God being the transcendent center to-ward which humanity, if it so chooses, will spiritually evolve. God has made the divine potential of human nature particularly mani-fest through the incarnation of Jesus Christ, whose function is to in-spire and draw an evolving humanity toward its spiritual destiny.

I made no attempt to conjecture in Mormon terms as to what dimensions of spirit the human brain might evolve toward, having referred to Teilhard de Chardin simply to establish that organic evolution can be viewed as having a spiritual aspect. I dwelt at greater length on Albert Schweitzer's principle of Reverence for Life, from which I extrapolated a number of applications to tradi-tional Christian tenets. Following Schweitzer's thesis that goodness includes altruistic service to all living things, I articulated the fol-lowing ethical postulates, which please me to this day for the suc-cinctness with which they establish a touchstone for judging right and wrong behavior: to live abundantly is to experience good, and to assist others to live abundantly is to do good; conversely, to die or suffer debility and pain is to experience evil, and to cause others to die or suffer debility and pain is to do evil.

From these postulates I redefined the Fall and original sin, con-cepts that I say are "as valid for the evolutionist as for any other Christian."[4] The Fall lies in the fated mortality in which living things have existed from the primordial beginning of life ages ago. Original sin lies in the fact that the vast majority of living things must nurture themselves on the substance of other living things; many of them kill the living things they ingest. Of necessity they must participate in the evil of killing in order to survive. I make a point of insisting that evil doing cannot be laid solely at the door of human beings. All life forms that kill other life forms participate in evil. Nonetheless, human beings stand in the unique situation of having a conscience and of therefore knowing that they must do evil in order to survive.

It is this last fact that makes another major Christian tenet, atonement, applicable within the scheme that I outline here. The Crucifixion does not serve to expiate my sins before an offended deity, who after all ordained a mortal world from the beginning, eons before conscience and a sense of responsibility evolved within that late-coming species we call Homo sapiens. Rather, the Crucifixion, with its symbolic suggestions of universal forgiveness, serves to enable me to forgive myself. Thus I say, as my essay nears its conclusion, that when I participate in the ceremony of the Lord's Last Supper, as a part of "my sacramental meditation I pray for no more than the ability to be reconciled to my fated sin." Having reminded my readers that I am no saint—and indeed do not aspire to be one—I nonetheless end the essay by returning briefly to the Christian tenet of an effacement and abnegation of the self in the service of others.

> The cross of our new ecologically oriented age is vaster, weightier, more hopeless of being borne than the old cross of earlier ages. We are asked by Christ to be eco-saints. Though our duty to our own kind is in nothing diminished, we are now asked to love and cherish the wild world as well. We are asked to covenant ourselves to the cause of clean air, pure water, and natural soil. We are asked to engage ourselves in behalf of snails, leeks, meadowlarks, kelp, moths, and earthworms too. The living world is our temple and we are asked to keep it holy.[5]

With that essay behind me, I went on during the summer of 1990 exploring topics on which, finally, I didn't write. One of these topics was the impact of economics and technology on wilderness. Predictably I read books on economics and paid a couple of visits to a colleague in the Department of Economics at Weber State. I soon realized that the economic system that prevails not only in Europe and the United States but also in much of the rest of the world as well does not allow for being reduced to a few clear principles. It is unfathomably complex, and its lines of cause and effect are largely conjectural. Nonetheless, this study reinforced my conviction that few human motivations threaten wilderness more strongly than the passion for wealth. "I have no hope of human beings halting the despoliation of the wilderness for aesthetic or spiritual reasons alone," I wrote to Don Walker.

To put it simply, people love wealth immeasurably more than wilderness. The massive domestications one sees everywhere in modern America are driven by economics. Wealth is central to the modern human spirit; it is the sum and substance of the modern personality. The modern heart passionately owns the suave, glittering spaces of a large department store as its true environment. Shopping is the American national sport.[6]

At the end of the summer of 1990, Althea and I made what I might call field trips to substantiate the impact of industrial technology in our own vicinity. We arranged a tour of the Geneva steel mill in Orem, where we saw coke ovens, blast furnaces, and a rolling mill in full operation. In the rolling mill we observed the process by which steel ingots were heated to two thousand degrees in furnaces fired by natural gas in preparation for being rolled into thin sheets. "The brick sides of the furnace from which the crane extracted an ingot glowed infernally," I wrote in my notes. "There were heat, fumes and clamor: quite disorienting and truly hellish, a volcanic drama."[7] This was only shortly after our visit to an active volcano in Hawaii, I will point out. Something in the incandescent glow of the molten metal struck me as inescapably wild.

A couple of weeks later we arranged a visit to the giant pumps on the west side of the Great Salt Lake, driving the last thirty or forty miles on gravel roads. Each of the motors driving the three pumps was large enough to fill the average living room. The pumps had been installed during the winter of 1987 in response to a succession of wet years in which the rising lake had inundated farms, subdivisions, and roadways along its borders. Ironically, the very year the pumps began to operate proved one of the driest on record. By the time Althea and I viewed them, the pumps sat more than a half mile from the lake's shore, a testimony to the ultimate futility of the human effort to control wild nature. Also visible from the pump station was the Union Pacific causeway that cut an incongruously straight line across the lake to the east and the salt flats to the west. Even here, in this remote and isolated desert, the human hand was unmistakable. "Every new construction, every new alteration in wilderness takes its toll," I wrote. "What we human beings are loath to recognize is the cumulative effect of our efforts. Each of us has such a small impact upon the wild world that it seems negligible. Taken together that impact is immense."[8]

Late in the afternoon on the same day, Althea and I also visited the Kennecott open-pit copper mine near the south end of the Oquirrh Mountains. The terraced pit was a half mile deep and two miles across. In it labored trucks as wide as a two-lane highway and electric shovels that loaded fifty tons of ore or overburden in a single scoop. "There is," I wrote, "a kind of grand scale to most modern heavy industry—giant machines at oil wells and on construction jobs, gargantuan removals of earth and ore, vast canyons cut and filled to make freeways, concrete dams that can hold back a hundred miles of lake." Of particular concern to me was the vast dump where the overburden from the mine was deposited. This dump, visible from many points in the Salt Lake valley, has grown in my lifetime from a modest heap on a lower shoulder of the Oquirrhs into a colossal accumulation, its horizontal base easily measuring five miles and its crest reaching two-thirds of the height of the range's highest peaks. This discolored rubble, composed largely of fragmented rock, supports little if any plant life. "When the already minimal percentage of copper plays out," I asked myself, "what will Kennecott do with slag heaps near its mills and this giant mountain of overburden? I fear they will remain as permanent legacies to the people of the Salt Lake valley, an enduring sign that they really didn't care if their once wild mountains were torn into rubble and left so by human activity."[9]

As I say, these field trips, like my other investigations of economics, led to no essay. Soon after we had made them, I turned to an attempt to define the word *wilderness,* feeling that my essay "A Woodlot in the Wasatch" had not accomplished that task. By mid-November 1990 I was lamenting "the confusion I find over the near synonyms wilderness and nature, a labyrinth I stumbled into without prior planning."[10] I did not in fact emerge from this labyrinth until February 1991, when I presented to my writing group a rough-hewn, convoluted essay titled "Pismires and Ants: Defining Wilderness." My friends received this draft with cordial disinterest. One of them spoke of it as "ponderous philology." Consequently I set the project aside and went on to other topics. I did not return to it until a year and a half later, when in a single day, I condensed it into a brief essay, titled "Wild Words," which, though still unpublished, strikes me as a balanced and readable differentiation between the words *wilderness* and *nature.*

In this brief essay I had little difficulty demonstrating that *nature,* a word of Latin origin passing into English from French during the twelfth century, had almost completely positive connotations in all its meanings. This was because, in its broadest sense, it signifies the creative forces underlying the entire material universe, interpreted by Christians as the handiwork of God and therefore to be revered and venerated. In this broadest sense, *nature* comprehends, as I put it in the essay, "not only every substantial thing that is, has been, or will be but every substantial thing that potentially could be or could have been." In this broadest—and most frequently used—sense, the word *nature* refers not only to the wild world but to the domesticated world as well. It was because I wished to avoid this equivocation and confusion, I went on to say, that I preferred the word *wilderness* to its sometime synonym *nature.*

It was only after four or five pages of perhaps dense ruminations on the distinctions to be made between *wilderness* and *nature* that I finally got around to making that simple explicit definition that had been my object all along, a definition that of necessity had to include the opposite of *wilderness:* "Wilderness is that order of nature existing independently of human manipulation; the domesticated is that order of nature existing because of human manipulation."

I ended the essay by raising the issue whether an exercise in abstract definition, such as I had just undertaken in the preceding paragraphs, could in some sense be construed as linking me and my reader concretely to wilderness. Words, I asserted, rise to consciousness from mysterious depths in the human mind. Furthermore, like the genes within living tissue, "words are mutant and viable; they have a native habitat, the collective human voice, wherein new meanings struggle against old and the fittest survive." Although it is true that "words can obliterate the wild from the human imagination, they can also plant it there. Where the human will bends toward a love of the wild, words become wild. As I write, I ask the wilderness to tincture my words. I hope the happy wild in me will, through words, awaken the happy wild in someone else."[11]

By the summer of 1991, I had moved on to a redaction of the parts of my wilderness journal that had been published in the

Possible Sack during the mid-1970s. I assumed that my intended collection would allow for something in this format, particularly because some of the longer journal entries were essentially essays with a date at the beginning. I believed I had made two important points in the journal entries. One was that my reverence for wilderness qualified me as religious despite my disbelief in the Christian deity. The other was that wilderness functioned as a vast, multifarious symbol for infinity, immortality, and omnipotence, allowing me to project vicariously into these qualities; that is, in beautiful wild places I was elevated and refreshed by the benign illusion that I share in these absolute qualities. For most of the entries the redaction I speak of consisted of minor stylistic changes—changes that I would abandon years later when I included a sampling of them in an earlier chapter of the present work. Most of my time on the redaction went to a single long entry that had stimulated me to investigate whether atomic theory, as understood by a layman, held any possibilities for a mystical response to nature. In late July, I wrote the following plaintive summary: "I read, thought, and wrote for weeks on the atomic nature of the elemental. The result was a few pages in a finished journal entry that seem almost childish in their simplicity. Why so long to know what little I wanted to say?"[12]

This entry, dated May 7, 1972, narrated a reflective hour I spent on the banks of the Green River in Red Canyon, a few miles below Flaming Gorge Dam. The river here was broad, tranquil, and, because the dam had allowed the mud of the upper river to settle, of a translucent blue. My mood was serene, and I felt myself in the presence of elemental force. By that term, *elemental force,* I had named something fascinating and attractive yet ultimately uncanny and incomprehensible. I paused particularly upon the word *elemental,* which I defined as that which is indivisible and irreducible, the ultimate unit of reality. I had long ago abandoned the attempt to understand the elemental through transcendental ideas. Now I attempted to profound it through scientific terms. I described the water of the river before me as a physicist might, alluding to the four forces commonly ascribed to matter—the strong force, the weak force, electromagnetic force, and gravity. "Through imagination I peer into the matter composing this water. I see it is a seething assemblage of energized particles, of tiny blobs of mass linked by pulsing energy fields. I see strings of atoms that coil and twine and twist. These atoms have no color, no texture, no odor, no sound. They are pure pulsation, sheer motion. There is enough energy in a thimble-full of them to blow up a city." Passages like the foregoing show why I had been so long in writing a redaction to this entry. I had read extensively and worked and reworked many passages only to finally realize that, for all my vivid imaginings about an inside view of matter, I was still locked within my senses and was therefore no closer to grasping the elemental than I had been before. Yet I believed in its reality, and, at that moment on the banks of the Green River, I felt myself intimately conjoined to it. It worked a particular magic there by rousing me to the experience of vicariously taking on the enormous power of the river. "Its magnitude awakens my respect for universal power. It reminds me of the simple, pure, elemental force that is everywhere applied in the universe, the force from which all other forces are compounded, the force that binds all things into the kinship of universal being. I am sobered and profoundly attracted. The river has aroused my thirst for omnipotence, for the power to do the all sufficient."[13]

As I neared the end of this redaction of my journal in mid-July, Leon and Gussie came from Arizona to visit their daughter Britt, who lived with her husband, Joe McFarlane, in rural Morgan County, about a half-hour drive from Ogden. On a bright Saturday Althea and I joined these four for an eleven-hour hike to the summit of Timpanogos. As we stood on the summit looking down into Utah Valley with its reputation for having one of the highest per-capita birth rates in the nation, the thought occurred to me of writing an essay on the impact of overpopulation upon wilderness, using this very hike as a frame.

In the subsequent essay, I cited statistics showing the world's population at just a little less than six billion and predicting many billions more within a half century. I gloomily predicted that "the part of the earth not immediately covered by human buildings and roadways will become a vast mine and refuse dump, and wilderness will be an unaffordable luxury. The national parks and designated wildernesses will be, relatively speaking, small, vulnerable, and off limits to the vast majority of people." My interest was not so much in a solution to the problem of overpopulation as in an explanation of how it had come about. That explanation had to do with my recognition of, as I put it, "the overwhelming importance of intimate associations with people to whom I am related by blood and marriage." It had been the presence of Britt and Joe that had brought this recognition to mind. With Karrin grown and departed from our home, the little children with whom we associated most closely were Britt and Joe's Jacci, Jed, and Casey, who reminded me repeatedly that I was at my happiest when in a stable relationship with children. I took that fact as typical of humanity. Human beings *want* more children than their natural environment can ultimately sustain.

> It isn't meanness, avarice, rapaciousness, or predatoriness on the part of human beings that is principally responsible for polluting this planet and killing off wild species of plants and animals by the hundreds of thousands. The greatest enemy of wilderness is the love of humanity for its own kind, especially the love for little children, multiplied as it is by billions everywhere across the face of the earth."[14]

I will reiterate that this was an indictment of humanity at large and not of Britt and Joe, who, I am pleased to say, have added a fourth child, Ned, to their affectionate, hospitable family.

As I said in an earlier chapter, I took an unplanned sabbatical from working on the wilderness collection in order to write *Aspen Marooney*. When I returned to work on the collection in the late summer of 1992, I began to work on an essay about the demise of traditional Indian culture, a topic relevant to my collection because, as I believed, culture descended from pre-Columbian roots had immersed Native Americans in wilderness. As I began to read on the displacement of aboriginal Indian culture in America, I took particular interest in the transmutation of the Hopi from a traditional Native American culture into a modern American subculture, being aware of the ironic role my father had played as a professional purveyor of white culture in northern Arizona. I decided in fact to make my father's life and career serve as the frame for my consideration of the extinction of traditional tribal culture generally. That decision led me to ponder whether I should be writing essays in which I appeared not as an individual but as a member of a family. Proceeding with a brief experimental preface to a collection of such essays, I wrote: "This book is the natural history of a western family. It's about the relationship of an individual and his kin to such wilderness as remains in a sizeable portion of the interior West."[15] Although my enthusiasm for a natural history of my family waned within a few days, my brief sortie in that direction had left me feeling that, instead of a collection of essays, I should be writing an autobiography.

The week before fall quarter of 1992 opened at Weber State, the English Department held a faculty retreat at a hotel in Park City. Preferring to be at home with Althea at night, I commuted each day between Ogden and Park City. While driving early one morning I became intrigued with the idea of writing a wilderness-oriented autobiography in the third person, in which I would speak of myself as he and him, as Henry Adams had done in his autobiography. Excited, I sat at the back during a couple of workshops that day and wrote experimental pages by hand. "Since thinking of this approach a couple of days ago, and spending some time, successfully, I feel, on a prefatory chapter," I wrote after the retreat had ended, "I respond with a slight euphoria and a foreboding sense of the problems to be confronted and solved if I am actually to write an entire book in this manner."[16] After a few days, these problems determined me to abandon the idea.

That I considered it at all is indicative of my dissatisfaction with writing wilderness essays, in which I had yet to establish a consistent voice and authentic persona. I had not had an experience comparable to the day I struck off a comic first chapter of *The Backslider,* inventing within a few hours' time a new Frank Windham whom I could both love and satirize. The problem now, however, was different: it was a new Levi Peterson whom I aspired to invent. My essays struck me as lackluster. What I said didn't startle, command, or compel. I noted the confident assertion of wilderness values in Edward Abbey's *Desert Solitaire,* Annie Dillard's *Pilgrim at Tinker Creek,* and, most recently, Terry Tempest Williams's *Refuge.* My essays were not an unequivocal endorsement of wilderness but an experiment in finding the position wilderness values should occupy in the hierarchy of values expected of a civilized person.

From the moment I had resolved to become a writer in the early 1970s, I planned on eventually writing an autobiography. I don't recall weighing whether there might be an audience for my life's story. I simply wanted to write it. It was acceptable to me that my fascination with wilderness become the predominant theme of that story. Quite quickly then, in September 1992, I began to view myself as writing not a collection of wilderness essays, but an autobiography. I did not plan to abandon my ideas about wilderness but rather sought to find a more coherent frame for them. I hoped a fuller account of my own life—and the lives of my family—would clarify those ideas and make them more interesting.

For some time I continued to write essays, intending eventually to convert them to chapters of my autobiography. I wrote the essay on my father and the Native Americans of northern Arizona in response to an invitation by my colleague Neila Seshachari, editor of *Weber Studies,* to submit something for a forthcoming issue dealing with the Mormons.[17] Eventually, I would reshape this essay into the second chapter of this autobiography. Other essays provided substantial parts of other chapters. Many of the essays, however, would languish unused in my files.

As I groped my way toward a satisfactory voice and persona for my autobiography, wilderness would become a distinctly lesser theme. I would come to realize that my predominant concern is with society, not wilderness. Family is at my emotional core. Furthermore, I have a strong need to follow and participate in the doings of decent people. As for my daily endeavors, my teaching and campus service have been of paramount importance; I thrived on success in both. Yet it is a fact that I have been sensitive to, and grateful for, the presence of wilderness throughout my adult life. I have noted its residual presence each day: a sky made clear by an all-night rain, the friendly bulk of Mount Ogden a half mile from my house, a sunset glinting on the Great Salt Lake. I have proved unable to translate that steady joy into a book of essays. But I respect myself for the endeavor, and I feel an affectionate regret for this stillborn child.

Retrenchment on the Liberal Mormon Front

IN MARCH 1993 Althea and I flew to Washington, D.C., for a conference of the American Association of Higher Education (AAHE). We arrived on a Friday night, a day early, in order to attend the sessions of a Sunstone symposium. A kind Mormon couple met us at the airport and conveyed us to their home, yielding their own bedroom to us, from whose large plate-glass windows we observed the beginnings of what came to be called the Great Blizzard of '93. The next morning we learned that wind and snow had closed airports across the entire eastern third of the nation.

At the end of the symposium on Saturday evening, our hosts dropped Althea and me off at the Hilton on Connecticut Avenue where the AAHE conference was to begin the next morning. The startled desk clerk, presiding over a nearly deserted lobby, asked how we had managed to arrive. On Sunday, freed by the cancellation of workshops, Althea and I made our way to the National Mall and visited various art museums and the National Archives. By evening the storm had halted. Sessions proceeded for the following three days, attended by increasing numbers. Colleagues from Weber State straggled in with a fund of horror stories to tell. One had spent two days in Houston. Another had hopped planes to five airports and had sat incarcerated for eight hours in a jet awaiting takeoff from Atlanta.

Karrin's wedding was on our mind throughout the spring of 1993. She spoke briefly of a ceremony on the summit of Bald Mountain in the Uintas, then settled, quite implacably, on our much neglected backyard, which, as she complacently granted—

and in fact insisted upon—would require enormous renovation. Althea and I launched into this hopeless task on evenings and weekends, trimming back our brush patch, grooming the edges of our lawn, digging and planting flower plots at both the front and the back of the house, and painting—for the first time in twenty-seven years of dwelling there—the garage, back porch, and window frames of the looming two-story house. Althea chose the color schemes and patterns and worked conscientiously at my side in executing them. We went on with this labor even when, during a brief visit in late March, Karrin and Mark decided—much to our relief—on the new Alumni House on the Weber State campus as the site of their wedding.

The wedding took place on June 19, 1993. Among the out-of-town guests were Mark's father, his maternal grandfather, and his best man, Kim Toy, a mountaineering friend. His grandfather Doktor Georg Engelbrecht was a retired petroleum chemist from Berlin. When we picked him up at the airport, this eighty-eight-year-old man skipped down the airport stairs two steps at a time. Georg proved an amiable, inquisitive guest, fluent in French and able to get along in English. At breakfast on the first morning he showed me photos of a recent vacation to a Caribbean island. In one, he is shown tall, blond, and stark naked, proudly posing on the beach with a companionable arm about the shoulder of a short, brown, fully clothed hotel maid. His Germanic insouciance toward nudity extended to the parking lot at a swimming beach along the Great Salt Lake where Mark took him for a swim. Georg stepped from the car and immediately began to strip, forestalled only by Mark's insistence that he utilize one of the nearby dressing huts.

The wedding was a gala affair. Mark, Gerhard, Kim, and I wore cutaway coats with tails, shirts with pleated fronts, and cravats. Karrin, Althea, and bridesmaid Sylvia Newman wore elegant ankle-length dresses of their own construction. We held a rehearsal, and a professional photographer took dozens of shots, which would result in a handsome album. The ceremony began with a prelude of harp music from a CD player, during which my stake-president brother, Roald, stood tall, dignified, and, as he later reported, somewhat embarrassed by the long wait at the front of the room. Gerhard and Mark marched solemnly to the front; then came Karrin and I. We had practiced only once the gait that Karrin prescribed, and I, possessed of no instinct for intricate pacing, got lamentably off step in the actual performance. More than a hundred relatives and loyal friends had assembled: all my living siblings except Mary were there, a considerable assortment of nephews and nieces, most of the English faculty, and many other friends from campus and town. An informal reception followed the ceremony. Dainty hors d'oeuvres (for the most part prepared at home) and sparkling cider appeared on waiting tables, placed there in constantly replenished supply by my commendably efficient female relatives. A set of hired musicians began to play Renaissance music. French doors were thrown open, and guests stood or took seats as they wished at patio tables. Karrin and Mark sat at a table with close friends, accepting congratulations from all who approached them—an informality that at first worried me as being too aloof but later, as the afternoon wore into a balmy evening, struck me as exactly right. Three hours after the ceremony had begun, as the bride and groom departed on the first leg of a honeymoon to Hawaii, many, many guests still lingered on. The event had come off perfectly—except for the ruin that my ill-cadenced step had inflicted upon the stately entrance of the bride.

The summer of 1993 saw the culmination of a campaign against liberal Mormonism that, because it affected many of my friends, also affected me. That a campaign was afoot had been evident since August 1991 when, following the August Sunstone symposium in Salt Lake City, the First Presidency and Quorum of the Twelve issued a statement against attendance at symposia and other unauthorized meetings. The most telling effect of this pronouncement was upon persons on a church payroll, most notably professors from BYU, whose representation in later Sunstone gatherings and in the pages of liberal journals dwindled appreciably.

The church proceeded to enforce its will by a simple mechanism. The ominously named Strengthening Church Members Committee sent samples of suspect writings to stake presidents and asked them to interview the authors regarding their attitude toward the church. It is safe to say that several dozen were interviewed. How many were quietly disciplined is impossible to say. Some, perhaps most, emerged unscathed from the experience. By the summer of 1993, however, six persons whose interviews had not gone well, or who had declined to be interviewed, were a topic of common discussion along the Wasatch Front. In September five of them were excommunicated, and one was disfellowshiped. These are spoken of still in liberal Mormon circles as the September Six.

One of the excommunicated was Lavina Fielding Anderson, whom I knew well. Her response to the edict of 1991 against symposia had been to begin a process of documenting instances of what she called "spiritual or ecclesiastical abuse"—the unnecessary coercion of individual conscience by a church governance notably lacking in due process. Predictably, after her paper on this topic, read at the Sunstone symposium of 1992, was published by *Dialogue* during the spring of 1993, she was summoned by her stake president.

Another dear friend whose life would be adversely affected was Gene England. He arose at the end of the Sunstone session in which Lavina had read her paper in 1992 and passionately declared that the Strengthening Church Members Committee, of whose existence he had only recently become aware, must be abolished. Gene's remarks were replayed on the evening TV news, and national newspapers took note of the committee. Gene had assumed that the committee was the ad hoc creation of underlings within the church bureaucracy. However, within a few days the First Presidency affirmed the standing of the committee by revealing that it consisted of two apostles (who, no doubt, were assisted by a host of functionaries). Recoiling with remorse, Gene wrote an apology to these two men and later published an essay that was partly a recantation of his fiery protest and partly a plea for reconciliation with those with whom he disagreed on church discipline.[1] In my judgment, Gene was in a double bind, circumstances having disproved his ardent faith in the harmony between free inquiry and the authority of the Brethren. He would remain puzzled and depressed till his death in 2001.

My own response to the rumors and newspaper reports that spread anxiety among the liberal Mormon community during the summer of 1993 was an essay read at the Salt Lake Sunstone symposium in August and later published in *Sunstone* magazine, offering untested advice on how to keep the spirit of loyal dissent and benign nonconformity alive during a trying period. I urged my fellow liberal Mormons to continue in full fellowship in their wards, emphasizing tolerance and respect for ideas in quiet and inoffensive ways. Those whose living derived from the church, I said emphatically, should not jeopardize their jobs for a liberal cause. This was aimed particularly at my close friends at BYU. In conclusion, I addressed those whose "particular identity and indignation demand a course of action that seems fated to lead to excommunication," urging them not to alter altogether their habits of worship and association with the church. "I fancy," I wrote, "that if I were excommunicated by a Church court on a weekday, I'd be back sleeping in sacrament meeting on the following Sunday."[2]

Could I have actually taken excommunication in stride and maintained something close to my customary participation in the life of my ward? I wasn't entirely sure. Lavina managed to do it, and I admired her enormously for the achievement—so much so that I would write an essay about her for the Sunstone symposium of 1995, which would later be published in *Dialogue*.[3]

On the eve of Lavina's excommunication in September, Sesh and I attended a prayer service on her behalf in Salt Lake City. Well over a hundred persons packed the benches of the restored pioneer Eighteenth Ward chapel on Capitol Hill. By now it was known that Paul Toscano, Maxine Hanks, Martha Bradley, and Michael Quinn had been excommunicated and Lynn Whitesides disfellowshiped. Many persons responded to the invitation to speak from the pulpit. A young woman read a declaration asking that her name be removed from the rolls of the church and invited other interested persons to sign. Scott Kenney, prominent in the founding of both *Sunstone* magazine and the liberal Mormon publishing firm of Signature Books, surprised us all by tearfully announcing that he had asked to have his name removed from the rolls of the church. He said a great burden had been lifted from his shoulders. Then, with deep feeling, he played a sad prayer by Bach on his cello, during which the crowd spontaneously arose and held hands. At the conclusion of the evening, the ever-vibrant Ardeen Watts, retired professor of music from the University of Utah, played the piano while directing us with loud insistence in a swelling rendition of the Lord's Prayer. On our way home, Sesh said this had been a unique and historical event. Certainly it had been an intensely moving experience—evidence, in my judgment, of the wild God's grace, which elevates and encourages Hindu and Christian alike. Above all, I felt entirely confirmed in the sentiment of the closing paragraph of my Sunstone address on the art of dissent among the Mormons:

> Though as a corporation the Church may be owned by its legally constituted officers, as a moral community Mormonism is beyond ownership.... I'll not let another human being, however highly placed, drive me from Mormonism.... I choose to stay where my heart is and to vent my disapproval of uncivilized beliefs and practices through a quiet but unrelenting resistance. There's a place within Mormonism for the loyal dissenter, and I for one intend to occupy it.[4]

Although I had worried that Karrin's marriage would diminish our association with her, events quickly proved otherwise. She invited us to come to Silverdale for the Fourth of July because Mark had decided to accompany his grandfather to his cousin's wedding in Canada. Karrin, Althea, and I had the good luck to be on a ferry in Elliott Bay while fireworks were shot from the top of the Space Needle. In mid-August, I climbed Mount Adams with Karrin and Mark while Althea waited in the apartment in Silverdale. At Labor Day, Karrin and Mark drove to Ogden and went backpacking with us to Red Castle Peak on the north slope of the Uintas. They spent a week with us, being—both of them—without jobs. At Thanksgiving we visited them in an apartment they had taken in Bellevue so that Mark could be closer to the job he had found in the accounting department of a bank. Disillusioned with law, Karrin had arranged to enter the teacher education program at the University of Washington. We had Thanksgiving dinner at Barbara's house in Issaquah. Barbara, completely bald from radiation treatment, bustled about her kitchen happily, only occasionally resorting to the cane she had recently begun to use. Also present was Mark's mother, Karin, whose acquaintance we only now made for the first time. She was thin, pleasant of countenance, capable of hearty laughter, knowledgeable on current issues, and prone to circumlocutions when asked about her own life and experience.

During the early winter of 1994 I wrote an essay on Bernard De Voto's *Across the Wide Missouri,* a history of the Rocky Mountain fur trade in the early 1830s. I presented the essay at a conference on De Voto in Ogden, emerging from the experience with a renewed assessment of my stand on the myth of the heroic frontier. I had read De Voto's book three or four times over the years, considering it a masterpiece of historiography, particularly in its literary qualities. Accordingly, I elaborated in my essay upon such literary effects as the book's "finely cadenced" style, finding "sheer poetry" in such a line as the following description of a mountain man's night watch: "Winter in the Montana plains—windless, no bottom to the thermometer, the stars eight feet away, tree branches booming like gunfire."[5]

I was gratified at the De Voto conference to make the acquaintance of Patricia Nelson Limerick, historian from the University of Colorado, who enjoyed national fame as a proponent of what newspapers were calling the new western history. Patty, as she preferred to be called, approached me warmly, praising *The Backslider* and telling me she had included it on a list of readings for a course on the history of the American West. She invited me to discuss my fiction at the conference of the Western History Association in Albuquerque during October—an invitation that I accepted. Before that event, however, I met Patty again at the conference of the Mormon History Association in Park City during May, where she joined Charles, his son John, and me in conversation over root beer. While Patty and John listened, Charles and I fell into a well-practiced routine of embellishing upon our family's past. A couple of weeks later Patty wrote her appreciation of "the Peterson Story Session," declaring it to be her favorite part of the conference and wishing it could have gone on longer. "It would, in fact, be an interesting experiment some day, to see at what point my thirst for high-quality anecdotes would be exhausted—at five hours? six hours? Whatever my limit is, we were a long ways away from it."[6]

A few weeks after the De Voto conference in February, Patty mailed me a signed copy of her book *The Legacy of Conquest: The Unbroken Past of the American West,* which I read with great interest—and with an ever-increasing respect for her. In an account that emphasizes conflict among diverse populations, Patty sides with the underdogs and losers of the West: dispossessed Indians; persecuted black, Hispanic, and Asian immigrants; and ignored, voiceless women of all races. Herein, as I understand it, is what is meant by the new western history, a historiography that departs from a traditional bias favoring the white male majority of Euro-Americans who settled the frontier and whose cultural descendants continue to dominate the modern West.[7]

It was a curious experience to read Patty's book within a couple of months of having made a close study of De Voto's. The two books, juxtaposed, forced me to confirm my attitude toward the American frontier and the civilization that has evolved from it. My conscience responds to Patty's bias. The legacy of the West, as of the rest of America, *is* a legacy of conquest, for which I feel guilty. But my heart responds to De Voto's sense that there was a grand and epic quality to the establishment of Euro-American civilization upon the American continent. As I say at the beginning of this book, I respond to the saga of the pioneers. They are part and parcel of my identity. Whatever the sins of the civilization that they founded, it is the civilization I was born to. I have no other.

In April 1994, I underwent what might be called a trial in an informal church tribunal. One afternoon my stake president, Ralph Ardema, a former student of mine who, if I recall correctly, was at that moment the principal of a middle school, asked by phone to visit me in my office on the following day, to which I assented. Anxious, I phoned Roald and Charles, asking whether his intent might be to deliver a letter summoning me to a church court. Roald, himself a stake president, thought not. He pointed out that two persons were required for the delivery of such a letter. Nonetheless, I spent a night in reflection on the value I set upon my church membership. I had not been a believer for forty years, yet I knew I would be deeply pained by excommunication.

President Ardema greeted me with a kindly deference as I came from behind my desk and joined him in my conference chairs. He was short, ruddy faced, and quietly self-confident. He said he had read my essay on hiking to Timpanogos and hoped to know more about my attitude toward the church. My reply is detailed in my diary:

I reviewed my ancestry and intimate connections in a large
Mormon family. I said I valued my membership. I wanted to
see the church flourish, accepted the sovereignty of the First
Presidency and the Twelve. I said I was a liberal Mormon and
certainly no anti-Mormon. I said my writings…were more belligerent than my actual feelings because I am trying to appeal
to belligerent people on their way out of Mormonism, trying to
say something to keep them in. I discussed my home teaching
and my affectionate connections with my ward. He asked my
views on the priesthood ordinances and alluded to the temple.
I said when I was asked to stand in the circle to bless a nephew
or niece I found it a holy experience. I said I valued partaking
of the sacrament. I broke down in my composure at this point
and found it difficult to speak. I said I valued the hope Christ
offers of immortality.

After perhaps twenty minutes President Ardema took leave of
me with such kind reassurance that I knew I had been acquitted of
sedition and apostasy. With great relief I phoned the good news to
Roald and Charles. Nevertheless, as my busy afternoon went forward, I felt sharply "the deep duplicity of my life—my possession
of distinctly different personas in conservative and liberal environ-
ments, and wondered again how I could bridge the two worlds
without being insane, and feeling again it is precisely because I do
bridge them that I'm not insane."[8]

In May 1994 I bought a new electric-blue Ford Ranger pickup
with a sluggish four-cylinder engine and a five-speed conventional
transmission. As it turned out, I would own this vehicle for ten
years to the day. The vinyl cover on the bench seat cracked early;
the gas mileage proved a disappointing twenty miles per gallon; the
absence of power steering afflicted me on a daily basis. Yet overall,
it was a serviceable and liberating companion.

In June, recruited by Karrin and Mark, Althea and I spent a
week in Maui with them and Mark's father. We stayed in a two-
bedroom condo on the arid southwest Maui coast. We feasted on
mangos and papayas, lolled on the beach, visited the crater of
Haleakala at ten thousand feet, and drove a couple of times in
our two rental cars to Hana on the rainy northeast coast. Mark,

Gerhard, and I took a catamaran to Molokai for snorkeling and, on another day, paid seventy dollars each for a morning of deep-sea fishing, a venture that produced, for the seven sportsmen aboard, one small tuna. On another day, Mark and I hiked for some sixteen miles in the bottom of Haleakala Crater through cinders, gray sand, and marvelous desert plants like the silversword.

My creative effort during the summer of 1994 was turned to writing about my mother. At first I planned on a chapter in my wilderness-oriented autobiography that would set her "into the context of the wild, narrating her life in its encounters and intimacies with, its escapes from, its effacements of the wild."[9] I quickly discovered, however, that the topic I truly wanted to write about was my mother's marriage to N. J. Smith. The result was an essay that I read at the Salt Lake Sunstone symposium in August. I didn't know at that moment whether I would make any further use of the essay's contents, having not entirely made up my mind to abandon my plan for an autobiography with a prevailing wilderness theme.

I mailed a copy of the essay to my siblings in July. Contrary to my expectation they did not protest my discussion of our mother's sexual relations with N. J. during the weeks before their final separation—until, at the end of a long day's trip to Mexico, Lenora and Leon learned that I intended to read the essay at the symposium. By 1994 Lenora and Marion had sold their house in Snowflake and had built a small house next to Gale's house in Solomon, near Safford. In late July Althea and I drove to Arizona, eventually making our way to Leon and Gussie's home in Thatcher, also near Safford. With Leon and Gussie we joined Lenora and Marion for a visit to the border town of Agua Prieta—ironically, taking lunch at a Taco Time restaurant on the Arizona side of the border. Late in the evening, as Lenora and I said good-bye, she asked me in a voice curiously mixed with pleading and command not to make a public matter of our mother's sexual relations with N. J. At breakfast the next morning Leon and Gussie gently reminded me that I would be accountable to our mother in the afterlife. Nonetheless, I decided to leave these intimate details in the essay—and, as my reader will recognize, I have included them in an early chapter of this book.

One reason for including them is that I believe I should account for the impact they had upon me when my elderly mother first made them known. "The facade of parent fell away from this aged person," I wrote in my essay, "and I saw a twenty-three year old woman, only a little past being a girl, who had passion and affection and, above all, pity for the man she had been married to for these three years."[10] Another reason is that I believe I honor, rather than dishonor, my mother by these intimate details. I make her worthiness more plausible, more enticing to readers who do not know her or her immediate society, by rendering her as a real rather than as an idealized person. What if I awaken from my own death to find myself in my mother's living presence? In the event of such a miracle I will expect a further miracle: that my mother will see history as I see it and will approve of what I have written.

Of greater significance, at least for me, was the perplexity I discerned in Lenora and Mary during that summer of 1994 as to whether they were Petersons or Smiths—or neither. Lenora was eighty, Mary seventy-eight. I, the inquirer, was sixty. While writing the essay, I frequently succumbed to the impulse to consult them on the spur of the moment—which meant, more often than not, a long-distance call from my office phone, conscientiously charged to my personal AT&T calling card. Lenora was interested enough in the project to phone me perhaps a half-dozen times. During one of these calls, she told me that only a month or two earlier, while imagining her reunion with Joseph and Lydia in the hereafter, she had experienced an intense desire to embrace them both. Immediately afterward, she thought of meeting and embracing N. J. there as well, and she felt "a quick, involuntary revulsion, saying 'No, not by him.'" A little later during the same conversation, Lenora admitted that the issues N. J. represented had traumatized her life. She went on to say that recently, while seated in the chapel of the Mesa temple, she had seen a woman whose traits were of the Smith family from which N. J. was descended, and a disembodied voice had said to her, "You were supposed to come through that lineage." I concluded that to some degree—despite Joseph's best efforts to reassure her—Lenora suffered a "sense of not belonging, being neither a Peterson nor a Smith."[11]

Mary denied feeling ambivalent, insisting forcefully that she was a Peterson, not a Smith. During our visit with her in Mesa I asked whether, if church policy should allow it, she would choose to be sealed to N. J. in eternity. With obvious emotion, Mary said, "Why would I want to be sealed to a perfect stranger?"[12] Yet she showed Althea and me, in a carefully arranged section of a photo album devoted to her Smith ancestors, the first photographs of N. J. we had ever seen.

I had reason to appreciate the depth of my own feelings about Lenora's and Mary's family allegiance at Lenora's burial in the Lakeside cemetery in September 2000. Among the mourners at the grave site were two Smith men from Snowflake. "It's kind of these old friends to come," I commented to Leon. "They are not here as friends," Leon said. "They are here as cousins." For the first time ever I realized that Lenora and Mary, who had passed most of their lives in Snowflake, must have been acutely aware of their numerous Smith cousins. Suddenly, I resented the presence of two of them at Lenora's burial. "You can't have her," I said to them in my imagination. "You can't have Mary either. They belong to us, not to you."

Near the end of fall quarter 1994, after a good half of our yearly funds had already been committed, the administration at Weber State announced a reduction in the departmental operating budgets. Warned over and over by both dean and provost that budget overruns would have to come from the next year's allocation, I decreed a number of unpopular belt-tightening procedures in the English Department. The most drastic came when, informed during the Christmas vacation of an immediate shortfall in our phone budget, I shut off all long-distance access for the English faculty—a measure whose notoriety raced across campus on the first day of winter quarter. By the third day of the new quarter, armed with additional funds from the dean, I restored long-distance access. "The faculty," I recorded, "are angry still. I am close to losing moral authority over them. My creative energy is consumed managing petty money and the daily frictions between students and faculty."[13] The dean and the provost were taken aback by my drastic measure. Their warning that they had no reserves for paying off budget overruns was obviously less than truthful. To this day I am puzzled how they expected me to understand that their warning was merely a ritual.

I was getting weary, not simply of my duties as chair, but of academic routines altogether. For years I had fancied I would teach until I was seventy. Now I was thinking I would do well to teach until I was sixty-five. I had enjoyed teaching Freshman English for decades. In fact, in the mid-1980s I wrote an essay asserting my pleasure in teaching basic composition for a history of Weber State. But the good humor and minor histrionics necessary to keep a captive audience alert were failing me. Furthermore, my general energy was waning noticeably, affecting, for example, the reliability of an intimate session with my wife as a means for relieving my tedium and stress. I find this entry in my diary after coming home from a long day on campus: "I suggested to Althea that we have a conjugal moment. She said, 'You'd never make it.' I agreed to wait till tomorrow night."[14]

Our interest turned ever more strongly toward the Northwest. During a phone conversation on a Wednesday evening in September, Karrin informed me that we would be grandparents in May. Althea had gone to bed early with a light fever. After I gave her the news, she kept me awake for an hour or two, exclaiming from time to time with evident pleasure.

In December, a day or two after fall quarter had ended at Weber State, Karrin phoned that Barbara was hospitalized and expected to die within a day or two. I attached sideboards to our pickup and tried on a new set of chains, and early the next morning, we set out for the Northwest. Snow was falling from Yakima to well beyond Snoqualmie Pass, a distance of more than a hundred miles. We arrived in Bellevue at midnight, about eighteen hours after our departure. Karrin and Mark drove us immediately to Overlake Hospital, where Barbara lay gasping in a near coma. Raymond and Amber sat on either side of the bed, holding her hands. We finished the night on Karrin and Mark's pullout sofa bed. In the morning Althea woke up weeping. She had dreamed she saw Barbara and Raymond climbing on a motorcycle. In the dream, Amber said to Barbara, "You forgot your coat." Althea said, "She won't need a coat where she is going."[15]

We returned to the hospital late that evening. Barbara was awake and spoke to us pleasantly. Early the next morning, my birthday, Amber phoned that she had died. A few days later thirty or forty persons attended a memorial service in the chapel of an Issaquah mortuary. There was no viewing, Barbara's body having been cremated. Mary and all of Barbara's siblings were present, as were friends from a flying club Barbara had belonged to.

A few days after our return to Ogden, Karrin and Mark followed. On Christmas Day we opened our usual plethora of gifts and, after lunch, went to Powder Mountain for an afternoon of skiing. Other happy days ensued, making our holiday memorable. As 1994 ended, my ambiguous spiritual condition is perhaps best summarized by an entry of my diary made following the annual Christmas sermon at a luncheon of the Kiwanis Club to which I belonged.

> I sensed a sudden new coherence to my intellectual being, seeing that my vast underlying drive is toward connection, not with God, but with competent, approving, affirming persons, of whom my mother was the prototype and my daughter and wife now stand as the dearest examples. I saw that happy moments of union, as occurred at my birthday dinner last week in Bellevue, where Karrin, Mark, Althea, and I had a happy baked chicken meal, are my ultimate happiness. God, whose Christian particulars we celebrate at Christmas, is merely this for me—a dimly hoped-for guarantor of that happy union between me and my loved ones through endless time. I speak of the transcendent God here—because in practical terms Nature has become my actual God, which I both worship and fear because in it lies both the sacred and the lethal.[16]

··· 27

Armchair Mountaineer

MOST, IF NOT ALL, MOUNTAINEERS ARE ENVIRONMENTALISTS. They love and respect the wild and want to preserve it. Presumably they share my happy, affirmative responses to the benign side of the wild. Yet the high, perilous terrain against which they pit themselves expresses the lethal side of the wild. That's why they are there. They are risk takers, and that environment provides plenty of risk, as an annual publication analyzing injuries and deaths in North American mountaineering will show.[1]

I can't entirely explain my fascination with the sport. Having an unsubdued fear of heights, I am at best an armchair mountaineer who occasionally does a little field testing of his theories about true mountaineers. Fundamentally, I disapprove of the sport because of its risk.

I have known three true mountaineers intimately, my brother Leon, my daughter, and my son-in-law. For years their devotion to the hazardous sport puzzled me. So when I was invited to participate in another wilderness conference at Weber State to be held in November 1994, I decided on a paper about the relationship between mountaineers and wilderness, hoping in the process to explain, at least to my own satisfaction, the workings of the mountaineer's psyche. From the start I planned on adapting my insights to a chapter of the wilderness-oriented autobiography I still intended to create.

The topic gripped me as few others have. I read many books on mountaineering during the fall of 1994, most of them about epic climbs that ended in tragedy. Sometimes I read compulsively till late at night, a thing I hadn't done since adolescence. The account that affected me most deeply was *Savage Arena* by Joe Tasker, an

Englishman who narrates a series of increasingly difficult climbs on world-class peaks. I particularly liked Tasker's candid ambivalence about climbing. He tells about his doubts, his regrets at having committed himself to a climb, his displeasures and sufferings while on a climb. But he also tells of becoming engaged by a climb, and it is obvious that greater challenges compulsively attract him once he has finished an arduous, dangerous climb. The obsession of mountaineering is rarely better demonstrated than in his book.

At the end of his book Tasker narrates a second attempt he and two friends made in 1980 to summit on K-2, a peak slightly lower than Everest but acknowledged to be more difficult. Reaching 26,500 feet, they were forced down by a raging storm. Though exhausted, they tried again and were again trapped by a storm. Making an epic retreat, they barely escaped with their lives. Tasker claims that afterward he and his friends showed none of "the soul-searching anxiety about whether we could have succeeded if we had tried harder. We had the satisfaction of knowing that we had tried to the utmost and that whatever had been lacking it was not anything in ourselves." Still, the experience had been harrowing enough that Tasker admits to a sense of having been reborn: "I shared the feelings of a Samurai brought back honourably from his suicide and knew the exalted state he would have been in on his reprieve. A whole new life was mine, as if the past was no more."[2] My feelings about Tasker were surprisingly personal. By the end of his book I felt something close to the affection of a brother for him. My sense of personal loss—and my disapproval of mountaineering as a sport—mounted as I progressed through the book, for I had been informed by a prefatory note that the manuscript for it had been delivered to the publisher as Tasker departed on what turned out to be a fatal attempt on a hitherto unclimbed approach to Everest.

Throughout the fall of 1994 I engaged in what seemed an endless production of elaborate notes, from which emerged readable draft essays on the subject of mountaineering and wilderness. Perhaps the most comprehensive was the essay I read before a session of the wilderness conference, on which I had been still at work that very morning. My key insight, for whatever it is worth, was that, despite their respect for the wild, mountaineers are defined by their adversarial stance toward wilderness. Mountaineers, I maintained, climb not because they have a death wish but because they wish to overcome their fear of death. Summitting, I said, is a symbolic conquest of the mountain, which in turn is a symbolic conquest of death and the mortal condition. Mountaineers practice a sport, I conclude, that "reinforces the human tendency to oppose and subdue the wild. They insist that human beings must stand in the wildest, most remote, most dangerous of places. Like most of the rest of us, they can't tolerate the idea of leaving some part of the earth unvisited by human beings."[3]

Another of the draft essays that I completed during the fall of 1994, titled "My Brother and the Mystique of the Summit," focused on Leon. It was Leon whose climbing first made me think about mountaineering—and whose climbing, I will add, gave Karrin her interest in the sport, which in turn led her to fall in love with and marry a Seattle mountaineer.

In the early 1970s, at a little past forty and known as an affectionate husband and father, dedicated teacher of English, and selfless church worker, Leon began doing scrambles and walk-ups on various summits around the West. I recall doing a scramble with him and his daughter Britt to the summit of Windham Peak, more than 14,000 feet, while his family and mine were on a backpack trip into the San Juan Mountains of Colorado. By the mid-1970s, he had taken up rock climbing and had begun to teach a class on basic climbing at Eastern Arizona College. I will admit that his interest in climbing took me by surprise. The assertiveness of such a risky sport seemed out of harmony with his mild and deferential personality. Adding to my surprise, Leon recruited a group of four fellow desert dwellers into what he called the Gila-Denali Expedition, a climb on Mount McKinley in Alaska, the highest point in North America. The successful climb, occurring in June 1981, impressed me beyond words, provoking me to query Leon about its details on every future meeting for years. Like my mother's first marriage, it seemed a family event of such importance that I had to write about it. Freshly informed by a photocopy of Leon's Denali diary, I devoted most of the essay I have named above to a narrative of his climb on that mountain.

Leon and his comrades flew to Anchorage by commercial jet and were deposited on the Kahiltna Glacier by a bush pilot. At this

point, one of them decided to abandon the climb and returned with
the bush pilot. For the next two weeks, the other four methodically
conveyed their considerable gear upward by sled and backpack,
typically taking two days to complete a move between campsites
because they wished to acclimate gradually to the altitude in order
to avoid pulmonary or cephalic edema. At last three of them—
leaving behind in camp the fourth who had suffered frostbite—
made a bid for the summit, turning back within a quarter mile of
their objective when a storm rolled in. During the next two days
they lay in their sleeping bags within their tent, emerging into the
storm briefly to melt snow for drinking water and cooking on their
tiny stoves. Afterward I asked Leon whether he wasn't claustrophobic during those days of enforced confinement. He said no, he
was just glad to be out of the storm. When the storm abated, Leon
and his comrades talked about turning back—after all, professional
guides allowed their clients to claim a successful climb if their party
managed to reach the final crest, which Leon's party had done before the storm set in. Despite a general weariness with their venture, they decided on a final attempt, this time succeeding. Although
Leon reported feeling something close to apathy while on top, he
later agreed with my surmise that he and his friends would have
spent the rest of their lives apologizing to others for the failure of
the Gila-Denali Expedition to achieve its objective. That is the way
it is with mountaineers. Only the summit counts.

Despite Leon's proven competence, risk finally caught up with
him when, in the spring of 1987, he fell about thirty feet from what
he had considered a cliff of easy grade. He was on belay, but the
protection he had placed pulled out when he fell. He broke his
neck, an elbow, an opposite shoulder blade, an ankle, and eleven
ribs. For three months he wore a body brace anchored to a metal
halo secured by four screws driven into his skull. He had to depend
on his wife to bathe him and help him use the toilet. He could sleep
only an hour or two at night before pain from his halo woke him.
He wore a strap-on brace for another three months and a full year
after his fall was only beginning to raise his arms as high as his
head.

My other mountaineers, Mark and Karrin, have had their share
of mishaps, though none so dire. Climbing has been the cement of

their marriage, releasing tension from their lives and making them more amicable mates. Both have completed the Mountaineers Club's basic and intermediate climbing courses and have participated in countless day and weekend climbs, mostly in the Cascade and Olympic ranges of Washington.

Mark's compact, muscular, well-coordinated body makes him a natural for technical climbing. Once while he and I traversed a snowfield on Timpanogos in Utah, I saw him suddenly catapult himself into a position of self-arrest. It was for practice. Yet there was an utter, instinctive grace to the gesture that I knew I could never duplicate. Mark is deeply versed in the lore of mountaineering and adheres strictly to the ethics of the sport. He was recently honored by the Climb Leader of the Year award of the Mountaineers Club, a recognition granted on the basis of votes from participants in climbs. In Mark's case, the honor was to be attributed partly to his emergency treatment on two occasions of climbers whose injuries would have been gravely complicated by a long wait. For both climbers, he reseated an arm pulled from its shoulder socket by a fall. Mark himself suffered a serious injury early in his climbing career. He fell while climbing on the glaciated northwest ridge of Mount Adams and injured a leg so severely that he required evacuation by helicopter. When, much later, I asked him why he had continued to climb, he said that immediately upon recovering consciousness from the fall he had made up his mind that he would accept whatever pain and inconvenience were required but would not quit. Such is the nature of a true mountaineer.

As for Karrin, she has suffered no serious injuries, but, like all climbers who stay in the game for long, she has had her share of narrow escapes. Of particular note was an exhausting twenty-hour climb on Mount Buckner in the northern Cascades, which she later narrated to me as an example of what is meant by the term *epic* when applied to a climb. Early in the morning, while she and Mark, though roped together, were doing a scramble at the edge of a cliff where a belay was impossible, a boulder on which she had just placed both her right hand and right foot gave way and tumbled into a deep abyss. Unbalanced, the right side of her body swung out in what mountaineers call the barn-door effect, her anchored left hand and foot serving as pivots like the hinges on a barn door.

Responding with a counterinstinctive maneuver in which she had been trained, she bent her right leg behind her so that her raised right foot struck the cliff, halting the pivot. If she had fallen, she of course would have dragged Mark with her. An hour or so later their party chose to ascend through a dangerous snow-covered couloir or gully. While they were in progress, the early sun struck an icy cliff above the couloir, releasing a shower of broken rock. Looking up, Karrin saw a volley of large stones tumbling directly toward her. At the last instant the volley of rock tumbled into a crevasse invisible to the climbers below—another of the unlikely providences by which climbers survive.

On a recent hike I made with Karrin—who is a strong if unconventional believer in Mormonism—she told me that an apparition of my father sustained her in the aftermath of an exceptionally grueling climb on the Brothers in the Olympic Mountains. She had carried a heavy pack along a nineteen-mile trail to reach the base of the peak, had climbed it, and was now on the return leg of the trail. Long before the end of the trail, she felt herself to be at the limit of her strength. Suddenly she discovered that my father, whom she recognized from photographs, was walking beside her. He was about my height and had gray hair rather than the silvery hair that I remember. He told her to tell me that he loved me and that he was proud of my writing. He remained with her, conversing, until she was within a mile or two of the trailhead. I was deeply touched by the account. In fact, I have difficulty writing about it without weeping.

As for my own attitude toward mountaineering, it is perhaps best expressed in another of the draft essays I completed during the fall of 1994. In this essay, "Climbing Peaks of Another Sort," I narrated an unsuccessful climb I made with Leon and one of his Denali comrades during the summer of 1994. As the essay makes clear, the positive meaning of my mountaineering experiences, such as they were, had to do with the companionship they offered me with loved ones who had more ardent motives for climbing. It was simply because I wanted to be with Leon that I accepted his invitation to accompany him on what he called a scramble to Gannett Peak in the Wind River Mountains that summer.[4]

At 13,804 feet, Gannett is the highest point in Wyoming. It is one of the few peaks in the Rockies almost entirely encircled by glaciers. The standard routes defined by the guidebooks call for glacier procedures and some rock climbing. Leon said ours wouldn't be a technical climb. His friend Ward Belliston, who had been with him on Denali, had proposed a rarely used route from the northwest, involving a long hike up a stream called Tourist Creek, a brief traverse of a snowfield, and a final scramble up the peak. None of the guidebooks mentioned this route. However, the word *scramble* was reassuring. I judged it meant clambering over jumbled boulders like those on King's Peak in the Uintas.

Leon and I left the house of his daughter Britt near Ogden early on a Monday morning. At noon we met Ward, two of his sons, and a friend of the eldest son at a trailhead where the Green River emerges from the Wind River Mountains. For a while we followed a comfortable trail along the Green River, which, flowing here between precipitous granite walls, did seem *green*—a milky greenish color probably derived from the grinding of glaciers and boulder fields. Keeping to the east side of the river, we left the trail and bushwhacked our way through trees and brush in a sporadic rain, the first that had fallen in almost two months. While we made camp on a bench above the river, Ward kept up the good-humored encouragement he had been voicing all afternoon: "Aren't we having fun now?" and "Oh, it hurts so good!" and "You gotta love it!" I found it easy to like Ward, who was a professor of engineering technology at Utah State University and, like Leon, a devout Mormon.

Leon and I shared my tent, also my Optimus stove that operates on tiny canisters of propane gas. At bedtime I took off my contact lenses, always a precarious process in the mountains, and put on my thick spectacles, whose narrow field of vision and magnification made night ambulation in the woods uncertain. Up at dawn, I took a couple of Anacin and heated water for a cup of Cream of Wheat. Soon we shouldered our packs and set out. Almost immediately we turned eastward off the river, entering Tourist Creek, a steep declivity with a rushing stream in the bottom and a vast boulder field tumbling down from the base of high cliffs on either side. We settled into a long scramble—a term that here came to have a quite different meaning than I had attached to it formerly. It grew on me that this was no hike but an arduous, exhausting labor only a little short of a technical climb. I was always the last in the line of six climbers. Leon stayed patiently with me, and I found it useful to watch his foot and hand moves. Every few minutes I was faced with exposure—empty space between me and the rocks below—and I surprised myself by heedlessly leaping from boulder to boulder. Nonetheless, unbalanced by my fifty-pound pack, I kept asking myself how alpinists manage to climb technical rock with full packs.

Late in the afternoon we turned southeastward out of Tourist Creek, taking a side gorge that was a little less steep and offered stretches where grass alternated with boulders. Toward evening we arrived at a crescent-shaped lake perhaps an eighth of a mile wide and a half mile long, which stood, according to Leon's altimeter, at 11,000 feet. We made camp with difficulty, there being only sparse spots of grass in a terrain composed mostly of rock. As we heated water for supper, the clouds that had covered the sky most of the day parted and a late sun came out. To the southeast stood the high final peaks on the Continental Divide with snowfields and glaciers, Gannett itself being still out of sight. For supper Leon and I shared his freeze-dried potatoes, beef, and gravy—not entirely inedible—and also one of my small cans of diced fruit. I was pleased to see Leon eat the fruit with evident relish.

We were up at dawn under a perfectly clear sky. Leaving camp at seven, we skirted the west side of the lake. I immediately fell behind the others, who seemed eager to explore the route ahead. I was unable to hasten over even relatively flat ground, where protruding rocks required that I pick my way meticulously. With some irritation I found my companions waiting on a rocky saddle beyond the end of the lake. Before us stretched a narrow, deep defile, whose rock-jumbled bottom would more or less serve as our route. This defile quickly passed out of sight around a giant buttress of rock. Beyond the buttress stood Gannett and other scarcely less formidable peaks, reaching 3,000 feet above our current elevation. The Wind River crest, of which they formed the most prominent part, was a mighty wall of rock, utterly devoid of visible vegetation, serrated, fractured, corrugated, riven into uncountable irregularities by frost, sun, and gravity. On the flanks of the peaks lay snowfields and a vast rubble of rocky talus.

A cliff prevented an easy descent from the saddle on which we stood. Leon soon found a route with secure footing and adequate handholds, and my companions climbed carefully down. As for me, the sheer drop below had engaged my fear of heights. Foreseeing such tenuous paths throughout the day, and believing myself destined to prove a drag on the pace of the group, I shouted to Leon that I was turning back. Leon shouted back a brief remonstrance, then shrugged his shoulders and went on.

I remained on the saddle till the group disappeared around the buttress. Just before they passed from my sight, Leon turned and waved and I, moved by ambiguous emotions, waved in return. The rocky abyss between me and my brother seemed an apt figure for the distances that had separated us physically throughout our adulthood and that had perhaps separated us emotionally even during childhood, when we shared a bed and sat side by side at the dinner table.

I headed back to camp, knowing already I would not have a pleasant day. I felt strongly the press of solitude. I was anxious, as if, like Robinson Crusoe, I had been irretrievably cut off from humankind. In fact, my anxiety was of the old pathological sort—that all too familiar impulse to break into an irrational run. Throughout a long day, I resisted the impulse with little confidence that I would be successful in controlling it. Calming myself as best I could, I went about a succession of simple activities. I opened the screens on my tent in order to air it, took a brief nap, and made a cup of soup. At midday and again in the late afternoon, I sat on a rock and wrote my impressions in a small notebook. Curiously, I felt a degree of security in the process of writing. Here are some of the impressions I recorded:

> Noon. The sun is bright and the dark lake is placid. Rock stands everywhere about. This wild place rouses dread rather than reverence in me—though I recognize its stark beauty. Althea is on my mind a good deal. I wish she were here.

• • •

> It's an obvious truth that climbers go to wilder places than hikers. The path we followed in getting here is no beaten track but is a trailless jumble of wild rock awaiting those disposed to meet their challenge.

• • •

Leon says there's a famous climber Rienhold Messner who has done many major peaks in the world solo, including Everest. He went up McKinley solo in a single day from the camp from which Leon spent a week in making the summit. Leon says Messner called that route a tourist promenade—a nice contempt indeed. I said luck was also involved for the man. Leon said yes. Messner's brother died in an avalanche on a climb they were doing together in the Himalayas.

◆ ◆ ◆

Evening. I took a hike this afternoon and looked back down on the narrow valley in which our lake lies. Everywhere is rock with minor spaces of short grass, flowers, and a crusty moss—tundra, perhaps. Our lake rather fills its narrow valley, rocks tumbling to its edge from many cliffs. I hiked to a ridge that looked as if it might overlook another gorge. Instead it led to a slight declivity with another ridge to look over. It was a high jumbled place and I came back. The Wind Rivers are a rock fantasy. This is the physical rather than the living wilderness—rock, water, and sky. If those who named the Rockies first saw these mountains, they had good reason to choose such a name.

◆ ◆ ◆

I have watched the day progress here, much aware that wilderness has no special regard for me. Clouds are forming now, high ones. The lake remains quiet, slightly rippled by a cool breeze. The great stony ridges all around and the towering peaks to the south preserve a perfect silence. A few flies and bees hum. I saw one bird. I heard two or three times what I thought was a pika—no sight of one.[5]

At seven, I heard a shout and answered. I could see no one and wondered whether in my loneliness I had hallucinated the shout. Soon, however, Leon, Ward, and Ward's younger son arrived, having turned back in the early afternoon at an elevation only a few hundred feet below the peak. The youngster, about thirteen, had simply sat down and refused to go farther. About an hour later, as night fell, the older son and his friend arrived, reporting that they had made the summit. I could see Leon, though he seemed completely fatigued, regretted not having gone on with them.

At dawn a light rain was falling—ominous because moisture would triple the difficulty of getting down the rocks of Tourist Creek. But by the time we broke camp, the sky had cleared. We hiked down the side gorge, beautiful on this sunny morning. We came into Tourist Creek, staying closer to the trough of the gorge than on our ascent. At times we had to take boldly to the rocks. Leon seemed tired and at one moment spoke angrily to himself. As for me, my heavy pack drove each step down with a vengeance, giving little chance for subtlety of footing. However, I again surprised myself by accepting exposure rather than backtracking to look for a safer passage. My left hip and thigh began to ache. A painful member of the body has a mind of its own, and I had to make an extra effort to make my left leg function. Later I would find my knees swollen from the downward pounding of our journey.

We made it down to our first campsite in about five hours, where Leon and Ward expressed relief at our having gotten down the rocks without an accident. It made me feel a little better about myself to see that even these veteran climbers had found the boulders of Tourist Creek a challenge. After lunch, we pushed on to the trail on the Green, which we followed at a steady pace. We halted in the early evening—about three hours from the trailhead—to make a pleasant camp among the pines on the banks of the river.

While we cooked and ate our supper, we discussed mountaineering. I said it appeared to me a mountaineer has to have advanced skills of three kinds: backpacking, rock climbing, and glacier travel. Leon agreed. The discussion got around to grades of severity in rock climbs. Ward's eldest son, who practiced in a climbing gym, said he had led on a 5.9 climb. Leon said that was steeper than he liked to lead. He talked about his near-fatal fall, saying the college where he teaches English had abolished his rock climbing class after his fall.

I asked whether the sourdoughs who had climbed Denali in a single lucky day but chose the second slightly lower summit deserved to be barred from recognition as the first climbers of that difficult mountain. Leon said he didn't have an opinion on that matter. He said he and Ward and their companions had planned to do both the lower and higher peaks but found time only for the higher. Ward's eldest son said in his opinion the sourdoughs had failed to climb Denali. Anything short of the top is a failure.

I asked Ward whether he had ever considered turning back during their three-week climb on Denali. He said no. I asked how they had settled the matter of leadership. He said there had never been a question about a leader. From the start, Leon had been in charge. He said Leon was a hard driver, keeping the party on the move and oriented to its goal. He said Leon was invariably levelheaded and took no chances.

Soon after dark we got into our sleeping bags. As we were drifting into sleep, Leon said in his calm, deferential voice, "When I waved good-bye to you on that saddle yesterday morning, I had the tenderest feelings toward you." I was deeply moved. Among the Peterson brothers, affection for one another, though manifest in our behavior, is rarely spoken aloud.

The next morning our trail led through a terrain of marvelous beauty—broad green meadows, pine forests, the wide rushing river, the rugged ridges, the serene expanses of two lakes near the trailhead. At the trailhead we said good-bye to Ward, his sons, and their friend and drove away. We paused in the little town of Pinedale for a hamburger, french fries, and a milk shake at a drive-in that announced itself as the "Home of the Roadkill Burger."

Driving homeward, Leon and I had perhaps the best conversation of our trip. We talked about some of his experiences as a Mormon bishop and as a counselor in a stake presidency. We talked about my precarious stance as a liberal Mormon and about random happenings from our boyhood. As for our trip to Gannett Peak, Leon said he regretted I had experienced only the work of getting near the peak and none of the reward of making the summit. "I wish you could have felt the exhilaration that comes when you make a summit," he said.

By no means did I consider our climb a failure. As far as I was concerned, that instant in which we waved good-bye on the saddle, that instant which had conditioned and preordained the happy moment when Leon's affection had been communicated to me in our tent, was the point, the summit, toward which our entire climb had tended.

··· 28

Aspen Marooney

THREE EVENTS MADE 1995 MEMORABLE: Lars was born, my deteriorating eyesight was dramatically restored, and *Aspen Marooney*
was published.

Having driven to Washington between quarters in March, Althea and I found Karrin "plentifully pregnant, showing her round
belly quite candidly under walking pants and a T shirt." In April,
while we chatted on the phone, Karrin reported having assisted in
a rappelling class for the Mountaineers Club. A little more than
seven months pregnant, she had tethered herself to a tree as she instructed at the edge of a cliff. One of her students, a female obstetrician, asked what her doctor thought of such activity. Karrin said
she hadn't told him. The obstetrician said, "Well, I just can't look
at you. It scares me too much."[1] Karrin insisted on a high level of
activity until the latest moment of her pregnancy. A photo taken
only days before her delivery shows her in hiking gear, striding
along a snowy trail duly preceded by an enormous, horizontally
extended abdomen.

On a Sunday morning in early June, Mark phoned to tell us
that Karrin was in labor. Late that night he phoned from the hospital to say that her labor continued. Having had no further word by
midmorning, I phoned the hospital where a nurse put Mark on the
phone. He sounded so tired and depressed that for a few moments
I feared the worst. As it turned out, the baby, a boy to be named
Lars, had been taken by C-section a few hours earlier. Karrin and
the baby appeared to be all right. Mark obviously wasn't. By noon
Althea and I were on our way to Bellevue, and a little after midnight, we arrived at the hospital and had our first look at Lars,
whom I described in my diary as "a handsome infant with quite

fine features." I went on to say, "Though I have held him only an instant, I have already bonded with him—but of course I had bonded with him before he was born."[2]

Returning to the hospital the next morning, we persuaded a reluctant Mark—who had been at the hospital for forty-eight hours with next to no sleep—to accompany me to their apartment while Althea stayed with Karrin and Lars. Mark awoke that evening from a long sleep and, before returning to the hospital, shared a spaghetti supper I had prepared. While we ate, he clarified the distress he felt over the advent of Lars. As I recorded in my diary, he "explained how much he loved Karrin, how much he admired her, how futile all her intense suffering had seemed when it ended in surgery. He said he had resented the baby as the ordeal came to its climax, weeping a little as he told me, and I could see why he had sounded as if tragedy had struck on the phone the day before."[3] I sympathized entirely, recalling the utter trauma of Karrin's advent in my life in 1965.

Althea stayed with Karrin and Mark for three weeks. I flew home, leaving our Corolla behind for Althea's use. I returned briefly in the middle of this period, recording in my diary that, despite the tensions of our crowded circumstances, "Lars remains the center of anxiety and love. I feel vastly privileged to be here seeing his entrance upon life. He has fine features and touches an adult's feelings profoundly by his tiny yawns, grimaces, and frowns."[4] I came back at the end of the period and drove home with Althea. As we said our good-byes, Karrin sat nursing Lars with tears trickling down her cheeks. Upon leaving for work earlier that morning, Mark had given us a strong whiskery hug.

Toward the end of the summer I approached my bishop for permission to give Lars his name and blessing according to Mormon custom. My bishop asked whether I kept the commandments. I reminded him that, because he had recently joined the Kiwanis Club, he was fully aware that I drank coffee. He said he had wondered what I was trying to prove by drinking coffee in front of him. I said I wasn't trying to prove anything; having drunk coffee at the Kiwanis luncheons for fifteen years, I had decided not to change my habit simply because my bishop had joined the club. He said he could respect that. I said that if he preferred that I not give Lars his blessing, my brother Roald, who was a stake president, would do it. He said I must be the one. I left, feeling triumphant over having secured his permission yet violated for having conceded his moral superiority by submitting to his interrogation.

Karrin, Mark, and Lars flew to Utah a few days before Labor Day. It was reassuring to see how affectionate Karrin had become with her three-month-old son. "She calls her child Dude, Noodle, Doodle, and a host of other names," I recorded. "She says tenderly, 'You're just hanging out, aren't you, Doodle? Doing what you do best, being a baby.'" One day we drove to the Uintas and climbed Bald Mountain with Lars. "These are *my* mountains," Karrin asserted, "and I want him to get to know them." On another day I sat in a chair on the back lawn with Lars in my arms. I fed him formula from a bottle and watched him stare at our trees for a while and then go to sleep. That night I recorded: "He has added a new degree of holiness to our house—it being, as my mother often said of her house, the births, gatherings, deaths, that sanctify a house." On Sunday, assisted by the bishop and a number of my male relatives, I blessed Lars in fast meeting, asking in a few brief sentences that he "be intelligent, good, and healthy and have a passion for truth." We held an open house that afternoon, to which a crowd of friends and relatives came. I had by now recognized a love for Lars of an astonishing, entirely unanticipated strength. As I would put it on a later visit: "Lars' round expressive face elicits my deepest—an almost desperate—affection."[5] In him I sensed a symbolic restoration of the infant I had once been. In holding, feeding, and cherishing him, I set aright the old crime against my mother of having grown up and gone away.

My enjoyment of the Labor Day weekend was marred by my poor eyesight and by my anxiety over pending surgery to correct it. I had worn contact lenses during my waking hours since the mid-1970s, when I had undergone cataract surgery. At night I had removed the contact lenses and gotten about the house by means of thick-lensed cataract glasses. For years the contact lenses had proved functional but always annoying. For example, while camping I accidentally dropped a brown-tinted lens on ground covered by brown pine needles. I put on my cataract glasses and searched the ground without success until I thought of my flashlight. Sure enough, the beam glinted off the lens, which had perversely landed in a vertical position among the needles. On another occasion, I accidentally flicked a lens off my left eye with an unthinking gesture of my hand, and it flew out the open window of a car I was driving.

By the autumn of 1995 my eyes had become so sensitive that the lenses were a constant irritant, blurring my vision to the point of making me a dangerous driver. One evening when I had been at Roald's house for a haircut, I exited from the freeway onto a dark city street, desperate to pull over and wet my lenses yet unable to make out the side of the street clearly enough to stop. At last I came to the brightly lit entrance to a gas station where I could see well enough to pull in. Within a few days I admitted the full failure of my contact lenses and began to wear my cataract glasses constantly. These glasses had double the magnification of ordinary eyesight, therefore offering a narrow field of view and requiring an adjustment to the fact that objects looked closer than they were. Furthermore, they injured my vanity, giving me the appearance, as I esteemed, of a dolt.

At last I arranged for intraocular implants, an eventuality I had rejected for years from worry that this elective surgery might cost me what vision I had. Although tests showed the cell count of my corneas to be minimal for such an operation, my ophthalmologist agreed to perform the surgery. The first operation, performed on the right eye in early October, went well. My vision improved each day following surgery, stabilizing at last at 20/30. In the meantime the techniques of modern surgery, done on an outpatient basis, allowed me much greater freedom than I had enjoyed during the 1970s. I rested a good deal during the first week and didn't drive, stoop, or lift heavy objects for two more weeks. But I could read and watch TV instantly, and after a couple of days I began to grade papers and spend a few hours at my office.

Consequently, I approached the operation on my left eye in mid-November with a relaxed insouciance. As before I walked about the house immediately following surgery, read a bit, and watched TV. However, by evening a red hue in my vision informed me of internal bleeding. The next morning, the ophthalmologist confirmed that the tiny suture had not closed entirely, causing not only the bleeding but also a dangerous loss of pressure within the eyeball. Rigid with anxiety, I spent the remainder of that day in a recliner with my eyes closed, hoping the suture would close. Copies of *Aspen Marooney* arrived in the mail that day, but I didn't look at them. The next morning the ophthalmologist decided on emergency surgery.

Althea and I went into the McKay-Dee Hospital at four in the afternoon and did not emerge till two the following morning. Because other operations preempted the operating room, I lay on a bed, prepared for surgery, for many hours. Mercifully, Althea read aloud two and a half chapters from my novel, a distraction that made the time pass unnoticed. At his office early the next morning, the ophthalmologist examined my eye at length, then reassured me by exclaiming, "I'll sleep better tonight!" During the surgery he had found that the lens had slipped from its proper position in my eye and one of the tiny springs intended to hold it in place had punctured the suture. Now, the pressure in my eye was at an appropriate level and the suture appeared fully closed.

Nonetheless, for a couple of weeks I behaved with the utter circumspection I had practiced during my convalescence from eye surgery during the 1970s. I made no pretense at grading papers or running affairs in the English Department. I didn't watch TV, and I moved about the house very little. I spent most of my time on the recliner with my eyes closed, listening to novels on tape that Althea checked out from the county library. In time my confidence returned, and I resumed my usual labors. During the ten years since this surgery, I have steadily congratulated myself for venturing on the rehabilitation of my eyes. My vision without correction is 20/25. I carry corrective bifocals in my shirt pocket. Occasionally while watching TV, I put them on to bring faces into slightly better focus, but by and large I use them only for reading or the scrutiny of small objects. I ordinarily work at the computer without them. My eyes require little more care than they did when I was twenty— with only this deficiency, that I am unable to rub my eyes when they itch.

During December 1995, I was engaged by a round of signings for *Aspen Marooney* at local bookstores. Sales went on at a modest rate, certainly not exhilarating yet no less than I had expected,

reassuring me that I was by no means finished as a writer. A gratifying number of readers informed me of their pleasure with the
book. Rob Van Wagoner, a talented fiction writer with whom I
would associate closely in later years, wrote that he had read the
book in a single sitting. "As usual your characters & their predica-
ments moved me. Your work brings peace & comfort to my soul."
An anonymous reviewer in the *Deseret News* was ambivalent,
praising the novel for it fast-paced plot and in-depth study of character, yet detailing various "literary transgressions," which included "a knee-jerk impulse to shock" and an academic tendency
to be "enamored of symbols." My friend and good-humored critic
Richard Cracroft did not find the work offensive, asserting that
"Levi, after awhoring after strange Gods, finally turns down his
volume and shock-fiction to turn up his Mormon sensitivities and
give us a wonderful examination of Mormon guilt and expiation
and persuades God to bend a little for two goodhearted and
well-meaning latter-day Saints." A number of other reviewers and
friends commented favorably on the novel's mellowness and mod-
eration, leading me to comment during a reading that perhaps I
had "got over a need for raw edges in my fiction."[6] It is true that
Durfey and Aspen reopen old wounds by coming together for the
first time in forty years at their high school reunion, compounding
both the guilt and the frustration of their ineradicable love for each
other. But when the reunion is over, they retreat to the comfortable
regularities of their respective marriages with Elaine and Roger, resigned if not happy. The book is not a tragedy but a study of personality deeply divided between passion and duty.

As I said in an earlier chapter, I had returned from my class reunion in 1991 determined to interrupt the writing of wilderness essays only briefly by writing a short story set at the reunion of a
rural high school in Utah. By the time I finished the story, told in
Durfey's voice, it had become so long that I judged it to have little
chance for publication in a magazine or journal. So I went on with
the project, narrating the same events in Aspen's voice. While I
worked on this enlargement, I realized that Aspen's forty-year concealment of the fact that Durfey, rather than her husband, was the
father of her eldest child had greater dramatic potential than the
ineradicable nature of Durfey's love. From then on, Aspen was
fully Durfey's equal in my intentions.

When the writing group considered Aspen's side of the story during the spring of 1992, Bruce Jorgensen let fall a musing, only half-serious suggestion that the entire tale might be broken into alternating chapters. That struck me as a good idea, and I went on, creating chapters in which Durfey and Aspen alternate in narrating parts of their history as each understands it. I also gave a chapter each to Elaine and Roger, allowing them to express a fundamental decency that makes the infidelity of their spouses even less justifiable. Inevitably, my narrative expanded in unpredictable ways, illustrating the old truth that form begets content. The chapters that I mailed to the writing group in July 1992 were accompanied by a cover letter in which I spoke of the astonishment I felt over "all the detail I have generated without the slightest shred of forethought and anticipation." I spoke of the intermingling of real life and imagination—of actuality and invention, as I called them in the letter—in the creation of a work of fiction:

> The motors of fictional invention include the desperate and intense things real people do. The drama of actuality is the driving center of the story: a woman, who hides her pregnancy through a temple marriage, birth, and a growing family; a couple who grasp a perfervid moment to commit adultery. The motors of invention include plausibility, the requirement that all characters shall resemble, though not duplicate, people from real life. The motors of invention include texture. You can't set your chief characters on a sparse and unadorned stage. The motors of invention included proportion, a major principle. You can't bring your characters to a climactic moment at the end of the chapter without a certain degree of filler. And it has to be pertinent filler, filler that counts and may in fact supersede in interest the major events for which it serves as a separator and buffer.[7]

Yielding to my old fantasy of a national readership, I submitted the novel first to Alfred A. Knopf and then to W. W. Norton during the early fall of 1992. Both firms promptly rejected it with a form letter. With that I resigned myself once again to aspiring to a regional readership, which indeed, as Althea reminded me, represented no mean achievement. In late October, after a little more polishing, I submitted the manuscript to Signature Books in Salt

Lake City. Although I now turned my attention to writing wilderness essays, I kept thinking about the difficulties of having four characters recount events each in his or her unique personal voice, difficulties that I did not feel I had resolved despite revisions aimed expressly at doing so. Concluding I simply wasn't a good enough writer to give each a truly distinguishing voice, I decided quite suddenly in March 1993 to recast the entire novel in the third person, trusting that the single overriding voice that I seemed fated to use would sound natural and appropriate. Each chapter would remain focused upon the character who had narrated it in the first-person version, and my third-person narrator would adopt fully the bias of the character at hand.

Warning Gary Bergera that the reader to whom Signature Books had assigned my manuscript might well wish to wait for the new version, I presented revised chapters 1 and 2 to my writing group near the end of April 1993. The first chapter, told in the third person from Durfey's point of view, was easy to revise. The second, told from Aspen's, wasn't so easy. Hitherto, I had explained Aspen's refusal to confess the sin of marrying Roger while pregnant with Durfey's child by reference to a covert feminism: she was angry with men—and with a male deity—and found her sin a convenient revenge. I didn't like this Aspen entirely. I liked her better as a would-be penitent whose resistance to confession defies her own understanding. Already I could see structural possibilities in such a personality. Being a believer, she wants to confess and prepares to do so, but at last understands that the unconfessed sin, though worthy of damnation, is essential to her integrity. *Integrity* was a word my friends in the writing group were not eager to apply to Aspen. Donna Jorgensen, I recorded, "rejects the idea that integrity derives from sin. We are free to choose good or evil, Donna said, and Aspen negates her freedom by choosing evil. I of course think decisions such as Aspen's are not decisions at all, but compulsory workings out of ingrained and fated animal nature. Choice is limited to trifling things where we are of two nearly balanced opinions or motivations."[8]

I didn't stop tinkering with the manuscript until the end of the editing stage of its production in the late summer of 1995. When an edited copy of the manuscript arrived by mail, I knew from previous experience that I must allocate plenty of time to a close scrutiny of it because, as I recorded, "those rascals at Signature" were entirely capable of making changes that they hoped I wouldn't detect. The next day my suspicions proved well founded. Comparing the edited manuscript with the one I had submitted, I found so many changes in the first chapter that I drove to Salt Lake—wearing my cataract glasses—and came away with the edited version on a floppy disk so that I could restore my original sentences more readily on the computer screen. While at Signature's office, I chatted briefly with Ron Priddis, who made a plea that I not compare the versions but satisfy myself with restoring the original only when something in the edited version jarred my sensibility. He defended his changes as smoothing the "flow" of my sentences. I refused to comply, as I wrote in my diary that night. "Frequently I agree that a dropped word or phrase is better or at least neutral. But when my sense of *flow* is interrupted by the change, why should I accept it? I won't."[9]

A couple of days later Ron phoned to tell me that any restorations I wished to make were acceptable to him. I was still grumbling over the excessive changes he had made. Yet by now I was beginning to concede that, as his revisions implied, my style was prolix and cumbersome. Although I continued to alter some of his changes, I fell into "the spirit that shorter is better" and paid closer attention even to sentences he had left untouched, sometimes deleting them altogether and, more often, recrafting them to make them more succinct. Finishing, I granted that "I like the improvement very much."[10] I repented now of having thought of Ron and Gary as "those rascals at Signature," recognizing that I had undergone this same change of heart from resistance to acceptance of editorial changes with every book I have had published.

The book Signature produced, a copy of which, as I have said, came fortuitously into my hands at the trying moment of emergency eye surgery, looked good and read well. It was of trade-book size with a glossy front depicting three jars of bottled fruit. One jar contained peeled, cooked pears; another contained peeled, cooked peaches; the third—placed in the middle—contained a single fresh apple with a large bite taken from it, an allusion to the fall of Adam and Eve, a minor motif that Durfey applies to himself and

Aspen from time to time in his part of the narrative. I admired the artist who had created this depiction for Signature, being instantly struck with its propriety.

The novel has two large themes. One is the astonishing durability of the love between Durfey and Aspen; the other is the guilt they suffer because of it. After my brother Leon read an early draft, he said that its conclusion was grim; it led to no redemption. I wrestled from then on with the details of the plot, experimenting with ways in which Durfey and Aspen might find absolution. It had seemed to me from the beginning that their meeting at the reunion had to lead to a compulsive, unpremeditated adultery, which of course was a far cry from redemption. Responding to Leon's quiet observation, I considered some other ending over and over. The best I could do was to have Aspen interrupt the adultery in midcourse because she can see that it will devastate Durfey. Later, as the novel ends, she engages in unfamiliar prayer, asking God to assuage Durfey's guilt. She makes no such request in her own behalf, having long since consigned herself to damnation. As she only now recognizes, guilt is essential to her integrity. Only in defiance can she be her own person.

Their guilt, as one reviewer observed, is "not the sort that will do the sufferer any good." Interpreting the novel by means of a conventional Mormon sensibility, Benson Parkinson found it objectionable on the grounds that guilt should lead to repentance and repentance to a restored innocence.

> In poeticizing [their guilt], Peterson can be accused of ennobling their adultery. In their minds Aspen and Durfey are willing to sacrifice their integrity and their hope of salvation for the good of others, continuing to go to the temple rather than arouse suspicion, refusing to confess and have it wreck their homes. This is a Mormon novel, yet there is no evidence in it that there might exist a repentance capable of healing them and their families."[11]

I am of course at odds with the conventional Mormon procedures of repentance, which, as my reader will recall, I once carried out by confessing myself a fornicator to my bishop. I now consider an intermediary between God and a repentant adulterer as unnecessary and morally debilitating to both the sinner and the inter-mediary, who is susceptible to the role of a voyeur. My Mormon confreres cheerfully discount the humiliation accompanying con-fession, interpreting it as a prelude to a restored innocence. Aspen knows better than that. Confession will make herself something less than herself. My Mormon confreres also discount the severe attrition to domestic harmony that results from an errant spouse's mandatory confession to his or her mate. Durfey perceives the fal-lacy in that. He sees that his true duty toward Elaine lies precisely in not confessing. Accordingly, I end Durfey's part of the novel by writing that, as he sat beside Elaine on a lawn, "she leaned her cheek against his shoulder and he was greatly comforted."

Passion and guilt energize much of my other fiction as well. Considered separately, neither one interests me much. Together, they give me something to write about. Passion, as I mean it here, is sexual. Among my own appetites, sex has always been one of the strongest and by far the most dubious. My sexual fantasies have al-ways been colored by the illegitimate. My reader will recall that as a teen I created elaborate fantasies about getting the girl I was cur-rently in love with pregnant and being forced to marry her. Why, I ask myself, did I lose interest in fantasizing about sex with her at the point where we had married and it had become legitimate? I can't explain. I surmise that my early conditioning left me with the feeling that permissible sex isn't quite real or is somehow incom-plete and unfulfilling. This, I surmise further, is my Christian inher-itance. I do not pretend to know how other religions feel about sex. But Christianity has traditionally interpreted the sex drive as an instinct to be severely delimited.

Whatever the source of my inhibition, it has been strong. I owe my wife a debt of gratitude for not exploiting my inhibition. Over and over, she has been willing to make love when she had no par-ticular desire for it. I have often pondered what my sex life would have been had I married a woman who shared my inhibitions. As it is, although I have committed adultery ten thousand times over in imagination, I have never done so in fact—nor have I ever come close to doing so. I have had good sense enough to recognize that, in the real world, fidelity to a loving and generous wife pays divi-dends far beyond the simple rewards of honesty.

In any event, as I say, passion and guilt have driven much of my fiction. For example, "The Confessions of Augustine," one of my first pieces of fiction, may be seen as an amplification of the sexual fantasies from my teen years with the added complication that Annie, the girl whom Fremont makes pregnant, is a Gentile and therefore doubly forbidden. Obviously, I exploited the same motif in *The Backslider*. There, however, Frank's Gentile wife, Marianne, converts, and the cowboy Jesus advises him to ease up on his guilt. For Arabella in my story "The Canyons of Grace," illegitimate sex functions as a mode of revolt against the Christian God. In "The Goats of Timpanogos," unpremeditated sex in a garage leads the errant Clifford and Sheila to an unconventional union.

I can't assess the degree to which my preoccupation with illegitimate sex pleases or displeases readers. I do know that passion and guilt have been an indispensable inspiration for me. Writing about them, I have been able to transfuse my sentences with unfeigned emotion. That, I think, is very important for any writer. Writers need to be ardent about their topics. Otherwise, the best they can achieve is expository competence.

··· 29

Good-bye to Utah

ALTHEA AND I LEFT UTAH because we wanted to live close to Karrin and her family. We could have waited a while before making our move. But we wanted to be on hand to watch Lars (and, as it would turn out, his brother, Hans) grow up. We also wanted to make the move into the congestion of the Seattle metro area while we had enough vigor to adapt. Obviously, our move was costly, in emotion if not in money. Both of us had come to Utah on the threshold of our adulthood. It had offered itself as our home, and we had accepted. We were young in Utah, and we grew old there. Its vistas and spaces, its forested slopes, sage-filled valleys, and shimmering wastes lurk at the fringes of ten thousand memories.

I returned to full-time teaching in the fall of 1996, convinced that I would find more time for writing than I had enjoyed as department chair. I continued to engage closely with my students, yet my zest for teaching waned steadily, especially in the basic writing courses. More and more I doubted that I would teach beyond sixty-five, an age I was quickly approaching.

However, I didn't behave entirely like a person headed for retirement. Sesh, who had been reappointed as chair, asked me to develop an online course during the spring of 1997, and I accepted. Weber State was launching what would evolve into a large offering of online courses from many departments. I got into the project, as I wrote in my diary, "for the pay and for the enforced familiarity with the Internet and with the many complex functions of my computer's software that this project will bring." I went on to note, ruefully, that for me "at 63 the learning vista opens wide and confusing and tension-creating rather than closing into briefer doses of familiar procedures and learning."[1]

My attainments with the computer to this point were unimpressive. I had begun using e-mail while serving as department chair, and I had surfed the fledgling World Wide Web enough to know that it was a resource of unimaginable potential. However, I had no personal account for accessing the Internet from home, and I was mystified by most of the programs on my computer. Relying on technicians, I prepared an online version of what was then English 111, the first of the department's two basic writing courses. The weekly assignments consisted of extensive reading in a conventional textbook, a comment posted on a class bulletin board that I called the Discussion Forum, and an essay, submitted and returned by e-mail. Later I would prepare online versions of the second basic writing course and of my upper-division course in British literature of the neoclassical era. The literature course took much more time to prepare than either writing course because I felt obliged to infuse the assignments with elaborate written lectures and numerous questions requiring responses to assigned works of literature, which each student posted on an online portfolio accessible only to that student and me.

I was often frustrated in my attempts to make the first course function. Luckily, technicians were at hand, and before long I could recognize my growing competence in online pedagogy. Finding myself rejuvenated by this new kind of instruction, I ruminated philosophically in my diary during my first quarter of instructing the course: "There is a fascination with simply mastering the computer. This becomes an end in itself and explains in part why [software] programs become constantly more complicated.... Mastery of the computer must be seen, therefore, as one of the civilized pursuits, like pole vaulting or acting or music."[2] A year later, I wrote of my regret over having so few years left to experiment with online instruction:

> I think the techniques of teaching I have acquired over the years
> have come so slowly and so singly, my chief methodology being
> internalized from the example of my professors, that I have had
> little sense of adventure in the art of teaching. Now, however,
> I see a confusing multiplicity of ways to induce learning in students via e-mail, the Web, and the much vaunted facility called
> multi-media—confusing and exciting.[3]

Off campus, I continued to engage in a variety of quaint causes. I still served as newsletter editor for the Association for Mormon Letters. I attended church with some consistency and took lunch every Thursday with the Kiwanis Club at the Mansion House. I continued to serve on the board of the Weber County Library, finding considerable satisfactions, as the following episode illustrates.

> After class today as I approached my office a young woman approached me. She was short, dark haired, and dressed in the uniform of a Davis County sheriff's officer with pistol, handcuffs, and so on. She said, "Are you Levi Peterson." I said I was. She said, "I've been looking for you for five years. Do you remember me?" I said no. She took a chair and told this story. She was in the middle of a divorce, had four children, and had come to the Weber County library board to appeal a $20 charge for damaged books. "You paid that fine for me," she said. "You can't imagine what that has meant to me." She said she couldn't have mustered 20¢ let alone the $20 at that time. Her eyes teared as she spoke as did mine. "I want to pay you back," she said pulling out two $10 bills. I declined. She said, "Use them to pay somebody else's fine." I agreed and took the money. She arose and embraced me as I sat in my chair. I returned her long hug, patting her back and murmuring, "God bless you, God bless you." Strange that there could be such instant intimacy, strange to be hugged by a cop. Strange that a kind gesture could encourage a poor woman in the midst of divorce far beyond the cash value of $20 for that is what she implied it meant.[4]

Amid all the foregoing activities and distractions, did I find the hoped-for time and tranquillity for writing? Fortunately, yes. At long last I settled into the creation of my autobiography, now writing the chapters that, much refined, touched up, and otherwise tinkered with, appear in this volume.

However, before I got consistently into work on my autobiography, I tried my hand at a few short stories. Only one of them—to be counted among the most dark and troubling things I have ever written—strikes me as worth further attention. The story is about two men who go for a Sunday ride in the Cedar Mountains to see—and hopefully chase—wild horses. My interest in this setting derived from rides I had taken with Roald in those mountains. But the sinister action of the story—an attempt of one of the riders to rape a female scientist making a field study of wild horses—was inspired by a book about a field study made of wild horses in Nevada, a book I had read several years earlier with an eye toward writing a wilderness essay about wild horses. That book had particularly impressed me with the fact that a wild stallion will breed the mares of his harem only when they come in estrous, but if he encounters a stray mare, he rapes her over and over till she aborts any fetus she may be carrying. Similarly, bachelor stallions—those too young or weak to win a harem for themselves—will rape a stray mare over and over.

The two riders in my story are a giant fellow named Mort, who has only contempt for women, and a defenseless loser named Irvin whom Mort has befriended. Mort takes umbrage at the female scientist because, backed by a regulation, she orders them to leave the mountain range before they disturb the wild horses she is studying. The idea of raping her occurs to him while they observe four bachelor stallions in the process of raping a stray mare. Irvin dislikes the idea but is powerless to change his companion's mind, there being "this other, more subtle matter, that when they were out on a ride Irvin fused with Mort. There was no provision for anything else. One was not without the other. They were two fetuses in a womb or, as Irvin esteemed, two prisoners in a cell, two corpses in a body bag."[5] Mort disarms the woman through a trick. Before the rape can proceed, however, she escapes afoot. Mort insists that Irvin take her pistol while they pursue her on their horses. "If you want to be merciful, you find her first and shoot her," Mort says. "Because if I find her first I'll drag her to death with this rope." Irvin is the first to find her, cowering in a shrub, so paralyzed by fear that she urinates in her pants. At this point, with the story ending, he becomes resolute and makes what for him is a wrenching decision. Mort is his only friend, yet the woman has to be saved.

> "You'll have to help yourself," he said [to her]. He leaned from the saddle and dropped the pistol onto a crown of bunch grass.

"Better check the chamber," he said. "Make sure it's still loaded."

He reined in the gelding, which was eager to leave. The woman still stared wildly around. "If you can't help yourself, you are sunk," he said. "I couldn't shoot him in a hundred years."

He turned the gelding and trotted toward the bottom of the canyon. When he last saw the woman, she was standing with the pistol in her hands. In the bottom, he made the gelding gallop.

A single shot sounded with an echoing expansion. A horse began to scream and a man shouted. Three more shots sounded. The horse went on screaming. Then a final shot and all he could hear was the thudding of the gelding's hooves.[6]

The story deals with both rape and the influence of a dominant over a dependent personality. Sparse and elliptical, it does little by way of explaining them. I had hoped that at least my own attitude toward them would be clear in the fact that the woman, though brutally threatened, is not raped and Irvin consigns his companion to death by returning the pistol to her. However, the women of our writing group objected to the story strenuously.

"As I read," Donna said angrily, "I was thinking why is my good friend Levi subjecting me to this?" Karla said, "I felt you were manipulating me." They objected to the near rape, the obscene dialogue, the description of the terrified woman so completely that only Charlotte seemed to have registered that the story ends with the rape averted and Mort, the chief assailant, dead. "Why would you want to document a rape?" Valerie asked. "What's the point?" Althea abstained from this discussion, not having read the story. She left the room and returned several times to relieve the tension she felt over the heated discussion, as she told me later.[7]

Though the men of the writing group were less than enthusiastic about the story, it obviously had not disturbed them as it had the women, for whom the story was, as I wrote, "an unredeemed negative experience." As I went on to admit, I had long felt guilty "for my gender's instinct for coercing women." The instinct was, I believed, universal among men despite the propensity of the pious and refined to mask its existence behind elevated thoughts. As for myself, I had long recognized the instinct within myself, fortunately kept in check by "an inhibiting guilt and a deeply conditioned empathy for women." I believed, in fact, that a candid confrontation of the instinct gives moral men more control over it. My story had been a gesture toward that confrontation. Ironically, it had missed its mark. "I would like to write a story in atonement of the male propensity for rape," I said in my diary, "yet see now I have written one that heightens fear and anger in women readers."[8]

I considered this story finished by New Year's 1997, and returned immediately to my autobiography. I say *returned* because I had in fact been intermittently at work on it since the fall of 1992 when, disillusioned with my wilderness essays, I had decided to make my own life the frame for my reflections on wilderness. The chapter on which I now began to work was the one about my early college years. I had covered my life from birth to graduation from high school in a single long chapter titled "Bound for the City, Fed on the Wild," completed by March 1993. At that moment, I planned on treating only selected periods of my later life bearing on the wilderness themes I had developed while still projecting a collection of essays. But by 1997 I had determined on a full autobiography. It is true that I could still write: "I must remember, as I begin a draft, that my overriding purpose is to illuminate the wild in my life."[9] However, I had already admitted being impressed "by the multitude of conflicts and contradictions" that infused the pages of my journals from my early college years.

> I show the deep, conventional piety of a Mormon. I show a strong ascetic streak, frequently expressing guilt for my physical (erotic) indiscretions. I distinguish between the spiritual and the sensual. I show a rising interest in a life of the mind and in following the humanistic pattern I see in certain professors. Sometimes I am arrogant toward those who fail to appreciate an intellectual life. I frequently react to the conflict between my faith and this new pattern of mind, always with anxiety, sometimes with a resolute determination to face the anxiety, sometimes with a declaration that I will abandon a life of the mind if necessary to preserve my faith.[10]

Inevitably wilderness became, in the chapter I now wrote, a subordinate theme to my relationship with Mormonism, the humanistic worldview, sexual morality, and my family.

I regard the chapter on my early college years as doubly important because it defined a pattern for my later chapters, establishing not only predominant themes but also a style and tone. I liken it to what is now the first chapter of *The Backslider*, which I wrote only after having drafted the four chapters that presently follow it. Having written this new first chapter, I knew the slant, the tone, the style of the chapters to follow. Similarly, having written this chapter on my early college years, I knew far more precisely than ever before the kind of autobiography I wanted to write.

Among the important issues I had to settle while writing the chapter was candor. I knew in advance that many of my likely readers would feel uncomfortable with the revelation that my ascetic mastery of masturbation had failed when I awoke from sleep in the midst of the act or that I had made a futile attempt at sexual intercourse with a girl in the front seat of a car. Yet I decided to include these facts in my chapter, thereby licensing myself to include similar facts in my later chapters.

My impulse to make such facts known derives, in part, from a resentment I have felt since early childhood toward the mandatory silence polite society imposes upon matters of sex and personal hygiene. It has puzzled me that people can't talk about instincts and behaviors known to be common to all of them. My impulse to reveal such facts also derives from my sense that, without a due portion of them, my life's story is incomplete. I don't want to present myself as something I am not. I want my readers to know about the moral ambivalence in which I existed as an undergraduate at BYU, preoccupied by a monkish compulsion to master my appetites yet obviously susceptible to the usual enticements of those appetites. I want my readers to know about my conditioning to church regulation, which was so thorough that I overcame an enormous reluctance to confess my fornication, fearing as I did that my confession to my bishop would lead to public humiliation. I do not present these facts for others either to emulate or to repudiate. I present them simply because they reveal the person I was, and that is the purpose of an autobiography.[11]

In the meantime, Althea and I continued to pay a good deal of attention to our daughter and her family. During the summer of 1996 Karrin and Mark moved from an apartment in Bellevue to a house on the Sammamish Plateau, about fifteen miles east of Seattle. The Plateau, as locals call it, is a forested elevation immediately east of long, sinuous Lake Sammamish. Among its towering firs and cedars were plots of expensive, high-vaulted houses. Real estate on the Plateau was, in fact, among the most expensive in the entire Puget Sound region, made so, at least according to local folklore, by an influx of Microsoft employees, who liked its proximity to the Microsoft campus in nearby Redmond.

At Christmas 1996, Althea and I spent nearly three weeks with Karrin and Mark, helping them carry out an improbable project of finishing the drywall work inside a new modular house, a project that Karrin promoted in hopes that Mark, restless as an accountant, would find it congenial work. On the day Karrin and I first went to the job site, a record snowstorm struck the Puget Sound, which was immediately followed by a freezing rain. As we returned from a second day on the job, Karrin drove through a flooded dip in a road, splashing water into the air intake of her pickup and ruining its engine. Pressing my pickup into service, we went on with the project. As it turned out, insurance would pay for replacing the ruined engine, which was fortunate because, when all the bills were paid, Karrin and Mark showed no profit for the job. Eventually, however, Karrin's surmise that Mark would find construction congenial proved true. As I write, some seven years later, Mark has turned with no regrets from accounting to freelance jobs in the repair and renovation of existing houses.

We returned to the Northwest for a few days at the break between winter and spring quarters of 1997. We spent our days tending Lars while his parents worked, deepening our attachment to our grandson. One night I wrote in my diary:

> While watching him devour a cheese sandwich for lunch I reflected on how deeply I loved this little creature who focuses intently on the animal needs and pleasures and engages in no abstract discussions of any sort. His potential for future higher level activity is part of my love for his present being—but not all of it. His simple animal existence is a great comfort and delight.[12]

I had an almost unlimited capacity for being with Lars. His presence eased my pathological need to be within a parent-child circle, and I longed to be with him more often. Months earlier, I had begun to think about securing inexpensive quarters where Althea and I could come for more extended visits without intruding upon the privacy of our daughter and son-in-law. I hatched the idea of renting a room in someone's basement year-round but was baffled by the process of locating one. I considered buying a used travel trailer and parking it in a nearby RV park but discovered that a space with hookup required a year's lease and cost as much as the rent of a one-bedroom apartment. Moreover, all these possibilities were conjectural. Leaving Utah for long periods of time was unimaginable. I wasn't sure I wanted to retire. All our friends lived there. Leaving our old house empty seemed a rank infidelity.

Nonetheless, as we drove eastward out of the Cascades at the conclusion of our March visit—with Lars fresh in my mind—the hitherto unthinkable suddenly seemed feasible. I proposed to Althea that we close our house, hire a neighbor to water and mow our lawn, and move to the Northwest for the summer. Althea agreed. So it happened that we loaded our small pickup and sedan with rudimentary furnishings and drove in tandem to the Northwest in mid-June. We rented an expensive one-bedroom apartment in Klahanie, a mammoth development about five miles from Karrin and Mark's house. We placed our bed in the living room, letting it double as a daytime sofa. Our dining table was a folding card table, and lawn chairs served as our seats. We turned the bedroom into a workplace, placing my computer on a light modular desk I had constructed and Althea's portable sewing machine on another card table. We had a balcony looking into a grove of firs and cedars, on which we often took our meals on warm summer days.

We quickly established a pleasant routine. I arose before dawn and worked on my autobiography for at least several hours every day. By August I had completed the chapter about my mission, which I read at the Salt Lake Sunstone symposium during a quick trip to Utah. After that I went on with a chapter about my early years with Althea. Althea and I also found time to explore Seattle and the nearby countryside, sometimes following narrow highways that threaded their way through towering stands of timber. We took walks almost every day and occasionally accompanied Karrin and Mark (with Lars in a child carrier) to nearby hiking destinations such as Tiger Mountain and Mount Si. We tended Lars for at least a few hours four or five days a week because Mark had an accounting job and Karrin had rented an office in Seattle and was trying her hand at family law. Lars liked to drop heavy rocks into a large bucket half filled with water, a diversion he pursued on the driveway for several hours at a time. He also liked to visit playgrounds, where he played on swings and slides while I watched in silence among a variety of young mothers who fell into easy conversation with one another.

One Wednesday evening I was surprised by a phone call from Mark, who requested that I baptize him. He had been taking lessons from a couple of Mormon missionaries, who had challenged him to be baptized on the following Saturday. He had said he would if his father-in-law would perform the ceremony. I agreed and immediately phoned my bishop in Ogden, "who, after an impromptu interview, which elicited some satisfactory equivocations on my part, said he would recommend me to Karrin's bishop, who will oversee the baptism."[13]

The baptism occurred in a stake center located behind the temple in Bellevue. The brief service, attended by about thirty persons, included hymns and several sermons. Karrin gave one of the talks, which I characterized in my diary as "an absorbing, intellectual sermon." I went on to worry in my diary over the toxic effect that my disbelief might have on Karrin and my other loved ones, finding it ironic that the topic I had recently been pursuing in my autobiography was the solidification of my disbelief during the early months of my mission. I declined to conjecture on the effect my disbelief might have had on Mark, commenting only that he "seemed very appreciative of my performance of the ordinance."[14]

In mid-September 1997 Althea and I went home to Ogden. As we traveled the eight hundred miles, I reflected on the fact that, for me, at least, the question now was not whether, but when, we should retire and move permanently to the Northwest. All in all, our summer had met my expectations.

I worked on a chapter about my early years with Althea throughout the fall. On the Sunday afternoon of General Conference in October, I listened to sermons while taking up carpet in our living room. "Somehow," I recorded, "the combination of these sermons, my tedious labor on this house at Althea's instigation, and my morning's summary of our letters of 40 years ago—which reminded that it was the new presence of Althea in my thoughts that influenced, shaped, and encouraged me to create a way of life beyond the expectations of my Mormon raising—filled me with a grieving appreciation for Althea." Reminding myself afresh that my identity required disbelief, I reflected sadly on the inevitable approach of a permanent separation between Althea and me. As if to console myself for this dismal recognition, I went on to articulate in fresh terms a familiar fact: however painful truth may be, morality requires that I confront its implications in my public life. "What is, is—recognizing this truth honestly is the heart of my moral being. As Althea said to me today, she was the one who believed me when I said it was a violation of my integrity to play the full role of believer as I had done on my mission. My relatives believed that role playing was the better part for me. By marrying Althea I expressed my integrity."[15]

Writing my autobiography seemed a deepening of my own spirit, as I recorded in my diary, "a spiritual act of gathering, recollecting, weighing, reflecting, discovering, generalizing, and abstracting. It will not be a celebrated book but I must write it for my own spiritual completion." It also stimulated eventualities not strictly spiritual. For example, throughout an evening of grading papers I paused from time to time to reflect on the as yet unrequited lust with which my early letters to Althea are replete. The result was, as I cryptically noted, that I "felt desire for my wife and late, around 10:30, asked her if, and she said yes." Her cheerful acquiescence to my impromptu request was characteristic. However, she was not above affectionate derision. One afternoon while I graded papers at home, she entered the room and, after looking me over, said, "Grading papers? You poor son of a bitch!"[16] What could I do but laugh?

During the spring of 1998 we made plans for another summer in the Northwest. I had an automatic sprinkling system installed in our lawn and again hired a neighbor to mow our lawn, also turning our garden plot over to his use. In June we again loaded our vehicles with sparse furnishings and made our migration. This time, however, we had no luck in renting an apartment by the month and finally signed a year's lease on a very small, plain apartment in the center of Issaquah, a couple of miles from the Plateau. Again I occupied my days with writing and tending Lars. I also spent a good deal of time helping Karrin and Mark make improvements in a house they had bought on the Plateau—an exceptional find because, though small, it was structurally sound and stood on a hillside lot offering glimpses of Lake Sammamish through towering trees.

By the end of the summer I knew that I wanted to retire and move to the Northwest before long. One Sunday immediately after we had returned to Ogden, Althea and I discussed moving as soon as possible. Only within the past few days, Althea said, had she realized that my talk of selling our house and moving was more than conjecture. She said that she had been crying about the prospect, also that she had wanted to be home in Ogden throughout our stay in the Northwest. I said we could rent the house rather than sell it. "She said it would be better to cut our connections irrevocably so that she could begin to be reconciled to being in the Northwest."[17] A week later I found her weeping again, saddened, as she told me, by pruning our belongings with an eye to selling the house, a process she had begun of her own initiative. My own grief over selling the house, though genuine, would not be as intense as hers. I had always worried too much about its deficiencies. The porch roof sagged, a radiator had burst, the bastions where the foundation met the wall on one side of the house appeared to be crumbling. But Althea loved the old house without reservation. She loved to sit at her desk and read while the leaves on the giant poplars outside the study windows danced in the breeze. The house was her refuge and friend.

Without our deciding definitively on retirement, I made arrangements to return to our apartment in Issaquah in January 1999. I had first asked Sesh to let me teach an entire class load online from Issaquah. The dean and the provost denied the request; no one from Weber State had ever taught a full load online, and allowing me to do it could set an unmanageable precedent. Sesh suggested that I take a two-quarter sabbatical. Accordingly, Althea and I moved back to the Northwest in January 1999. Taking advantage of my sabbatical, I made rapid progress with my autobiography. By February I was at work on an advanced draft about my mission. I felt satisfied with both the style and the mode of development I had arrived at. I intended to avoid the density of detail with which some critics claimed I had overloaded my biography of Juanita Brooks. "Facts and chronology," I said in my diary, "are no more than outlined. I strive to make it readable and indicative, not exhaustive.... I try to make my sentences simple where possible and, where a choice is before me, to select the more ordinary and colloquial word, trusting that I'll still manage to include many words that distinguish my personality and characteristic diction from other writers."[18]

We liked many things about Issaquah. There was a creek near our apartment where I often took Lars and let him throw rocks into the rushing water. Within easy walking distance were a library with a playground, a grocery store, and a community center. Sheltered by umbrellas, we took long walks on trails along the flank of Tiger Mountain. Also, temperatures rarely got below freezing. Inevitably, however, this long Puget Sound winter, our first, was depressing. Althea, who kept count of rainy days, declared we had gone fifty-six consecutive days without seeing the sun. One day in March I complained in my diary that "my life here has constricted borders: the same routines seven days a week, a tiny apartment, a congested cityscape, rainy skies, towering trees in most wild places. I foresee no escape." I went on in the same entry, however, to put our situation in a more positive light. It posed a stimulating challenge, I said, to be taken "as an opportunity for growth into new skills, attitudes, and perceptions."[19] I was sincere in this optimistic sentiment. I doubted that I would ever learn to love Seattle and its vicinity. Yet what was happening to Seattle was happening to all of the United States, and I wanted to know about it firsthand.

I ended the foregoing entry by declaring that "I would like the *adventure* of buying a new residence." It was not long before the adventure began. Pursuing what I considered an "unlikely scheme," we arranged to borrow a large down payment on a condo, using our house in Ogden as collateral. From the start it was clear that we would have to be content with modest quarters. What had been a generous retirement in Utah translated into a rather sparse one on the Plateau, where the standard new house cost close to three times the worth of our house in Ogden. After inspecting a variety of condominiums on the Plateau and in Issaquah, we settled on a one-bedroom condo in Providence Point, a large association composed of something like 1,350 residents dwelling in 900 units. It was a gated retirement community located on the edge of the Plateau, at that moment in unincorporated King County, later to be annexed into Issaquah. We chose Providence Point largely because it offered more space between its well-landscaped buildings than most condominiums. Also, a small forested ravine with a rushing creek, a dedicated greenbelt, ran through our village only a couple of hundred yards from our building. We chose the one-bedroom apartment because it was more spacious in effect than two-bedroom units that fell within our financial range.

We closed on this condo in June 1999, and by the end of that month, when our lease on the Dogwood apartment ended, we had moved into it. Unquestionably, the cramped inconvenience of the Dogwood place had conditioned us to feel good about our new quarters. Our spirits were also elevated by our first hike along the edge of our forested ravine and rushing creek. Many times since then Althea has said that this first hike along the gulch, as we came to call it, helped reconcile her to our new situation. Our pleasure was only enhanced when, hardly more than two weeks after we had moved in, we encountered a family of coyotes near the end of the trail. "Returning, as a fire truck siren sounded on the nearby highway, we heard a great cacophony of coyotes. We peered into the trees and saw five or six of them. One was grey rather than tawny and had a husky-like tail, perhaps a feral dog or a cross. We were deeply moved, both apprehensive and pleased by this manifestation of the wild so close to our condo."[20]

I am not sure to this day whether we did well by our own spirituality by moving into Providence Point, where, by the size and appointments of their condos and their display of luxury cars and the frequency with which they take world cruises and other kinds of vacations, many residents demonstrate an affluence far above ours. The opulence of the Plateau generally worked to make me feel "paltry and insignificant.... Uprooted from my teaching environment, living in the most meager kind of apartment, owning two aging cars, I have nothing to bolster a flagging self assurance." I voiced the same sense of inferiority one day following a walk through the opulent neighborhoods south of Providence Point: "There is a curious effect upon me in all the elegance and luxury now that they are in my own neighborhood and immediacy. I cannot ignore them but must to some degree measure myself against them. I feel a great inadequacy as I see how humble a place I am able to command." However, on these occasions and many others, I felt the need to resist my sense of inferiority. In the earlier entry, I ended by insisting "that attitude, ideas, matters of learning, of spirit, of individuality are primary and imperative. I must turn to the cultivation of my own aging spirit as the chief purpose of my life and it makes the venality of modern consumer civilization irrelevant." Similarly, I followed my expression of inferiority in the later entry by declaring that I must "resist a scale based on income and wealth. My purpose is not to possess status through consumption but to rejoice in the health and presence of my loved ones."[21]

Althea and I returned to Ogden in mid-August because the public institutions of higher education in Utah had established the semester as their basic academic term and Weber State was starting its academic year a month earlier than customary for a quarter. Our plan was to sell our house by the end of the semester and return to the Northwest, where I would instruct a full load of online courses during the spring semester 2000, a privilege I had secured by applying for retirement at the conclusion of the semester. The fall was frantic, worrisome, and sad. On campus I taught a usual load of classes in the morning and spent my afternoons preparing my online classes for the spring semester. Evenings and weekends, I joined Althea in preparing our house for sale. Among our many renovations was a brick project. On the west side of our house sizable chunks of concrete had broken away from the wall at the ground level. I called in a structural engineer who, to my vast relief, assured me that the defect was not the foundation or the brick wall that it supported but the concrete facade that covered the brick wall. Nonetheless, prospective buyers would have interpreted the defect as serious, and it had to be remedied. I dug a trench, mixed concrete in my wheelbarrow and poured footings, rented a trailer-mounted brick saw, cut and laid brick on the footings, filled the narrow gap between the sound facade and the brick with concrete, and smoothed the joint lines with a trowel, effectively remedying the defect by providing a solid support beneath the facade. To my satisfaction, not a single person—neither inspecting officials nor prospective buyers—made any comment on the repaired wall, evidence that the defect had vanished.

Throughout the fall, Althea and I cleaned, painted, and carted away books, furniture, and goods. I installed a new dishwasher and cooktop in the kitchen. We hired other renovations done. We had the front porch reroofed and had aluminum caps mounted over the crumbling brick atop the three chimneys. We had the asbestos removed from our old furnace and hired a plumber to install a new furnace and connect it to the radiator system. We had a concrete pad laid over the floor of the wood room in our basement, hitherto bare earth. We were forced to have a radon pump installed in our basement and to have a termite treatment consisting of poison injected into dozens of holes drilled along the walls both inside and outside our house.

Ironically, these renovations made our departure from the house more difficult. They struck us as beautiful, and we grieved that we had not completed them earlier so that we ourselves could have enjoyed them. We were of course in a constant mood of saying good-bye to the old house. On the very day of our return from the Northwest in August, I wrote in my diary:

> I feel, as I consider the enormous task of preparing this old house for sale, as if I am involved in an involuntary divorce action. I don't want to be divorced from this house. I disliked many things about it—most of them having to do with its antique structure. But half my life has been spent while dwelling in this domicile. The comings and goings of innumerable loved ones and events—the countless heartwarming experiences—have bonded me to the house.[22]

The young couple to whom we sold our house took possession of it on December 16, 1999. We stayed with Roald and Luana that night, "already feeling like dispossessed aliens in a land formerly our own." We stayed three more nights. On the last, Roald cut my hair very short on the hope that I wouldn't need another haircut till we made it back to Utah in the spring. The next morning, a Sunday, as we prepared to climb into our fully loaded vehicles, Roald said, "Now I know how Mother used to feel when we left after a visit."[23]

Our good-byes had been said to a land as well as to a house and loved ones. Our love for Utah had been brought freshly to mind on many occasions throughout the fall. In October we had driven via Price and Monticello to an academic conference in Santa Fe. "Nostalgia visited us along a familiar old landscape. Spanish Fork Canyon, the Book Cliffs, the LaSal Mountains spoke the same beguiling language as long ago....More than once Althea expressed her joy at driving this old road with me. The two of us in a rolling car, amidst a beautiful landscape, evading anxiety and duty at home, moving, moving, moving toward the promises of the future."[24]

A couple of weeks before that, we had taken our friend Jean Anne Waterstradt on a drive to the vicinity of Monte Cristo, some forty miles northeast of Ogden. I parked the car on a prominence from which we could see in all directions. I walked from the car and stood a while. That evening I recorded in my diary the sentiments that came to me while I viewed the vast panorama, sentiments that I think Althea fully shared:

> I was hungry for the scene around me—receding ridges, canyons; alternations of sagebrush, yellowing aspen, dark fir. I felt the wild, felt my belonging. I had an image of a man who had hunted this country every fall from boyhood on; an image of a man who had cast his youthful aspirations on it; for whom it had represented a rich anticipation of unspeakable happiness; who had grown old in an annual renewal of that epiphany. I grieved over my sense of farewell: of possibly never again seeing this scene. A sense of loyalty to Utah came over me and I felt, though I will no longer be a Utah resident, in my heart I will not be a resident of any other place. I will just be a generic resident, one who is on the earth with no bonding to the place he lives.[25]

I will report, writing some five years later, that both Althea and I can admit to periods of feeling bonded to the coastal Northwest. There is no question, however, that Utah remains at the core of our emotions.

··· 30

Running Out of Sunsets

IT IS TIME TO END THE ACCOUNT OF MY LIFE. I have enjoyed chroni-
cling my personal history, but with increasing frequency its eventualities repeat themselves. I will offer a few more of them here by
way of characterizing the six years Althea and I have lived in the
Northwest and then conclude with some reflections on the themes
it has traced.

I am seventy-one, Althea is sixty-nine. We are in good health
and essentially happy. Our daughter and son-in-law treat us well.
We have two grandsons, Lars and Hans, and we spend much time
fraternizing with them. We have accumulated new friends. We attend an occasional play or ballet in Seattle. We travel to Utah three
or four times a year, and we make it to Arizona on the average of
once a year.

Having a lot of tolerance for one another, we have not felt
cramped in our one-bedroom condo. Our living room and bedroom do double duty. We eat, watch TV, and receive guests in the
first and sleep, study, and write in the latter. Although Althea
grieved for our Ogden house for the first year or two, she has applied herself consistently to the decoration and improvement of our
condo. We have installed the heavy brass chandelier from our
Ogden house over the dining space of the living room and, in the
entrance hall, the small antique chandelier that we removed from
my parents' house in Snowflake during the 1970s. We have installed custom-built shutters in our living room windows and, in
our bedroom, store-grade shutters from our Ogden house. Both
sets are stained the pomegranate orange that Althea favors.

We continue to have adventures, some of them adverse. Although the Sammamish Plateau, where we live, is heavily wooded,

its streets and thoroughfares are congested, a fact vividly under-scored for us by a collision Althea had on a rainy night in an inter-section only a mile from our condo. This was only six weeks after our move from Utah. Our Corolla was totaled, and Althea suffered a broken kneecap, two broken fingers, and chest and shoulder con-tusions from the seat belt. She was not at fault for the collision and fortunately did not require hospitalization. However, within a few days of the accident, she developed blood clots in her injured leg and a few days after that had an allergic reaction to an anticoagu-lant. Eventually, she recovered from her afflictions and, as I have said, enjoys good health today. The car with which we replaced the Corolla was a similarly humble Ford Escort, an inglorious convey-ance on the Sammamish Plateau, where SUVs and luxury cars are abundant.

Ironically, Althea recently suffered a second collision in which the 2004 Corolla with which we replaced our aging pickup was totaled when struck from behind by an automobile driven by a drunk driver. Again she was not at fault. Luckily, she recovered quickly from a whiplash injury, and we have replaced the wrecked Corolla with a 2006 Corolla that looks almost precisely like its predecessor.

Our first year at Providence Point was made particularly mem-orable by Hans's birth. Within a couple of weeks of our move from Utah, Karrin announced that she was pregnant. As she had during her pregnancy with Lars, she remained highly active, enlisting me as a hiking companion three or four times a week. I found our long, intimate conversations particularly gratifying. On September 15, 2000, Karrin was once again delivered of a child by a C-section following a long, unsuccessful labor. Hans (pronounced Hahnz) proved a handsome infant of blue eyes and fine blond hair, a close replica, it seemed to all of us, of Lars and also of Mark at the same age. During the wee hours of the night following Hans's arrival, I took a turn at changing his diaper and bringing him to Karrin for nursing. Occupying a bassinet in her room, he cried or made other noises so often that Karrin slept little. I spent most of the next night holding him in the corridor adjoining her room so that she could sleep. Sometimes I sat, sometimes walked, with this tiny, flan-nel-swathed bundle in my arms, feeling closely connected to our second grandson, happy to forego sleep for such an eminently good cause as his welfare.

As the foregoing incident suggests, Althea and I have been much engaged in the domestic life of Karrin and Mark. They have tolerated the incursions upon their sovereignty that our presence implies, we hope rewarded by the help about their house and the convenient child care we have provided. Singly or together, Althea and I tend Hans while his parents work, and we are often at their house to greet Lars after school, getting him a snack and helping him with his homework. We read to Hans, play games with Lars, and watch videos with both of them on subjects ranging from Pooh Bear and Bambi to Star Wars and Harry Potter.

Predictably, I find myself tolerant of long hours in the presence of my grandsons. With Hans as with Lars, I find the magic circle of child and parent completed and consider myself a fortunate man to have as much exposure to them as I have. Furthermore, I deem it no small matter that I have mastered the art of feeding formula to an infant, changing a diaper, engaging in conversation at the level of a three year old, and accompanying an eight year old to a soccer practice or a chess tournament. I did such things long ago with Karrin but without my current appreciation of their primacy over almost any other achievement I can boast of.

Althea and I have also helped Mark's parents participate in family affairs. Debilitated by a stroke, Gerhard has stopped driving. Accordingly, I drive across Seattle to the Ballard neighborhood once a week and take him shopping or fetch him back to dinner at Mark and Karrin's house, following which Mark takes him home. In 2003 we helped Mark's mother, Karin, move from Seattle into subsidized housing in Issaquah that I had located. Mark and I helped her move. Karrin and Althea worked long hours to make the new apartment pleasant and convenient. Closer at hand now and possessed of a phone, she sees her son and his family much more often.

Amid these domestic preoccupations, Althea and I have remained intellectually active. Three years ago Althea took a three-quarter course in German; recently it has been French. She is the most proficient student of foreign language that I have ever met—certainly much more so than I ever was. Ranging far beyond the assigned material, she makes comparative lists of nouns, verbs, adjectives, and so on. She acquires tapes and CDs, watches the news from Paris on the international channel, and prints off articles from foreign Web sites. I have been the beneficiary of her passion for French, refreshing my lapsed fluency by mere proximity to my linguistically dedicated wife.

As for me, although I am retired, I continue to teach a single online class for Weber State each semester. I have helped organize two writing groups with an eye toward securing a sympathetic critique of my writing. I have continued to work on my autobiography, pausing to write an occasional essay for a Sunstone symposium in Salt Lake City, Los Angeles, or Seattle. During 2003, I joined a colleague from Weber State, Karen Moloney, in the task of editing *Dialogue: A Journal of Mormon Thought,* the most venerable of liberal Mormon publications. Karen was appointed as editor in chief, I as associate editor. Although our appointment was not officially scheduled till January 2004, we were obliged to launch a complete editorial process months in advance. By January, my partner had resigned because of professional and family commitments and I had been appointed sole editor. Hence I have entered upon a demanding new endeavor for what I expect to be a five-year term. If my wits and energy remain, I intend to return to writing fiction when my stint as editor has ended. My subject will be the elderly, I think. I see no reason the study of sin and turmoil I have applied to the young or middle-aged in my fiction to this point will not prove fertile among the old. Passion, I observe, does not die in human beings merely because the capacity to carry it out dwindles.

The writing groups to which Althea and I belong have yielded intimate friends. We assemble with each group for a monthly dinner and discussion in one or another of our domiciles. We also gather somewhat more irregularly for dinner and wide-ranging conversation on Mormon topics with a discussion group formed by a young couple from my ward. I have found other friends, cordial if not intimate, in the Issaquah Second Ward where I attend meetings once or twice a month and serve as a home teacher. I have also found friends in the Kiwanis Club of Issaquah. Meeting for lunch on Wednesdays, club members sing rally songs with lusty vigor and pay a dollar toward a charitable fund for the privilege of informing one another of their triumphs and reversals. Sometimes when I am about to leave on a trip to Utah, I pay my dollar and tell my colleagues that I am off in search of a polygamous wife. When I return, I pay another dollar and tell them that I had no luck finding a woman who wished to switch patriarchs.

As I say, I regard myself as essentially happy. Obviously, a close, steady engagement with my daughter and her family contributes a great deal to my happiness. Nonetheless, I find myself periodically gloomy over the evident decline of my abilities and the increasing probability that my joys will become, one by one, untenable.

I can't help being depressed by an increasingly violent world. The *Seattle Times*, through which I browse every morning, offers a steady diet of crime at home and war abroad. My own nation has been at war since September 11, 2001. An angry, weeping Karrin phoned us on that day, telling us to turn on our TV. For hours we watched replays of those horrifying moments when the hijacked jetliners crashed into the World Trade Towers. That evening, Karrin put on her uniform, drove to the base where her navy reserve unit served, and spent the night on volunteer duty. Later she served eight months on active duty. Fortunately for her family, she was stationed at this base and able to commute home three or four nights of the week.

The United States will never again, at least in my lifetime, be as free and tolerant as before the attack. The majority of my compatriots appear to want aggressive rather than defensive war. I supported the invasion of Afghanistan in October 2001 because it appeared that the ruling Taliban party had indeed sheltered the Al-Qaeda terrorists responsible for the attack of September 11. I did not support the invasion of Iraq in the spring of 2003. For one thing, I believed our preemptive strike made us the aggressors. For another thing, I feared precisely what has in fact transpired since the collapse of the Iraqi Army three short weeks following our invasion. The newspaper carries daily accounts of attacks upon U.S. and collaborating Iraqi forces. There is little protection from terrorists willing to engage in suicide bombings. I foresee years of mutual destruction between, on the one hand, U.S. troops and their Iraqi allies and, on the other hand, guerrilla fighters recruited from a disaffected Iraqi populace. Sooner or later there will be a monument to U.S. troops killed in the Middle East rivaling the monument in our nation's capital dedicated to the dead of the Vietnam War.

My periodic melancholy is also fueled by the inevitable attrition among those whom I have loved the most. My relatives and friends depart at a faster rate now. The effect is that I have less confidence in retaining those who survive. Watching my friends and siblings adjust to the roles of widow and widower has not been entirely reassuring. I have little hope of coping well with that role were I required to do so.

My sister Lenora and sister-in-law Betty died in September 2000. Luckily, Althea and I had a chance to say something of a good-bye to both of them. In August we drove to Utah and persuaded Roald to join us for a trip to Arizona. Our express purpose was to see all our living siblings and their spouses—Lenora and Marion, Wanda, Mary, Charles and Betty, and Leon and Gussie— a purpose conditioned by a determination to "love that well which thou must leave ere long," to borrow a line from Shakespeare's sonnet 73. Driving with Roald was memorable. We conversed endlessly, removing all tedium from our journey. We paused to visit Wanda at a daughter's ranch near Snowflake. Though afflicted with diabetes, Wanda remained her former affable, affectionate self. Driving on toward Thatcher, we encountered a fierce thunderstorm on our descent into Salt River Canyon. Wind drove the rain in torrents, lightning flashed on all hands, and thunder crashed incessantly in our ears. Boulders tumbled to the roadway from the cliffs above, and we negotiated the tight curves with a full expectation of being struck at any instant. Because there was no place to park that wasn't at the base of a cliff, we could only drive on. Emerging unscathed from the storm at the bottom of the canyon, we exulted in our triumph. From then on, our trip had a sacramental quality.

While we were in Thatcher with Leon and Gussie, we visited Lenora and Marion in nearby Safford. Nearly eighty-six, Lenora was confined to a wheelchair by a broken hip. A gaunt, thin Marion, ninety-three, suffered from senility, obeying—and disobeying— like a little child. One day Leon and Gussie took us all, including Lenora's daughter and son-in-law Gale and Rex Barney, for a picnic on their forested property in New Mexico. I remember our lunch, sheltered from a light rain by a tarp, as a happy moment.

428   A RASCAL BY NATURE, A CHRISTIAN BY YEARNING

My father and mother's family were together again, conversing, laughing, communing. Only Marion sat silent, lost in senility.

Roald, Althea, and I routed back to Utah via Mesa, where we had lunch with Mary, who at eighty-four was fragile and stooped yet alert of mind and living alone. She suffered from loneliness, yet I judged her to be coping with Waldo's absence much better than our mother had predicted that she would. We drove on the next day to St. George, where Charles and his daughter Colette Spackman took us to the hospital to see Betty. A long, painful history lay behind this, Betty's last hospitalization. She had suffered from arthritis for twenty years, consulting many doctors and requiring heavy medication. For perhaps half of that period she had suffered from severe pain in the muscles of her shoulders and back with no hope from her doctors for improvement. On this, our last visit, Betty asked for a blessing. Charles anointed, Roald blessed, I assisted in the laying on of hands. Our good-bye was emotional. Both Althea and I kissed Betty and wept. Betty said to Althea, "You are my sister," a reference to the fact that both were single children with no siblings. There had indeed been a special bond between the two. Within six weeks of our visit, both Lenora and Betty were dead, with the consequence that Althea and I made two quick trips by air to attend their funerals.

The major loss Althea and I suffered during 2001 was Eugene England. His illness and death were preceded by a remarkable visit he, Charlotte, and their daughter Jennifer paid to our condo in January of that year. After lunch, Gene and I took a walk. He said he was very depressed and alarmed by the fact that he no longer found pleasure in work. That evening I recorded in my diary:

> He attributes his collapse to the opposition from orthodox Mormons to his efforts to establish a flourishing center for Mormon studies at Utah Valley State College, where he sought vindication after his humiliating forced retirement from BYU. "I have a testimony," he said to me on a brief walk down our gulch road. "That is the problem. How can I reconcile the fact that apostles have treated me like shit?"[1]

He said this final word with a savage emphasis. I was startled, it being the only time in our entire relationship that I ever heard him utter any word that could not be said over a pulpit.

About a month later, Gene collapsed in his home in Provo and underwent surgery for the removal of several cysts and a tumor in his frontal lobe. Treated by radiation and chemotherapy, he made a slow recovery during the following spring. On a trip to Utah in early May, Althea and I, in company with Bruce and Donna Jorgensen, visited Gene and Charlotte at home. Althea and I visited them again in August when we had come to Utah to attend the Salt Lake Sunstone symposium. By now, Gene was in a near coma, heavily sedated and obviously dying. Attended by their children, Charlotte had been staying beside him day and night, cherishing every moment of his presence and unable to resign him to death. I recorded: "I bent over his wasted, sleeping form and kissed his nearly bald head and said, 'I love you, Gene.' He opened his eyes and gave me a piercing look and Althea too. I said, kissing him again, 'You made a Christian of me. Put in a good word for me with God.' Althea, Charlotte, and I wept."[2]

About a week later, Gene died and was buried with a private family service. A week after that, a public memorial was held in the Provo Tabernacle, which Althea and I attended. I was one of the speakers, delivering an address that would later be published in an issue of *Dialogue* devoted to Gene.[3]

A major loss struck us again during August of 2003 with the accidental death of my brother Roald. On our trips to Utah Althea and I had consistently lodged with Roald and Luana in West Point. On our visits I went walking with Roald at six every morning and later leaned on the pole fence at his corral watching while he fed his dog, two horses, chickens, and pigeons. I worried about him. He had abandoned the effort to keep trim and fit, accumulating close to 280 pounds on a frame of six foot four. "What am I saving myself for?" he grimly asked when Luana chided him for not observing a healthy diet. His ankles swelled and he limped painfully. At the end of every visit, Althea and I wondered if he would be alive when we came back.

In early August 2003, Karrin and Mark and their boys drove to Utah with us, and we stayed with Roald and Luana for a few days. Lars struck it off well with Roald, gathering eggs with him in the hen coop and sitting by him on a bench and receiving instruction on solstices and equinoxes. I myself sat on that bench with Roald on a Sunday morning after he had already put on the white shirt he would wear to church. Blur, Roald's large black horse, put his head over the pole fence, hanging it within inches of Roald's face, a thing he often did for minutes at a time, as Roald told me. This time he snorted a shower of alfalfa-tinted saliva across Roald's white shirt. Then he turned his rump to his vexed but acquiescent master and waited for a belly scratch with a stick Roald kept handy for just this purpose. Obviously, man and horse had an affection for each other.

On the following Tuesday morning, we followed Karrin and Mark to Charles's cabin in Pine Valley, intending to return on Friday so that Karrin could attend the twentieth-year reunion of her high school class in Ogden. Before we left for southern Utah, I walked with Roald at dawn, watched him care for his animals in the early slant of the sun, and, returning to the house, ate a breakfast of fried eggs and toast, which he prepared. A little later, he and Luana stood on their porch and waved good-bye. Planning on a speedy return, Althea and I didn't consider that this might be our last good-bye.

On Thursday, Leon and Gussie joined us at Charles's cabin among the piñons. They were preparing for a second eighteen-month mission to Thailand and wanted to say good-bye. They intended to catch Roald for a good-bye after entering the Missionary Training Center in Provo at the end of the month. The next day, a little before noon we said another round of good-byes. While we were taking photos, Althea said, "Roald ought to be in this lineup." Unknown to us at about this moment our grievously injured brother was dying in an Ogden hospital, Luana and her children having just made the decision to remove him from life support. On the previous afternoon, following a ride in the mountains, he fell asleep at the wheel of his pickup on a rural freeway. His horse trailer separated from the pickup before the latter rolled over. Strangely, the trailer came to rest, upright and with the horses uninjured, on top of the pickup in the median. Inside the crushed cab, Roald was battered beyond recovery.

The coffin was closed at the viewing on Monday evening. Luana and their children received condolences and expressions of respect for five hours. Lars asked me where the body was. I led him to the coffin and explained why it wasn't open. He wept. The funeral was held on Tuesday in a stake center less than a quarter mile from Roald's house. Both meeting hall and adjoining recreation hall were filled to capacity.

On the Saturday before Roald died, the descendants of Luana's parents had gathered for their annual reunion in the West Point city park. We travelers from the Northwest were there, having arrived the night before. Among the participants was Jim McFarlane, husband of Luana's twin sister, Lolita. Jim told us later that as he had seated himself beside Roald at a picnic table, Roald said, "Jim, we're running out of sunsets." It was just like Roald to say that. He often spoke in metaphor. Sunsets stood for all the things that make life bearable. During the early decades of their residence in West Point, Roald and Luana looked out their kitchen window at brilliant sunsets developing over the Great Salt Lake. Later, houses were built in the alfalfa field across the street and blocked their view. But I don't think his obstructed view was on Roald's mind when he spoke to Jim. Old age was on his mind. A distinct melancholy is reserved for old people. In poetry it creates elegy, which celebrates the beauty that used to be. The young can appreciate nostalgia too. But the old specialize in it.

I find it helps enormously to be attached to Lars and Hans. They have a future and therefore I do too, as I was reminded by a minor episode at Roald's burial. Sixty or seventy people were crowded around the open grave. An honor guard from Hill Air Force Base stood at attention before the coffin. Commands were given. Airmen folded an American flag that had covered the coffin and handed it to Luana. A bugler sounded taps. Perhaps thirty yards away, a rank of airmen, with rifles aimed into the air in the direction of the crowd, prepared to fire. Just then, Hans bolted from the crowd and ran toward the riflemen. Karrin, Mark, Althea, and I all dashed after him, I in the lead. I got to him just as the first volley was fired. He began to cry. I picked him up and tried to cover his ears while a second volley boomed. Hans elevated the decibels of his protest. Then the leader ordered the squad to face about and fire their final volley in the opposite direction. I don't know whether this was normal protocol or a gesture designed to reduce the crash of the volley in Hans's ears. Regardless, the solemnity of the occasion was demolished as far as I was concerned. As I carried Hans away at a run, I began to laugh, my grief effaced by my desperate effort to quiet the disturbance Hans was bent on making. There is something refreshing about the indifference of the very young to protocol and propriety. With Hans about, I couldn't take even a burial too seriously.

Something else that helps me retain a modicum of cheerfulness about being old is the resilience I see among other old people. For example, I am happy to report that, after three and a half years of loneliness, Charles remarried during the spring of 2004. His new spouse is May Kemp, a neighbor whose husband died not long before Betty. Althea and I quickly became attached to May when we first met her on an auto trip to St. George in March. In mid-April, we returned to St. George by air and drove on to Snowflake with Charles and May to attend a formal celebration of the ninetieth birthday of our sister Wanda. Only three days before our trip to Snowflake, Charles and May decided to make it the occasion of their wedding, performed, as it turned out, by our cousin Fred Peterson, justice of the peace.

What is to be said now by way of some final reflections on the themes and preoccupations of my life? Am I satisfied with what has happened? What more is to be said on wilderness, on my vexed and vexing relationship with Mormonism, and on my family?

It was my interest in wilderness that led me into the writing of this autobiography in the first place. Ironically, as I have said, wilderness has steadily waned in importance, both as a theme in this work and as a fact in my life. For a long time now, I have been preoccupied by human relationships that are not routine and secure enough to free my mind for thinking much about wilderness. Furthermore, my opportunities to be in wild places have dwindled greatly.

Relentlessly, with little reservation, the Euro-American civilization into which I was born has transformed the wild into the domesticated. Wherever I have traveled, wherever I have lived, I have seen steady *development*—that is, the turning of wild or rural places into roads, buildings, and countless other human artifacts. I have only to return to Snowflake to be starkly reminded of this truth, or, for that matter, to the neighborhoods in which I lived in Provo, Berkeley, Salt Lake City, and Ogden. I have only to walk out my condo door and look down the street to see a hillside on which looming megahouses have within a mere six years replaced a flourishing forest. This ultimate generalization about my culture saddens me, of course. Though I have been preoccupied by many things other than wilderness, still it ranks high in the hierarchy of my personal values. I regret that Lars and Hans will find and relish less of it.

Despite all that, I rejoice that I have experienced as much of the benign wild as I have. The nearby wild touches and blesses my existence in Washington as it did in Utah. On the Olympic coast I have watched a gray, angry surf toss gigantic tree trunks about like matchsticks. I have hiked in the rugged Cascades from trailheads lying an hour or less from where I live. I have gone snowshoeing with Karrin and Mark beneath the snow-laden boughs of towering firs and cedars. But far more often—almost daily, in fact—I enjoy brief accessions of what I called the backyard wilderness when I lived in Ogden. The greenbelt running through Forest Village continues to delight us. Hiking the edge of its forested ravine, we can hear the sibilant rush of the creek a hundred yards below. We have seen owls, woodpeckers, opossums, weasels, voles, mice, and a variety of songbirds. I have mentioned the coyote family we saw during our first summer here. A couple of years later, another pair of coyotes denned in the ravine, and we saw them and their pups along the road. I saw an adult bear on one occasion and a half-grown cub on another. I saw the adult bear at the head of the ravine, about three hundred yards from our condo door.

Lars and I heard coyotes one night when he was sleeping over. We lay on pads on the living room floor, still awake. Lars didn't recognize the sounds, but I did. I called him to an open window, and we listened. I remembered a camp at City of Rocks in Idaho long ago when Lars's mother was his age or a little younger. Althea and Karrin were asleep inside the camper. I sat on the tailgate of the pickup, enjoying my thoughts. An astonishing relay of coyote sounds—yips, barks, something close to off-key howls—ricocheted through the moon-drenched night from coyotes in at least three places. At the window with Lars or sitting beside a camper in which his mother-to-be slept, I heard the same sounds—ancient, primordial, forever wild.

What more is to be said about my relationship with Mormonism?

As I have said, the closest friends Althea and I have in the Northwest are Mormons, active and inactive. Certainly I have intensified my engagement with Mormonism, quite unexpectedly, by becoming editor of *Dialogue*. I often fancy that, just as my relatives and friends are called to be missionaries and temple workers, I have been called to oversee this forum for a wide-ranging study of Mormonism.

As for my attitude toward the church, it remains steady. I have undergone little change from 1982, when I read my essay "The Civilizing of Mormondom: The Indispensable Role of the Intellectual" before a session of the Association for Mormon Letters. In that essay, I said that, like all other cultures, the Mormon Church stands in need of continual change for the better. Now as then, I think people who are both faithful to Mormonism yet believe in the free play of the mind are the most effective agents of beneficial change within the church. I admit that a frightful attrition occurs among the ranks of liberal Mormons. Sooner or later, disillusionment threatens their enthusiasm if not their membership. The strength of my position in the cause of liberal Mormonism is that I underwent my disillusionment long, long ago, beginning in late 1954 with my arrival in the French mission. I am rarely astonished by anything church authorities do to stifle independent thought and initiative among church members. I have expected it from the start.

I grant a certain degree of perversity in my insistence on taking an active role in the liberal Mormon cause. I could enjoy the social benefits of Mormonism simply by loitering in the background, attending meetings and associating with the multitude of relatives and friends who have anchored me to Mormonism all along. There is indeed some ego in my determination to exert an influence upon the restrictive ethos to which their love and friendship have shackled me. That influence is, of course, in the direction of making the church a more hospitable home for the likes of Gene England and Lavina Fielding Anderson.

What more is to be said about the primacy of family and friends in the overall account of my life?

I am a social animal, first and foremost. Unquestionably, family and friends have been and remain the center of my existence, especially family. I ended an early chapter from this book with this sentence: "It was a blessing to grow up with the sense that a large, inclusive family is a fixed feature of the cosmos, its ranks filled with persons to whom you can rightfully turn for any necessity." During these seventy years I have not lost my appetite for being among my relatives. My siblings have often remarked on the assiduousness with which Althea and I have maintained our connections with them. Without rancor, I will observe that she and I have initiated the majority of our visits. The simple truth is, I think, that we need them more than they need us. It doesn't bother me to admit that fact. I am happy that they have affectionately responded to our initiatives.

Often when I drive to Ballard and take Gerhard shopping, he and I have a meal at an inexpensive restaurant. I see solitary diners there, most of them elderly. They are implacably somber, as if they survive only by cauterizing the enormity of their loneliness. Loneliness is another quality in which the elderly excel. Like any other skill, the skill for creating attachments atrophies with age. I don't think even younger Americans manage this skill well. Unfortunately, all too often they fail to cultivate that built-in source of attachments, an extended family. Spouses sequester themselves into nuclear families; then, finding themselves incompatible with one another, split their nuclear families. Long before they are old, they begin to know what loneliness is. I saw my mother work at keeping strong the ties of her extended family, and I internalized the impulse, as has Althea. We have worked at conveying this value to Karrin, who I think is equally determined to convey it to Lars and Hans. The benefits of maintaining family ties are moral as well as practical. I for one feel a deep propriety about the instinct for family. It is the voice of nature, confirming that my first obligation is to my genetic kind.

From that branch of my extended family deriving from my father and mother I count not only twelve siblings but also sixty-four nephews and nieces who are alive or who lived long enough for me to know them. All my siblings have been closely attached to Mormonism, as have been the large majority of my nephews and nieces. How have I managed to maintain a close, affectionate relationship with all of them despite my evident violation of a good many of the commandments they adhere to?

The chief commandment I have failed to respect is temple marriage. Althea's presence in the family these forty-seven years after our wedding is a constant reminder that, according to their strong conviction, I will not be among them in eternity. Althea and I will be consigned to a lesser kingdom. Even there, it is possible that, not being married in the temple, we will not be allowed to be together. Though none of them speak of this matter, I know they think about it. They wouldn't be Mormons if they didn't. As I have said, I need this distinction between us. A telling sign that I don't believe as they do has been essential to my continuing affection for them. To their credit, they have accepted me on these terms. And, as I have shown over and over in the preceding pages, they have accepted Althea.

One day years ago, I was startled to receive a letter from my sister Lenora, who rarely wrote letters. It contained a single sentence: "Thanks for bringing Althea into the family." Needless to say, I was touched to the point of tears. It was, of course, a high tribute to Althea, who from the start made her own way into the affections of my brothers and sisters. That I have myself managed to stay there is shown by a statement of Charles's son Joe, who reported that a friend of his, who knew of my doings on the liberal Mormon circuit, asked him how my family responded to me. "The family has its reservations about what Levi writes," Joe told his friend. "But it has no reservations about Levi." Again I was deeply touched.

For whatever it is worth, I will add that I have no anxiety over being separated from my loved ones in eternity. If I awaken from death into the miracle of eternal life, I will expect to be greeted by all of them, including Althea. I know very little about what God is, but I know a great deal about what God is not. God will not be so petty and mean-spirited as to deny those who have loved each other in mortality to continue their love in immortality. It is love that sanctifies and seals a relationship, not a ritual conducted before an altar made by human beings.

The account of any life followed far enough turns tragic. That is a simple fact. All the more reason, then, to end this account of my life now. I am glad to have lived. I have been very lucky. I have had love and friendship in abundance. I haven't suffered more affliction or tragedy than I could bear. I have been largely able to live up to the primary dictates of my conscience. I have enjoyed a sufficient livelihood. I chose a profession that satisfied me, and I have no regrets whatsoever as to Weber State, the locale where I pursued that profession.

I consider myself a religious person. I have been blessed with reverence and with a sense of the sacred. I believe in the natural, though I often yearn for the supernatural. I believe in the scientific worldview, though it offers no answers to ultimate questions. Despite the astounding accomplishments of a technology devolving from the scientific worldview, nature stolidly deflects the senses, defying any human attempt to peer into its essence. In closing this autobiography, I recognize the absolute mystery underlying existence. It has always seemed to me a vast anomaly that anything exists. No one can explain why nature has uttered this brown, blue, and green planet called Earth and called forth living things to inhabit its land, water, and atmosphere. Nonetheless, I am grateful to be among those living things. I have seen my share of sunsets. I rejoice in the prospect of a few more. I hope, most ardently, for the resolve to be at peace when my last is upon me.

◆ ◆ ◆

Notes

Chapter 1. My Ancestors

1. Lynn M. Hilton, comp., *Levi Savage, Jr. Journal* (Salt Lake City: John Savage Family Organization, 1966), 75.

2. Levi S. Peterson, "A Mormon and Wilderness: The Saga of the Savages," *Sunstone* 17, no. 18 (December 1979): 69–72. The present chapter draws upon parts of this essay.

Chapter 2. That Failed Anthropologist, My Father

1. Parts of this chapter are drawn from my essay "The Native American," *Weber Studies* 10, no. 3 (Fall 1993): 101–15.

2. H. R. Voth, *The Oraibi Summer Snake Ceremony,* Anthropological Series 3.4 (Chicago: Field Columbian Museum, 1903).

3. Theodora Kroeber, *Alfred Kroeber: A Personal Configuration* (Berkeley and Los Angeles: University of California Press, 1970), 51.

4. Joseph Peterson to Lydia Savage Smith, typescript of letter, ca. July 30, 1924, Joseph Peterson File, Levi S. Peterson Collection, Archives, Weber State University, Ogden, Utah. Hereafter cited as LSP Collection.

5. Joseph Peterson to A. L. Kroeber, typescript of letters in the Phoebe A. Hearst Museum of Anthropology, University of California at Berkeley, Joseph Peterson File, LSP Collection.

6. *Geronimo,* manuscript of high school pageant, 1939, Joseph Peterson File, LSP Collection.

Chapter 3. The Ranch

1. Joseph Peterson to Arley Peterson, October 30, 1910, photocopy, Joseph Peterson File, LSP Collection.

2. J. Arley Peterson, interview by Charles S. Peterson, "Farming and Homesteading of Joseph Peterson," April 9, 1972, Western Studies Oral History Community Improvement through Local History: Kellogg Project, Department of History, Utah State University, Logan, photocopy, Joseph Peterson File, LSP Collection.

3. Department of Interior, Homestead Entry, U.S. Land Office, Phoenix, AZ, no. 0190, Final Proof, Testimony of Claimant, Receipt no. 962691, Joseph Peterson, November 19, 1912, U.S. Homestead Record Center, Suitland, MD.

4. Joseph Peterson to Arley Peterson, August 10, 1916, Joseph Peterson File, LSP Collection.

5. Elwood Peterson, "History of Elwood Lynn Peterson," dittoed document, n.p., n.d., 7–8, Joseph Peterson File, LSP Collection.

6. Leora Peterson Schuck, *Leora's Quest: Lakeside and Beyond* (self-published, 1980), 70. I rely greatly on this articulate and detailed autobiography for the history of the family at Lakeside and Holbrook.

7. Wanda Peterson Tenney, comp., *Histories of Joseph, Amanda A., and Lydia S. Peterson,* photocopied anthology of letters, genealogy, photographs, reminiscences, diary extracts, and personal narratives about the Peterson, Andelin, and Savage families, hardbound, 1998. Personal note added to "Excerpt from Diary of Loretta Hansen." Though loosely organized and without page numbering, this vast work is replete with useful information. For example, it reproduces more than a hundred letters exchanged between Joseph and Amanda in 1897 and 1898.

8. Schuck, *Leora's Quest,* 72.

9. Ibid., 80–81.

10. Ibid., 83–84.

11. E. Peterson, "History of Elwood Peterson," 10.

Chapter 4. My Mother's First Marriage

1. Lydia S. Peterson, "Autobiography of Lydia Jane Savage Peterson," photocopied typescript, 1980, 25. In the present chapter I have amplified my memories, tenaciously gathered from conversations with my mother over many years, by frequent reference to this eighty-page autobiography.

2. Ibid., 26.

3. Ibid., 27.

4. Ibid., 28.

5. Ibid.

6. Samuel F. Smith to Lydia S. Smith, July 7, 1916, photocopy, My Mother's First Marriage File, LSP Collection.

7. L. S. Peterson, "Autobiography," 29.

8. Lydia S. Smith to Lydia Lenora Savage, n.d., photocopy, My Mother's First Marriage File, LSP Collection.

9. L. S. Peterson, "Autobiography," 30.

10. Ibid.

11. Quoted in Lydia S. Smith to Levi M. and Lydia Lenora Savage, September 6, 1916, photocopy, My Mother's First Marriage File, LSP Collection.

12. Jesse N. Smith III to Lydia S. Smith, September 15, 1916, telegram, photocopy, My Mother's First Marriage File, LSP Collection.

13. L. S. Peterson, "Autobiography," 33.

CHAPTER 5. The Family I Was Born Into

1. Joseph Peterson to Lydia S. Smith, January 23, 1924, Joseph Peterson File, LSP Collection.

CHAPTER 9. My Early College Years

1. An earlier version of this chapter, titled "My Early College Years: From the Autobiography of Levi S. Peterson," was published in *Dialogue: A Journal of Mormon Thought* 33, no. 3 (Fall 2000): 153–69.

2. Bertrand Russell, "A Free Man's Worship," in *Patterns for Living,* edited by Oscar James Campbell, Justine Van Gundy, and Caroline Shrodes, 3d ed. (New York: Macmillan, 1949), 343–49.

3. LSP, "Journal: A Record of My Life," vol. 1, 1952–1954, January 6, February 4, 1953, Journals/Diaries File, LSP Collection.

4. Ibid., November 23, 1953.

5. Ibid., December 24, 1953.

6. Ibid., March 11, 1954.

7. Ibid., vol. 2, April 28, 1954.

8. Ibid., May 10, 1954.

9. Ibid., May 1, 1954.

10. Ibid., October 9, 1954.

11. Ibid.

12. Ibid.

CHAPTER 10. A Missionary

1. LSP, "Journal," vol. 2, December 17, 1954, Journals/Diaries File, LSP Collection.

2. LSP, "Missionary Journal," February 23, 1955, Journals/Diaries File, LSP Collection.

3. Harold W. Lee to LSP, August 24, 1955, Correspondence File, LSP Collection. Unless otherwise noted, all letters cited throughout this book are in this chronologically arranged file.

4. LSP to Lydia Peterson, August 27, 1955.

5. Jerry Brown to Lydia Peterson, May 2, 1955.

6. LSP to Lydia Peterson, December 18, 1955.

7. Ibid., August 6, 1956.

8. Ibid., August 1, 1956.

CHAPTER 11. Althea

1. Althea Sand to LSP, July 6, 1957, Althea Sand File, LSP Collection. Letters from Althea cited hereafter are in this file.

2. LSP to Althea Sand, August 29, 1957; Althea Sand to LSP, September 2, 1957.
3. LSP to Althea Sand, July 19, 1957.
4. Ibid., August 2, 1957.
5. Ibid.
6. Ibid., August 13, 1957.
7. Ibid., August 11, 25, 1957.
8. Ibid., September 10, 1957.
9. Althea Sand to LSP, November 20, 1957.
10. Ibid., December 3, 1957.
11. LSP to Althea Sand, July 3, September 17, 1957.

CHAPTER 12. Nebo by Moonlight

1. LSP to Larry and Louise Peterson, February 16, 1959.
2. LSP to Roald Peterson, April 15, 1961.
3. LSP to Arvid and Stella Sand, June 16, 1961.
4. Ibid., June 26, 1961.
5. LSP to Leon Peterson, July 3, 1961.

CHAPTER 13. A Grasshopper's Way of Life

1. LSP, "The Development of Utah Livestock Law, 1849–1896," *Utah Historical Quarterly* 32, no. 3 (Summer 1964): 198–216.
2. LSP to Peterson Family Newsletter, January 20, 1964.

CHAPTER 15. An Entire Landscape of Possibilities

1. Lydia Peterson to LSP, January 23, 1966.
2. LSP, "The Primitive and the Civilized in Western Fiction," *Western American Literature* 1, no. 3 (Fall 1966): 197–207.
3. LSP, "Tragedy and Western American Literature," *Western American Literature* 6, no. 4 (Winter 1972): 243–49.
4. LSP to Leon Peterson, October 11, 1970.

CHAPTER 17. Becoming a Writer

1. LSP, "The Confessions of Augustine," *Denver Quarterly* 12, no. 4 (Winter 1978): 35–55; LSP, "Road to Damascus," *Dialogue: A Journal of Mormon Thought* 11, no. 4 (Winter 1978): 88–89.

CHAPTER 18. Putting a Pathology to Use

1. LSP, "Wilderness and Isolation," unpublished manuscript, October 20, 1970, box 6, folder 17, p. 15, LSP Collection.

CHAPTER 19. *The Canyons of Grace*

1. LPS to Don Walker, July 20, 1980.

2. Joan Washburn to LSP, October 1, 1980; Lydia Peterson to LSP, November 23, 1980.

3. LSP to Peggy Fletcher and Allen Roberts, February 18, 1980.

4. LSP introduction to *Greening Wheat: Fifteen Mormon Short Stories* (Midvale, UT: Orion Books, 1983), ix–x.

5. LSP to Charles Peterson, February 5, 1982.

6. Leon Peterson to LSP, September 23, 1970.

7. LSP, "The Civilizing of Mormondom: The Indispensable Role of the Intellectual," *Sunstone* 7, no. 3 (May–June 1982): 9.

8. LSP to Lydia Peterson, April 21, 1983.

9. Leora Schuck to LSP, January 29, 1983.

10. Lydia Peterson to LSP, January 19, 1983.

11. Mary Ray to LSP, February 28, 1983.

12. LSP to Mary Ray, March 22, 1982.

CHAPTER 20. *The Backslider*

1. LSP to Linda Sillitoe, March 24, 1982.

2. LSP to Karrin Peterson, November 3, 1983.

3. LSP to Leora Schuck, January 8, 1984.

4. Kathleen Anderson to LSP, July 18, 1984.

5. LSP to Bruce Jorgensen et al., November 1, 1984.

6. Nat Sobel to LSP, May 5, 1986.

7. Lenora Hansen to LSP, December 17, 1986.

CHAPTER 21. My Mother's House

1. LSP to Marcella Peterson, August 17, 1986.

2. LSP to Don and Marjorie Walker, August 13, 1986.

3. LSP to Leon Peterson, October 13, 1986.

4. LSP to Mary Ray, June 18, 1987; Mary Ray to LSP, June 25, 1987.

5. LSP, "My Mother's House," *Dialogue: A Journal of Mormon Thought* 24, no. 3 (Fall 1991): 79–88.

CHAPTER 22. Juanita Brooks

1. LSP, "Juanita Brooks: The Mormon Historian as Tragedian," *Journal of Mormon History* 3 (1977): 47–54.

2. LSP, *Juanita Brooks: Mormon Woman Historian* (Salt Lake City: University of Utah Press, 1988), 284.

3. LSP, "A Tribute to *Dialogue*," *Dialogue: A Journal of Mormon Thought* 21, no. 2 (Summer 1988): 141.

4. LSP, "A Christian by Yearning," in *The Wilderness of Faith*, edited by John Sillito (Salt Lake City: Signature Books, 1991), 132. First published in *Sunstone* 12 (September 1988): 19–22.

5. LSP to Mignon Probst, February 18, 1989; Tracie Lamb-Kwon to LSP, April 20, 1989.

6. Don Walker to LSP, September 25, 1988.

CHAPTER 23. *Night Soil*

1. LSP, "Night Soil," in *Night Soil: New Stories* (Salt Lake City: Signature Books, 1990), 192.

2. LSP, "The Third Nephite" in ibid., 19.

3. Alexandra R. Haslam and Gerald W. Haslam, comps., *Where Coyotes Howl and Wind Blows Free: Growing Up in the West* (Reno: University of Nevada Press, 1995), 57–73.

4. LSP, notes, December 4, 1989, Correspondence File, LSP Collection. Notes identified only by date will be found chronologically filed in my Correspondence File.

5. LSP, "Night Soil," 188.

6. Gary Bergera to LSP, September 10, 1990; LSP to Gary Bergera, July 23, 1990; LSP, notes, September 16, 1990.

7. Marilyn Abildskov, "A Local Author Spins Some Earthy Tales in New Book," *Ogden Standard-Examiner,* December 2, 1999, 4E.

8. LSP, diary, December 8, 1990, Journals/Diaries File, LSP Collection. All diaries cited hereafter may be found in this file.

9. Eugene England, "A Coming of Age," *This People* (Summer 1990): 38; England, review of *Night Soil, Weber Studies* 8, no. 2 (Fall 1991): 99.

CHAPTER 24. Our Compass Swings Northwest

1. LSP, diary, July 31, 1990.

2. Linda Sillitoe to LSP, December 31, 1990.

3. LSP, diary, July 3, 1991.

4. LSP to Marylee Mitcham, October 8, 1991.

5. LSP, notes, July 24, 1991.

6. LSP, diary, September 6, 1992.

7. Ibid., December 26, 1992.

CHAPTER 25. A Stillborn Book

1. LSP, "Notes on Wilderness," November 7, 1989, Wilderness Essays File, LSP Collection.

2. LSP, "A Woodlot on the Wasatch," manuscript essay, August 21, 1995, Woodlot on the Wasatch File, LSP Collection.

3. LSP, "A Mormon Evolutionist and the Wild God's Grace," *Sunstone* 14, no. 4 (August 1990): 28.

4. Ibid., 27.

5. Ibid., 30.

6. LSP to Don Walker, July 22, 1990, Economics File, LSP Collection.

7. LSP, "Tour of Geneva Steel," August 29, 1990, in ibid.

8. LSP, "Visit to the Pumps on the Great Salt Lake," September 7, 1990, in ibid.

9. LSP, "Visit to Bingham Open Pit Copper Mine," notes, September 9, 1990, in ibid.

10. LSP, "Notes on the Difficulty of Defining Wilderness," November 13, 1990, Defining Wilderness File, LSP Collection.

11. LSP, "Wild Words," unpublished essay, August 23, 1992, Wild Words File, LSP Collection.

12. LSP, "Notes on the Laws of Physics," June 22, 1991, with hand-written notes dated July 27, 1991, in Wilderness Journal: Redaction 1991 File, LSP Collection.

13. LSP, "Entries from a Wilderness Journal," July 29, 1991, unpublished entry for May 7, 1972, in ibid.

14. LSP, "Hike to Timpanogos, unpublished essay, August 16, 1991, Hike to Timpanogos File, LSP Collection. Published version slightly revised and retitled "Hiking to Timpanogos: How Charity, Affection, and Sex Are Killing the Wilderness," *Sunstone* 16, no. 6 (November 1993): 22–30.

15. LSP, "Notes toward a Preface," September 1, 1992, Transition to Autobiography File, LSP Collection.

16. LSP, "Notes on Third Person Wilderness Autobiography," September 13, 1992, Transition to Autobiography File, LSP Collection.

17. LSP, "The Native American," *Weber Studies* 10, no. 3 (Fall 1993): 101–15.

CHAPTER 26. Retrenchment on the Liberal Mormon Front

1. Eugene England, "On Spectral Evidence, Scapegoating, and False Accusation," in *Making Peace: Personal Essays* (Salt Lake City: Signature Books, 1995), 23–42.

2. LSP, "The Art of Dissent among the Mormons," *Sunstone* 16, no. 8 (February 1994): 39.

3. LSP, "Lavina Fielding Anderson and the Power of a Church in Exile," *Dialogue: A Journal of Mormon Thought* 29, no. 4 (Winter 1996): 169–78.

4. LSP, "Art of Dissent," 39.

5. LSP, "The Literary Qualities of *Across the Wide Missouri*," unpublished essay, February 16, 1994, De Voto File, LSP Collection; Bernard De Voto, *Across the Wide Missouri* (Boston: Houghton Mifflin, 1947), 303.

6. Patricia Nelson Limerick to LSP, June 11, 1994, De Voto File, LSP Collection.

7. LSP, "Notes on Patricia Limerick's *Legacy of Conquest*," April 16, 1994, in ibid.

8. LSP, diary, April 19, 1994.

9. LSP, "Notes on My Mother and the Wild," May 10, 1994, My Mother's First Marriage File, LSP Collection.

10. LSP, "My Mother's First Marriage," unpublished manuscript, p. 14, in ibid.

11. LSP, "Phone Conversation with My Sister Lenora Hansen, 9:30 p.m.," in ibid.

12. LSP, diary, July 27, 1994.

13. Ibid., January 4, 1995.

14. LSP, "Subduing the Barbarian: Freshman English at Weber State," in *Weber State College: A Centennial History,* edited by Richard Sadler (Salt Lake City: Publisher's Press, 1988), 240–46; LSP, diary, November 21, 1994.

15. Ibid., December 12, 1994.

16. Ibid., December 22, 1994.

CHAPTER 27. Armchair Mountaineer

1. *Accidents in North American Mountaineering,* published annually by the American Alpine Club of Golden, Colorado, and the Alpine Club of Canada of Banff, Alberta.

2. Joe Tasker, *Savage Arena* (New York: St. Martin's Press, 1982), 255, 256.

3. LSP, "Is It Wilder on the Summits? Meanings of Wilderness for Mountaineers," draft essay, November 11, 1994, p. 11, Mountaineering File, LSP Collection.

4. LSP, "Climbing Peaks of Another Sort," unpublished essay, in ibid. Much of the following narrative is drawn verbatim from this essay.

5. LSP, "Bio. Report on Trek to Gannett Peak," typescript of handwritten diary, August 13, 1994, in ibid.

CHAPTER 28. *Aspen Marooney*

1. LSP, diary, March 17, April 16, 1995.

2. Ibid., June 6, 1995.

3. Ibid.

4. Ibid., June 15, 1995.

5. Ibid., August 29, September 2, 3, October 11, 1995.

6. Robert H. Van Wagoner to LSP, January 12, 1996, Aspen Marooney File, LSP Collection; "Levi's Tribe of Outsiders," *Deseret News,* January 14, 1996, E1, E8; Richard H. Cracroft, comment on AML-List, December 29, 1995; LSP, "Adaptation for a Reading at the Marriott Library, University of Utah," unpublished manuscript, February 11, 1996, Aspen Marooney File, LSP Collection.

7. LSP to writing group, July 10, 1992, Aspen Marooney File, LSP Collection.

8. LSP, "Notes on My Comrades' Critique of Early Chapters of Aspen Marooney," unpublished notes, April 27, 1993, in ibid.

9. LSP, diary, August 24, 25, 1995.

10. Ibid., August 27, 30, 1995.

11. Benson Y. Parkinson, review of *Aspen Marooney, Weber Studies* 13, no. 3 (Fall 1996): 134.

CHAPTER 29. Good-bye to Utah

1. LSP, diary, June 3, 1997.

2. Ibid., October 2, 1997.

3. Ibid., March 5, 1998.

4. Ibid., January 27, 1997.

5. LSP, "Bachelor Stallions of the Cedar Mountains," unpublished story, 1992, 2. Revision of version of October 13, 1996. Bachelor Stallions File, LSP Collection.

6. Ibid., 5.

7. LSP, diary, October 20, 1996.

8. Ibid.

9. LSP, "Chapter Two: Bound for the City, Fed on the Wild," unpublished manuscript, March 4, 1993, Boyhood File, LSP Collection; LSP, diary, January 25, 1997.

10. LSP, "Chronology of My Life, 1951–1954," unpublished notes, January 16, 1997, 1, Autobiography 1951–1954 File, LSP Collection.

11. LSP, "In Favor of Candor," unpublished address, August 4, 2003, Evans Biography Address 2003 File, LSP Collection. My comments on candor are drawn in part from this address, which I delivered at a biography workshop at Utah State University.

12. LSP, diary, March 19, 1997.

13. Ibid., July 30, 1997.

14. Ibid., August 2, 1997.

15. Ibid., October 5, 1997.

16. Ibid., October 9, November 3, 4, 1997.

17. Ibid., September 13, 1998.

18. Ibid., February 10, 1999.

19. Ibid., March 2, 1999.

20. Ibid., July 15, 1999.

21. Ibid., March 24, July 22, March 24, July 22, 1999.

22. Ibid., August 13, 1999.

23. Ibid., December 16, 19, 1999.

24. Ibid., October 14, 1999.

25. Ibid., September 22, 1999.

CHAPTER 30. Running Out of Sunsets

1. LSP, diary, January 23, 2001.

2. Ibid., August 11, 2001.

3. LSP, "Salvaged for Mormonism," *Dialogue: A Journal of Mormon Thought* 35, no. 1 (Spring 2002): 10.

• • •

Levi S. Peterson: A Bibliography

Books

1982 *The Canyons of Grace*. Urbana: University of Illinois Press; reprinted by Orion Books, a division of Signature Books, Midvale, Utah, n.d. [stories]

1983 *Greening Wheat: Fifteen Mormon Short Stories*, edited by Levi S. Peterson. Midvale, Utah: Orion Books, a division of Signature Books. [anthology]

1986 *The Backslider*. Salt Lake City: Signature Books; reprinted 1990 as a mass market paperback. [novel]

1988 *Juanita Brooks: Mormon Woman Historian*. Salt Lake City: The University of Utah Press. [biography]

1990 *Night Soil: New Stories*. Salt Lake City: Signature Books. [stories]

1995 *Aspen Marooney*. Salt Lake City: Signature Books. [novel]

Stories

1957 "Le Visage de la Vie." *Wye* 16, no. 1 (Fall): 20–23.

1958 "Justice on the Salt, 1865." *Wye* 16, no. 3 (Spring): 2–5.

1978 "The Confessions of Augustine." *Denver Quarterly* 12, no. 4 (Winter): 35–55; reprinted in *The Canyons of Grace*, 1–26.

1978 "Road to Damascus." *Dialogue: A Journal of Mormon Thought* 11, no. 4 (Winter): 88–99; reprinted in *The Canyons of Grace*, 35–56.

1981 "Trinity." *Ascent* 7, no. 1: 1–8; reprinted in *The Canyons of Grace*, 27–34.

1981 "The Shriveprice." *Sunstone* 6, no. 4 (September–October): 50–58; reprinted in *The Canyons of Grace*, 57–78.

1982 "The Canyons of Grace." *Ascent* 7, no. 3 (Spring): 1–34; reprinted in *The Canyons of Grace*, 102–35; and in *Great & Peculiar Beauty*, edited by Thomas Lyon & Terry Tempest Williams, 791–823 (Salt Lake City: Gibbs-Smith Publisher, 1995); reprinted fragment from "Canyons of Grace" in *Stories and Stone*, edited by Reuben Ellis, 185–92 (Boulder, Colorado: Pruett Publishing Company, 1997).

1982 "The Gift." *Dialogue: A Journal of Mormon Thought* 15, no. 2 (Summer): 92–117; reprinted in *Greening Wheat: Fifteen Mormon Short Stories*, 91–117.

1985 "Night Soil." *Utah Holiday* 15 (December): 6, 83–88; reprinted in *Night Soil: New Stories*, 177–92.

1986 "Sunswath." *Sunstone* 10, no. 12: 13–22; reprinted in *Night Soil: New Stories*, 117–42.

1986 "The Third Nephite." *Dialogue: A Journal of Mormon Thought* 19, no. 4 (Winter): 159–71; reprinted in *Night Soil: New Stories*, 19–39.

1988 "The Newsboy." *Weber Studies* 5 (Fall): 41–57; reprinted in *Night Soil* 1–18; and in *Where Coyotes Howl and Wind Blows Free,* edited by Alexandra R. Haslam and Gerald W. Haslam, 57–73 (Reno: University of Nevada Press, 1995).

1992 "Durfey Renews an Interest in Rodeo." *Utah Holiday* 22, no. 2 (December): 44–49; reprinted in *In Our Lovely Deseret: Mormon Fictions*, edited by Robert Raleigh, 47–61 (Salt Lake City: Signature Books, 1998).

1992 "The Christianizing of Coburn Heights" in *Bright Angels and Familiars: Contemporary Mormon Stories,* edited by Eugene England. Salt Lake City: Signature Books, 109–32; first published in *The Canyons of Grace*, 79–101.

1993 "Elaine and Durfey Visit the Old Farm." *Rough Draft* (Spring): 7–11.

Articles and Essays

1964 "The Development of Utah Livestock Law, 1848–1896." *Utah Historical Quarterly* 32, no. 3 (Summer): 198–216.

1966 "The Primitive and the Civilized in Western Fiction." *Western American Literature* 1, no. 3 (Fall): 197–207.

1972 "Tragedy and Western American Literature." *Western American Literature* 6, no. 4 (Winter): 243–49.

1974 "Wilderness Journal." *Rocky Mountain Review* 2: 6–11.

1975 "Wilderness Journal." *Rocky Mountain Review* 3: 52–55.

1976 "Juanita Brooks: The Mormon Historian as Tragedian." *Journal of Mormon History* 3: 47–54; reprinted in *Tending the Garden*, edited by Eugene England and Lavina Fielding Anderson, 135–45 (Salt Lake City: Signature Books, 1996).

1977 "Editorial." *Encyclia* 54, no. 1 (Spring): v–vi; reprinted in *Encyclia: A Retrospective - 75th Anniversary* (1983): 216–17.

1979 "Vardis Fisher's *Children of God*: A Second Look." *Sunstone* 4, no. 1 (January–February): 30–32.

1979 "A Mormon and Wilderness: The Saga of the Savages." *Sunstone* 4, nos. 5 & 6 (December): 69–72; reprinted in *Sunstone* 10, no. 5 (May 1985): 66–69.

1982   "The Civilizing of Mormondom: The Indispensable Role of the Intel-
       lectual." *Sunstone* 7, no. 3 (May–June): 8–15; reprinted in *Restora-
       tion Studies III*, edited by Maurice L. Draper, 73–83 (Independence,
       Missouri: Herald Publishing House, 1986).

1983   "Overhauling Mormon Aesthetics." *Sunstone* 8, nos. 1 & 2
       (January–April): 13–14.

1985   "The Lamb and the Lion." *Weber Studies* 2 (Spring): 21–26.

1987   "Juanita Brooks's *Quicksand and Cactus*: The Evolution of a Liter-
       ary Memoir." *Dialogue: A Journal of Mormon Thought* 20, no. 1
       (Spring): 145–55.

1987   "In Defense of a Mormon Erotica." *Dialogue: A Journal of Mor-
       mon Thought* 20, no. 4 (Winter): 122–27; reprinted in *Multiply and
       Replenish*, edited by Brent Corcoran, 239–47 (Salt Lake City: Signa-
       ture Books, 1994).

1987   "Introduction to Section IV: The Rocky Mountains" in *A Liter-
       ary History of the American West*, edited by Thomas J. Lyon. Fort
       Worth: Texas Christian University Press, 822–48.

1988   "Subduing the Barbarian: Freshman English at Weber State" in
       Weber State College…A Centennial History, edited by Richard W.
       Sadler. Salt Lake City: Publishers Press, 240–46.

1988   "Juanita Brooks as a Mormon Dissenter." *The John Whitmer Histor-
       ical Association Journal* 8: 13–29; reprinted in *Mormon Mavericks:
       Essays on Dissenters*, edited by John Sillito & Susan Staker, 215–41
       (Salt Lake City: Signature Books, 2002).

1988   "A Tribute to *Dialogue*." *Dialogue: A Journal of Mormon Thought*
       21, no. 2 (Summer): 140–42.

1988   "A Christian by Yearning." *Sunstone* 12, no. 5 (September): 19–22;
       reprinted in *The Wilderness of Faith*, edited by John Sillito, 125–34
       (Salt Lake City: Signature Books, 1991).

1989   "Juanita Brooks, My Subject, My Sister." *Dialogue: A Journal of
       Mormon Thought* 22, no. 1 (Spring): 16–28.

1989   "In Memoriam: Juanita Brooks." *Sunstone* 13, no. 5 (October): 6–8.

1990   "Eternity with a Dry-Land Mormon." *Dialogue: A Journal of Mor-
       mon Thought* 23, no. 2 (Summer): 110–15.

1990   "A Mormon Evolutionist and the Wild God's Grace." *Sunstone* 14,
       no. 4 (August): 24–30.

1991   "My Mother's House." *Dialogue: A Journal of Mormon Thought*
       24, no. 3 (Fall): 79–88.

1993   "The Native American." *Weber Studies* 10, no. 3 (Fall): 101–15.

1993   "Hiking to Timpanogos: How Charity, Affection, and Sex Are Kill-
       ing the Wilderness." *Sunstone* 16, no. 6 (November): 22–30.

1994   "The Art of Dissent among the Mormons." *Sunstone* 16, no. 8
       (February): 33–39.

1996 "Preface: Notes of a Weber County Writer" in *The Word from Weber County*, edited by Bob Sawatzki. Salt Lake City: Publisher's Press, xix–xxii.

1996 "Freedom and Bondage in Utah's West Desert" in *The Word from Weber County*, edited by Bob Sawatzki. Salt Lake City: Publisher's Press, 94–104.

1996 "Lavina Fielding Anderson and the Power of a Church in Exile." *Dialogue: A Journal of Mormon Thought* 29, no. 4 (Winter): 169–78.

1997 "A Woodlot in the Wasatch." *Rough Draft* 17, no. 3 (Fall & Winter): 45–48; reprinted in *"Proving Contraries": A Collection of Writings in Honor of Eugene England*, edited by Robert A. Reese, 79–88 (Salt Lake City: Signature Books, 2005).

1998 "In Memoriam: Samuel W. Taylor." *Sunstone* 21, no. 3 (August): 11.

2000 "Growing Up in Snowflake." *Weber Studies* 17, no. 3 (Spring): 2–10.

2000 "My Early College Years: From the Autobiography of Levi S. Peterson." *Dialogue: A Journal of Mormon Thought* 33, no. 3 (Fall): 153–69.

2002 "In Memoriam: Neila Seshachari." *Sunstone*, Issue 123 (July): 5–6.

2003 "Resolving Problems for Missionaries Who Return Early." *Sunstone*, Issue 127 (May): 42–45.

Poetry

1978 "Poem on a Saturday Ride." *Mountainwest* 4, no. 1 (January): 20–21.

Reviews

1965 *"The American West: An Appraisal,* edited by Robert G. Ferris." *Western Humanities Review* 19, no. 1 (Winter): 93–94.

1970 *"The Sound of Mountain Water* by Wallace Stegner." *Utah Historical Quarterly* 38, no. 1 (Winter): 92–93.

1984 "Panorama, Drama, and PG at Last: *A Woman of Destiny* by Orson Scott Card." *Dialogue: A Journal of Mormon Thought* 17, no. 4 (Winter): 157–59.

1985 "Mystery, Violence, and Sex: *The Tenth Virgin* by Gary Stewart." *Sunstone* 10, no. 2 (March): 62.

1985 "Vine Deloria Jr., editor, *A Sender of Words: Essays in Memory of John G. Neihardt.*" *Utah Historical Quarterly* 53, no. 3 (Summer): 296–98.

1987 "Famous Writer Tells Amazing Stories: *News of the World* by Ron Carlson." *Sunstone* 11, no. 4 (July): 34–35.

1990 "Plight and Promise: *Windows on the Sea and Other Stories* by Linda Sillitoe." *Dialogue: A Journal of Mormon Thought* 23, no. 4 (Winter): 177–78.

1991 "Stopping the Flow: *And the Desert Shall Blossom* by Phyllis Barber." *Sunstone* 15, no. 6 (December): 56–57.

1992 "Young at Heart: *Set for Life* by Judith Freeman." *Dialogue: A Journal of Mormon Thought* 25, no. 3 (Fall): 190–92.

Interview

1999 Ure, James W. *Leaving the Fold: Candid Conversations with Inactive Mormons.* Salt Lake City: Signature Books, 43–56.

Criticism of Works

1983 Jorgensen, Bruce W. "Maverick Fiction: *The Canyons of Grace* by Levi S. Peterson." *Dialogue: A Journal of Mormon Thought* 16, no. 2 (Summer): 121–24.

1984 Hales, John. "Peterson, *The Canyons of Grace*." *Western Humanities Review* 38, no. 1 (Spring): 84–86.

1985 Lynn, Karen. "Hope and Hesitation: *Greening Wheat: Fifteen Mormon Short Stories* edited by Levi S. Peterson." *Sunstone* 10, no. 1 (January): 63–64.

1985 Geary, Edward A. "The Varieties of Grace, review of *The Canyons of Grace* by Levi S. Peterson." *Sunstone* 10, no. 2 (March): 59–61.

1987 Swenson, Paul. "Levi Peterson: Piling on the Paradoxes in an Existential Parfait." *Utah Holiday* 16, no. 8 (May): 35, 41–42.

1987 Wright, Charlotte M. "Book Review of *The Backslider* by Levi S. Peterson." *Weber Studies* 4, no. 2 (Fall): 78–79.

1989 Aikens, Patricia Truxler. "Book Review of *Juanita Brooks: Mormon Woman Historian* by Levi S. Peterson." *Weber Studies* 6, no. 1 (Spring): 77–78.

1989 Peterson, Paul H., Newell G. Bringhurst, Maureen U. Beecher, and Louis C. Midgley. "Editor's Introduction and Book Reviews of *Juanita Brooks: Mormon Woman Historian* by Levi S. Peterson." *Brigham Young University Studies* 29, no. 4 (Fall): 115–35.

1996 Parkinson, Benson Y. "Book Review of *Aspen Marooney* by Levi S. Peterson." *Weber Studies* 13, no. 3 (Fall): 133–34.

2000 Austin, Michael. "Are Mormons Really Christians?: Levi Peterson and The Paradox of Mormon Identity." *Sunstone* 117 (May): 64–66.

Index